S0-BSJ-051

Date Due

THE GREAT POWERS
IN WORLD POLITICS

INTERNATIONAL RELATIONS AND ECONOMIC NATIONALISM

BY

FRANK H. SIMONDS, Litt. D.

JOURNALIST; AUTHOR OF *"History of the World War," "Can America
Stay at Home?" "Can Europe Keep the Peace?"* ETC.

AND

BROOKS EMENY, Ph.D.

FORMERLY INSTRUCTOR IN INTERNATIONAL POLITICS, YALE UNIVERSITY
AUTHOR OF *"The Strategy of Raw Materials: A Study of
America in Peace and War"*

AMERICAN BOOK COMPANY

NEW YORK · CINCINNATI · CHICAGO · BOSTON · ATLANTA

TO
BETTY BROOKS
AND
JUDY HEYWARD

PREFACE

This text undertakes the study of international relations from a new vantage point. Instead of approaching the contemporary situation by means of an extended survey of the historical background the authors focus attention upon the present national policies of the great powers whose influence is dominating in international relations. These national policies they seek to interpret in the light of their basic factors, economic, ethnic, geographic, and historic.

The fundamental objective is thus *to resolve the Present* into its essential elements, both current and past. This departure from the more conventional type of treatment is, moreover, demanded not merely because of its pedagogical advantages but also by reason of its practical merits at a moment when so many aspects of the subject itself have hitherto been slighted or still remain uninterpreted.

The years which have elapsed since the onset of the Great Depression have witnessed a swift and striking transformation in the nature of the problem of world peace. For the old questions of nationality which dominated the Paris Peace Conference there have been substituted economic issues that have today become all-important. And whereas the old questions were exclusively European in their bearing, the new issues are world-wide in their implications.

This book constitutes an attempt to examine the causes and circumstances of this transition from the political chaos of the immediate postwar years to the economic catastrophe which has accompanied the Great Depression. It undertakes to prove that precisely as European peace was impermanent a century ago because of the political inequalities existing in the condition of the nationalities of the Continent, so, today, world peace is precarious because of the economic disparities in the circumstances of nations everywhere.

The argument of this volume is that Fascism and National Socialism, although on the surface indistinguishable from familiar nineteenth-century imperialisms, are at bottom, at least in their latest stages, the characteristic expressions of great peoples in revolt against the limitations placed upon their national prosperity by their poverty in national resources. The aim of the authors is not to prove that new wars have already become inevitable but simply to demonstrate that no viable system of organized peace can be founded upon the contemporary status quo of economic inequality.

The purpose of this book is to make clear how real and great are the disparities between material resources of the several Great Powers, how disastrous are the consequences of these disparities for the material and social conditions of the peoples of the less favored countries, and, finally, how idle is the hope that the world can escape new wars so long as no peaceful means can be discovered to abolish inequalities which in the eyes of those who suffer from them seem the proof positive of intolerable injustice. Its further purpose is to explain how all the experiments of the postwar period for insuring peace have eventually collapsed because in effect if not in design they would perpetuate rather than amend the economic status quo despite the patent resolution of more than one great people to resort to war rather than to endure inequality.

The text was written by Mr. Simonds in constant consultation with Dr. Emeny, who supplied the economic background, maps, and charts—also the Bibliography which lists (with indication of the publishers) the various books, periodicals, and pamphlets mentioned in the footnotes accompanying the text. The authors acknowledge their indebtedness to Miss Ethel Peterson for drafting the maps, to Miss Phyllis Parker for stenographic services, and to Mrs. Lovell Thompson for authoritative editorial direction.

F.H.S.
B.E.

Louisiana Purchase,
  Snowville, N.H.
    January, 1935.

CONTENTS

LIST OF MAPS AND CHARTS

The fifteen years which followed the coming into effect of the treaties made at the Paris Conference (1919) naturally fall into three well-defined periods of approximately equal length. Each of these periods, too, was marked by a characteristic event of special importance. In the first, the occupation of the Ruhr epitomized the years between 1920 and 1925; in the second, the Truce of Locarno was equally illuminating; and in the last, the rise of Hitler and of National Socialism in Germany was similarly significant.

The first and last periods, moreover, were times of revolt, while the middle span was a brief but brilliant era of reconstruction. The first revolt was precipitated by the response of the German people to the Treaty of Versailles. Instinctively and violently they strove to break the chains which had been imposed upon them by the Settlement of Paris. Inevitably, however, that attempt brought them into direct collision with France, and the consequence of that collision was the occupation of the Ruhr, which for Germany was a defeat even more disastrous than the World War itself.

Beaten, the Germans were again compelled to sue for peace. This time, however, they were fortunate enough to find a statesman at once abler and wiser than any they had possessed since Bismarck. The next period, so far as

German policy was concerned, was therefore dominated by Gustav Stresemann, and the German policy of that period was based upon the clear perception that for all calculable time Germany could not hope to escape from the restraints of the Treaty of Versailles, and that her immediate problem was to escape from the social perils which threatened as a consequence alike of the disaster of the World War and of the occupation of the Ruhr.

Fortunately by 1925 not only Great Britain but France as well had begun to emerge from the shadow of war psychology, and both were now looking forward and not backward. Even the United States, while still resolute in its determination to avoid all political association with the Old World, was in a mood to participate financially in European reconstruction. In Briand and Sir Austen Chamberlain, too, France and Great Britain found statesmen animated by the new spirit and ready to co-operate with Stresemann.

The stage was thus set for a complete change in course, and that change was symbolized by the various accords signed at Locarno in the autumn of 1925. In effect, these accords adjourned to the future all the territorial disputes arising from the Treaty of Versailles save the question of Alsace-Lorraine. In this detail, Germany renounced voluntarily all purpose to recover the provinces which she had taken by the Treaty of Frankfort and lost by the Treaty of Versailles. Great Britain and Italy, for their part, guaranteed the status quo at the Rhine against either German or French aggression.

Germany also entered the League of Nations, in the autumn of 1926, and for the next few years, in fact until the death of Stresemann in 1929 and the fall of the Tory Ministry to which Chamberlain belonged in the same year, Geneva became the scene of the close association of this great triumvirate of peace, in which Briand was the acknowledged chief. The dominating purpose of these statesmen, too, was to restore peace by re-establishing prosperity. And the re-establishment of German prosperity was the first task, because it was self-evident that unless Germany was able to live tolerably in her new circumstances, she was sure in the end to revert to that program of violence which had characterized the years between Versailles and Locarno.

During the next few years economic recovery was rapid, and as German prosperity returned, German passion and despair, awakened by the effects of the World War and of the Ruhr, were largely dissipated. Insensibly the entire atmosphere of Europe changed, and throughout the whole world there spread the conviction that genuine peace had at last been restored and that in the League of Nations mankind had at last found an effective instrument to prevent war in the future.

All of this new structure, however, was built not upon rock but upon sand; for the German prosperity actually had its origin not in the restoration of the old circumstances of the prewar era, which had witnessed the almost fabulous growth of German industry, trade, and commerce, but, instead, in the vast influx of American and British loans. Germany was able to keep her industrial machine in full operation because, first, these foreign loans furnished her with the resources necessary not merely to pay reparations but also to purchase abroad the essential raw materials which she lacked, and, second, the payments in kind which she was making on account of reparations also provided a fictitious prosperity.

When, however, events in the United States produced a sudden arrest of American lending, and the British loans also terminated simultaneously, the fundamental insecurity of German prosperity was disclosed with tragic clarity, and there ensued a collapse followed by a further disintegration in the economic life of the Reich which continued for several years. And with that crash the whole program of Stresemann fell also, for that program had been based upon the major assumption that if Germany accepted the terms of Versailles loyally she would be able to find material prosperity in association with her former foes.

The financial prostration and the economic paralysis which marked the course of the Great Depression in 1930 and 1931, however, constituted in German eyes a clear demonstration of the fallacy of Stresemann's policy and the futility of any attempt to live up to the terms of the Treaty of Versailles. Thus a fresh revolt set in and found its expression in the person of Adolf Hitler and in the program of National Socialism.

In point of fact, Germany's new plight was only to a slight degree the consequence of the Treaty of Versailles. On the contrary she was now suffering primarily and chiefly from the ultimate consequences of the Industrial Revolution, and not from the immediate effects of the World War. The difficulties which confronted her were economic and not political, and they were not to be exorcised by restoration of her old frontiers or removal of the restrictions placed upon her means of defense.

The calamity which had now overtaken the Reich was actually a detail in a world calamity. But the German people saw their new hardships and handicaps in terms of their old grievances. They were really suffering from evils which were inherent in their material circumstances, but instinctively they responded to the repetition of the old slogans of the pre-Locarnian era. Wrongs had been done them in the peace treaty. Removal of these wrongs they were justly entitled to demand, but that bestowal of justice could not bring about a restoration of prosperity.

Explosion, however, had become inevitable; and to understand that explosion, which is the dominating circumstance of the third postwar period and responsible for the contemporary problem of peace, it is necessary to turn back to the years between Waterloo and the Marne. During those years the world had been evolving politically and economically in accordance with principles which had been asserted by the three great Revolutions, the English, American, and French. Together these had prepared the way for the contemporary national state in which equality in political rights and security in property are assured to all citizens or subjects irrespective of distinctions of class or condition.

The eventual effect of the three revolutions, therefore, was to strip Aristocracy of the political power which it had inherited from the age of Feudalism and to transfer that power to the masses of national populations. And since by the close of the World War universal suffrage had been generally adopted, the right of majorities to rule, and therefore the power of the masses to control, had thus been established.

In the meantime the Industrial Revolution, in its turn, had transformed the circumstances of the world in respect of property. In the place of a society in which land had been the chief element in production and the masses largely composed of peasants who lived in the country and worked the soil, there had been gradually developed a system whose characteristic feature was a huge urban population which dwelt beside factories and mines and was dependent upon employment in these for its existence. And in exactly the same fashion the old mercantile class, which had been largely occupied in trade and commerce, had evolved into a capitalistic class, now chiefly the owners of the new instruments of production.

Between Capital and Labor, thus defined, there was, on the whole, no open break before the World War. The former enjoyed the benefits of rapidly expanding industry and consequent increase of wealth. The latter, in turn, enjoyed the blessings of a steadily mounting standard of living. Between the two, a certain balance of power was exercised by the political parties which had developed. Dependent upon the capitalist for their financial contributions and upon the proletariat for their electoral support, these parties bestowed upon the former protection from confiscatory legislation and upon the latter relief from extreme exploitation.

As a consequence, the real issue in the prewar years was not over the distribution of property but over the extent to which the possessors of property should share their profits with the working masses. Decade by decade, too, the workers saw their conditions improving and the outlook for their children widening. They became increasingly conscious of the power residing in their political rights. The whole social system was fluid; its obvious inequalities did not assume the aspect of irremediable injustice, because, like Napoleon's soldiers, the workers carried the baton of a marshal, if not in their knapsacks, at least in their dinner pails.

On the heels of the World War, however, the Russian Revolution, having adopted the program of Karl Marx, undertook to abolish the whole democratic system. For political liberty it substituted the domination of the workers; for private property, state ownership; and for the national state it aimed to substitute the world community. The design of this threefold program was to take the machinery of production out of private hands and transfer it to a state that was exclusively directed by and for the workers, and to replace the old rivalry between sovereign states by a struggle between Capital and Labor within one world-wide state.

This challenge of Communism was a direct threat to the owners of property who constituted the capitalist class. Under the democratic system the right of the majority to rule had been made effective by the adoption of universal suffrage. As a consequence, merely by employing the existing political machinery, the workers in Great Britain, France, and elsewhere could, if they chose, follow the Russian example and destroy the whole capitalistic system. In a word, they could substitute for the progress by evolution of the prewar era the new tactic of revolution. And danger that this might happen arose from the possibility that the workers, who had supplied the cannon fodder in all armies, might rise against the system which had sent them to battle.

In point of fact, however, nothing of the sort happened in Great Britain or France. Alarmed by the obvious threat of the Red Revolution, the governments of the Allied nations furtively financed and secretly favored the counter-revolutionary campaigns of the White Russians. All of these, however, came to nothing. The Russian Revolution, like the French, succeeded in making good its control at home. On the other hand, it was unsuccessful abroad, and the defeat of the Red army under the walls of Warsaw in 1920 broke the invasive power of Bolshevism. As a consequence, a military truce presently ensued between western democracy and eastern revolution at the frontiers fixed by the Treaty of Riga.

Defeated on the battlefield, the Russian Bolshevists did not at once abandon the struggle. On the contrary, they undertook to promote world revolution by means of the Communists within the democratic countries, financing campaigns of sabotage and strikes from the Kremlin. This second offensive, however, was no more successful than the first in the western countries where the economic structure was strong. In these states the workers looked with disapproval upon the excesses of the Bolshevists and manifested no inclination to follow their example; and as Labor remained loyal to the democratic faith, Capital had no reason to desert it.

In Italy, however, quite a different situation existed. There the strain of a war too long protracted had produced genuine unrest among the masses. Again, the disappointments awakened by a victory too little rewarded in the peace treaties had aroused a violent resentment among the veterans. Thus there was, on the one hand, a decided drift toward Communism, and on the other a violent nationalism which found a leader in Mussolini and expression in Fascism.

At the same moment, Italian Finance and Big Business, taking alarm at the apparent inability of the existing parliamentary regime to preserve order or to protect property, decided to throw its lot in with Mussolini and his movement. And this turn to Fascism was made not merely by the owners of property, as Marx had foretold, but also by those who held posts of profit and dignity under the capitalistic system and were not ready to join the manual workers. On the contrary, as their employers were alarmed for property, they were concerned for position. Thanks to this double reinforcement, Fascism triumphed and liberty was thus sacrificed to the double desire for national greatness and domestic order.

What happened in Italy in 1922 was, moreover, a close repetition of what had occurred in France a little more than a century before. Then the Bourgeoisie, which had made the French Revolution to overthrow Aristocracy, having subsequently become weary of the excesses of the Republic, appealed from chaos to Caesar and assisted in the overthrow of the Republic and the establishment of the Empire. In 1804, Napoleon was thus commissioned to re-establish domestic peace and order. In 1922, Mussolini accepted a similar mandate. And in both instances, since the instrument of reaction was a man of genius, his personality invested that reaction with a character all its own.

Like Napoleon, Mussolini addressed his appeal to national pride. In place of a free Italy, he proposed to make a great Italy. And in undertaking his task he returned to the traditions of the Risorgimento. His march on Rome was thus conducted in the spirit of the Expedition of the Thousand to Sicily, two generations earlier; and as Garibaldi had been the symbol of Italian unification, Mussolini now became the incarnation of Italian greatness.

Arrived at the seat of power, Mussolini, like Napoleon, proceeded to sweep away those democratic institutions which, while they existed, would have constituted a constant peril to his regime. Parliament was abolished, free speech ended, the press regimented. The workers were deprived of their power to establish a Communist regime by the exercise of their voting rights. All this domestic reaction, however, was accomplished in the name of a fiery and frenzied nationalism. Fascism promised to Italy that glory and those rewards which democracy had failed to gain for it, either in battle during the World War or around the green table at the Paris Conference.

To the internationalism of Communism, Fascism opposed Italian nationalism. Lenin's revolution had sought to move horizontally through all the workers of the world. Mussolini's operated vertically up through all the strata of the Italian population. Communism called upon the masses everywhere to march to class warfare under the Red Flag. Fascism summoned Italians to march to victory in a new national war under the Tricolor of Savoy. Common to both, moreover, was hostility to democracy. The Russian Revolution destroyed democracy to gain power, and the Italian Reaction abolished it to prevent a Communist triumph.

Like Communism, however, Fascism failed to effect any immediate lodgment in the western democracies. As the workers there had rejected Communism, the employers now rejected Fascism. Feeling its position as yet unchallenged, Capital continued to view without alarm the possession of the instruments of political power by Labor. And Labor, in its turn, remained confident that under the gradualness of democratic processes it would achieve greater and more lasting benefits than through the violence of the Communist tactics.

By 1926, therefore, it seemed as if Revolution and Reaction had come and gone without serious consequences
for democracy in the world at large. Communism and
Fascism both appeared domestic experiments without
exportable value. Under the direction of Stalin, too, the
Russian Revolution was moving toward the Five-Year
Plan, and thus away from the program of World Revolution. And, in a similar fashion, Fascism, under the
guidance of Mussolini, was more and more concentrating
its attention upon domestic reorganization.

As early as 1925, too, Germany, under the inspiration
of Stresemann, had made the Pacts of Locarno in association with her French and British foes of the war. Thus,
as in November, 1918, the Social Democrats, led by
Ebert, had crushed the brief Red Revolt, so now the less
extreme Nationalists seemed to be following Stresemann
and putting aside the program of *revanche*, which had its
origin in the passions provoked by a lost war and a
Punic peace. When, too, in 1926, Germany came to
Geneva, welcomed by Briand and Chamberlain, the
world at last seemed safe for Democracy and equally insured against Communism and against Fascism.

Three years later, however, the Great Depression suddenly cast its shadow over the world; and that shadow
rested first upon the Reich. The German workers, who
during the years of the Truce of Locarno had begun to
enjoy a rising standard of living and had therefore, in
increasing numbers, deserted the Communist for the Republican cause and parties, now turned to the Left. Capitalism in Germany, as in Italy, was thus confronted by
the possibility of domestic revolution. Immediate or
remote, as the danger may have been, this Red Peril
constituted the basis for a German Reaction conducted

in faithful imitation of the Italian; and as Mussolini had been the instrument of the Italian Reaction, Hitler became the agent of the German.

In Germany as in Italy, therefore, Capital aided and abetted in the overthrow of the existing democratic regime, in an effort to prevent the possible employment of the democratic machinery by the workers, who constituted the political majorities, to establish a Communist system. And having mounted to power, National Socialism followed the example of Fascism and swept away the institutions of democracy—parliament, free speech, and an unshackled press. All political parties, save the dominant National Socialist, were abolished; and Republican and Communist met in the same concentration camp.

To gain power, National Socialism exploited patriotic emotions as Fascism had done. Upon the democratic elements in the country was thrust the responsibility for the collapse of 1918, for the submission to the Treaty of Versailles, and for the continuing humiliations of the postwar period. As Mussolini had revived the memory of the glories of Ancient Rome in the very name of Fascism, Hitler now recalled the greatness of the First Reich in his prospectus for a Third in which were to be gathered all the lands formerly included within the limits of the Holy Roman Empire. Once more unity was exalted above liberty, and again the objective of domestic unity was represented to be foreign conquest.

Internationally, the repercussions of the German Reaction were immediate and important. While the triumph in Italy of a man and a movement proclaiming the gospel of intransigent nationalism did not have decisive influence in the world at large, the conquest of Germany by a leader and a party dedicated to the same gospel more than doubled the danger of war and necessarily arrested all the experiments of Geneva—experiments based upon the twofold assumption of a continued sway of democracy in the world and of the enduring supremacy of international ideals within the various democracies.

When, however, first Italy and then Germany renounced democracy for dictatorship and adopted a program of immediate armament and eventual war, there remained no basis for co-operation between them and the British, French, and American democracies which still sought to evangelize the world by their own prospectus of peace. Between the ideal of conquest and that of co-operation, there could be no common ground. And for the neighbors of Italy and Germany there was left no alternative but to prepare themselves for that conflict which seemed impending and would in the end prove inevitable if Italian and German purposes long went unmodified.

On the political side, therefore, the World Crisis of 1934 had its origin in the two Reactions, the Italian and the German, both in turn provoked by the Russian Revolution. Each of these Reactions borrowed the same ideology of nationalism to overthrow Democracy, in order to forestall Communism. The inescapable consequence of such strategy was, moreover, to arouse the fears of those nations which lay in the pathway of the national aspirations and ambitions thus aroused, and to drive them to military preparations calculated to guarantee their own security against threatened aggression.

Apprehensions awakened among the nations adjacent to Germany and Italy by the nationalistic purposes proclaimed by the dictators and the dominant political parties of these states, were likewise intensified by the course of Japan in Manchuria in 1931. That course was, in effect, no more than the translation into action, by the masters of Japan, of a nationalistic program indistinguishable from the prospectuses of the German and Italian dictatorships. What the German and Italian dictators publicly announced an intention of doing, the Japanese government actually did; and what their government did, the Japanese people approved.

The Japanese people thus disassociated themselves from all the endeavors of the democracies of the western world to establish a system of peace and order internationally by means of the Covenant of the League of Nations and the Pact of Paris. They set national interest above respect either for the specific obligations undertaken by treaty or the general restraints of public international law. The withdrawal of Japan from the League (1933), and that of Germany in the same year, were decisive disclosures of the pursuit by both countries of national policies irreconcilable with the whole international conception of Geneva, and incompatible with the assumptions upon which the League had been based.

The political crisis, moreover, was intensified by an economic crisis not less acute. While the Great Depression, like the Russian Revolution, failed to disturb the political institutions of the western democracies, it did, in a later stage, bring about a complete transformation in their economic practices. The evils attendant upon growing domestic unemployment and shrinking foreign trade, which accompanied the "Economic Blizzard," were so threatening that Great Britain, France, and the United States broke with all the traditions of *laissez-*

faire and launched themselves upon programs of inflation, currency manipulations, high tariffs, and quotas.

These programs constituted an appeal to the instincts of economic nationalism quite as open as the German or Italian appeal to political nationalism—and the effect was hardly less disastrous. International trade everywhere languished, and the nations of the world were presently engaged in a struggle with one another for existence, waged only by economic weapons but fought in the same spirit as armed conflict and producing a devastation hardly less complete than that of military battle.

While all countries suffered heavily from this new upheaval, the situation of some was very much more serious than that of others. Among the Great Powers, the plight of Germany and Italy was by far the most unhappy, since their resources in the essential raw materials of industry were inadequate to their needs and they were therefore dependent upon foreign supplies which were to be obtained by Germany only through the sale of domestic manufactures and by Italy through the export of labor.

As, under the stimulus of the Great Depression, countries necessarily sought to expand their own industrial output and to restrict their use of foreign goods and labor and thereby to relieve domestic unemployment, the consequences for the Germans and Italians were disproportionately severe. While Great Britain, France, and the United States, thanks to their resources and wealth, were able to purchase or dispense with foreign manufactures and labor and yet to maintain their own industrial life, Germany and Italy were faced by the prospect of a declining standard of living if their supplies

of foreign raw materials were cut off. Economic necessity therefore gave fresh impulsion to policies which
had their origin in territorial aspirations, and thus
bestowed a new aspect upon the problem of world
peace.

To understand that contemporary aspect, therefore, the
student of international relations is confronted by a
double task. First, he must examine the origin and development of those political issues and traditions to
which both Fascism and National Socialism appealed in
the face of a real or imagined threat of Russian Communism; for only through the knowledge of the territorial,
ethnic, and psychological issues dividing European
peoples is it possible to comprehend how Mussolini and
Hitler were able to mobilize the passions and patriot-
isms of their two great peoples and thus capture the
power to destroy democratic institutions. Second, the
student must, in the same fashion, acquire knowledge of
the nature of the material circumstances of the Great
Powers, of their resources and deficiencies in the essentials of industry and in foodstuffs, and of their possession
or lack of means to make good their wants in this respect; for only such knowledge can explain the economic
aspects of their national policies. And to comprehend
the problem of world peace it is further necessary to examine the various programs for the organization of that
peace in the light of the political and economic circumstances of the Great Powers.

Always in considering the postwar circumstances, it
must also be remembered that the twenty-year period of
1914–1934 constituted an era of convulsion without parallel since the period of the French Revolution and the
First Empire.

Twenty years after the summoning of the States-General, which marked the opening stage of the earlier upheaval, the attention of the world was concentrated upon the figure of Napoleon Bonaparte and the fortunes of Imperial France. The future of both, moreover, was then necessarily interpreted in the light of Wagram which had just been won and without suspicion of the retreat from Moscow less than four years distant. In 1809 the idea that the French Revolution, but recently ended, and the Industrial Revolution, not yet well begun, would together shape the affairs of mankind throughout the century that was to follow, and bestow new and unimagined forms alike upon political and upon economic life, must have seemed incredible. And to the contemporary audience of 1809 any suggestion that the Napoleonic drama was destined to prove but a brief if brilliant episode, without lasting meaning, would have appeared absurd.

The same limitations of perspective manifestly existed on New Year's Day, 1935. Unmistakably the world was again in crisis and, as a result, the present was as obscure and the future as unfathomable as it had been a century and a quarter earlier. It is this uncertainty, however, that invests living with the character of genuine adventure and bestows upon the study of current events the charm of an authentic voyage of discovery.

PART ONE

FOUNDATIONS OF INTERNATIONAL
RELATIONS

Chapter I

THE NATION STATES SYSTEM

THE contemporary world is organized upon the basis of the nation states system; that is, each of the countries among which the surface of the earth is divided constitutes a politically self-governing national state asserting itself to be sovereign. What are commonly described as international relations are no more than the sum of the contacts between the national policies of these sovereign states.

National policies are systems of strategy employed by states to insure security,[1] promote prosperity, or attain ethnic unity where this last is lacking. Sometimes a distinction is made between the foreign and the domestic phases of national policy, but in reality such a distinction is largely imaginary; for what a state does at home and what it does abroad will invariably be dictated by

[1] While "security," used in this sense, refers primarily to that of a nation's territory, states are also concerned with the protection of the property and persons of its citizens abroad. (Borchard, E. M., *The Diplomatic Protection of Citizens Abroad*, 1927; Ladas, S. P., *The International Protection of Industrial Property*, 1930; Liu Shih Shun, *Extraterritoriality, Its Rise and Its Decline*, 1925; Offutt, Milton, *The Protection of Citizens Abroad by the Armed Forces of the United States*, 1928; Stowell, E. C., *Intervention in International Law*, 1921.)

exclusive concern for its domestic interests. In such matters as currency and tariff, however, attempts to serve domestic interests can have world-wide repercussions.

There are now more than sixty sovereign states, and since their interests not only vary ordinarily but are also often directly opposed, collisions between national policies are frequent. But whereas the citizens of states, although claiming equality in the eyes of their domestic law, nevertheless acknowledge a common duty to obey that law or are speedily brought to obedience by local courts and police, no similar situation exists in the case of sovereign states.

On the contrary, in conformity with the doctrine of absolute sovereignty,[1] nations have so far resisted all attempts to subject their national policies to the restrictions of any system of public international law or to the restraints of any form of international police. They have identified such attempts as constituting a direct challenge to their own sovereignty.

During the past five centuries which have witnessed the development of the nation states system,[2] there has been evolved, concomitantly, a body of public international law.[3] From the days of Machiavelli and Grotius to the present hour, this body of principles and precedents, to which treaties between nations belong, has been expanding continuously. But it has not yet acquired the force internationally that domestic law possesses within countries.

[1] For further analysis and critique of the doctrine of sovereignty, see: Laski, H. J., *Studies in the Problem of Sovereignty*, 1917; MacIver, R. M., *The Modern State*, 1926; Mattern, Johannes, *Concepts of State Sovereignty and International Law*, 1928.

[2] Mowat, R. B., *The European States System*, 1929, enl. ed.

[3] Brierly, J. L., *The Law of Nations*, 1928; Butler, Sir G. G., and Maccoby, Simon, *The Development of International Law*, 1928; Stowell, E. C., *International Law; A Restatement of Principles in Conformity with Actual Practice*, 1931.

As a consequence, for the settlement of disputes between nations, the use of so-called public international law is purely voluntary, whereas between citizens of a state the legal determination of disputed issues is compulsory. In practice, too, although states not infrequently make use of international law when they find such use convenient, it is only in issues which are relatively insignificant. By contrast, when national honor, security, or other vital questions are at stake, states invariably hold national interests above the restraints of public international law.[1]

The classic example of this practice was the German invasion of Belgium in 1914. Even the German Chancellor himself admitted publicly and frankly that this action was illegal, judged by the precedents of international law. But he discovered complete justification for it, nevertheless, in the fact that Germany, at the moment, found herself in a "state of necessity"[2]; and although the declaration of Bethmann-Hollweg was widely and roundly denounced as a cynical defiance of the conscience of mankind, it was in fact no more than a stupid but honest assertion of the doctrine states invariably follow in similar circumstances.[3]

Again, although Great Britain cited the Belgian episode as justification for her declaration of war upon Ger-

[1] Lauterpacht, H., *The Function of Law in the International Community*, 1933.

[2] "Gentlemen, we are now in a state of necessity (*Notwehr*), and necessity (*Not*) knows no law. Our troops have occupied Luxemburg and perhaps have already entered Belgian territory.

"Gentlemen, that is a breach of international law. It is true that the French Government declared at Brussels that France would respect Belgian neutrality as long as her adversary respected it. We knew, however, that France stood ready for an invasion. France could wait, we could not . . . . He who is menaced as we are and is fighting for his highest possession can only consider how he is to hack his way through (*durchhauen*)." (From the speech of the German Chancellor von Bethmann-Hollweg, delivered before the Reichstag, August 4, 1914.)

[3] Rodick, B. C., *The Doctrine of Necessity in International Law*, 1928.

many and made much of her championship of the principles of international law and of the sanctity of treaties, she and her allies during the World War frequently showed equal disregard for both. As a consequence, protests against open violations of international law, lodged by the United States while it was neutral, produced no practical result and were forgotten when, at last, the United States also became a belligerent.[1]

Thus before the World War and during that struggle, public international law exerted no effective restraint upon the national policies of states. Nor has the post-war period seen any material change. On the contrary, although the world is today far more richly endowed with means for settling international disputes by law and not by war than it was before 1914, states still disclose the same complete unwillingness to subject their sovereignty to the restraints of the League of Nations that they formerly did to subordinate it to the limitations of public international law.[2]

That unwillingness was clearly illustrated in the history of the Pact of Paris (1928). While all nations readily ratified this pact, which constituted a formal renunciation of war as an instrument of national policy,[3] none

[1] Garner, J. W., *Prize Law During the World War*, 1927; same author, *International Law and the World War*, 1920; Moore, J. B., *International Law and Some Current Illusions*, 1924.

[2] Hawtrey, R. G., *Economic Aspects of Sovereignty*, 1930; Madariaga, Salvador de, *Disarmament*, 1929; Williams, Sir J. F., *International Change and International Peace*, 1932.

[3] The two articles of faith, without benefit of sanction, contained in the Pact of Paris, are as follows:

Article I

"The High Contracting Parties solemnly declare in the names of their respective peoples that they condemn recourse to war for the solution of international controversies, and renounce it as an instrument of national policy in their relations with one another.

Article II

"The High Contracting Parties agree that the settlement or solution of all disputes or conflicts of whatever nature or of whatever origin they may be, which may arise among them, shall never be sought except by pacific means."

consented to the modification of national policies which could reach their goal only through war.[1] Nor was any state ready to provide force to insure the keeping of the pledge which the pact constituted. Instead, when Japan invaded Manchuria, in clear violation of the Pact and of the Treaty of Washington as well, the states which had ratified both engagements limited their action to weak and vain protests.

For the student of international relations, therefore, the point of departure must be a clear perception of the paradox disclosed by the performances of nations in the postwar period. On the one hand, they have indulged in an incredible multiplication of the instruments for insuring peace, but on the other hand they have consistently rejected all responsibility for the employment of these instruments where their own interests were not advantaged thereby. Between the various means for preventing conflict and the evident desire of peoples to escape war, it has therefore been impossible to establish any connection. But without some belt stretching from machinery to motive power, only paralysis has resulted.

There has, too, been a second paradox even more strik-

---

[1] Sir Austen Chamberlain's note of May 19, 1928, to the American Secretary of State, defining the British interpretation of the meaning of the Pact, has become the classic definition of national foreign policy under the prevailing international system.—

"The language of Article I, as to the renunciation of war as an instrument of national policy, renders it desirable that I should remind your Excellency that there are certain regions of the world the welfare and integrity of which constitute a special and vital interest for our peace and safety. His Majesty's Government have been at pains to make it clear in the past that interference with these regions cannot be suffered. Their protection against attack is to the British Empire a measure of self-defence. It must be clearly understood that His Majesty's Government in Great Britain accept the new treaty upon the distinct understanding that it does not prejudice their freedom of action in this respect. The Government of the United States have comparable interests any disregard of which by a foreign power they have declared that they would regard as an unfriendly act. His Majesty's Government believe, therefore, that in defining their position they are expressing the intention and meaning of the United States Government."

ing than the one above stated. Along with the unprecedented expansion of the machinery for preserving peace,
there has also gone an equally impressive spread of the
spirit of intransigent nationalism. In fact, precisely as
the French Revolution was followed by an enormous
wave of ethnic nationalism, the aftermath of the World
War has been an explosion of economic nationalism not
less destructive.[1]

In effect, then, the world of today is a lawless world,
not because a system of public international law and a
world court are lacking, but because nations refuse to
shape their national policies to conform to that law, or
to submit their disputes to that court, or, finally, to invest the existing machinery with the necessary police
power. But in a lawless world, force must be the ultimate means of pursuing policy, and resort to force must
mean war.

War, too, has actually been the unfailing concomitant
of the nation states system throughout its history, as of
the city states system which preceded it. In fact, the
western world has known but two periods of peace; one
absolute, when it was united under the single sovereignty
of Rome; the other relative, when the medieval Papacy
was able to moderate the conflicting ambitions of
princes.[2] And in both instances the sovereign states
were lacking.

Since states are unwilling to subject their national
policies to international restraints, it follows naturally
that they must seek to clothe these policies with force.

---

[1] Angell, Sir Norman, *The Unseen Assassins*, 1932; Foreman, Clark, *The New Internationalism*, 1934; Hayes, C. J. H., *Essays on Nationalism*, 1926; same author, *The
Historical Evolution of Modern Nationalism*, 1931; Woolf, L. S., *After the Deluge*, 1931.

[2] Wright, R. F., *Medieval Internationalism, the Contribution of the Medieval Church
to International Law and Peace*, 1930.

In fact, armaments have always been the most familiar and characteristic prerogative of sovereignty. Thus, even in peace, nations are commonly engaged in strengthening their armies and navies, thereby unconsciously disclosing their conviction that war will continue a recurrent feature of international relations.

Differing as they do in extent of territory, size of population, and amount of natural resources, however, states also vary in the degree to which they can clothe their national policies with force. As a consequence, only a few—and these the most considerable—will possess the force necessary to support their national policies effectively; and these alone constitute the Great Powers. Thus, ours is not only a world without law but also a Great-Power world.

Such, too, it has always been during the centuries which have seen the development of the modern nation states system. In that time, it is true, there have been many changes in the ranks and even in the regional location of the Great Powers. Nevertheless, the interplay of the national policies of these powers has constantly had a disproportionate and even a dominant influence upon international relations.

It is equally evident, despite popular conviction to the contrary, that while rulers and forms of government within nation states have changed frequently, national policies, by contrast, have varied surprisingly little from century to century. Such modifications as have occurred have been due far more often to economic than to political causes.

Mutual comprehension of national policies by people of different nation states, however, is rendered difficult, if not impossible, by the fact that, while for every people its own policies are far more a matter of instinct than of conscious calculation, those of others are invariably measured by their effect abroad rather than by their cause at home. Thus people think of the objectives expressed in their own national policies as their rights and identify challenge or resistance to these rights by other states as constituting injuries; although such opposition must in its turn appear, in the eyes of the peoples responsible for it, no more than legitimate defense of their similarly self-determined rights.

The student of international affairs, therefore, must dismiss any question of right or wrong in the consideration of the national policies of all states, beginning with his own.[1] The universal assertion of the doctrine of absolute sovereignty, preventing, as it does, the existence of any world court of competent jurisdiction, precludes objective and impartial appraisal of national policies. And the student must similarly note the significant detail that, not infrequently, those nations which most uncompromisingly resist all foreign interference with their own national policies most insistently assert their right and competence to meddle with those of others.

The implications of the nation states system are clear. It insures the existence of a world without an effective system of public international law, in which force is the determining factor between nations. In that world, also, only Great Powers, by reason of their disproportionate strength, can invest their national policies with real international importance.

[1] "The simple formula of right and wrong does not afford an adequate basis for the settlement of international disputes. It presupposes that perfect independence and that formal equality of sovereign authorities, which are in reality the foundation of the international anarchy." (Hawtrey, R. G., *Economic Aspects of Sovereignty*, 1930, p. 145.)

Chapter II

NATIONAL POLICY

In the preceding chapter (page 21) national policy was defined as the system of strategy employed by a state to insure its security, promote its prosperity, or complete its ethnic unification. In addition, states are naturally concerned with their honor and prestige, but in practice these are seldom called into question when more material interests are not also at stake.[1]

Implicit in the use of the word "strategy" is the suggestion that even in peace states commonly conduct their international relations in the same spirit as their military operations in war. That point of view was clearly set forth by Clausewitz in his famous definition of war as "the pursuit of policy by other means."[2] What he had in mind when he framed his definition was that the vital interests of the European states of his day were essentially competitive, and that, as a consequence, these states continuously pursued conflicting national policies. Ordinarily they sought to advance their rival

[1] Bratt, K. A., *That Next War?*, 1931; Custance, Sir R. N., *A Study of War*, 1924; Hawtrey, R. G., *Economic Aspects of Sovereignty*, 1930.

[2] Clausewitz, Karl von, *On War* (translation by Col. J. J. Graham), 1911.

purposes by other means than arms, that is, by diplomacy, financial pressure, or alliances, but on occasion,
when the issue at stake was vital and all other means
had failed, they resorted to war.[1]

This view of international relations as a condition of
continuous conflict was once universal, and accordingly,
although war was even then regarded as the ultimate
instrument of policy, it was also deemed legitimate.
Today, however, public opinion, at least in democracies,
holds resort to war, save in cases of actual aggression
and therefore in self-defense, to be an act of violence
both legally and morally without justification.

In the postwar period that conviction has found various expressions. The British and the Americans have
sought to outlaw war and also to prevent it by self-
denying ordinances. The French, for their part, have
striven to bind all nations to a pledge of collective action
through the League of Nations in case of aggression.
These attempts, however, have so far proved without
practical result, and the explanation of their failure is discoverable in the physical circumstances of various states.

By reason of these physical circumstances, states are
divided into two classes. Of these, the first is composed
of the nations whose territories are large and rich and
whose ethnic unity has been achieved; the second, of
the nations whose lands are exiguous and poor and whose
unification is uncompleted. For the former, which are
the sated and therefore contented states, security is the
sole objective of national policy. For the latter, which
are naturally dissatisfied, the chief goal must be the acquisition of what they lack.

[1] Cowan, A. R., *War in World History*, 1929; Fuller, J. F. C., *War and Western Civilization, 1832-1932*, 1932; Hull, W. I., *The War Method and the Peace Method*, 1929; Porritt,
Arthur, *ed.*, *The Causes of War*, 1932.

A similar disparity between the circumstances of the Haves and of the Have-nots has always existed among the individuals within national frontiers. But whereas the individual citizen almost always has a chance to better his condition, no similar opportunity, as a rule, exists for a state. On the contrary, the earth is already divided among the several nations. In theory, the existing disparity might be abolished in one of two ways: the sated states might consent to sacrifice a portion of their territory, or to share with the discontented the exploitation of their own superior resources on terms of equality. In practice, however, no relief is discoverable for the less fortunate countries; for both solutions run counter to that basic principle of sovereignty which holds national territory to be inalienable. Faithful to that principle, too, states are rarely willing to cede their lands to others, and never to surrender any part of their right to the exclusive exploitation of their own national resources.

As a consequence, the less fortunate states are often confronted by the choice between war and acceptance of their present condition of material inferiority as permanent. And to choose the latter horn of the dilemma is politically impracticable for any regime, whether democratic or dictatorial, because it involves an undertaking to persuade the people to renounce all hope of escape from conditions which inevitably impose upon them a lower standard of living than that prevailing in adjoining countries.

The fact that forty-two millions of French not merely possess a homeland area large and rich enough to satisfy their needs and their aspirations, but also own an extensive colonial empire as well, while an equal number of Italians are crowded into a narrow peninsula and in addition lack any considerable colonial territories, is clearly the consequence of accidents of history and not of the operation of any divine law.

In the same way, the fact that the sixty-five millions who constitute the white population of the British Commonwealth own and exploit the well-nigh inexhaustible resources of an empire on which the sun never sets, while the same number of Germans are cooped up in the relatively insignificant and economically insufficient region between the Rhine and the Oder, the Alps and the Baltic, is explicable only in terms of luck, of the good fortune which enabled Great Britain to achieve national unity centuries before Germany.

It is customary to think of the territory of a state in the same fashion as of the private property of an individual; but it is evident that there is here a double contrast. Within states, courts and police uphold titles and maintain lawful owners in possession of their land, which was acquired by the lawful processes of inheritance, purchase, or barter. By contrast, in the matter of national territory not only is there lacking any international authority to maintain the present owner in possession, but also that nation's title almost invariably derives from war.

In Europe, at least, all present frontiers are derived from former conquests. As a consequence, states which were anciently possessors of provinces from which they were evicted because of defeat in war, still regard the present tenure as based upon neither legal nor moral warrant. Furthermore, such states are entitled to believe that the present tenure may also prove transitory like the past. For example, the Italy of the Roman era ruled all of what is today France and England, while the frontiers of the original German Empire—called the Holy Roman Empire—enclosed a third of contemporary France and half of modern Italy. To take a more recent illustration, between 1912 and 1922 Adrianople belonged to Turkey, Bulgaria, and Greece in turn and ultimately became Turkish again.

The student of international affairs, then, is confronted with two mutually exclusive conceptions of national policy, the first static, and the second dynamic.[1] Here, too, he also touches the very heart of the problem of peace in the contemporary world, which is posed by the demand of one group of peoples for security based upon the status quo, and of another for a prosperity or unity attainable only by a modification of that status quo. And the collision between these conceptions is as old as history and has obviously been, hitherto, an inescapable concomitant of the nation states system.

Today, as always in the past, the static theory is naturally embraced by those states which already have prosperity and now seek security. For these, their present fortunes conform to their own estimates of national necessities. Having, their single ambition is to hold. It is, too, the familiar thesis of the peoples of such states that mankind has, at last, reached the point where the territorial division of the earth's surface has become immutable because the title of the present possessors is both legally and morally imprescriptible; legally, because it is established by treaty; morally, because it can be assailed only by war—and war has now been adjudged a crime. Furthermore, it is alleged that war has become so terrible in its destructiveness that even the victors in

[1] Balla, V. de, *The New Balance of Power in Europe*, 1932.; Simonds, Frank H., *Can Europe Keep the Peace?*, 1934, rev. ed.; Williams, Sir J. F., *International Change and International Peace*, 1932.

the next struggle must, on balance, prove actual losers, whatever their nominal gains in territory or prestige.[1]

Against that thesis, however, there must be set the contention of those countries which, being dissatisfied with the status quo, advance the dynamic theory. They assert that for centuries history has been no more than the record of struggles between states. In these struggles nations have risen to power, ruled, and ultimately fallen. But why, Italian Fascism and German National Socialism today demand, should the traditional ebb and flow in the fortunes of states be interrupted merely to suit the views of those peoples which happen at the moment to be sated and therefore satisfied? As to the argument, so frequently on the lips of the fortunate peoples, that war has in the contemporary era become more terrible than ever before: to that Mussolini and Hitler reply with one voice that war has always been in the process of becoming more terrible, but this fact has never yet exercised effective restraint upon the resolution of peoples to achieve liberty, unity, or well-being.

After each of the many general wars in Europe, the victors have, without exception, attempted to exploit the immediate war weariness and horror of the world, due to recent agony, to make the terms lately imposed upon the vanquished a basis for perpetual peace, seeking thereby to consolidate the gains which they have achieved upon the battlefield. Hitherto, however, all such attempts have failed, because the vanquished have eventually recovered their strength without ever

[1] Angell, Sir Norman, *The Great Illusion*, 1933; Bogart, E. L., *Direct and Indirect Costs of the Great World War*, 1920; Dumas, Samuel, and Vedel-Petersen, K. O., *Losses of Life Caused by War*, 1923; Folks, Homer, *The Human Costs of the War*, 1920. For detailed study of national losses to individual belligerents during the World War, see Carnegie Series, *Economic and Social History of the World War*, under the nation in question.

accepting as final those decisions which were the consequence of military defeat.

Accordingly, the old drama has presently been repeated and a fresh challenge has been directed at another status quo. In the eyes of the peoples still satisfied, such undertakings to revise the existing order by violence have always seemed crimes both legally and morally: legally, because they inevitably involve a breach of existing treaties; morally, because they lead to war. But in the eyes of the peoples who embark upon them, they express the inalienable right of nations to resort to force in the presence of injustice.

Nor can it be questioned that, in the past, the various attempts to make immutable a contemporary state of European frontiers, had they been successful, would have perpetuated injustices and wrongs which today would appear intolerable. Thus, had the effort of the conquerors of Napoleon to perpetuate the system of the Congress of Vienna prevailed, the German people would have been denied unity; the Italians, liberty; and the Poles, like many smaller nationalities, would still be subjected to alien tyranny.

Again, although the spirit disclosed today alike by the Italian, Japanese, and German peoples seems, in the eyes of the citizens of the sated states, compounded of imperialism and of barbarism, to these peoples themselves it is indistinguishable from the spirit which created the British or the French empire beyond the seas. Between British occupation of Egypt or American seizure of Panama, on the one hand, and Japanese operations in Manchuria, on the other, to all but Anglo-Saxon eyes the difference is one of calendar and not of conscience.

Precisely in the same fashion, the long-standing Italian ambition to replace France in Tunisia as France replaced Turkey in Algeria, legally and morally abhorrent as that aspiration seems in the eyes of all Frenchmen, can be pronounced unethical by an objective mind only if it be assumed that in recent times there has been a revolution in international morals. And even in such case, it is not to be mistaken that this moral transformation inures exclusively to the benefit of nations which were forehanded with their imperialism as well as with their idealism.

In any event, the fact is unmistakable. After 1918, as after 1815, the victors have undertaken to organize the world on the basis of a settlement imposed upon the vanquished by force. All the several programs of peace, the League of Nations, the Kellogg Pact, the fugitive Protocol of Geneva, have been sponsored by the successful and satisfied powers. By contrast, all the violent reactions against the status quo have been among nations which were either actually defeated or later disillusioned as to the status quo of 1919.

A century ago, it was the defeated French, the irreconcilable Italians, the victorious Prussians who in turn challenged the Settlement of Vienna; today it is the vanquished Germans, the dissatisfied Japanese, and the victorious Italians who have called the Settlement of Paris or the principles of Geneva into question. But while the actors have changed, the lines of the drama remain unmodified.

It is apparent also that the developments of the postwar era have enormously strengthened the demand for a change in the existing situation because they have rendered progressively less favorable the condition of the dissatisfied nations.[1] In that period the Great Depression has produced a spirit of economic nationalism everywhere, and inevitably the effect of that spirit has borne most heavily upon countries which are relatively poor in the essentials of industrial life.

What is novel in this spirit of economic nationalism, too, is that it dominates whole peoples. And the explanation of this phenomenon is to be found in the fact that within a relatively brief time the masses have everywhere risen, not merely to political power, but also to national consciousness. It is, therefore, no longer the kings, cabinets, or ruling minorities who alone grasp the implications for their own country of the national policies of other states. On the contrary, peoples everywhere have become acutely aware that their very standard of living can be profoundly influenced for evil by the policies or pretensions of their neighbors.

Under the conditions of the contemporary industrial era, the traditional rivalry between nations has, in reality, become a life-and-death struggle; and of the nature and stakes of that struggle, peoples are today universally aware. As a consequence the masses demand of their governments that, on the one hand, they enforce and defend national rights uncompromisingly, and on the other, at all hazards, insure tolerable conditions of national existence. And where democratic regimes have failed to satisfy popular demands, peoples have flung themselves unhesitatingly into the arms of dictators, identifying in programs of violence the promise of the realization of their aspirations.

[1] Douglass, P. F., *The Economic Dilemma of Politics: A Study of the Consequences of the Strangulation of Germany*, 1932; Einzig, Paul, *The Economic Foundations of Fascism*, 1933; McGuire, C. E., *Italy's International Economic Position*, 1926; Orchard, J. E., *Japan's Economic Position*, 1930; Rohde, Hans, *Franco-German Factors of Power*, 1932.

The difference between the rivalries dividing states in the prewar era and the issues separating them today is profound. In the former age, it was in Asia and Africa that the Great Powers were quarreling over colonial empires and spheres of interest. The stakes of that game were power, prestige, and profit, and the game itself was a clash of imperialisms in which national existence was never in the balance. Even in Europe, where territorial rivalries were acute, the gage of battle was still only border provinces.

Today, however, the face of things has greatly altered. Rivalries between nations no longer have their basic cause in a race for the possession of distant colonies but in the struggle for the control of the sources of those raw materials and foodstuffs which are essential, not merely or mainly to national greatness, but to national existence itself. National policies no longer have their origin exclusively in the search for power and prestige; rather they have become expressions of the resolution of peoples to survive.

Nevertheless, it must be evident that British and American national policies, like French and Russian, are founded upon a determination to retain existing and disproportionate material advantages. That British and American publics are less aroused and articulate in the matter of security than the French and Russian is due solely to the fact that the challenge to their well-being inherent in the purposes of dynamic powers is less direct and apparent. And it is less apparent because both of the Anglo-Saxon nations seem today far beyond the reach of nations at once less fortunately circumstanced and determined to better their conditions by force if other means fail.

In all their conceptions of world peace and international order, however, both the British and American publics instinctively adopt the static conception, accept present possession, in their own case at least, as proof of moral as well as legal right, and never even dream of any modification of their sovereignty or sacrifice of their territory to satisfy the necessities of less well favored peoples. Such a point of view, however, ignores the actual problem of peace which is posed by the fact that for at least three of the Great Powers and many more of the smaller, their present situation seems both unequal and inequitable and for them war provides the only present means of escape from that situation.

Chapter III

THE GEOGRAPHIC FACTOR

THE basic factors of national policy are threefold: the geographic, the economic, and the demographic. Of these, the first is constituted by the land of a state, viewed from the standpoint of its position; the second, by its land and people considered from the aspects of self-sufficiency and population pressure; the third, by the population examined in respect to size and ethnic make-up.

First among these factors is the geographic. In theory, of course, all of the physical circumstances of the territory of a state have at least a measure of importance for the policy of that state. Thus the organization of national defense must be influenced by the fact that the surface of its land is mountainous, or is level, or is broken, and by the further fact that its frontiers are covered by natural barriers, whether mountains or rivers, or are open because of the absence of such barriers; and, finally, by its possession or its lack of navigable rivers. Nevertheless, these details have relatively slight significance for national policy in international relations, and only position exercises decisive influence in regard thereto.

The position of the territories of a state must be considered from three standpoints: world, regional, and inter-regional.

As to the *world* aspect, history discloses that the occupation by city and nation states of situations advantageous for trade and commerce has insured them prosperity and power. Extension of the known and exploitable world, by discovery and changes in methods of production and means of transportation due to invention, have, in their turn, weakened the positions of some states and enhanced those of others. And the result has been a decline in the fortunes of the former and a rise in the power and prosperity of the latter.[1]

Accordingly, when the known and exploited world was practically limited to the eastern half of the Mediterranean region, Athens, because of its obviously favorable position in that world, seated as it was midway between Asia Minor and Italy and opposite Egypt, enjoyed its hour of prosperity and power.[2] Later, however, when the frontiers of civilization were extended to include the whole of the Mediterranean Basin, Rome, by reason of its central and therefore more advantageous situation in this larger world, prospered, while Athens declined in wealth and power.[3]

[1] For general discussion of the influence of geography upon the history and development of states, see: Brunhes, Jean, and Vallaux, Camille, *La Géographie de L'Histoire*, 1921; Fairgrieve, James, *Geography and World Power*, 1924; Febvre, L. P. V., and Bataillon, Lionel, *A Geographical Introduction to History*, 1925; Hennig, Richard, *Geopolitik*, 1931; Mackinder, H. J., *Democratic Ideals and Reality*, 1919; Thomas, Franklin, *The Environmental Basis of Society*, 1925; Whitbeck, R. H., and Thomas, O. J., *The Geographic Factor; Its Rôle in Life and Civilization*, 1932.

[2] Ferguson, W. S., *Greek Imperialism*, 1913.

[3] Frank, Tenney, *Roman Imperialism*, 1914; Semple, E. C., *The Geography of the Mediterranean Region*, 1931; Newbigin, M. I., *The Mediterranean Lands*, 1924.

In the same fashion, more than a thousand years after the fall of Rome and following the further extension of the limits of the world due to the discovery of America and the sea route to the Far East, England, advantageously situated at the edge of the Old World and facing the New, and also fortunately located in respect of the ocean road to India, rose to commercial importance and political power.[1] Concomitantly, the importance of Venice and Genoa, the great trading city states of the Mediterranean, declined.[2]

Today, when the limits of the known and exploited world have become almost conterminous with those of the planet itself, it is manifest that the position of the United States in respect of Europe, Asia, and Latin America strikingly recalls that of Rome in respect of Europe, Asia, and North Africa when the world was restricted to the Mediterranean Basin.[3] Similarly, the position of Japan in relation to the mainland of Asia, on the one hand, and to America and Europe, on the other, largely reproduces that of England in respect of Europe, Asia, and America three centuries ago. Nor is it less evident that both in the case of the United States and in the case of Japan, a commercially advantageous position has once more produced familiar results.

In fact, the mere extension of the frontiers of the world to their present and ultimate limits has produced a change of prodigious import. Whereas from the days of Imperial Rome to those of Victorian Britain only those

[1] Day, Clive, *A History of Commerce*, 1928; Hayes, C. J. H., *A Political and Social History of Modern Europe*, 1924, Vol. I; Sargent, A. J., *Seaways of Empire, Notes on the Geography of Transport*, 1930, rev. ed.

[2] Bryce, James, *The Holy Roman Empire*, 1919.

[3] Brigham, A. P., *Geographic Influences in American History*, 1903; Semple, E. C., *American History and Its Geographic Conditions*, 1933; Turner, F. J., *The Frontier in American History*, 1921.

states, the seats of whose governments and power were in Europe, were reckoned Great Powers, today the accession of the United States and Japan to that rank is universally recognized.

With the arrival of the Industrial Era, however, the significance of position in its world aspect underwent a revolutionary change. Before that time states had owed their material prosperity and consequent political power largely to the advantageous situation of their territories in relation to the principal trade routes and commercial centers of the globe, but thenceforth another consideration acquired far greater importance. This was the situation of the territories of states in respect of what can perhaps best be described as "the world that matters."

The explanation of the change, moreover, is simple in the extreme. It is clear that in the present Machine Age the development of the national industry has become a matter of supreme importance for every state, because upon the extent of that development must turn not only its prosperity in peace but also its strength in war.[1] In fact, only those states which have reached a comparatively high degree of industrial development can now hold the rank of Great Powers, with all the implications that this circumstance has for national policy.

But the extent of the industrial development of a state must obviously be conditioned by the degree of accessibility of its territories to the reserves of energy, primarily in coal and secondarily in water power,[2] and by the possession or ready availability of iron and the other

[1] Emeny, Brooks, *The Strategy of Raw Materials; A Study of America in Peace and War*, 1934; Inter-Parliamentary Union, *What Would be the Character of a New War?*, 1931; Tryon, F. G., and Eckel, E. C., *eds., Mineral Economics*, 1932.

[2] Although water power may be used as a source of energy for the establishment of light industries such as textiles, it cannot form the basis of the heavier industries for which coal and iron are the indispensable prerequisites.

raw material resources essential to industry; reserves and resources which constitute "the world that matters." In addition, a factor of primary importance is the climate of a nation's territory, since for all practical purposes effective large-scale exploitation of industrial resources is conditional upon location within a temperate zone.[1]

Obviously, the question of accessibility to the essential raw materials is twofold, since states may actually possess within their own frontiers a considerable share of the primary elements of industry, or their territories may be located in close proximity to those of states enjoying such advantages. In all respects, the former situation will obviously be more fortunate than the latter. Thus, the condition of the United States, for example, which possesses vast reserves in coal and huge deposits of iron, will be more advantageous than that of France, which has much iron but insufficient coal, or that of Germany, which has much coal but little iron. Nevertheless, since the frontiers of France march with those of Germany, their respective resources will be mutually accessible in time of peace. Italy, too, while deficient in coal and iron, is near enough to Great Britain, Germany, and France to draw upon them and thus to support a considerable industry of her own.

By contrast, the situation of all South American states, located as they are upon a continent singularly lacking in the basic essentials of industry such as coal and iron, renders them incapable of achieving considerable industrial development and therefore of attaining the status of Great Powers, despite the fact that several are advantageously situated in respect of trade routes.

[1] Huntington, Ellsworth, *The Pulse of Progress*, 1926; Taylor, T. G., *Environment and Race*, 1927.

It follows, therefore, that while states whose territories have easy access to "the world that matters" (page 51) and are thus capable of relatively great industrial development will, even today, benefit also from a favorable location in respect of the great trade routes and the chief commercial centers of the world, nations deprived of the former advantage will not be compensated for that lack by the possession of the latter.

Position, then, in its *world* aspect, must be defined as the situation of the territory of a state, first in its relation to "the world that matters," and, second, in its relation to the principal trade routes and chief commercial centers of the earth. In both respects the influence of position upon national policy must therefore be evident; for, on the one hand, it will be an important factor in determining the ability of a nation to play the role of a Great Power, and, on the other hand, it will have a large part in deciding the nature and importance of its relations with other countries.

From the *regional* standpoint, the question of position relates to the continental location of a state's territorial base which is the seat of its government and the center of its wealth. In this respect it is obvious that in order to be a Great Power a state must be situated in Europe, Asia, or the Americas.[1] Since, moreover, the political circumstances in each of these continental regions differ greatly from those in the other two, it is evident that

[1] In international politics, Africa must be considered as a continental region apart, being composed politically of European colonial possessions and of states having a unique position in that they either are without political or economic importance, such as Ethiopia and Liberia, or are members of the British Commonwealth of Nations, with Dominion status, such as the Union of South Africa and Southern Rhodesia, or enjoy only limited sovereignty, as Egypt, which, although independent in law, in fact is under British control. Precisely the same detachment also characterizes the Australian continent.

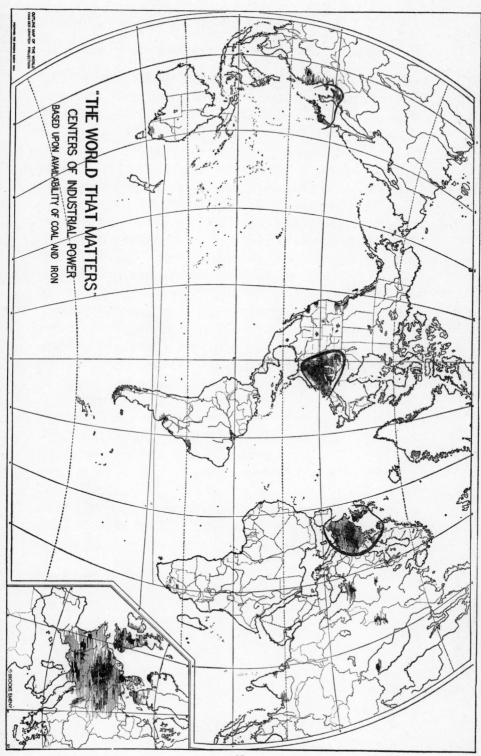

OUTLINE MAP OF THE WORLD
CHAU DER GRIATEN PROJECTION

PREPARED FOR BROOKS EMENY 1934

"THE WORLD THAT MATTERS"
CENTERS OF INDUSTRIAL POWER
BASED UPON AVAILABILITY OF COAL AND IRON

© BROOKS EMENY

very different consequences to national policy will result from the location of the territorial base of a state in Europe, in Asia, or in the Americas.

Thus, in the case of Europe, traditions of rivalry and persistence of territorial disputes have produced political conditions which necessarily exercise a decisive influence upon the policies of all states having their territorial bases in that continent. Accordingly the problem of national security and even of national existence is always an immediate concern of European governments. That problem, too, is posed by dangers peculiarly European and existing just beyond the frontiers of every Continental state.

In the Americas, by contrast, while economically the United States has manifestly the same concern with Mexican or Canadian conditions as have European states with those of their neighbors, politically the absence of all territorial disputes or of any serious national rivalries spares it regional anxieties. And the same is, of course, true in the case of both Mexico and Canada. In Central America and South America, to be sure, territorial disputes sometimes disturb the relations between states. Certain suspicions and jealousies do thus, in fact, exist in the New World, but the national policies of the considerable countries of North and South America, alike, are not dominated by the fears and dangers which necessarily shape the policies of European states.

In Asia, Japanese national policy is similarly shaped by conditions peculiar to the Far East. And these conditions also explain the possession by western nations of large continental and insular areas in the Asiatic region. For Japan, which alone of the Great Powers has its territorial base in that region, the policies of the western nations as they relate to Far Eastern questions are of vital importance. By contrast, since the Japanese possess no territory beyond the Asiatic region, their policy is without considerable European or American implications.

The significance of position in its regional aspect is therefore evident. Each of the three important continental regions, the European, American, and Asiatic, possesses a set of political conditions which differ profoundly from those of the others. As a consequence, the national policies of states, since they are shaped by their regional circumstances, will vary correspondingly. For all of the Great Powers save the United States, moreover, their regional circumstances constitute a restriction upon their policy elsewhere. For the United States, by contrast, the conditions of the American region constitute a guarantee of freedom of action everywhere, abroad as well as at home.

There remains for consideration the *inter-regional* aspect of position. Two states, Great Britain and France, possess territories in all five regions—European, American, Asiatic, Australasian, and African. Others, including Italy and Soviet Russia, hold lands in two regions. To this category the United States belongs, at least nominally, so long as it still retains the Philippines. It follows, therefore, that, the territory of these nations being located in several regions, their national policies will be affected by inter-regional conditions wherever they have possessions, and their policy will have an imperial as well as a purely regional phase.

Of course, even in the case of such states, the political conditions existing in the regions in which their territorial bases are situated will have first importance, so far

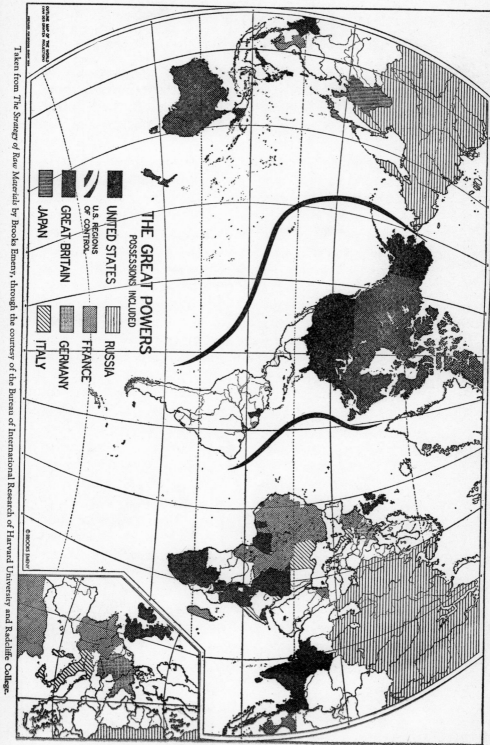

THE GREAT POWERS
POSSESSIONS INCLUDED

UNITED STATES

U.S. REGIONS
OF CONTROL

GREAT BRITAIN

JAPAN

RUSSIA

FRANCE

GERMANY

ITALY

OUTLINE MAP OF THE WORLD
(VAN DER GRINTEN PROJECTIONS)
PREPARED FOR BROOKS EMENY 1934

© BROOKS EMENY

as national policy is concerned. Nevertheless, for Great Britain and Soviet Russia, because their Asiatic possessions are of such vast extent and of such great value as well, political conditions within the Asiatic region must influence their national policies only a little less than do those in Europe. For France, by contrast, although her Asiatic possessions are considerable, it is the African portion of her empire which constitutes the greater consideration, so far as national policy is concerned. As for Italy, her overseas territories are mainly limited to the African continent and chiefly to portions of that continent so near to European shores as to be a detail in her regional, rather than her inter-regional, policy.

Viewed either from the regional or from the inter-regional standpoint, too, the contrast between the position of the United States and that of every other nation of the globe is at once striking and illuminating. The regional position of the United States gives it complete immunity from all those concerns and dangers which dominate and dictate the national policies of every European or Asiatic state. And the fact that, aside from the Philippines, it has no inter-regional position, leaves it utterly unconcerned on the political side with conditions in Europe, in Asia, or in Africa, so far as its own vital interests are directly concerned. Thus it has no dangers to guard against at home and no important exposed possessions to protect abroad. Accordingly, whatever dangers threaten it, if there actually be such, have their origin at a distance and where it has no territorial stake.

Yet such is the world position of the United States, and so great a share of "the world that matters" lies within its own frontiers, that its national policy must be a matter of concern alike for European and for Asiatic nations. Thus, while American policy can and does largely ignore that of every other nation, no great or small power of Europe or Asia can ever afford to ignore an American policy, which, although it may be determined by purely regional considerations, frequently has almost incalculable repercussions abroad.

In relation to national policy, the question of position has importance in certain other respects, both regional and inter-regional. As the territorial base of a state is insular or continental, that fact will exercise a decisive influence in the matter of national defense, for insular position must obviously bestow a measure of immunity from danger of invasion by military forces, while proportionately increasing the dangers of attack by hostile navies. Thus, for both Great Britain and Japan, the naval branch of national defense is of primary importance. For postwar Germany, by contrast, the military branch is of chief importance and the dangers of attack from the sea are very small.

Since both Great Britain and Japan, despite the fact that their territorial bases are insular, also possess large and vitally important lands whose situation is continental, they are therefore compelled to maintain considerable armies to defend these lands. By contrast, France and Italy, since their Mediterranean islands are of small relative value, are to all intents and purposes purely continental and therefore primarily military powers, although their possession of overseas lands also compels them to give serious attention to naval strength as well. Nevertheless, because for Great Britain and Japan communication with their overseas lands is a question of vital importance, while for France and Italy defense of the homeland territory is the primary concern, position takes on a different aspect in the case of these insular and continental states.

Here, again, the situation of the United States is unique; for while in fact the American position is continental, the conditions which exist within its region invest that position with the immunities of insularity. In addition, since the United States has no important possessions beyond its own region, it is freed from the necessity of maintaining large military forces abroad to defend such possessions. Whereas for Great Britain and Japan the naval branch of national defense is of primary importance and the military also is of great value, for the United States the military branch has practically no importance as an instrument of national policy, and the naval has value solely as a barrier against attack originating at a distance and directed at the American territorial base itself, or against its sea lines of communication about that base.

Russia, on the other hand, its regional and interregional situation being completely continental, can with utmost safety continue to ignore the naval branch of national defense and concentrate its attention upon the military. And in this respect, although Russia possesses vast territories outside the European region, which is the site of its territorial base, it is nevertheless in the same situation as Germany, which today holds no lands beyond European limits.

The problems of national defense will also be materially affected as the position of the territorial base of a state within its continental region is central or eccentric. Thus, postwar Germany, since its situation is central, has to reckon with political conditions on the Vistula, the Danube, and the Rhine, that is, on three sides, while

French concern is restricted directly to the regions of the Rhine and the western Alps, and Italian to those of the eastern and western Alps, because the position of both countries is eccentric.

Japan at the eastern edge of the Asiatic continent, and Great Britain at the western limit of the European, can disregard conditions at the opposite ends of their continental regions. As for the United States, the conditions within its own region permit it, although its position is actually central, to give almost as little military attention to its Mexican and Canadian frontiers as to its Atlantic and Pacific boundaries.

Position, too, exercises a decisive influence upon national policy in yet another respect. Thus, as a nation's access to the sea is direct or indirect, its policy will be free or subject to grave restrictions. These limitations will, of course, be far more crippling if the territories of a state are actually landlocked. But since completely landlocked states are both few in number and without primary importance, internationally, they can be ignored and attention directed to those possessing direct or indirect access to the sea. By direct access is meant possession of territories fronting open seas and endowed with ice-free harbors; while indirect access means possession of harbors upon enclosed waters whose outlets to the open seas are controlled by another state.

The situation of Great Britain, as of France, in this respect, supplies a sufficient example of direct access to the sea, since the approach of both to the Atlantic is not dominated by the territory of another state. By contrast, the Italian road to the open seas is closed on the west by Gibraltar and on the east by Suez, both of which are in British hands. As for the Germans, their way to the Atlantic is blocked by the British Isles. Italian policy has therefore always to take account of British command of its sea lines of communication, and for that reason, in its prewar alliance with Germany and Austria, it expressly stipulated that the treaty establishing this partnership would be inoperative if the Central Powers engaged in war with Great Britain. And the desire to break the strangle hold of the British was one of the reasons for the creation of the German navy in the prewar era.

In the same fashion, Russia finds its way out of the Baltic blocked by Germany, its road to the Mediterranean commanded by Turkey, and its free access to the Pacific closed by the Japanese Islands. It was the desire to obtain direct access to the open sea through ice-free harbors that dominated and shaped Russian policy from the Napoleonic era to the Revolution of 1917, as it was also the lack of such harbors that was responsible for Russian defeat in the World War.

The United States, by contrast, possesses direct access to both the Atlantic and the Pacific oceans and at Panama controls the canal between the two, while its naval bases give it practical mastery of the Caribbean Sea. Thus, its position in respect of access to the sea insures the maximum of freedom of action in the matter of national policy, alike in peace and in war.

It must then be evident how important in relation to the national policy of a state is the position of its territory; for upon this circumstance must turn the character of its national policy and the nature and extent of its organization for national defense.

Chapter IV

THE ECONOMIC FACTOR

SECOND among the basic factors of national policy (page 41) is the economic, the primary elements of which, land and people, must be considered respectively from the point of view of production and of numbers. As the geographic factor is largely a question of position, the economic is almost exclusively a matter of self-sufficiency and population pressure.

States, by reason of the types of their production, fall naturally into three groups, the agrarian, the industrial, and the balanced.[1]

To the first group, the agrarian, belong those nations which are capable of feeding themselves and also of

[1] For general comparative studies of the raw material and industrial situation of states, see: American Academy of Political and Social Science, "Raw Materials and Foodstuffs in the Commercial Policies of Nations," *The Annals*, Vol. CXII, March, 1924; Bain, H. F., *Ores and Industry in the Far East*, 1933; Bowman, Isaiah, *The New World*, 1928, 4th ed.; Delaisi, Francis, *Les Deux Europes; Europe Industrielle et Europe Agricole*, 1929; Emeny, Brooks, *The Strategy of Raw Materials; A Study of America in Peace and War*, 1934; Furness, J. W., and Jones, L. M., *Mineral Raw Materials*, Trade Promotion Series No. 76, Bureau of Foreign and Domestic Commerce, 1929; Gini, C., *Report on Certain Aspects of the Raw Materials Problem*, League of Nations, 1922; Leith, C. K., *World Minerals and World Politics*, 1931; Lippincott, I., *Economic Resources and Industries of the World*, 1929; Zimmermann, E. W., *World Resources and Industries*, 1933.

producing an exportable surplus of one or more kinds—foodstuffs, raw materials, minerals—but which, by reason of their lack of resources in coal and iron in exploitable quantities and combination, and by reason, also, of their distance from such resources on foreign territory, are unable to support any considerable national industry.

To the second group, the industrial, belong those states which, while lacking most of the essentials of industry on their own soil and, in certain cases, also foodstuffs in sufficient quantities to feed their own populations or support their national industries, have nevertheless been able to build up great industrial establishments by reason of the accessibility of their home-land territory to foreign reserves and resources in the essentials of motive power and in the necessary raw materials and ores.

To the third group, the balanced, belong those states which are advantageously situated in respect of the needs both of their people and of their industry, being, on the one hand, able to feed their population and, on the other, to support their industries from the resources of their own territory.

To the agrarian group belong all the states in South America and those in continental Asia, as well as many of the smaller European countries; to the industrial group, Great Britain, Germany, Italy, Japan, and France; and to the balanced group, the United States, the Soviet Union, and the British Empire taken as a whole.

It will be noted at once that no purely agrarian country takes rank as a Great Power, and the reason for this is obvious: Today, war has become largely a question,

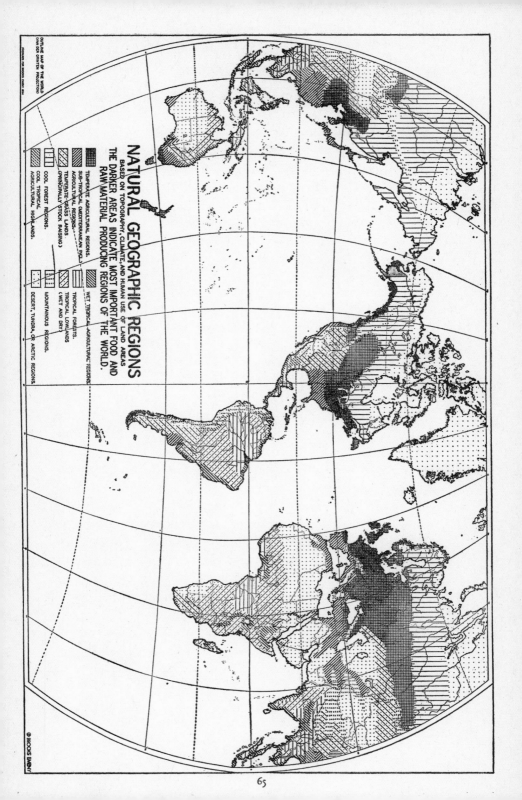

NATURAL GEOGRAPHIC REGIONS

BASED ON TOPOGRAPHY, CLIMATE, AND HUMAN USE OF LAND AREAS

THE DARKER AREAS INDICATE MOST IMPORTANT FOOD AND
RAW MATERIAL PRODUCING REGIONS OF THE WORLD.

TEMPERATE AGRICULTURAL REGIONS.

SUB-TROPICAL MEDITERRANEAN AGRICULTURAL REGIONS.

AGRICULTURAL REGIONS.

TEMPERATE GRASS LANDS (PRINCIPALLY STOCK RAISING)

WET TROPICAL AGRICULTURAL REGIONS.

TROPICAL FORESTS.

TROPICAL LOWLANDS (WET AND DRY)

MOUNTAINOUS REGIONS.

COOL FOREST REGIONS.

COOL TROPICAL AGRICULTURAL HIGHLANDS.

DESERT, TUNDRA, OR ARCTIC REGIONS.

OUTLINE MAP OF THE WORLD
(ON GOR GINTER PROJECTION)

PREPARED FOR BROOKS BARNEY 1934

© BROOKS BARNEY

not of man power but of machine power,[1] and as a consequence, states incapable of developing considerable national industries are also incapable of playing the role
of a Great Power.[2] It is, moreover, this absence of considerable industrial establishments which explains the
relative political insignificance of all states belonging
to the predominantly agrarian group. So far from being
self-sufficient, therefore, these states are manifestly de-

[1] The important relation of the industrial and economic development of a state to
its strength in war is clearly defined in the report of Sub-Committee A of the Preparatory Commission on Disarmament, of which the following statement of the basic
factors of national power is directly pertinent (League of Nations, C739. M278.
1926 IX No. 16 CPD 28 p. 12 *et seq.;* italics, however, by authors):

"A complete list of the factors which come into operation in modern war would
have to include *all the factors of the national life in time of peace.*

"It is, however, necessary to determine the *factors which are of main importance in
war and on which consequently the strength of a country in war time essentially depends.*

"These fundamental factors are as follows in the case of any country at war:

"(1) The quantity, quality, and the degree of preparation for war of the land, sea,
and air forces in existence at the opening of the war or formed in the course of the war;
also the armament, equipment, and upkeep of those forces;

"(2) The number, composition, and distribution of its inhabitants, taking into
account the resources in men that might be obtained from overseas territories, and
also the resources in men that would, on the contrary, have to be kept in those territories;

"(3) *The extent to which it is self-supporting (for instance, as regards fuel, foodstuffs,
raw material, and manufactured goods), and the extent to which, as a result of its means of
transport and the freedom of its communications, especially its communications by sea, and of
its financial strength, it can obtain the commodities of every kind in which it is deficient from
abroad;*

"(4) The geographical situation, the configuration of its territory, and the development of its system of means of communication of every kind, which may enable or
prevent it from rapidly moving and supplying its forces;

"(5) Fixed defensive systems of the mother country and colonies (fortifications,
naval and air bases, naval stations, etc.);

"(6) The time which is at its disposal to prepare and bring its forces into operation
or to allow of outside help reaching the country without danger of invasion, due to:
either the natural protection afforded it by the sea or strong frontiers; or its peacetime
armaments . . . *or the measures which it has been able to adopt in order to expedite the mobilization of at least a part of its resources;*

"(7) *The capacity of the country to produce or import* war materials in war time (ships,
aircraft, war material of every kind);

"(8) The internal and external political situation."

[2] Eckel, E. C., *Coal, Iron and War,* 1930; Emeny, Brooks, *The Strategy of Raw Materials; A Study of America in Peace and War,* 1934; Inter-Parliamentary Union, *What
Would Be the Character of a New War?,* 1931.

pendent upon the industrial establishments of other countries, alike in peace and in war.

The situation of the second group of states, those which are the possessors of relatively considerable industries but are dependent upon foreign sources for foodstuffs or for many of the essentials of industry, is, from the standpoint of self-sufficiency in war, equally significant. Thus Germany and Great Britain are to a large but unequal degree dependent upon the outside world for the food to sustain their populations. In addition, while both are rich in coal, both are poor alike in iron and in most of the other raw materials and minerals necessary to their industries.

Italy, Japan, and France are largely self-supporting in the matter of food, although on the basis of widely varying standards of living. In this respect, therefore, their situation is vastly better than that of Great Britain or of Germany. But Italy and Japan are almost wholly deficient both in coal and in iron, while France, although extremely rich in iron, has insufficient coal reserve to support its national industry. And all three share the limitations of Great Britain and of Germany in the matter of most raw materials and essential minerals.

Only the United States and the Soviet Union actually possess, in their homeland territory, both the resources in foodstuffs requisite to support their populations and the reserves in motive power and resources in raw materials and minerals necessary to support their industries on present or prospective scales of output. Between these two Great Powers, however, there is an important difference, due to the fact that the United States already has developed a national industry commensurate with

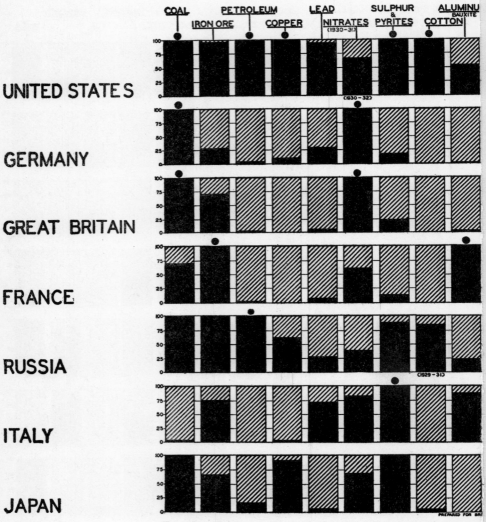

STRATEGIC SITUATION O

NATIONAL SELF-SUFFICIENCY IN ESSEN

EXPRESSED IN PERCENTAGES OF DOMESTIC PRODUC

■ DOMESTIC PRODUCTION.   ▨ NET IMPORTS.

UNLESS OTHERWISE NOTED PERCENTAGES FOR ALL POWERS ARE YEAR

Taken from *The Strategy of Raw Materials* by Brooks Emeny, through the courte,

F THE GREAT POWERS

TIAL INDUSTRIAL RAW MATERIALS

TION AND NET IMPORTS TO CONSUMPTION

⬤ NET EXPORTS LARGER THAN TWO PERCENT OF THE TOTAL
APPARENT CONSUMPTION OF THE SEVEN POWERS.

LY AVERAGES FOR 1925–29 INCLUSIVE (EXCEPT RUSSIA, 1929–32)

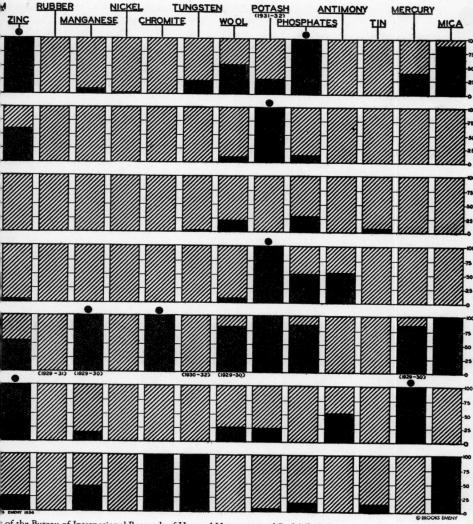

of the Bureau of International Research of Harvard University and Radcliffe College.

national needs, while Russian industrialization is only in an early stage.

A clear distinction must also be noted in the matter of the extent of the industrial establishments of the seven Great Powers, for the size of a nation's industry has today become the indication of its potential strength in war.[1] While for Great Britain, Germany, and France industrial production suffices for national needs and would be adequate to support national defense in time of war, and while the industrial output of Italy, Japan, and Russia is important though insufficient for domestic needs, the national capacity of any one of those six powers is relatively inconsiderable in comparison with that of the United States. In fact, American production and domestic consumption each constitutes approximately half of the aggregate of the entire world.

In considering Great Britain, however, it is necessary to emphasize the difference between the situation of the United Kingdom and that of the British Empire as a whole.[2] Although in the matter of foodstuffs and raw materials Great Britain suffers from much the same poverty as Germany, her greatest industrial rival in Europe, the situation of the British Empire is quite otherwise. Like the United States and the Soviet Union, the British Empire is largely self-sufficient in all respects and also, unlike the Soviet Union, is already the possessor of a great industrial establishment. On the other hand, while the territories of the United States and of the Soviet Union are compact, those of the British Empire are scattered about the Seven Seas.

[1] Emeny, Brooks, *The Strategy of Raw Materials; A Study of America in Peace and War,* 1934.
[2] Boycott, A. G., *Elements of Imperial Defence,* 1931; Cole, Captain D. H., *Imperial Military Geography,* 1930, 6th ed.

Viewed from the standpoint of self-sufficiency, it is plain, then, that the three groups of states (page 63) are on a very unequal footing. Only the United States and the Soviet Union, within their homeland areas, are capable, the first actually, the second potentially, of feeding their populations and also of supporting their industries with only the slightest measure of dependence upon the outside world. Much the same measure of self-sufficiency is possessed by the British Empire, with the difference, however, that the accessibility of imperial resources for the United Kingdom, which is the seat of the wealth and power of the Empire, is subject in time of peace to the control of price as affected by transportation costs, and in time of war is contingent upon the maintenance of command of the sea lanes of communication.

The control of the seas by enemy fleets would carry small threat to the Soviet Union and little or none to the United States, so far as national life or national industry is concerned; but for Great Britain, with only six months of foodstuffs normally available from domestic production and with practically all the necessities of industry save coal lacking in sufficient quantities, blockade would spell starvation, paralysis, and therefore surrender in war. For Germany, which feeds its population for eight months of the year, the effect of blockade would be less immediate in this respect but equally fatal in all else.

The weakness of the British and German situations was plainly revealed during the World War.[1] When the

[1] Baker, C. W., *Government Control and Operation of Industry in Great Britain and the United States During the World War*, 1921; Beveridge, Sir W. H., *British Food Control*, 1928; Delbrück, Clemens von, *Die Wirtschaftliche Mobilmachung in Deutschland*, 1924; Goebel, O. H., *Deutsche Rohstoffwirtschaft im Weltkrieg*, 1930; Guichard, Louis, *The Naval Blockade*, 1930; Salter, Sir Arthur, *Allied Shipping Control: An Experiment in International Administration*, 1921; Smith, G. O., *The Strategy of Minerals*, 1919; Surface, F. M., *The Grain Trade During the World War*, 1928.

submarine campaign reached its highest point of effectiveness, Great Britain was within hailing distance of starvation and surrender. And it was the British blockade that, by closing all German doors opening on the outer world, eventually compelled a German surrender dictated by undernourishment of the population and by complete exhaustion of stocks of many essential raw materials.

The Italian situation is much worse than either the German or the British in the matter of minerals and of raw materials alike, for coal is lacking, together with most of the other essential commodities. Thus, while in a pinch Italy might feed herself, under the pressure of a blockade her industry would collapse almost immediately.[1]

As for the French colonial empire, although a valuable source of foodstuffs and of a few raw materials, it contributes relatively little to national self-sufficiency. Economically, however, it is an important outlet for French industrial production; and on the military side, it forms an important reservoir of man power. This latter circumstance, moreover, invests French colonial lines of communication with much the same importance as the British.[2]

In the matter of self-sufficiency, therefore, France, while better off than Great Britain, Germany, Italy, or even Japan, is far inferior to the United States, the British Empire, or the Soviet Union. Completely blockaded by land and sea, France could hold out for a considerable time, but in the end, while her supplies of food, iron, and even coal might suffice, her shortage of other supplies would ultimately prove decisive.

[1] See Chapter XIII.   [2] See Chapter XI.

The vulnerability of Great Britain, the fact that it is a matter of life or death for her to keep open her sea lanes, has, for Germany, Italy, and even measurably for France as well, a profound significance in the field of national policy. The lack of self-sufficiency imposes upon Great Britain the necessity to possess naval supremacy in European waters, a supremacy which she is financially able to support; and this naval supremacy, coupled with the British position alike on the North Sea and in the Mediterranean, permits the British to forbid all sea approach to Germany and to Italy, and also to the Mediterranean and Channel coasts of France. In addition, it permits them to interrupt at will the communication between France and her North African colonies, whence come the bulk of her overseas military contingents.

Since Germany and Italy are wholly, and France to a considerable degree, dependent upon the outside world, and particularly upon transoceanic lands, for necessary minerals and raw materials, and since, also, it lies within the power of the British fleet to prevent or gravely to hamper communication with these foreign sources of supply, it follows that German, Italian, and French national policies will necessarily be shaped in such fashion as to avoid conflict with the British. It was the failure of Germany, in 1914, to adhere to this traditional course, that insured German defeat in the World War.

It must be noted, however, that the extreme vulnerability of Great Britain in the matter of sea blockade bestows upon France, by reason of her geographic position and therefore of her ability to strike quickly either by airplane or by submarine, a certain degree of independence in the matter of national policy lacking alike in the case of Italy and in the case of Germany. And this circumstance also dictates British concern for French security to the extent of opposing the occupation of the French coast by any state which might exploit that vantage point to British disadvantage. The same concern is naturally felt also for Belgian and Dutch neutrality.

The situation of Japan in the matter of self-sufficiency is, in the main, comparable with that of Great Britain. Although Japan is able to feed herself to a vastly greater extent at present, the rapid growth of her population is steadily increasing her dependence upon the outside world for foodstuffs, while within her island kingdom she is to an even greater extent than Great Britain without the necessary raw materials and minerals essential to industry.[1] For her, as for Italy or Germany, therefore, a blockade would be fatal, as, of course, it would be for Great Britain far more promptly.

Unlike all of the European states save the Soviet Union, however, Japan finds herself adjacent to lands easily accessible and provided with many of the raw materials which she lacks, together with precious resources in foodstuffs. Therefore, while Japan suffers from most if not all of the limitations of Germany and Italy, in the matter of self-sufficiency, she can largely remedy her lack, provided she can both dominate the seas separating her from China and control the Chinese provinces north of the Great Wall. Thus naval supremacy in the waters of eastern Asia is as vital for Japan as similar supremacy in European waters is for Great Britain.[2]

[1] Orchard, J. E., *Japan's Economic Position*, 1930; Penrose, E. F., *Food Supply and Raw Materials in Japan*, 1930.

[2] See Chapter XX.

So far the question of self-sufficiency has been considered chiefly from the standpoint of war, where its significance must be obvious. The further fact that all states, large and small, give clear proof of their recognition that conflict is always possible, also explains the concern of every country to be economically self-sufficient in the largest measure possible. And that fact is equally illuminating as it explains the resolution of certain Great Powers, today hopelessly dependent upon the outside world for the necessities of national life and industry, to escape from their present condition of inferiority; for it is manifest that in the next great war, as in the last, victory will in all human probability belong, not to the side which counts the biggest battalions, as in the Napoleonic era, but to the coalition that possesses the greatest economic resources.[1]

Looking now to the implications of the economic factor in times of peace, it must be recognized at once that in recent years, at least, these implications have become well-nigh identical with those in time of war. During the postwar period, and particularly after the onset of the Great Depression of 1929, those states possessing the largest degree of self-sufficiency, and therefore the major share of the world's reserves in motive power and resources in raw materials and minerals, have progressively adopted a policy of exclusive exploitation of their resources.[2] As a consequence, the situation of

[1] Eckel, E. C., *Coal, Iron and War*, 1930; Inter-Parliamentary Union, *What Would Be the Character of a New War?*, 1931.

[2] Hawtrey, R. G., *Economic Aspects of Sovereignty*, 1930; International Institute of Intellectual Co-operation, *The State and Economic Life*, 1934; League of Nations, *Report and Proceedings of the World Economic Conference*, 1927; Patterson, E. M., *The World's Economic Dilemma*, 1930; Rawles, W. P., *The Nationality of Commercial Control of World Minerals*, 1933; Simpson, Kemper, *Introduction to World Economics*, 1934; Wallace, B. B., and Edminster, L. R., *International Control of Raw Materials*, 1930.

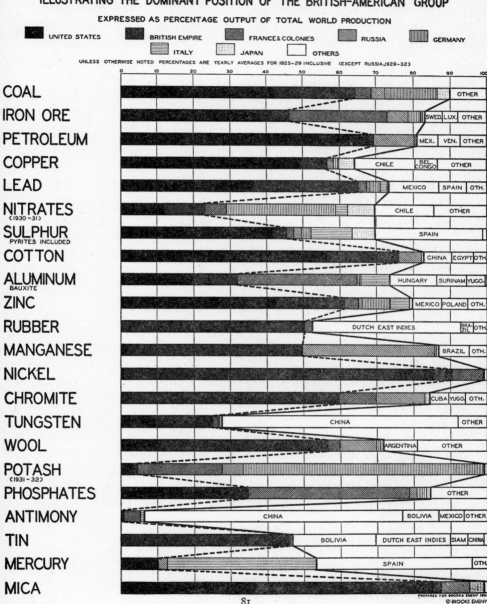

RAW MATERIAL MONOPOLY OF THE POWERS
ILLUSTRATING THE DOMINANT POSITION OF THE BRITISH-AMERICAN GROUP

EXPRESSED AS PERCENTAGE OUTPUT OF TOTAL WORLD PRODUCTION

UNITED STATES   BRITISH EMPIRE   FRANCE & COLONIES   RUSSIA   GERMANY

ITALY   JAPAN   OTHERS

UNLESS OTHERWISE NOTED PERCENTAGES ARE YEARLY AVERAGES FOR 1925-29 INCLUSIVE (EXCEPT RUSSIA) 1929-32)

0   10   20   30   40   50   60   70   80   90   100

COAL — OTHER

IRON ORE — SWED. LUX. OTHER

PETROLEUM — MEX. VEN. OTHER

COPPER — CHILE BEL. CONGO OTHER

LEAD — MEXICO SPAIN OTH.

NITRATES (1930-31) — CHILE OTHER

SULPHUR PYRITES INCLUDED — SPAIN

COTTON — CHINA EGYPT OTH.

ALUMINUM BAUXITE — HUNGARY SURINAM YUGO.

ZINC — MEXICO POLAND OTH.

RUBBER — DUTCH EAST INDIES BRAZIL OTH.

MANGANESE — BRAZIL OTH.

NICKEL

CHROMITE — CUBA YUGO. OTH.

TUNGSTEN — CHINA OTHER

WOOL — ARGENTINA OTHER

POTASH

PHOSPHATES — OTHER

ANTIMONY — CHINA BOLIVIA MEXICO OTHER

TIN — BOLIVIA DUTCH EAST INDIES SIAM CHINA

MERCURY — SPAIN OTH.

MICA

PREPARED FOR BROOKS EMENY 1934
© BROOKS EMENY

the less fortunate has inevitably and progressively worsened.

These less richly endowed states, notably Germany, Italy, and Japan, can obviously purchase abroad the raw materials which they lack at home, only as they are also able to sell abroad the goods which they produce; or, in the case of Italy, only as they export emigrants whose remittances from abroad balance necessary foreign purchases. The fact that Great Britain has abandoned free trade and the further fact that the United States has shut out foreign immigration and still further heightened tariff walls, while the Soviet Union has undertaken a vast program of industrial action, have produced alarming repercussions, not only in Germany, Italy, and Japan but also among smaller countries similarly situated. And the results for France, if less considerable, have been hardly pleasant.

What the consequences of this contemporary phenomenon of economic nationalism may be, can perhaps be best indicated by examination of the situations of the several Great Powers individually.

The United States, possessing as it does the richest and most extensive domestic market in the world, as a result of the size of its population and the extent of its consuming power and also of the high degree of its self-sufficiency in industrial raw materials, finds itself confronted largely with a problem of distribution.[1] It can feed its population, it can supply its industry, it possesses surpluses in many things which other states require in

[1] Crowther, Samuel, *America Self-Contained*, 1933; Donham, W. B., *Business Adrift*, 1931; Foreign Policy Association and World Peace Foundation, "America Must Choose" by Wallace, H. A., *World Affairs Pamphlets No. 3*, 1934; Foreman, Clark, *The New Internationalism*, 1934; Lautman, Jules, *Les Aspects Nouveaux du Protectionnisme*, 1933; Roorbach, G. B., *Problems in Foreign Trade*, 1933.

sufficient quantity to enable it by trade to fill the gaps in national production. Thus it was perhaps only natural that, possessing self-sufficiency to the extent it does, the United States should have been the nation to give the first signal for the start of the present march toward autarky.[1]

The example set by the United States was followed not only by the British Isles, but also by the Dominions of the British Empire generally. Thus, where the United States raised its tariffs, Great Britain not only abandoned free trade but also undertook by the Ottawa Agreement to establish a system of imperial preference.[2] In this fashion, the British strove to establish within their empire the same kind of economic unit, based upon a similar measure of economic self-sufficiency, which the United States already constituted.

In the case of the Soviet Union, much the same experiment was adopted under circumstances which were very different. The objective of the Soviet Union was to establish a balance between its agriculture and its industry and thus to attain complete self-sufficiency and thereby political as well as economic independence. And once more, as in the case of the United States and of the British Commonwealth of Nations, the physical circumstances of the Soviet Union are adequate to insure the success of the experiment; Russia is capable of a high degree of self-sufficiency.

[1] The word "autarky," meaning "self-sufficiency," is from the Greek *autarkeia*, while "autarchy," meaning "absolute sovereignty," is from the Greek *autarchia*. The roots are different: *ark-*, "suffice," and *arch-*, "rule." But as the two English words "autarky" and "autarchy" are pronounced alike, they have been confused, and "autarky" is written "autarchy" by most authors.

[2] Cole, G. D. H., *British Trade and Industry*, 1932; Foreign Policy Association, "Ottawa Conference," *Foreign Policy Reports*, Vol. VIII, No. 21, 1932; Imperial Economic Conference, *Report of the Conference*, 1932; Tryon, G. C., *A Short History of Imperial Preference*, 1931.

In all three instances, moreover, it is evident that the basic conditions are substantially the same on the economic side. Each state possesses a relatively large population and actual wealth alike in minerals, foodstuffs, and raw materials. Geographically and politically, the circumstances of the United States and of the Soviet Union are more advantageous than those of the British Commonwealth, since the territories of the former are compact, while that of the latter is scattered. In consequence, the whole area of the United States and the whole area of the Soviet Union are each under a single government, while that of the British Commonwealth is divided among self-governing dominions. Nevertheless, in theory at least, self-sufficiency is possible to a very large degree in the cases of all three.

As to France, her situation is far less satisfactory, although her colonial empire is vast in extent and rich in certain of the resources which she lacks. In the matter of foodstuffs France is self-supporting, while her colonies constitute, together with the homeland area, a market sufficient to support the larger part of the present national industrial establishment. But in many of the essential raw materials her empire is singularly lacking, and her dependence for them upon foreign sources, particularly British and American, remains highly important.

However, so long as French policy rigidly avoids conflict with the Anglo-Saxon powers—and with them there is no clash in vital interests—French access to the raw materials and minerals which are lacking within her empire is assured. Her position is strengthened, furthermore, by the fact that she possesses sufficient resources to produce an adequate supply of many of the industrial commodities in demand abroad, thus enabling her to purchase what she needs in foreign markets. Accordingly, the French Empire constitutes the fourth among the political units of the world capable of being self-sufficient alike in peace and in war, so long as relations with Great Britain, and to a lesser degree with the United States, are satisfactory.

To the United States, the British Commonwealth, the Soviet Union, and the French Empire, then, the extent of their economic self-sufficiency dictates a static national policy. Within their present territorial limits, these powers have reserves and resources sufficient to insure prosperity in peace, while in war they possess or can normally obtain the essentials of modern combat in adequate quantities. The primary concern of national policy in each case must therefore be to conserve what is already possessed.

The situation of the other three Great Powers is utterly different. As to Germany, the size of her domestic population and the relative poverty of her territory in most of the essentials of industry compel her to expand her foreign markets.[1] To do this she possesses the requisite industrial plant, but her capacity to produce at home and also to sell abroad is obviously conditioned upon her access both to those reserves in raw materials and to those markets which are mainly controlled by the more fortunate Great Powers.[2]

In Italy and Japan, the situation has been aggravated by the growing effect of population pressure, which has begun to make itself felt in Germany as well. Population pressure, of course, is determined primarily neither

[1] Angell, J. W., *The Recovery of Germany*, 1932; Michels, R. K., *Cartels, Combines and Trusts in Post-war Germany*, 1928; Sombart, Werner, *ed.*, *Volk und Raum*, 1928.
[2] Douglass, P. F., *The Economic Dilemma of Politics*, 1932.

by the size nor by the density of population, but by the relation existing between these and national productivity.[1] The existing situation will manifestly be affected by the rate of the annual increase in numbers of people in relation to the expansion in production. The fact that Great Britain and Germany are far more densely populated than the United States or Russia is not, in itself, significant. But when, as in the case of Germany at least temporarily, and of Japan and Italy permanently, population has passed the saturation point, regard being had to the capacity of the territories of each country to maintain the present standard of living, then the effect upon national policy of this condition of density must be immediate and far-reaching. For each country will, as at least one solution of the problem, seek lands abroad on which to establish its surplus population, and in order to retain that surplus as an element of national power it will also strive to include those lands within its own empire.

Exactly the same results will be discoverable, but in an even greater degree, when, the population of a state having actually reached or passed the point of saturation, every year sees a further increase due to a surplus of births over deaths. The rate of natural increase, too, will have a direct influence upon the energy with which the national policy pursues the primary objective of acquiring lands suitable for colonization. In this cir-

[1] For books dealing with the broad aspects of the problem of population pressure, see: Carr-Saunders, A. M., *Population*, 1925; Crocker, W. R., *The Japanese Population Problem, The Coming Crisis*, 1931; Dennery, Étienne, *Asia's Teeming Millions*, 1931; Dublin, L. I., ed., *Population Problems*, 1926; East, E. M., *Mankind at the Crossroads*, 1923; Gini, Corrado *et al. Population*, 1930; International Union for the Scientific Investigation of Population Problems, 2d Assembly, *Problems of Population*, 1932; Pitt-Rivers, G. H. L. F., ed., *Problems of Population*, 1932; Roberts, S. H., *Population Problems of the Pacific*, 1927; Thompson, W. S., *Danger Spots in World Population*, 1929; Uyeda, Teijiro, *The Future of Japanese Population*, 1933.

cumstance it is possible, for example, to discover an explanation for the familiar insistence on the part of various Italian and German statesmen upon a redivision of the earth's surface.

For France, Soviet Russia, and the United States, by contrast, neither density of population nor rate of natural increase has importance in relation to national policy. France not only has a low density and a practically stationary population in her homeland area, but also possesses vast colonial territories capable of absorbing any present or future surplus. The situation of Russia and the United States is even more favorable, because, although each has a growing population, nevertheless its density of population is low and the point of saturation for its territory is still far removed. Great Britain, too, although its density of population is high, still finds a certain outlet for her surplus in her Dominions, and in addition the rate of increase of population has already or nearly reached the vanishing point owing to voluntary but not less effective exercise of birth control. As a consequence, for her the population problem is hardly acute.

The desire to acquire markets and to possess new lands rich in natural resources, to insure the prosperity of larger populations at home quite as much as to obtain territories abroad suitable for colonization, was also one of the compelling motives of national policy in the case of certain of the Great Powers of Europe in the closing quarter of the nineteenth century, and in fact to the very eve of the World War itself. And this motive has again been revealed in the case of Japan in Manchuria, where the underlying cause is discoverable in a deliberate attempt to counteract the effect of population pressure.

The population of Japan has already passed the point of saturation, while the rate of annual increase is still relatively very high indeed. Hence, as a substitute for acquiring lands upon which to establish her surplus population, Japan has undertaken to control territories whose markets and resources appear in her eyes sufficient to make it possible for her to maintain her great and growing population at home. Germany's demand for the return of her lost colonies is likewise based quite as much upon the need of markets and of raw materials as upon the need of lands suitable for colonization, although by contrast the Ukrainian projects of Hitler are frankly based upon a program of colonization.

LAND UTILIZATION AND POPULATION PRESSURE OF THE SEVEN GREAT POWERS

	United States	Germany	Great Britain	France	Russia	Italy	Japan
Total area in square miles.............	3,088,519	180,972	94,400	212,700	8,439,000	119,700	152,360
Per cent of arable and pasture land.......	42.0	63.4	80.0	67.0	30.0	73.5	18.9
Per cent of total area cultivated.........	18.8	59.0	31.0	46.6	15.0	68.6	15.5
Millions of population (000,000 omitted)..	125	66	45	42	165	42	67
Population per square mile of arable land.	100	578	596	294	66	477	2,418
Average annual increase in population	756,000	336,000	170,000	55,000	2,500,000*	423,000	908,000

*Estimated.

Density and the rate of increase of the population, as these produce population pressure, must therefore profoundly affect the national policy of Great Powers.

They will drive powers subjected to such pressure to seek changes in the territorial status quo of the world and thus bring them into collision with the states whose interest lies in maintaining the status quo both in respect of their own territories and in respect of those of other states.

Within limits, too, population pressure operating in smaller states will, like lack of economic self-sufficiency, produce disturbing consequences. But the weakness of these countries will deprive their discontent of importance save as it constitutes a temptation to the Great Powers to intervene in their political affairs. On the other hand, the existence of misery and social unrest in the smaller states contributes to disturb the general regional situation, as events in the Danubian Basin in Europe have plainly demonstrated.

The relation between the development of explosive nationalistic movements in Italy, Germany, and Japan, and the economic circumstances of these states, has found too little recognition as yet in the United States and Great Britain. Thus Fascism has been explained in terms of the personality of Mussolini and the national characteristics of the Italian people. In the same manner, National Socialism has been ascribed to the personality of Hitler and to the consequences of a Punic peace for Germany. And the Japanese seizure of Manchuria has been explained as a relapse to old-fashioned imperialism due to the temporary ascendancy of the military element in Japan.

Despite the present habit of ascribing Italian events to the ambition of the Duce and the delight of the Italian people in drama, the fact cannot be blinked that Italy today faces a choice between drastic reduction of

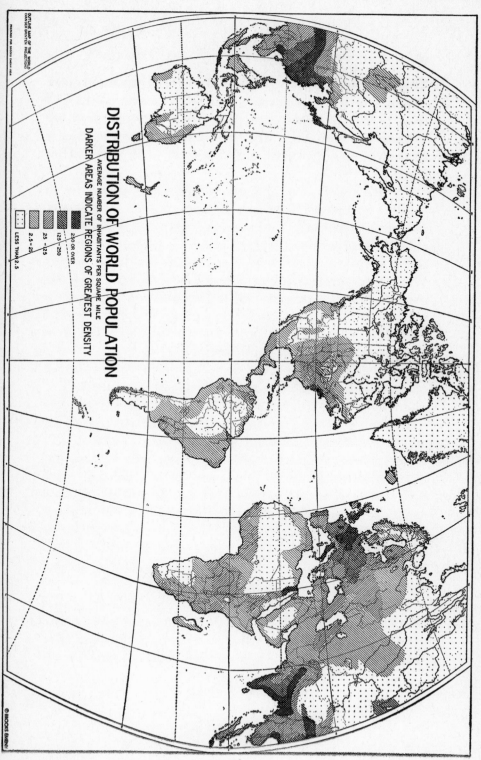

DISTRIBUTION OF WORLD POPULATION

AVERAGE NUMBER OF INHABITANTS PER SQUARE MILE

DARKER AREAS INDICATE REGIONS OF GREATEST DENSITY

250 OR OVER
125 - 250
25 - 125
2.5 - 25
LESS THAN 2.5

OUTLINE MAP OF THE WORLD
(CRATTER GRINTEN PROJECTION)

PREPARED FOR BUDDIE SMIXY 1934

© BROOKS SMIXY

91

population by birth control and passive acceptance of a declining standard of living. Such a reduction of population plainly foreshadows a progressive decline in Italian political importance, while a falling standard of living would threaten eventual, if not immediate, social upheaval.

It is equally evident that, although the German people have by resort to birth control brought their birth rate below the French, and thus greatly reduced the annual increment to population,[1] the effect of population pressure continues to be felt. In the east, too, the unchecked birth rate of the Poles is having present effect and forecasts future results far from attractive to the cause of Germanism in the Vistula and Baltic regions.

The double effect, upon German material existence, of the world-wide depression and of the Jewish boycott provoked by the Hitler Revolution has, moreover, served to emphasize to all Germans the weakness of their economic situation. Together, these two events, depression and boycott, have had the character of a blockade and the results have been the same, because, being unable to sell abroad, Germany has been unable to purchase in necessary quantities the raw materials she requires.

In Japan, population pressure is far more seriously felt than in Germany or as yet even in Italy. And, of course, relatively the same poverty in foodstuffs and raw materials exists; for although, like Italy, Japan still feeds itself, the limit of possibility has about been reached and the level of subsistence is comparatively low. Although

---

[1] In 1932 the birth and death rates per 1,000 in Germany and France stood as follows:

	Birth Rate	Death Rate
Germany	15.5	11.2
France	17.2	15.7

Fascist Italy and National Socialist Germany have not
so far been able to translate their program of national
expansion into action, it is certainly the promise of
Mussolini and Hitler to remove present restraints by
force that has won them a large part of their present
popularity and power.

The far-reaching nature of the implications of the
economic factor of national policy must therefore be
evident, for these must determine whether the national
policy of a state is to be static or dynamic.

Chapter V

THE DEMOGRAPHIC FACTOR

THIRD among the basic factors of national policy (page 41) is the demographic, which is constituted by the people of a state considered from the two aspects of numbers and ethnic circumstances. Another aspect, that of race, is likewise to be noted.[1] There is, however, no considerable state whose population is predominantly black, while the differences between the yellow and white races, as these affect national policy, have their origin in varying levels of political and economic attainment rather than in any fundamental inequality in capacity for development due to racial characteristics.[2]

In recent years there has developed a considerable

[1] For general descriptive studies of the character and history of the various racial groups, see: Bean, R. B., *The Races of Man: Differentiation and Dispersal of Man*, 1932; Dixon, Roland, *The Racial History of Man*, 1923; Duncan, H. G., *Race and Population Problems*, 1929; Haddon, A. C., *The Races of Man and Their Distribution*, 1925; Huntington, E., *The Character of Races*, 1924; Reuter, E. B., *Race Mixture*, 1931; Taylor, T. G., *Environment and Race*, 1927. For discussions of race as a political factor, both national and international, see: Finot, Jean, *Race Prejudice*, 1924; Garth, T. R., *Race Psychology*, 1930; Gregory, J. W., *Race as a Political Factor*, 1931; Remington, W. E., *World States of the Machine Age*, 1932; Wrench, G. T., *The Causes of War and Peace*, 1926.

[2] For general books on the racial basis of civilization, see: Cornéjo, M. H., *The Balance of the Continents*, 1932; Muret, Maurice, *The Twilight of the White Races*, 1926; Spengler, Oswald, *The Decline of the West*, 1926-28, 2 vols.

literature devoted to the discussion of the question of future collision between different racial groups.[1] In its relation to contemporary international relations, however, this question has immediate importance only in the case of the Japanese. Discrimination between the yellow and white races in the immigration laws of the United States, Canada, and Australia has unquestionably been responsible for a state of mind which finds expression, to a degree at least, in Japanese policy. Yet even here the Japanese feeling is national rather than racial and as such is analogous to the ethnic passions of Central Europe.

The rise of the National Socialists to power in Germany has been accompanied by an outbreak of persecution of the Jewish minority which has been justified by appeal to racial considerations. Actually, however, the Aryan and Nordic myths,[2] so solemnly paraded in Germany today, are without real foundation and find credence only among the followers of Hitler. Nor is it necessary to attach greater importance to the legends of the "yellow peril," which is equally imaginary and similarly without importance save as a means of sowing prejudice and arousing passions which, however un-

[1] See: Chidell, Fleetwood, *Australia—White or Yellow*, 1926; Duboscq, André, *Le Pacifique et le Rencontre des Races*, 1929; Gregory, J. W., *The Menace of Colour*, 1925; Hall, J. W., *The Revolt of Asia: The End of the White Man's World Dominance*, 1927; Kohn, Hans, *Orient and Occident*, 1934; Miller, H. A., *Races, Nations and Classes*, 1924; Muntz, E. E., *Race Contact*, 1927; Pitt-Rivers, G. H. L. F., *The Clash of Culture and the Contact of Races*, 1927; Shiel, M. P., *The Yellow Peril*, 1929; Stoddard, Lothrop, *The Rising Tide of Color*, 1920; Woolf, L. S., *Imperialism and Civilization*, 1928.

[2] The outstanding classic on the inequality of races was written by J. A. de Gobineau (*The Inequality of Human Races*, 1915). Madison Grant (*The Passing of the Great Race*, 1921) and Lothrop Stoddard (*The Rising Tide of Color*, 1920) are the principal American protagonists of the doctrine. As to the literature on criticisms of various theories of racial superiority, see: Hankins, F. H., *The Racial Basis of Civilization: A Critique of the Nordic Doctrine*, 1931; Hertz, F. O., *Race and Civilization*, 1928; Josey, C. C., *Race and National Solidarity*, 1923; Radin, Paul, *The Racial Myth*, 1934.

pleasant in their immediate consequences, have little permanent importance.

As to the first aspect of the demographic factor, that of *numbers*, two elements, size of population and degree of development in production technique, must be considered. Thus, to be a Great Power it is evident that a nation must possess a relatively large population and that its people must have achieved a high degree of efficiency in industrial output.

France and Italy, for example, each containing approximately forty-two millions of inhabitants and having developed national industries to a relatively high degree of efficiency, count as Great Powers, whereas China and Brazil, with four hundred fifty millions and forty millions respectively, despite their great numbers, are internationally insignificant because of the low stage of their industrial development. Again, while both the Soviet Union and the United States are reckoned as Great Powers, the superiority of the former in numbers constitutes no counterbalance to the almost incalculable superiority of the American population in technological skill, as well as the corresponding superiority in industrial development.

In yet another respect, the implication of size in the matter of the population of nations is significant. Primary importance attaches only to the population of that portion of a state which may be defined as its territorial base, that is, as the seat of its government and the principal center of its wealth. Thus, while the total population of the British Empire approximates four hundred fifty millions and that of the French is above one hundred millions, it is the forty-five millions of Great Britain and the forty-two millions of the French homeland area that constitute the decisive element in establishing each as a Great Power.

Again, while the white populations of the British Dominions can and will contribute materially to imperial defense, as was demonstrated in the World War, the situation of the sixty-five millions in Germany, concentrated as they are upon the homeland territory of the Reich, gives these millions a war value far in excess of that of the substantially equal number of white British subjects scattered about the Seven Seas.

Finally, for nations whose territories and populations are scattered, there must be a diversity and even a conflict of interests among the various parts, resulting in trade restrictions through the raising of tariff barriers, and in a limitation upon the freedom of international policy, particularly of the homeland. Thus in the British Empire, for example, the burden of imperial defense is unequally shared between the Dominions and the United Kingdom, and inter-imperial trade is adversely affected by the tariff walls which the Dominions maintain against the mother country and against each other. In the United States, by contrast, a compact national territory insures an equal division of the costs of national defense and, what is even more important, a common market for all sections of the country.

Finally, the inter-regional position of the British Empire, as contrasted with the regional location of the United States, deprives British imperial policy of the unity which is possessed by the American. The distance of Australia, South Africa, New Zealand, and Canada from Europe gives their peoples far different points of view in respect of Europe, for example, than proximity imposes upon the inhabitants of the British Isles.

In the United States it is true that there are shades of difference between the views of the Atlantic Seaboard and of the Middle and Far West concerning Europe, and likewise between the Eastern and Western interest in Asiatic affairs; yet, in the main, community of national public opinion imposes community of action in American policy. On the contrary, British policy must always represent a necessary compromise between the conflicting interests and opinions of the European, American, African, and Australasian fractions of the Empire.

The second important aspect of the demographic factor is that of the *ethnic make-up* of nations. Thus for Germany and for her Continental neighbors the dispersal of the German-speaking populations of the Continent has an even more compelling importance than the dispersal of the English about the Seven Seas has for Great Britain. In fact, in Europe the ethnic circumstances have an importance at least as great as the economic.[1]

The reason is simple. On the one hand, so inextricably intermingled are the several nationalities dwelling in Central Europe that it is impossible to draw political frontiers without creating ethnic minorities; and on the other hand, to such heights has the passion of ethnic nationalism been raised in postwar Europe that compromise between the quarreling nationalities has so far been impossible, and economic prostration has accompanied ethnic conflict.

Of the ethnic minorities in contemporary Europe, the German are the most considerable. By virtue of the

[1] See: Friedman, Samuel, *Le Problème des Minorités Ethniques*, 1927; Junghann, Otto, *National Minorities in Europe*, 1932; Lessing, O. E., *ed.*, *Minorities and Boundaries*, 1931; Trampler, Kurt, *Die Krise des Nationalstaates*, 1932.

Peace of Paris,[1] the ten millions of German-speaking people who formerly constituted the ruling fraction of the Austrian Empire have been dispersed, seven millions transferred to the Austrian Republic and more than three millions to the new Czechoslovakian state, although all, at the end of the war, sought union with the Germans of the Reich. There are also German minorities of considerable size in the borderlands of Poland and France.

Similar and even harsher terms were imposed upon the Magyars,[2] since a third of the Hungarians were scattered among the Czechs, the Rumanians, and the Yugoslavs. In the same fashion, too, the Bulgarians of Macedonia were handed over to Greece and Yugoslavia.[3] Central and southeastern Europe were thus Balkanized, and in the new Balkans all the old feuds of the original have been reproduced on an even larger scale.

As a consequence, the desire of the Germans, the Hungarians, and the Bulgarians to recover their lost provinces and unhappy minorities has become a dominating circumstance in the national policies of all three. In Germany, the erection of the Polish Corridor, which not only created a German minority but also shattered territorial unity as well, has produced the most acute postwar problem in Europe.

In all of these questions of nationality, too, it must be perceived that it is the test of language which must be applied. Of course it is true that the German, French,

[1] Feinberg, Nathan, La Question des Minorités à la Conférence de la Paix, 1929; Foreign Policy Association, "Protection of Minorities in Europe," Information Service, Vol. II, No. 19, 1926; Ladas, S. P., The Exchange of Minorities: Bulgaria, Greece and Turkey, 1932; Rouček, J. S., The Working of the Minorities System Under the League of Nations, 1929; Stone, Julius, International Guarantees of Minority Rights, 1932.

[2] Apponyi, Albert, Gróf et al., Justice for Hungary, 1928; Buday, László, Dismembered Hungary, 1923; Seton-Watson, R. W., Treaty Revision and the Hungarian Frontiers, 1934.

[3] Reiss, R. A., The Comitadji Question in Southern Serbia, 1924; Strupp, Karl, La Situation Juridique des Macédoniens en Yougoslavie, 1930.

and Italian elements in the population of Switzerland all claim a common Swiss nationality. In the same way, the Flemings and Walloons of Belgium both count themselves as Belgian. Nevertheless, despite these and other relatively unimportant exceptions, the presence of linguistic minorities within the frontiers of a state usually constitutes an obstacle to domestic political unity and always a danger of partition following unsuccessful war.

Again, the effect of the presence, just across the frontiers of a state, of minorities speaking the same tongue as its own people usually resembles that of population pressure, since it inspires the government and people of such a state with the hope of expanding their boundaries to include these minorities, thereby to achieve ethnic unity. Thus the aspiration of France in the prewar era to recover the French-speaking districts of German Lorraine and that of Italy to liberate the Latin populations of Trieste and the Trentino directly influenced French and Italian national policies. And today the irredentist ambitions of Germany, Hungary, and Bulgaria have similar effects.

The fact that European ethnic circumstances find no parallel in America or, for that matter, in the various parts of the British Commonwealth having white populations, has always served to blind Anglo-Saxon publics almost completely to the importance and the reality of this question of nationality in Europe. Anglo-Saxon peoples habitually identify the irredentist aspirations of European states as no more than ambitions to acquire new markets, fresh sources of raw materials, and wider lands for colonization or for the enhancement of power and prestige.

To assign economic or purely imperialistic causes for policies which have their origin in ethnic circumstances is, however, to err fatally. And the same must also be said of the not less familiar Anglo-Saxon interpretation which explains in terms of mere militarism the European differences due to these same circumstances of nationality. For although economic, strategic, and political considerations are usually present, it is the ethnic which invests these aspirations with a moral value in the eyes of peoples which cherish them wholly distinct from the material considerations.

The importance of the demographic factor in its relation to the national policy of states must be clearly realized. As the population of a state is homogenous or mixed, the national policy of that state will be free from or will be dominated by dangers threatening both the unity of its domestic political life and the security of its title to its territories. Again, as the political frontiers of a state differ from or coincide with the ethnic, the national policy of that state will be with or without an irredentist aspect, and therefore in this respect dynamic or static.

In Europe, too, because quarrels between nationalities have endured for centuries and have been marked by many tragic episodes, their psychological consequences and therefore their influence upon national policies cannot be ignored. Thus, even present possession of ethnic unity and territorial satiety cannot serve fully to dissipate the moral effects of fears which have their origin in the memory of past partitions or mutilations. And these fears take the form of continuing and anxious concern for national security.

That is why, in France and Poland, for example, although the former has recovered Alsace-Lorraine and the latter has regained national unity and independence, the recollection of recent events continues to exercise a profound influence upon national policy. In the same fashion, for the German people the present spectacle of the alien possession of lands which before 1919 were their own, and the further sight of millions of people who are German by tongue but are denied the exercise of the right of self-determination, constitute evidences of an injustice at once indefensible and intolerable.

In its European phase, at least, German national policy is therefore dominated by the purpose of bringing about a unification of the German nationality by combining in one state the seventy-five millions of Teutons of Central Europe. But the fact that such union would make the new Germany the most powerful state on the Continent has led the French and Italians to undertake to preserve the status quo; the French by guaranteeing the territorial integrity of the Slav states, and the Italians by defending the independence of the Austrian Republic.

However irrational and incomprehensible these ethnic rivalries may appear in the eyes of Anglo-Saxons, and however unfortunate their influence upon European peace and international order, they are a dominating circumstance in Europe today. In fact, they are the reefs upon which many of the postwar peace programs have been wrecked.

The significance of the demographic factor must therefore be plain. Upon the question of size of population and the degree of development of that population in the technique of production will depend the ability of a state to play the role of a Great Power; and the ethnic make-up of its population, together with that of adjoining states, will go far to determine whether its policy is to be dynamic or static; for lack of ethnic unity operates like absence of economic self-sufficiency and presence of population pressure.

Chapter VI

INSTRUMENTS OF POLICY

NEXT in order of natural sequence (after the discussion of the factors of national policy) must come a consideration of the instruments by which states undertake to carry out their policies. In practice, the most important of these instruments may be divided into four classes: economic, financial, political, and military. Of these, the economic and the financial are primarily the weapons of peace, while the political is used often, and the military mainly, in war.

The *economic* means of pursuing national policy are many and varied. The most familiar is, of course, the tariff. By imposing duties upon goods and raw materials originating abroad, states frequently undertake to insure for themselves the exclusive exploitation of their domestic markets. The double objective of this undertaking is to achieve the fullest measure of prosperity in time of peace and the largest measure of national self-sufficiency alike in peace and in war.

Before the World War and for more than a decade thereafter, Great Britain followed a policy of free trade, which for her was traditional. It had become traditional because, on the one hand, Great Britain had experienced the Industrial Revolution far in advance of other countries and thus acquired a long lead in the field of industrialization, and, on the other hand, her abandonment of all attempts to feed her growing population mainly from the agricultural production of her own homeland territory enabled her to accept the production of agrarian states in return for her manufactures.[1] In addition, her surplus production of coal and her ownership of the great bulk of the world's shipping provided her with further resources which, in the aggregate, enabled her not only to trade abroad advantageously but also to occupy the situation of a creditor nation, by virtue of her practice of investing abroad, annually, the difference between what she paid and what she earned.

All the other considerable states, on the contrary, by the imposition of duties upon foreign manufactures, adopted policies originally directed chiefly at Great Britain, and designed to develop national industries of their own.[2] Again, for obvious reasons, no considerable state followed the example of the British in sacrificing its agriculture. All sought to protect their agrarian production against foreign competition by the same resort to tariffs, when this seemed necessary.

Even before the onset of the World War, however, the United States and Germany had reached and passed

---

[1] Clapham, J. H., *An Economic History of Modern Britain*, 1931–32; Cunningham, William, *The Rise and Decline of the Free Trade Movement*, 1912; Derry, Kingston, *Outlines of English Economic History*, 1932; Hirst, F. W., *From Adam Smith to Philip Snowden*, 1925.

[2] Boggs, T. H., *The International Trade Balance*, 1923; Culbertson, W. S., *International Economic Policies; A Survey of the Economics of Diplomacy*, 1925; Taussig, F. W., and White, H. D., *Some Aspects of the Tariff Question; An Examination of the Development of American Industries Under Protection*, 1931, 3d enlarged ed.; Williams, B. H., *Economic Foreign Policy of the United States*, 1929.

Great Britain in the field of industry; and Germany, before the war, and the United States, in the postwar period, began to invade the British domestic market with their manufactures, while the British situation in the world markets became less and less satisfactory. As a consequence, by the close of the first decade after the great conflict, the British were forced to follow the example of the other Great Powers in protecting their domestic markets, and to seek sure outlets for their manufactures by arranging preferential tariffs with their self-governing Dominions.[1]

Free trade thus disappeared from the world, and all states, by similar means, undertook to protect their home markets, while also engaging in a bitter struggle with one another for foreign trade. In this struggle, the combatants inevitably had recourse to quotas and contingents, which were devices designed to force those states from which they bought largely to buy a proportionate amount of their own products. At the same time, every state instinctively sought to reduce its foreign purchases and thus to defend its currency and also to preserve its domestic market for exclusive national exploitation.[2]

In addition, certain groups of citizens, more or less without governmental sanction or encouragement, undertook to strike at countries whose policies were re-

[1] Amery, Rt. Hon. L. S., *Empire and Prosperity*, 1931; Beaverbrook, W. M. A., Baron, *My Case for Empire Free Trade*, 1930; Beveridge, Sir W. H., ed., *Tariffs; The Case Examined*, 1931; McCurdy, C. A., *Empire Free Trade*, 1930; Ramsay, Alexander, *The Economics of Safe-guarding*, 1930; Williams, H. G., *Through Tariffs to Prosperity*, 1931, 2d ed.

[2] Daye, Pierre, *L'Europe en Morceaux*, 1932; Delle-Donne, O., *European Tariff Policies Since the World War*, 1928; Donham, W. B., *Business Adrift*, 1931; Hodgson, J. G., *Economic Nationalism*, 1933; Jones, J. M., *Tariff Retaliation*, 1934; Morrison-Bell, Sir Clive, *Tariff Walls; A European Crusade*, 1930; Patterson, E. M., *The World's Economic Dilemma*, 1930; Rogers, J. H., *America Weighs Her Gold*, 1931; Salter, Sir Arthur, *Recovery, The Second Effort*, 1932; Simpson, Kemper, *Introduction to World Economics*, 1934.

pugnant to them, by means of boycotts. The Chinese employed this means first against the British and then against the Japanese,[1] while the Jews, all over the world, had recourse to it against Germany. Since it was possible, in all instances, for prospective purchasers to obtain elsewhere the things which they required, the result was disastrous for the nation against which the boycott was declared. Not only were its foreign sales reduced, but as it sold less abroad it was also compelled to reduce its purchases of the things which it lacked and required to feed its population or support its industry.

Again, in certain cases, such, for example, as those of Bolivia and Paraguay, the Great Powers undertook, by declaring an embargo in war materials, to compel warring states to make peace. And the employment of an embargo as a peaceful means of exerting coercion upon states which were guilty of aggression was widely discussed. Thus the embargo, like the boycott, was established as a means of pursuing national policy, and also was considered as a means of preserving international order.[2]

It must be evident, however, that while all of these economic means of pursuing national policy are nominally peaceful, in effect they can be only less disastrous than the methods of war. Nor is it less clear, how unequally severe is the operation of these means in the case of various Great Powers. Upon those states whose poverty in foodstuffs or raw materials compels them to buy largely abroad, and to pay for such purchases by the sale

[1] Hyde, Charles C., "The Boycott in Foreign Affairs," *American Journal of International Law*, 1933, Vol. 27, pp. 1-10; Remer, C. F., and Palmer, W. B., *A Study of Chinese Boycotts with Special Reference to their Economic Effectiveness*, 1933.

[2] Clark, Evans, *ed.*, *Boycotts and Peace*, 1932; Geneva Research Center, "Sanctions and Security; an Analysis of the French and American Views," *Geneva Special Studies*, Vol. III, No 2, 1932.

of their own manufactures, services, or labor, the effect
of the progressive reduction of the foreign demand for
their exports is to insure, in the end, a reduction in the
national standard of living—a reduction from which
there is no escape by peaceful means.

By contrast, although the great states which are self-
sufficient—the United States in large measure, the
British Empire at least in theory, the Soviet Union potentially—must suffer from the general reduction of international trade, their discomforts can be largely counterbalanced by a new adjustment in the matter of domestic
distribution. Even if it be true (as is today both asserted
and denied) that these fortunate states cannot preserve
their existing standards of living under present circumstances, none of them, at least, is confronted by the prospect of a catastrophic drop such as faces Germany and
Italy.

The *financial* instrument of national policy has several
aspects, one of which closely resembles in its operation
the economic instrument. By reducing the value of
national currency in relation to gold, states can, temporarily at least, reduce the costs of domestic production
and thereby enjoy advantages in the foreign market.
Ultimately, of course, progressive reduction leads to ex-
cessive inflation and to eventual domestic catastrophe,
but if currency manipulation be skillfully employed and
wisely restricted, it can at least bestow temporary advantages, which in their effects are analogous to a
similar employment of tariffs.[1]

[1] Copeland, M. T., *International Raw Commodity Prices and the Devaluation of the Dollar*, 1934; Einzig, Paul, *The Sterling-Dollar-Franc Tangle*, 1933; Geneva Research Center,
"Problem of World Economic Conference," *Geneva Special Studies*, Vol. IV, No. 3,
1933; Gregory, T. E. G., *The Gold Standard and Its Future*, 1932; McIver, D. T., *Debased
Currency and the London Monetary Conference*, 1933; Rowland, S. W., *Depreciation Reconsidered*, 1933; Stamp, Sir J. C., *The Financial Aftermath of War*, 1932.

In the end, all Great Powers are usually driven to adopt a like policy in the matter of currency manipulation; and this restores the original state of balance, as has recently happened in Great Britain and the United States. On the other hand, when states, for reasons of domestic public opinion, feel themselves compelled to remain on the gold standard, the consequent high costs of production must restrict their sales abroad and increase unemployment at home, as France has lately demonstrated.

What is clear about a subject which is even today still largely unexplored, is that states can, if they choose, by debasing and manipulating their currencies, gain temporary advantage in the foreign markets and thereby, to that extent, promote national prosperity at the expense of other countries. Currency manipulation must therefore be reckoned an instrument of national policy, although its employment is dangerous and may also bring disaster to other states.

In a similar fashion, states may seek to promote national prosperity by the payment of subsidies to shipping or bounties to certain industries. The effect of these largesses is to enable national shipping to compete on advantageous terms with the merchant marine of foreign countries, and to enable national industries to resort to dumping, which is the sale abroad of domestic products below the price charged at home or even below the actual cost of production. This last device is commonly and significantly described as "cutthroat competition."[1]

Another and more familiar form of employment of the financial instrument of policy should be noted, of which

[1] Viner, Jacob, *Dumping: A Problem in International Trade*, 1923.

several different types are distinguishable.[1] For example, a state having made public and private loans to backward countries may interfere in their internal affairs either to protect these investments or for the more subtle purpose of obtaining concessions, either economic or strategic. Such has been in considerable part the history of the imperialist expansion of the Great Powers as exemplified by the establishment of British hegemony in the Near East and Middle East, of domination by the United States in Central America and the Caribbean lands, and of Japanese control of Manchuria and northern China.

A second and even more calculated application of money power is the use of loans or outright subsidies of one state to another to obtain political or military advantages. Of this type, France has supplied outstanding examples in her loans to Czarist Russia before the World War and to her allies of the Little Entente and to Poland since the war[2]—loans that strengthened her political alliances and also enabled her allies to make military preparations of advantage to her in case of war.

[1] The literature existing upon various aspects of financial imperialism is extremely large. Among the more important, the following may be noted for reference: Barnes, H. E., *World Politics in Modern Civilization*, 1930; Bau, M. J., *The Foreign Relations of China*, 1922; Bérard, Victor, *British Imperialism and Commercial Supremacy*, 1906; Carter, J. F., *Conquest: America's Painless Imperialism*, 1928; Earle, E. M., *Turkey, the Great Powers, and the Bagdad Railway; A Study in Imperialism*, 1923; Feis, Herbert, *Europe the World's Banker; 1870-1914*, 1930; Hoskins, H. L., *European Imperialism in Africa*, 1930; Jones, C. L., *Caribbean Backgrounds and Prospects*, 1931; Moon, P. T., *Imperialism and World Politics*, 1926; Motherwell, Hiram, *The Imperial Dollar*, 1929; Nearing, Scott, and Freeman, Joseph, *Dollar Diplomacy*, 1925; Owen, D. E., *Imperialism and Nationalism in the Far East*, 1929; Peffer, N., *The White Man's Dilemma*, 1927; Rohde, Hans, *Der Kampf um Asien*, 1924–26, 2 vols.; Viallate, A., *Economic Imperialism and International Relations During the Past Fifty Years*, 1923; Winkler, Max, *Investments of United States Capital in Latin America*, 1929; Woolf, L. S., *Imperialism and Civilization*, 1928; Young, C. W., *Japan's Special Position in Manchuria*, 1931.

[2] Feis, Herbert, *Europe the World's Banker, 1870-1914*, 1930; Langer, W. L., *European Alliances and Alignments*, 1931; Mowat, R. B., *The Concert of Europe*, 1931; Perquel, Jules, *Les Vicissitudes des Placements Français à l'Etranger*, 1929; White, H. D., *The French International Accounts, 1880-1913*, 1933.

In the third place, money power can be used as a direct means of coercion.[1] Thus the French, by refusing to carry out the terms of loans to Austria in 1931, forced that state to abandon its program of tariff union with Germany. And a similar refusal to make loans to Germany in the same year, unless repaid by political concessions, defeated all Anglo-American efforts to salvage the finances of the Reich. By bestowing or refusing loans, then, states can serve their national policies. On the economic side, too, the British have always exacted material advantages where they have extended monetary favors, with the result that those who have borrowed in London have bought chiefly in the British market. The experience of Argentina is a familiar case in point.[2]

Finally, states whose nationals have lent largely to another country on short term, can, either directly by pressure for repayment or indirectly by precipitating a war scare, gravely compromise the financial situation of that country, by thus forcing a rapid liquidation and repatriation of these loans and a consequent strain upon solvency. France has been in recent years charged with such a course, directed successfully against the United States, Germany, and Great Britain. Thus, money power can be employed to serve national policy either to shake the financial stability of a state or, by the threat of accomplishing this end, to compel that state to modify its own national policy.[3]

[1] Einzig, Paul, *Behind the Scenes of International Finance*, 1931; same author, *Finance and Politics*, 1932.

[2] McCrea, R. C., *et al.*, *International Competition in the Trade of Argentina*, 1931; Schuman, F. L., *War and Diplomacy in the French Republic*, 1931.

[3] Coste, Pierre, *La Lutte pour la Suprématie Financière*, 1932; Einzig, Paul, *Behind the Scenes of International Finance*, 1931; same author, *The Fight for Financial Supremacy*, 1931.

It is apparent, therefore, that the financial instrument of national policy, like the economic, is not only important, but is available to none but the more fortunate powers. As the economic instrument is uniquely at the service of the relatively self-sufficient nation, so the financial instrument is within the reach of but a few states which by reason of their national prosperity have been able to accumulate the necessary resources in capital for foreign lending.

Ruthlessly and efficiently employed, moreover, money power in peace can be as effective as man power in war and can produce a catastrophe in a rival nation as complete as the economic instrument—and produce it far more quickly. Thus, in both cases, the distinction between peaceful and military instruments of national policy is less striking than is commonly believed and, in the contemporary age, is becoming ever more inconsiderable.

In respect of the *political* instrument of national policy, it is apparent that this may be employed either to prepare for war or to preserve peace. Diplomacy, which constitutes one of the political resources, has in the past been used as often to arrange the circumstances of future conflict as to assist in the perpetuation of peace. Today, however, diplomacy has largely lost its importance in international relations as a consequence of the progressive march of people to political power, on the one hand, and the consequent growth of the system of international conference, on the other.[1]

These developments, together with the revolution in the means of communication and transport, have created

[1] Cambon, J. M., *The Diplomatist*, 1931; Redlich, M. D. de, *International Law as a Substitute for Diplomacy*, 1929; Reinsch, P. S., *Secret Diplomacy*, 1922; Satow, Sir Ernest M., *A Guide to Diplomatic Practice*, 1932, 3d ed. rev., 2 vols.; Toynbee, A. J., *The World After the Peace Conference*, 1925; Young, George, *Diplomacy Old and New*, 1921.

a situation in which it is the prime ministers, foreign ministers, and secretaries of state who negotiate, and negotiate directly, while the ambassadors and ministers plenipotentiary have been reduced to the status of messenger boys who communicate statements which they are customarily permitted to decode but seldom to draft. When London can communicate with Washington by telephone and by wireless, and the British prime minister can reach Berlin, Paris, or Geneva in a few hours by airplane, the mission of the diplomat has obviously been restricted to narrow limits.

As late as the period just preceding the World War, French diplomacy, by reason of the ability of its ambassadors alike in Berlin, London, Rome, and Washington, rendered its country great services, while by contrast the course of the German government at home deprived its representatives abroad of all possibility of serving the Fatherland similarly, even had they been of the caliber of the French, which they obviously were not.[1] In the postwar period, however, all the Great Powers have followed the example of Germany rather than of France, and conducted their international relations in important instances directly, rather than through diplomats.

Aside from the field of diplomacy, the political instrument of national policy is employed in several ways. Thus, recognition or non-recognition of newly established governments may be used to exact concessions or to overthrow a regime inimical to national interests. In the Americas, refusal by the United States to recognize revolutionary governments in certain of the smaller countries has in many instances been an effective means of exerting decisive influence upon the internal affairs of

[1] Charles-Roux, François, *Trois Ambassades Françaises à la Veille de la Guerre*, 1928.

such states.[1] On the other hand, the policy initially pursued by most countries in refusing to recognize the Soviet regime eventually collapsed, thus demonstrating the ineffectiveness of this practice when applied to a Great Power. Nor does the refusal to recognize Manchukuo give promise of proving more efficacious in the case of Japan.

More important, however, is the use of the political instrument of national policy through the medium of alliances, both general and merely defensive, and of that less tangible form of international partnership which is termed an *entente*. Through the medium of such agreements, states pool their military resources in advance of wars which they believe imminent, and co-ordinate their international action and harmonize their national policies in international conferences and elsewhere. All these alliances and understandings, however general in terms, are in fact directed at other nations in whose purposes the allies discover a menace to themselves.

The Great Powers, too, not only make such alliances between themselves but also contract similar engagements with the lesser states. Thus, in the postwar period, France has made alliances with Poland and the three nations of the Little Entente, while Italy has entered into somewhat less precise arrangements with Austria and Hungary. And, apart from community in dangers, the cement which has served to bind these bargains has been, for the allies of France, the power of money, and for those of Italy, the inducements of concessions in trade.

[1] Geneva Research Center, "Duties of Non-Recognition in Practice, 1775–1934," *Geneva Special Studies*, Vol. V, No. 4, 1934; Hervey, J. G., *The Legal Effects of Recognition in International Law*, 1928; Hill, Chesney, *Recent Policies of Non-Recognition*, 1933; Jaffe, L. L., *Judicial Aspects of Foreign Relations, in Particular of the Recognition of Foreign Powers*, 1933; Graham, M. W., *The League of Nations and the Recognition of States*, 1933.

Nominally these associations are organized in the name of peace; actually, however, they are invariably made with an eye to war and usually, if by no means always, contain military clauses. Obviously, the hope of the formal allies or of the partners on a limited scale is that the collective force represented by the alliance or entente will discourage challenge; but victory in war is as clearly an objective as the perpetuation of a peace, which the very fact of the alliance discloses to be precarious.[1]

Last of all we come to the *military* means for pursuing national policy.[2] It is true that, technically, by the terms of the Kellogg Pact, or Pact of Paris, war has been outlawed and recourse to it pronounced illegal. In point of fact, however, the rapid expansion of armaments following the ratification of that Pact, indulged in by all nations, great and small alike, has clearly demonstrated how little practical importance nations attached to their formal and solemn pledges.

Thus, as the Japanese action in Manchuria demonstrated, a state which has ratified the Kellogg Pact may refrain from declaring war formally, but otherwise proceed as before. Moreover, even in signing and ratifying that Pact, the Great Powers in several instances hedged their acceptance about with reservations which took back with one hand, unobtrusively, what with ostentation had been relinquished by the other.

[1] Armstrong, H. F., *Europe Between Wars?*, 1934; Balla, V. de, *The New Balance of Power in Europe*, 1932; Langer, W. L., *European Alliances and Alignments*, 1931.

[2] Carter, J. F., *Man is War*, 1926; Dawson, W. H., *The Future of Empire; the World Price of Peace*, 1930; Fuller, J. F. C., *War and Western Civilization 1832-1932*, 1932; Maurice, Sir Fredrick, *Governments and War*, 1926; Nickerson, Hoffman, *Can We Limit War?*, 1934; Porritt, Arthur, ed., *The Causes of War*, 1932; Shotwell, J. T., *War as an Instrument of National Policy*, 1929; Sturzo, Luigi, *The International Community and the Right of War*, 1930.

In the light of the objectives of the national policies of the various great states, it is manifest that war still remains not merely one means but the only effective means of pursuing national policy to its logical end. And all states recognize this fact and expose their convictions by the preparations they make in the field of armaments, both military and naval. Hence, as long as one group of states hold to the dynamic conception and another to the static—that is to say, while one set of powers are resolved to extend their frontiers and another to defend their present territories—all the various so-called peaceful means of pursuing national policy, which have been here indicated, must in the end prove inadequate.

To abolish war, it would first be necessary to reconcile the conflicting national policies of states, and in this direction nothing has been accomplished and very little attempted in the postwar world, because the doctrine of absolute sovereignty, which is the foundation principle of the nation states system, squarely blocks the road.

It is, of course, necessary to distinguish clearly between preventible and inevitable wars. The Spanish-American War, for example, was clearly a preventible war, because the issues at stake were not vital; in fact, that conflict was very nearly avoided, as it could and should have been. On the contrary, the war between Serbia and Austria-Hungary, which in 1914 was the signal for general conflict, was, like the Italian Wars of Unification in the nineteenth century, inevitable, because the Southern Slavs were resolved to achieve unity and the masters of the Dual Monarchy were resolved to preserve their existing empire intact. Postponement, to be sure, was possible, but for Austria such postponement insured the further growth of a deadly peril.

Precisely in the same fashion, the programs of Italian Fascism, German National Socialism, and Japanese Imperialism point directly to future inevitable wars, as the Japanese have already demonstrated, because each of these programs is wholly unrealizable save by war, and all three peoples have committed themselves unreservedly to these national programs and policies. To persuade these peoples to renounce their national policies it would be necessary to convince them that their objectives were unattainable even by war, or that their ends were to be reached by some other available means, or, finally, that even if their goals were to be realized by war, the ultimate consequence of the conflict would be so ruinous as to leave them in a still more disadvantageous situation than before.

In practice, however, such persuasion is impossible. In the present situation of Europe, for example, there is no possibility of demonstrating to upwards of seventy-five millions of Germans that a condition of ethnic unity, which less than twenty-five millions of Poles achieved after a century of partition, and which thirty-odd millions of Italians realized in the last century, in the face of obstacles which, in both instances, seemed insuperable, is permanently beyond German strength. And it is likewise impossible to discover any other means for the realization either of ethnic unity or of that territorial expansion dictated by material needs, save war.

There remains the final argument that war has become so destructive today that there can be no victors and that the combatants are foredoomed to share in a common and unlimited disaster. But it is at least true that for the Poles, the Czechs, the Southern Slavs, and the Rumanians, the last war was very far from an unrelieved disaster, since it won them independence, or ethnic unity, or both blessings at once. Even for France, which recovered its lost provinces of Alsace-Lorraine and a far more defensible frontier, and for Italy, which redeemed its lost brethren of Trieste and the Trentino and carried its boundaries to the summits of the Julian Alps, the World War, despite all of its incidental destruction, was not without material profit.

But the real question goes far deeper. In fact, it turns upon the estimate which the dissatisfied peoples of the present hour themselves place upon their contemporary circumstances and future prospects. If they are convinced, as the Italian acceptance of Fascism and the German adoption of National Socialism would indicate, and as Mussolini and Hitler constantly proclaim, that a national existence restricted to present territorial limits and existing material resources is impossible, since it must prove no more than a long-drawn-out but inevitably losing struggle against conditions at once intolerable and inescapable by peaceful means, then all warnings of the horrors of war and all admonitions based upon legal and moral precepts are bound to fall on deaf ears.

Conflict for the American, British, French, or Russian peoples could prove only a disaster, for it could, even if successful, bring them little that they lack. But the situation of the Italian, German, and Japanese peoples is less clear, since for them a present which is far from attractive seems but the preface to a future even less appealing if the fortunate powers continue to reserve for themselves in every measure the advantages of their superior fortune.

Besides the economic, financial, political, and military instruments of national policy there are various others which will readily come to mind. Of these propaganda is perhaps the most important, as it certainly is the most familiar.[1] In recent years, too, with the enormous expansion of the reading public, which has occurred in every state, and with the arrival of the radio as well, this weapon has attained employment to an extent which it would be difficult to exaggerate.

Nevertheless, it is essential to note that, in time of peace, propaganda is mainly effective as an instrument of governments to consolidate domestic support behind their policies and to enlist public approval for the political regime. By use of it, also, statesmen have been able to counteract at home the effects of that world opinion of which so much was expected in the immediate post-war period as a means of exerting moral force against national policies inimical to the maintenance of international peace.

Thanks to propaganda, furthermore, the Mussolinis and the Hitlers have been able to arouse popular enthusiasm and exploit popular passions to their own vast personal profit. In peace, however, the influence of the propaganda of a nation beyond its own frontiers has been relatively slight, for it not only eventually awakens counter-propaganda but also immediately excites domestic suspicion, as the National Socialist efforts abroad have abundantly demonstrated.

That propaganda has enormous value as an instrument of national policy during a conflict, on the other hand, the events of the World War proved. But with it, as with the other so-called peaceful instruments of national

---

[1] Angell, Sir Norman, *The Press and the Organization of Society*, 1922; Cook, Sir Edward, *The Press in Wartime*, 1920; Lasswell, H. D., *Propaganda Technique in the World War*, 1927; Lowell, A. L., *Public Opinion in War and Peace*, 1923; Vieteck, G. S., *Spreading the Germs of Hate*, 1930; Wright, Quincy, ed., *Public Opinion and World Politics*, 1933.

policy, our concern lies simply in appraising its value as a possible substitute for arms and therefore for war. And from that standpoint it is manifest that propaganda, which may perhaps be termed the psychological instrument of policy, is as inadequate as the economic, the financial, or the political.

It is certain that, in time of peace, the superior material resources and therefore disproportionate means of the static powers will bestow upon them commensurate advantage in respect of all of the instruments of policy. In fact, if the existing disparity in fortune long endures, even the ultimate instrument of war may be forced from the hands of the dynamic powers; for an ever-increasing inferiority in material resources must, in an age in which Vulcan has replaced Mars as the god of war, carry with it the certainty of defeat on the battlefield where the armies of the future will be mechanized.

Chapter VII

FOUNDATIONS OF INTERNATIONAL RELATIONS—
SUMMARY

THE foregoing chapters together constitute a statement of the foundations of international relations in the contemporary world. Since they must also serve as the basis of the later discussions of this study it is essential to reassemble and briefly restate the facts set forth in them.

Important beyond all else is the fact that the world of today is organized in accordance with the nation states system and therefore in conformity with the doctrine of the absolute sovereignty of the individual state; for that doctrine precludes the creation of a universally accepted and effectively enforced system of public international law, of a world court of competent and conceded jurisdiction, and, finally, of an international police.

To this fact was due the international anarchy which existed in the prewar era and has continued throughout the postwar period; for in the absence of law, courts, and police, force necessarily constitutes the ultimate means by which states seek their ends. These ends, moreover, are sought by national policies which are the systems of strategy employed by states to maintain or acquire security, prosperity, and national unity.

As there are sixty-odd sovereign states in the world and their national policies are not only frequently at variance but also often in direct collision, controversy is the characteristic detail of international relations. And when controversies have their origin in questions affecting national honor, title to territory, or provisions of municipal[1] law, the doctrine of absolute sovereignty bars the way to ready settlement by arbitration.

In theory, nations under such circumstances have no other choice save resort to force. In practice, however, inasmuch as nations differ widely as to size, population, and resources, and therefore in strength, only the strongest are actually able to pursue their national policies uncompromisingly. Such states constitute the Great Powers, which at present are seven in number. Inevitably, then, in a world without law the role of the Great Powers is predominant.

Even among the various Great Powers, however, there exists a primary distinction which exercises a decisive influence in determining the character of their foreign policies. Thus, while the objectives of national policy are always security, prosperity, and unity, the Great Powers are divided into those who possess and those who seek to possess. Accordingly, the controlling purpose of the former must be to defend advantages already acquired, and of the latter, to acquire similar advantages. The national policies of the first group will therefore be static, and those of the second group, dynamic.

[1] "Of or pertaining to the internal or governmental affairs of a state, kingdom or nation;—used chiefly in the phrase *municipal law*." (*Webster's New International Dictionary*, 2d ed.)

Whether the policy of a state is static or dynamic will necessarily depend upon its physical circumstances from which are derived the basic factors of that policy, the geographic, the economic, and the demographic. In a word, the key to the policy of a state must be sought in the position of its land, the extent and nature of its material resources, and the economic and ethnic circumstances of its people.

Although force is the ultimate instrument of policy, there are others, especially the economic, the financial, and the political. Like the military, however, these are generally employed by one nation to enable it to profit at the expense of others. Even in time of peace, therefore, the relation between states is primarily competitive and not co-operative. But in such competition all the advantage lies with the static powers, for it is because their economic, financial, and political circumstances are satisfactory that their policies are static.

To pursue its national policies successfully, a dynamic power has no other choice but an appeal to force. To build a bridge between the static and dynamic powers and thus to establish a condition of actual peace, it would be necessary to bring about some compromise between the rights of the former and the claims of the latter; for, in the matter of world peace, as in all else in human relations, real partnership must be founded upon community of interest.

In the absence of any such compromise, partnership between the static and dynamic powers would obviously amount to a combination of the Haves and the Havenots which would keep the former forever rich and the latter eternally poor. Such a bargain being clearly out of the question, the only alternative is an alliance of the

Haves to impose the status quo upon the Have-nots permanently by means of their superior strength. But here again, the partnership of the Haves would be possible only on the basis of parity.

Today, however, it is self-evident that there is no possibility of real partnership between such static and dynamic peoples as the British and the German, or the French and the Italian, or the American and the Japanese. Hence the bases of a universal association to preserve peace do not exist. It is equally clear that the British behind the Channel and the Americans beyond the Atlantic are exposed to no such perils as the French at the Rhine and the Russians along the Amur. Hence the basis is lacking also for an alliance of the static powers to defend the status quo.

In theory that status quo, since it rests upon existing treaties, constitutes the public international law of the world. In practice, however, Germany, Japan, and Italy refuse to recognize or respect that law, because it is the foundation of the present inequality between their physical circumstances and those of Great Britain, France, Russia, and the United States. By contrast, France, the Soviet Union, and many smaller states refuse to permit a revision of that law, because of the sacrifices revision would impose upon them. The United States and Great Britain, while refusing to make sacrifices to satisfy Japan, Germany, or Italy, also decline to assume responsibilities for French or Russian security.

The peace programs of the postwar period have originated with the Anglo-Saxon nations. They have been based on the assumption that the desire for peace of all peoples, those of static and dynamic powers alike, is so dominating as, in itself, to constitute a parity of interest and therefore a basis of partnership for all of the Great Powers. Actually, however, while all peoples with equal sincerity desire to avoid war, all are primarily concerned either with the retention of advantages they possess or with the acquisition of those they lack.

As a consequence, the French and their allies have sought to amend the Anglo-Saxon programs to provide security for the status quo, while the Germans, the Japanese, and the Italians have rejected these programs because they would erect obstacles to the revision of that status quo.

The student of international relations must therefore be on his guard against confusing any program of peace which has yet been suggested, with genuine Internationalism. All the various forms of international cooperation that have ever been proposed have been designed to conform with the national interests of the proponent states. Genuine Internationalism, by contrast, would envisage the modification of the national policies of all of the powers to conform to some mutually accepted status quo, not only territorial but also economic. The static powers would have to surrender some part of their present disproportionate advantages; the dynamic would be compelled to forego the most extravagant of their claims.

Obviously the notion that Great Powers could today be persuaded to consent to such curtailment of sovereign rights is Utopian. But not less impractical is the assumption that any viable system of international cooperation can be established upon the basis of the present inequalities in the physical circumstances of the Great Powers, accentuated as these are by the economic policies and practices of the static countries.

Actually it is not because peoples are wise or stupid, educated or illiterate, good or bad, that their national policies are static or dynamic. Nor is it because their skins are white or yellow, or their language English, French, German, or Italian. Even forms of government, whether democratic, fascist, or communist, have little to do with the question, although they may dictate the spirit in which national policies are pursued. Navalism, militarism, imperialism, these are only convenient indictments nations hurl back and forth at each other. But in fact if the Frenchman and the German changed places they would exchange policies. And in the same way, in British or American circumstances the Frenchman would adopt the naval policies of the English-speaking powers; while in French circumstances the British and Americans would employ the military system of the French.

What counts is whether peoples live on islands or continents; whether their countries are situated in Europe, Asia, or America; whether they have natural resources to supply their industry and food supplies to feed their populations. If their title to these advantages is undisputed, they will also have security. Otherwise they will seek that security. A decent measure of prosperity, a reasonable degree of security, and in addition a fair measure of ethnic unity, these things together constitute the irreducible minimum of an acceptable national existence and therefore the sole basis for a real association between nations to insure peace.

To know the physical circumstances of a state is therefore to understand its national policy. To know the extent of its resources is to perceive the strength which it can mobilize to support that policy. To persuade a people to change its policy it is necessary to modify the circumstances which are responsible for that policy. To compel a state to abandon its policy it is necessary to muster a force decisively superior to the force of that state. These simple facts constitute the foundations of international relations and they have always to be considered in the light of the doctrine of the absolute sovereignty of the individual state.

PART TWO

REGIONAL AND WORLD POLITICS

Chapter VIII

PREWAR EUROPE[1]

THE next step in this study of international relations must be an examination in some detail of the circumstances of each of the Great Powers in respect of prosperity, security, and ethnic unity, as these explain their national policies. Since five of the seven Great Powers have their political capitals in Europe, that continent is the natural starting place for such an examination. But first it is necessary to consider the European Region as a whole and to contrast the Europe of tradition and of today, that is, prewar and postwar Europe.

Prewar Europe was organized under the nation states system and, within itself, constituted a Great-Power World. Such, too, had been its political circumstances from the Thirty Years War to the World War. In theory, therefore, by reason of the universal acceptance of the dogma of absolute sovereignty, Europe had existed in a

[1] In the study of prewar European politics, the student should have available for general reference the following: Hayes, C. J. H., *A Political and Social History of Modern Europe*, 1924, 2 vols.; Mowat, R. B., *The European States System; A Study of International Relations*, 1929, enl.; same author, *European Diplomacy, 1815-1914*, 1922; Phillimore, Sir W. G. F., *Three Centuries of Peace Treaties*, 1919; Satow, Sir E. M., *International Congresses*, 1920.

condition of anarchy, because there was lacking any established system of public international law and any form of central authority. In practice, however, this state of anarchy had been measurably mitigated by the gradual evolution of at least one guiding principle, that of the balance of power, and the development of a rudimentary form of authority, that of the Concert of Europe.

This guiding principle, the doctrine of the balance of power, had begun to take form as far back as the Treaty of Westphalia (1648). It had found clear expression in the Peace of Utrecht (1713), and it had been the dominating factor in the Settlement of the Congress of Vienna (1815). Three times, therefore, after general Continental conflicts, European statesmanship had sought to establish a system of order on the basis of a common political doctrine.

The doctrine of the balance of power, itself, was no more than the translation into practice of the bitter lessons Europe had learned in its struggles with Louis XIV and Napoleon Bonaparte. The sum of these lessons was that the possession by any single power of disproportionate strength must inevitably tempt its rulers to seek Continental hegemony and thus to disturb the peace and threaten the liberty of all Europe.

But after the War of the Spanish Succession (1702–1712), which was the final bid of Louis XIV for European hegemony, the victorious coalition was unable to give full application of the doctrine of the balance of power; for, although beaten, Louis was not helpless. On the contrary, his army was still in existence and his capital had not been captured by his foes. Consequently, while France was compelled to surrender many of her claims to regions adjacent to her own frontiers, she still remained far and away the most powerful state in Europe. Thus both the opportunity and the temptation to renew the old struggle for supremacy survived the defeat and disappearance of Louis the Grand.

A century later, however, the triumph of the new coalition was complete, Paris had fallen into the hands of the victors, Napoleon was on Elba, and the military strength of France was, for the moment, completely broken. Thus the sovereigns and statesmen of a successful alliance were able, as they were also resolved, so to reorganize Europe as to make it impossible for any future master of France, whether Bourbon, Revolutionary, or Bonapartist, to renew the old struggle for Continental hegemony.

To accomplish this end, it was obviously necessary to abolish the long-continued disparity in population between France and the other Great Powers of Europe. Unlike their successors a century later, however, the victors of 1815 did not attempt to achieve their purpose by mutilating the frontiers of their recent antagonist. On the contrary, in the first Treaty of Paris (May, 1814), which preceded Waterloo, and in the second (November, 1815), which followed it, they conceded to France the frontiers of 1789.[1] Thus, after twenty years of conflict,

---

[1] It is important in this connection to distinguish between the above treaties of Paris and the Congress of Vienna. The first were instruments for concluding the state of war existing between France and the Alliance, and for settling the problem of French frontiers. The Congress of Vienna, on the other hand, was assembled (September, 1814 to July, 1815) for the purpose of reconstructing the states system of Europe. Its object was defined in No. 1 of the Separate and Secret Articles of the first Peace of Paris as follows: "The disposal of the territories given up by His Most Christian Majesty, . . . and the relations from whence a real and permanent Balance of Power in Europe is to be derived, shall be regulated at the Congress upon the principles determined upon by the Allied Powers among themselves." (See Lockhart, J. G., *The Peace Makers, 1814-1815*, 1932).

France herself remained with no material territorial diminution.

But the victors did strip France of all of the conquests of the Revolution and of the Empire, and these territories, together with the possessions of the King of Saxony and other monarchs who had joined their fortunes to those of the Great Emperor, constituted the material out of which the statesmen of Vienna constructed their new system. In thus proceeding to destroy the traditional French superiority on the Continent, the Congress of Vienna, however, left France herself with no mutilated frontiers and no "lost provinces," a fact which counted incalculably in assuring permanence to their work.

In accordance with the doctrine of the balance of power, therefore, the Congress of Vienna bestowed upon Prussia the Rhineland, Westphalia, and the larger part of the kingdom of Saxony; upon Austria, Lombardy and Venetia; upon Russia, Finland and all of ethnic Poland save Galicia, Posen, and West Prussia. In addition, two of the smaller states in the pathway of French invasion were similarly strengthened. Thus Holland received Belgium, and Savoy obtained Genoa and Sardinia. As for the British, since they had no desire to hold Continental territory aside from Gibraltar, they took their share of the booty in the form of Malta and the Ionian Islands in European waters and of overseas lands, of which Cape Colony was the most considerable.

When the Congress of Vienna had completed its labors, therefore, the political situation on the Continent of Europe had been completely transformed. While the France of 1815 was still the France of 1789, Russia, Prussia, and Austria had been greatly expanded and were now individually far more nearly a match for their old foe than ever before. Again, as the Congress of Vienna, by dividing the spoils of victory evenly among the three victorious Continental powers, had also sought to preserve the balance among them, something like a state of balance actually existed among all of the European Great Powers of the time.

This system of Vienna not only survived the brief challenge of the Hundred Days but, with minor modifications, endured right down to the eve of the World War. During this period of nearly a hundred years, the unification of Italy was accomplished and the German Empire was established under the leadership of Prussia. But on the territorial side the changes were relatively slight. France acquired Nice and Savoy (1860), and lost Alsace-Lorraine (1871); Austria was forced to surrender Lombardy (1859) and Venice (1866), but was permitted to occupy Bosnia and Herzegovina (1878); Prussia took Alsace-Lorraine in the name of the new German Empire; and, finally, Russian frontiers in Europe remained virtually unchanged.

Meantime, with the unification of Italy (1859–1870) and the creation of the German Empire (1866–1871), France had irrevocably lost her old primacy. Russia, Germany, and Austria now surpassed her in population, and Italy was rapidly approaching parity in numbers. On the other hand, Russian increase in population was vastly greater than German, and the ability of any single Great Power to play the role which had for two centuries before Waterloo been French, was still lacking.

In one respect, the situation changed just before the outbreak of the World War. Again, as in the years before the French Revolution, Europe was divided into rival alliances: Germany, Austria, and Italy were united in the Triple Alliance, and Russia, France, and Great Britain in the Triple Entente.[1] But the balance between the two combinations appeared too nearly equal to tempt either to run the risks of a conflict which would now inevitably be general.

Beneath the surface, however, this state of balance was crumbling fatally. Under the influence of the centrifugal pull of nationality, the various subject peoples of the Hapsburg Monarchy were beginning to look beyond national boundaries to ethnic unities; and in the case of the Southern Slavs, at least, these aspirations found strong support in St. Petersburg. The two Balkan wars of 1912 and 1913, moreover, not only crystallized the resolution of the Serbs to repeat the achievement of Savoy, but also fired the ambition of the Rumanians to make the Regat[2] the instrument of unification of still another Latin people.

Subliminally, therefore, the balance of power in Europe was again threatened. If the Hapsburg Monarchy were resolved into its ethnic factors, then Germany was satisfied that she would find herself isolated between hostile Russia and irreconcilable France. To preserve the balance of power, Germany therefore undertook to protect the unity of the Dual Monarchy; and thereby, in the famous phrase of Napoleon III, she allied herself to a corpse, and in July, 1914, it was, in the bitter

[1] Among the important books dealing specifically with the history of the above alliances, the following may be noted: Coolidge, A. C., *Origins of the Triple Alliance*, 1926, 2d ed.; Gooch, G. P., *History of Modern Europe, 1878-1919*, 1923; Lanessan, J. L. de, *Histoire de l'Entente Cordiale Franco-Anglaise*, 1916; Langer, W. L., *European Alliances and Alignments, 1871-1890*, 1931; Michon, Georges, *The Franco-Russian Alliance, 1891-1917*, 1929.

[2] The Rumanian word *Regat*, meaning "kingdom," is used especially to mean prewar Rumania.

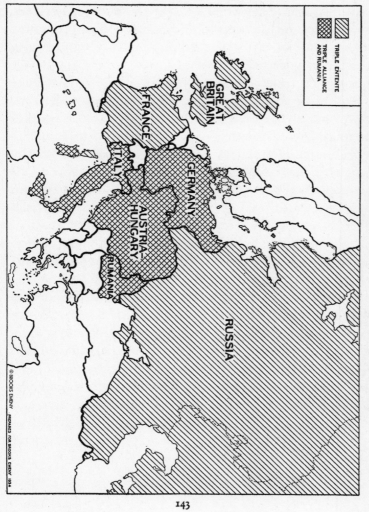

PREWAR EUROPEAN ALLIANCES

Legend:
- TRIPLE ENTENTE AND RUMANIA
- TRIPLE ALLIANCE

GREAT BRITAIN
FRANCE
ITALY
GERMANY
AUSTRIA-HUNGARY
RUMANIA
RUSSIA

© BROOKS EMENY   PREPARED FOR BROOKS EMENY 1934

words of Bülow, the dead hand which held the helm.[1]

What it is essential to perceive, however, is that as late as the onset of the World War the doctrine of the balance of power still exercised a profound influence upon European policy. In fact, it was to preserve the traditional balance established by the Congress of Vienna, that the German Empire took up arms in 1914.

Prewar Europe, moreover, had not only a doctrine but also a system of authority, and that was the Concert of Europe. Incomplete and shadowy as this system was, it did avail to prevent any general war between Waterloo and the Marne. At the root of this system lay the second of the guiding principles of Old Europe, the doctrine of Great-Power authority. Individually the Great Powers were to be equal; collectively theirs was the duty and right to keep order on the Continent. That was the law and the gospel of prewar Europe.

This system of the Concert of Europe had taken form during the last stages of the struggle against Napoleon, when the sovereigns and statesmen of the allied Great Powers were necessarily in close touch with one another. This habit of collaboration was immensely strengthened by the Congress of Vienna, and it persisted after the various treaties of peace had been ratified and applied;[2] for after Vienna, as after Paris a century later, many questions remained still unsettled.

In the seven years after the Congress of Vienna there were, accordingly, a succession of international conferences, of which the final meeting was that of Verona

---

[1] Bülow, B., Fürst von, *Memoirs*, 1931–32, 4 vols.; Wedel, O. H., *Austro-German Diplomatic Relations, 1908-1914,* 1932.

[2] Cresson, W. P., *The Holy Alliance; the European Background of the Monroe Doctrine,* 1922; same author, *Diplomatic Portraits: Europe and the Monroe Doctrine One Hundred Years Ago,* 1923.

in 1822.[1] Meantime, by 1818 France had been readmitted to the circle of the Great Powers on an equal footing. In fact, even in the Congress of Vienna, Talleyrand had reconquered for the recently vanquished foe a position which contrasts strikingly with that of the German position in the case of the Paris Conference of 1919. In these various conferences (of 1818, 1820, 1822), too, the representatives of the Great Powers undertook to administer the affairs of Europe by virtue of the authority which their collective strength bestowed upon them.

With the death of Castlereagh and the coming of Canning (1822), Great Britain, setting an example which the United States followed a century later, withdrew from the Continent and left it to the other four Great Powers to preserve order. Nevertheless, the Belgian Revolution of 1830, raising as it did, momentarily at least, the question of the permanence of the system of Vienna and therefore of the balance of power, was the occasion for a Conference of London.[2] In that conference, too, the five Great Powers both established the Belgian state and recognized and insured Greek independence.

Even as late as 1852, when the question of Schleswig-Holstein threatened to produce war, the five Great Powers, with Sweden, joined in a Treaty of London to

---

[1] Three congresses were held during this period. The first of them, Aix-la-Chapelle (1818), was notable for the fact that France was again admitted as a member of the Concert of Europe. The second, Troppau (1820), was called to consider the crisis in Europe arising from the revolutions in the kingdoms of Naples and Spain. And at the third and last, Verona (1822), at which Great Britain was represented only by an observer, a French army was ordered to pass beyond the Pyrenees for the purpose of suppressing the Spanish revolution. It was this latter act of interference with the aspirations of a people to settle their own internal affairs that gave impetus to the declaration of the Monroe Doctrine the following year.

[2] Treaty of London, November 15, 1831. The problem of the status of Belgium was not definitely settled until the second treaty of London, April 19, 1839, in which Holland finally recognized the independence of Belgium and the latter country was declared to "form an Independent and perpetually Neutral State."

regulate the succession to the Danish throne. Two years later, however, when the Crimean War ushered in the long series of conflicts between Great Powers which lasted until 1871, the Concert of Europe necessarily dissolved, and a quarter of a century of Continental anarchy followed as a consequence.[1]

After the Franco-Prussian War, however, all the Great Powers of the Continent were similarly exhausted by the several wars in which they had engaged. Hence, when the Russo-Turkish War threatened to precipitate a new —and this time a general—conflict, Bismarck had little difficulty in persuading all of the Great Powers to agree to attend a new international conference like those which had taken place in the years after Waterloo.

The Congress of Berlin (June 13–July 13, 1878), which was the consequence of the intervention of the Iron Chancellor, not merely revived the old system of the Concert of Europe, but imparted to it a vitality which endured for nearly four decades after 1878.[2] The means by which the Congress of Berlin resolved the difficulties having their origin in the Eastern Question require at least a passing glance, for they are as significant examples of traditional European statesmanship as the decisions of the Congress of Vienna itself.

[1] Although the Concert of Europe went into eclipse during this period and was not restored to vigor until the Congress of Berlin in 1878, an interesting recognition of its importance to the maintenance of European peace is contained in Protocol No. 23 of the Congress of Paris, 1856, which reads as follows: "The Plenipotentiaries do not hesitate to express, in the name of their Governments, the wish that States between which any serious misunderstanding may arise, should before appealing to Arms, have recourse, as far as circumstances might allow, to the Good Office of a friendly power." Although this protocol, when invoked by the British, both in 1866 and in 1870, did not prevent the Austro-Prussian and the Franco-Prussian wars, respectively, it has remained nevertheless an important pronouncement of the principle of the Concert of Powers and has now become a part of public international law in the form of Article XII of the Covenant of the League.

[2] Mowat, R. B., *The Concert of Europe*, 1931.

In 1878 the objective was to prevent a war visibly impending by reason of the terms of the Treaty of San Stefano (March 3, 1878), which Russia had imposed upon Turkey.[1] These terms, designed to give the Czar control of the Straits (the Dardanelles and the Bosporus), were equally unacceptable to London and to Vienna; and Disraeli had sent a British fleet through the Dardanelles and called Indian troops to Malta. His dramatic gestures had thus brought Europe to the very edge of conflict.

The crisis was resolved by a series of compromises and territorial adjustments. Russia was forced to abandon the Treaty of San Stefano but was permitted to annex Kars and Batum in Asia and the portion of Bessarabia she had been forced to cede after the Crimean War. Much, but not all, of the territory she had undertaken to bestow upon her protégé Bulgaria was granted to this small state, but Thrace and Macedonia, with their considerable Christian populations, were restored to the bloodstained hands of the Turks because the rivalries of the Great Powers in these regions were irreconcilable. Serbia, Montenegro, and Greece were also permitted to annex considerable areas of Turkish territory.

Of the other Great Powers, Austria was permitted to occupy the Turkish provinces of Bosnia and Herzegovina as solace for her still recent surrender of Venetia and Lombardy. France was invited to occupy Tunisia as consolation for the even more recent loss of Alsace-Lorraine. As for Great Britain, her prime minister, Disraeli, brought back Cyprus in his pocket. Italy, in her turn, had to be contented with the recognition of her accession to the status of a Great Power, bestowed by her in-

[1] Holland, T. E., *European Concert in the Eastern Question*, 1885.

clusion among the conferees. For Germany, Bismarck acquired the prestige incident to formal recognition that Berlin had replaced Paris as the center of European power.

The price of this quaintly termed "Peace with Honor" was necessarily paid by the weaker nations—by Turkey, first of all, which had to consent to territorial cessions both in Europe and in Asia. The Balkan states, however, paid their full share. Thus despite the services rendered to the Czar at Plevna by the Rumanian army, Rumania was forced to cede her Bessarabian lands to Russia. Bulgaria, in turn, was compelled to reimburse Rumania by surrendering the Dobrudja to her. As for the Serbs, the occupation of Bosnia-Herzegovina raised a barrier to their aspiration for national unity, while Austrian garrisons in the Sanjak of Novi Bazar separated Serbia from Montenegro.

At this price, however, war between Great Powers was avoided and Europe was assured of another generation of peace. The Eastern Question was not settled, to be sure.[1] On the contrary, in Serajevo, the capital of the Bosnian province which the Congress of Berlin had handed over to Austria, the signal fire for the World War would one day be lighted. Nevertheless, as the statesmen of the Congress of Vienna could claim for their handiwork the credit for forty years of European tranquillity, those of Berlin could claim for theirs the similar credit for a new pause which lasted from 1878 to 1914.

After the Congress of Berlin, too, the habit of collaboration persisted. In 1881 a Conference of Berlin was

[1] Durham, M. E., *Twenty Years of Balkan Tangle*, 1920; Earle, E. M., *Turkey, The Great Powers and the Bagdad Railway*, 1923; Miller, W., *The Ottoman Empire and Its Successors, 1801-1927*, 1927.

convoked to regulate the still unaccomplished decisions of the Conference three years before. Again in December of 1884, a third Berlin Conference was convened to arrange the diplomatic and legal basis for the partition of Africa among the colonial powers and to settle the difficult question of the international status of the Congo Basin. Nearly a quarter of a century later, the Conference of Algeciras (1906) for the moment preserved European peace by its resolution of the Moroccan crisis.[1] In 1911, however, the Turco-Italian War disclosed the growing weakness of the Concert, and its utter impotence was revealed when the Balkan states, despite the warning of the Great Powers, suddenly attacked Turkey in 1912 and by their own arms abolished the servitudes imposed upon them by the Congress of Berlin.[2]

Nevertheless, as late as the winter of 1913, a Council of Ambassadors successfully liquidated the disputes between Russia and Austria growing out of the First and Second Balkan Wars. The Treaty of Bucharest (August 10, 1913) was, therefore, a further monument to the efficacy of the system of the Concert. But, like the Treaty of London in 1852, which preceded the Crimean War by but three years, it proved only the preface to conflict. And this time the struggle became general.

The reason for the failure of Sir Edward Grey, when in July, 1914, he undertook once more to invoke the old

[1] Dickinson, G. L., *The International Anarchy, 1904-1914*, 1926; Stuart, G. H., *French Foreign Policy from Fashoda to Serajevo, 1898-1914*, 1921.

[2] In addition to the above conferences of European Powers, the World Conferences of The Hague of 1899 and 1907, which resulted in the establishment of an International Tribunal of Arbitration and in the codification of certain principles of the Laws of War, and the London Naval Conference of 1908, which drew up the famous Declaration of London defining the rights of neutrals in trade and contraband, should be mentioned. Although these agreements were virtually abrogated as a result of the World War, they represent an outstanding example of international co-operative effort during the prewar era for the solution of world problems.

machinery of the Concert of Europe, to prevent a clash
between Great Powers, was simple and must today be
unmistakable. For Austria, the situation which had
resulted from the Balkan Wars had become intolerable.
The purpose of the Serbs, now victorious in two wars, to
unite the Southern Slavs of the whole Danubian area,
thus stripping the Dual Monarchy of Bosnia, Herzegovina, Croatia, Slavonia, and Dalmatia, was undisguised
and its menace was evident. And behind Serbian purpose was Russian encouragement.

Serbian purpose, moreover, was matched by Rumanian, and accordingly Transylvania, the Banat, and
Bukovina were similarly in jeopardy. In Bohemia and
Moravia, too, the Czechs were stirred both by Pan-Slav
sympathies and by separatist ambitions.[1] Thus Vienna
seized upon the assassinations of Serajevo as a justification for a war of self-preservation, and rejected the appeals of Sir Edward Grey to come to conference as Russia
had come in 1878 and France in 1906. Berlin, too, paralyzed by the fear of losing its single sure ally, saw its
fate linked with that of Austria, and, at least until the
eleventh hour had passed unseized, permitted itself to
be dragged after Vienna.

With the outbreak of the World War, too, the Concert of Europe was inevitably abolished, while the disintegration of the Hapsburg Monarchy automatically
destroyed the balance of power in Europe. As a consequence, long after the Paris Conference had issued the
formal death certificate of the Austro-Hungarian Empire, European statesmanship continued to repeat in
mournful approbation Palacky's famous phrase—"if
Austria did not exist it would be necessary to invent it."

[1] Jászi, Oszkár, The Dissolution of the Hapsburg Monarchy, 1929.

Chapter IX

POSTWAR EUROPE[1]

WILSON's Fourteen Points and his later speeches[2] which together became the basis of the Armistice, contained two equally revolutionary proposals. Of these, the first was the principle of self-determination, and the second was the project for a League of Nations. Each of these

[1] In the study of the Peace Settlement and of postwar European politics, the student should have available for general reference, the following:

Peace Settlement—Baker, R. S., *Woodrow Wilson and the World Settlement*, 1922, 3 vols.; Beer, G. L., *African Questions at the Paris Peace Conference*, 1923; Haskins, C. H., and Lord, R. H., *Some Problems of the Peace Conference*, 1920; Howard-Ellis, Charles, *The Origin, Structure and Working of the League of Nations*, 1928; Nicolson, H. G., *Peacemaking, 1919*, 1933; Scott, J. B., ed., *Preliminary History of the Armistice*, 1924; Temperley, H. W., ed., *History of the Peace Conference of Paris*, 1920-24, 6 vols.

Postwar European Politics—Bogardus, J. F., *Europe, a Geographical Survey*, 1934; Burns, C. D., *1918-1928; A Short History of the World*, 1928; Cole, G. D. H., and Cole, Margaret, *The Intelligent Man's Review of Europe Today*, 1933; Langsam, W. C., *The World Since 1914*, 1933; Muir, Ramsay, *Political Consequences of the Great [War*, 1930; Ogg, F. A., *European Governments and Politics*, 1934, rev. ed.; Slosson, P. W., *Twentieth Century Europe*, 1927; Toynbee, A. J., *Survey of International Affairs*, annual; Wheeler-Bennett, J. W., ed., *Documents on International Affairs*, annual since 1930.

In addition to the above, the following secondary sources should prove useful for articles on special topics, references to which will be found in the collected indexes of each: *American Journal of International Law; Current History; Foreign Policy Reports; International Conciliation;* World Peace Foundation Publications.

[2] See the address of President Wilson to Congress, January 8, 1918, and his Mount Vernon address of July 4, 1914. (For text of the Fourteen Points, etc., and of a part of the Mount Vernon Address, see Appendix B.)

proposals deserves the description of revolutionary because each in its turn undertook to substitute for one of the oldest traditions of modern Europe a theory, now become American by adoption but as yet without practical test.

Thus the principle of self-determination envisaged the substitution for the doctrine of the balance of power, which asserted the supreme right of Europe collectively to security, of a system by which the rights of the individual peoples were proclaimed to be absolute.[1] Plebiscite was to decide the question of allegiance, even where the result might be to place in the hands of a single nationality power as disproportionate as that which had belonged to the France of Louis XIV and Napoleon.

Justice to Woodrow Wilson, the author of the Fourteen Points, must, however, compel recognition of the fact that when he uttered his famous prescriptions the European situation was far different from that which he discovered when the Paris Peace Conference convened. And to the Europe which existed on the Fourth of July, 1918, the principle of self-determination might perhaps have been applied without grave difficulties, for, even when the President spoke at Mount Vernon, the Central Powers were still undefeated, the Hapsburg Monarchy as yet was intact, and the possibility of its utter disintegration had not fully dawned upon Europe. What Wilson had in mind was to avoid the creation of other Alsace-Lorraines. During half a century the blunder of 1871 had poisoned the atmosphere of Europe. Not even the most ardent German champion of the Treaty of Frankfort could deny that the will of the population of the Reichsland to remain French had been unanimous or

[1] Mattern, Johannes, *The Employment of the Plebiscite in the Determination of Sovereignty*, 1920; Wambaugh, Sarah, *Plebiscites Since the World War*, 1933; Wittmann, Ernö, *Past and Future of the Right of National Self-Determination*, 1920.

that the refusal to permit these populations to determine their own allegiance had, in the end, been one of the potent factors in producing the World War.

Nor was Wilson less mindful of the evil consequences for Europe of the extinction of Polish independence, of the denial to the Balkan peoples of the right of each to be free and united, and, finally, of the failure of Italy to achieve complete unification in 1860, 1866, and 1870, which was witnessed by the irredentist sentiment in respect of Trieste and the Trentino, that had brought Italy into the war on the side of the Allies. And it was to remedy the old evils and to prevent the creation of new, that the American President fashioned his constitution for a reformed Europe.

When, however, between the Armistice and the assembling of the Paris Peace Conference, the Hapsburg Monarchy broke up, the Hungarians renouncing the old association with the Austrians, and the Czechs proclaiming their independence, the principle of self-determination acquired new and portentous implications. In fact, the traditional problem of the balance of power reappeared, in a new setting to be sure, but with all its old significance.

To apply the principle of self-determination to the Austria of July, 1918—which was also the Austria of July, 1914—would have involved no more than the transfer of the border provinces of the two halves of the Dual Monarchy to the Rumanians, the Serbs, and the Italians, besides the transfer of Galicia to the new Poland. But there would still have remained a central core made up of Austria proper, Hungary, and Bohemia, counting more than thirty millions of inhabitants about equally divided among Germans, Magyars, and Slavs.

When, however, these three nationalities of the old Dual Monarchy separated in November, 1918, the situation became far different. In Austria and Bohemia—to which of course Moravia and Austrian Silesia were joined—there were at least ten millions of people who were German by speech, and in Bohemia three millions of these Germans were intermingled with six millions of Slavs, constituting a large minority, which for three centuries had been the dominant nationality.

For these ten millions of German Austrians, now that the old monarchy had collapsed, there was no other tolerable solution of the new problem save union with the sixty millions of Germans of the Reich. Such unity had been prevented in the past by two accidents of history: the Reformation and the rivalry of the Hapsburgs and Hohenzollerns. But now both dynasties were gone and the religious issue had lost its centrifugal influence. *Anschluss* was thus the wish of the Austrian Germans, and from Vienna the victorious Allies were promptly put on notice that these ten millions of Germans claimed for themselves the benefits of Wilson's principle of self-determination. They claimed them as a matter of right, moreover, because the President's proposals had been the basis of the Armistice and thus of the terms upon which all of the Central Powers had surrendered.

A plebiscite in what remained of the Austrian half of the old Hapsburg Monarchy in January, 1919, when the Paris Conference assembled, would have insured a solid majority for union with the German Republic, since the Teutonic element outnumbered the Slavic in the ratio of ten to seven. But to transfer seventeen millions of people and upwards of sixty thousand square miles of territory to Germany would enable the nation which had been defeated in the war to emerge victorious from the Peace Conference.

In place of the old Germany of sixty-five millions of people and slightly more than two hundred thousand square miles, there would now be a new Germany of nearly eighty millions of inhabitants and close to two hundred and fifty thousand square miles, even when France had recovered Alsace-Lorraine and Poland had regained Posen. By contrast, postwar France would still count only forty millions of people and but little more than two hundred and ten thousand square miles, while United Italy would count the same number of inhabitants and an area barely half as great as the German.

If, however, the Teutonic and Slavic populations of Austria and Bohemia were separated and the ten millions of the former transferred to Germany and the seven millions of the latter combined in a separate and independent state, on the one hand postwar Germany would still be larger in area and population than the prewar Empire, while on the other, the new Czech state, almost completely surrounded by German territory and without natural frontiers, would be politically and economically no more than a satellite.

For the European powers which, after four years of desperate and doubtful battle, had seen victory fall to their cause by only the narrowest of margins, both of these solutions were equally impossible. Nor is there anything to suggest that Woodrow Wilson, himself, ever urged upon Clemenceau, Lloyd George, and Orlando, his associates of the Big Four, any such integral application of his principle of self-determination.

On the contrary, the Paris Conference condemned the seven millions of German-speaking people of Austria to an independence which was unsought, unwelcome, and later destined to prove economically if not politically impracticable. As for the three million Germans of Bohemia, they were transferred to the control of the Czechs, henceforth to constitute the most considerable but by no means the only minority in a state which, in fact, was to have no ethnic majority.

From the very outset, therefore, the application of the principle of self-determination universally on the European Continent proved politically impossible. But while denying the benefits of this dogma to the most powerful of all the European nationalities, the statesmen of Paris proceeded at the same time to extend its blessings to most other peoples. Thus among the Great Powers the French and the Italians profited materially, while of the smaller states the Rumanians, the Southern Slavs, the Czechs, and the Poles benefited enormously.

The victors of 1918 carried their inconsistency also one step further, for they broke completely with the precedent of their predecessors of 1815. Whereas the Congress of Vienna had left the France of 1789 intact, the Peace of the Conference of Paris mutilated the Germany of 1914 ruthlessly, chiefly to the advantage of the Poles. Such mutilation, however, was justified morally by citation of the unquestioned fact that the majority in the eastern provinces actually taken from the Reich was, even on the basis of German statistics, clearly Slavic.

Obviously, however, the statesmen of Paris could not have it both ways and preserve even the smallest semblance of concern for consistency or of regard for justice. To deny the ten millions of Germans of Austria the benefits which application of the principle of self-determination would insure and then in the name of that principle

POSTWAR EUROPE
THE POWERS AND THE SUCCESSION STATES

POSTWAR EUROPE
THE POWERS AND THE SUCCESSION STATES

to tear Germany's eastern frontiers to pieces and in addition to destroy German territorial unity by the creation of the Polish Corridor, was to present the beaten but still powerful German people with a moral issue of incalculable proportions.

To the natural and justified resentment provoked by the territorial decisions of Paris there were added other and not less exacerbating circumstances. Of these the impossible reparations claims, the unilateral disarmament requirements, and the notorious "Guilt" clause[1] were the most considerable. As a consequence of the sum of these decisions, the victors of 1919 failed to make a viable peace with their vanquished foe.

Nevertheless, when these victors had completed their labors and a new system was established upon the European continent, the German people still remained the most powerful single ethnic group and next to the Russian the most numerous. By 1934 there were not less than seventy-five millions of German-speaking people dwelling in the center of Europe and constituting a compact mass. And in the hearts of these millions the desire for ethnic unity survived.

Surviving also, however, was the threat to Europe collectively and to the individual states about the circle of German frontiers immanent in this German longing for unity. French security in Alsace-Lorraine and Italian in Trieste and the Upper Adige, Polish access to the sea through the Corridor, and the very existence of Czechoslovakia were thus conditioned, henceforth, upon the

[1] The English translation of the German text of Article 231 of the Versailles Treaty reads as follows:

"The Allied and Associated governments declare and Germany recognizes that Germany and its allies are responsible as originators for all losses and damages which the Allied and Associated governments and their nationals have sustained in consequence of the war imposed upon them by the attack of Germany and her allies."

preservation of the status quo of the Paris Conference. And when the National Socialist Revolution of March, 1933, overthrew the German Republic and brought to power a dictator who openly proclaimed his purpose to join to his new Third Reich the German populations of the old Austria, which had been his birthplace, and at the same time asserted Germany's right to rearm, the old problem of the balance of power in Europe was clearly posed once more.

At that moment, too, the resemblance between the European condition of 1933 and that of 1792 also awakened further apprehension alike in Paris, in Rome, and in London. When the wars of the French Revolution began, France was surrounded at her frontiers by small states and principalities incapable of resistance and even ready to welcome the invader. And to this situation must be ascribed, in no small part, the early victories in Belgium, the Rhineland, and Northern Italy, which were together to supply the springboard of the great Napoleonic adventure that led to Berlin, Vienna, Madrid and, eventually, to Moscow.

In 1933, likewise, all of Central Europe from the southern frontiers of the Reich to the shores of the Aegean presented a spectacle of political incoherence aggravated by ethnic feuds and economic prostration.[1] Was it not then to be feared, if not actually to be expected, that the armies of a rearmed Germany would find in Vienna, Budapest, and Sofia the same welcome which had greeted those of the French Revolution in Brussels, Mainz, and Milan? And out of the debris of the Hapsburg Monarchy was it not conceivable that

[1] Buell, R. L., ed., *New Governments in Europe*, 1934; Macartney, C. A., *National States and National Minorities*, 1934; Zurcher, A. J., *The Experiment with Democracy in Central Europe*, 1933.

the new German dictator might be able to construct a Mittel-europa comparable with that system which the great French Emperor had erected upon the ruins of the Holy Roman Empire?

The principle of self-determination, then, had brought no solution to the traditional problem of Europe. It had not even been tried, in the case of the most serious of all questions, namely, the German, because it would have opened the floodgates and left Europe without protection against new inundations like the old. But it is at least arguable that had the statesmen of Paris dealt with Germany as those of Vienna had done with France, even though Austro-German union were prohibited as Franco-Belgian had been prevented a century before, solid peace might have been re-established and Germany might have ended by accepting as definitive the separate existence of the Austrian population of the Danubian Republic, as France had accepted that of the Walloons of the Belgian kingdom.

Such speculations, however, need have no place here, for what concerns us is simply the fact that viable peace was not made with Germany, and that after the overthrow of the German Republic and the arrival of Adolf Hitler, the principle of self-determination, which had been the battle cry of the Allies of the World War, became the war cry of the former foe, in the postwar era.

Simultaneously, too, the doctrine of the balance of power, which had been anathema to the American President, became the guiding dogma of America's associates in the World War. Since tolerable peace was not made with the German people at Paris, and they eventually committed their destinies to a dictator who proclaimed his purpose to achieve German unity by force, National

Socialist Germany henceforth assumed in the eyes of its neighbors that position which Bourbon and Bonapartist France had once occupied in the eyes of all European states. And for such a menace, Europe, during three centuries, had been able to evolve no answer save coalition.

The proposal to substitute a League of Nations for the old Concert of Europe was also, in its turn, revolutionary, because it envisaged transferring the control of the Continental affairs of the Old World from the hands of the Great Powers of the European region to an international council in which all of the nations of the world would speak with authority. Thus, after centuries during which Europe had dominated the fortunes of the world, it was now itself to come under world control.[1]

But to substitute the League of Nations for the old Concert of Europe, in so far as the administration of Old World affairs was concerned, was possible only upon one of two assumptions: first, that a peace could be made at Paris satisfactory to victor and vanquished alike; second, failing such a settlement, that the non-Continental Great Powers—and in practice this meant the United States and Great Britain—would be ready to employ their military, naval, and financial resources to preserve order on the mainland of Europe. In a word, a state of peace had to be established either by common consent or by competent authority backed by adequate means.

Neither assumption, however, was justified by the event. And the explanation must be sought first in the circumstances of the Great Powers and secondly in the history of the several experiments in peace.

[1] Toynbee, A. J., *The World After the Peace Conference*, 1925.

Chapter X

GERMANY

HALF a generation after the close of the World War Germany was, despite defeat in war and unilateral disarmament in peace, potentially if not actually the first of the five Great Powers of the European region. In numbers, her population far exceeded that of France, Italy, or Great Britain. In the field of industry her superiority over Russia was so great that it effectively counterbalanced Slav numbers. As a consequence, in 1934, as at all times since the Settlement of Paris, the question of peace or war in the Old World turned upon the ultimate direction German national policy would take.[1] Germany, therefore, is obviously the nation to be studied first in a survey of the Great Powers of Europe.

In the examination of her national policy it is obvious that consideration must be given to the geographic, eco-

---

[1] The following books dealing with the general aspects of postwar German politics will prove useful for reference: Anonymous, *Der Kampf um die Deutsche Aussenpolitik*, 1931; Dawson, W. H., *Germany under the Peace Treaty*, 1933; Hoetzsch, Otto, *Germany's Domestic and Foreign Policies*, 1929; Koch-Weser, E. F. L., *Germany in the Post-War World*, 1930; Kühlmann, Richard von, *Thoughts on Germany*, 1932; Luehr, Elmer, *The New German Republic*, 1929; Rosenberg, Arthur, *The Birth of the German Republic*, 1931.

nomic, and demographic aspects of the German situation;[1] for upon these turn the questions of security, prosperity, and ethnic unity, the major objectives of all national policies.

Geographically, the German situation is the simplest in that, alone among the Great Powers of Europe, her territory is completely restricted to that Continent. Her central location, moreover, gives rise to a problem of security as old as history; for now, as always, the position of the Germans brings them into collision with the Latin in the West and the Slav in the East.[2]

In its contemporary form that struggle reverts to the Thirty Years War on the Rhine and to the Partition of Poland on the Vistula. Beyond these events, too, the Franco-German dispute goes back to the Treaty of Verdun which in the ninth century established the frontiers of the original German Reich at the Meuse.[3] Polish-Prussian conflict, in its turn, goes back to the thirteenth and fourteenth century adventures of the Teutonic Knights.

At the outbreak of the World War Germany was fortunately situated on both frontiers. The Congress of Vienna, by finally extinguishing Polish independence,

[1] Diesel, Eugen, *Germany and the Germans*, 1931.

[2] "Germany's central position in the heart of Europe is chiefly responsible for the disastrous reverses which have been so frequent in her history. They have balked her progress at every step, nipped every growing bud, doomed every hopeful development to a tragic ending. No one ever recognized this more clearly than did Bismarck himself. He saw that owing to her central position Germany might at any moment be endangered and overwhelmed by powerful coalitions, and the thought cost him many sleepless nights. The *cauchemar des coalitions* with which a Russian diplomat once teased the Prince was anything but an imaginary nightmare. It was his clear realization, based on history and experience, of the fact that a terrible danger continually hung over Germany's head. Viewed in this light, the foreign policy of the great chancellor, which sometimes seemed so complicated, becomes astonishingly clear and lucid." (Article by Richard von Kühlmann, Council on Foreign Relations, *Permanent Bases of Foreign Policy*, 1931, pp. 63–64.)

[3] Haller, Johannes, *France and Germany, the History of One Thousand Years*, 1932.

had given Prussia the control of the lower Vistula. From Thorn to the Baltic the Germans had doubled this natural line of defense by the fortresses of Danzig, Graudenz, and Thorn. In the gap between the lower Vistula and the upper Oder they had constructed the fortress of Posen. From Breslau to the Austrian frontier the Oder covered Germany, while Cracow, in the hands of an ally, anchored that line.

Relying upon the strength of this eastern system of defense, Germany in 1914 had sent all but a handful of her army to the western front. Nor had her judgment been mistaken, for the Russian invasion was broken at Tannenberg even before it reached the Vistula. In the south, too, Cracow had never been seriously menaced, and after the victory of the Dunajec in May, 1915, the Russian "steam roller" disappeared behind the Niemen and the Pripet marshes.

In the west the Treaty of Frankfort had bestowed similar strategic advantages upon the Germans. At Metz and Thionville, they commanded and covered the valley of the Moselle; at Strasbourg and Molsheim, that of the Rhine. Alsace, too, was further protected by the Vosges, and a French attempt to penetrate between Strasbourg and Metz had been broken in the great victory of Morhange-Sarrebourg in August, 1914. Thereafter the German defense system in the west was never seriously challenged, although American troops were within range of the outer forts of Metz at the moment of the Armistice.

The strength of her frontiers alike in the east and in the west had bestowed upon Germany the priceless advantage of the offensive in August, 1914. As a consequence, she was able to undertake her great turning movement through Belgium, prescribed by the famous Schlieffen Plan. Although by the narrowest margin victory escaped her in the Battle of the Marne, Germany was able to fight on French and Belgian soil to the end of the war. Thus the early successes due to the natural strength of her western frontier spared her the horrors of invasion and the consequent devastation incident to modern warfare.

East and west alike, however, the Treaty of Versailles stripped the Germans of all of the advantages of their position in 1914. In the west, the return of Alsace-Lorraine to France cost them Metz-Thionville and Strasbourg-Molsheim. It also opened to the French their old avenues of invasion down the Moselle to the Rhineland, into the Palatinate by the left bank of the Rhine, and into South Germany by the right. When, also, the French presently constructed a Hindenburg line in steel and concrete between the Rhine and the Moselle,[1] the Germans were faced with the fact that another war with France, unlike the last, would begin on German soil.

Finally, although the French were unsuccessful in their efforts to gain permanent occupation of the whole of the left bank of the Rhine from Alsace to the Netherlands, they were able to write into the Treaty of Versailles provisions creating a demilitarized zone west of that river, imposing the demolition of the existing fortifications on both of its banks, and forbidding their reconstruction.[2] Strategically, therefore, Germany was thrown back east of the Rhine, and her territories to the west were certain to become the No Man's Land of the next conflict.

[1] See map, Chapter XI, pages 208–209.
[2] Articles 42, 43 and 180 of the Treaty of Versailles; also see Toynbee, A. J., *Survey of International Affairs, 1920-23,* 1925.

In the east, the transformation was equally complete and disastrous, for the restoration of Poland deprived Germany both of the lower Vistula and of the fortress of Posen. The fortifications of Danzig were dismantled, and the city and its suburbs erected into a Free State; Graudenz and Thorn passed to Poland; Posen, which had covered Berlin from Slav invasion, now protected Warsaw from German attack; and the Polish frontiers were advanced to within a hundred miles of the German capital. Finally, while Breslau was left to Germany, Upper Silesia and Cracow passed to Poland.

Thus Germany was thrown back behind the Oder in the east, as she had been thrust back behind the Rhine in the west, East Prussia was cut off from the Reich by the Polish Corridor, and all Germany beyond the Oder was exposed to invasion upon the declaration of war. Last of all, an alliance between Poland and France, and a similar partnership between France and Czechoslovakia soon suggested that the next war, unlike the last, would be a war on three fronts. For not only had the Austrian ally vanished, but also a new foe had risen in the south, and strategically this was hardest of all the blows struck to German security by the Paris Settlement.

Bismarck had once observed that the possessor of Bohemia held the keys to Germany. And now these keys had been placed in the hands of a new Czechoslovak state which promptly allied itself with France. From the Bohemian plateau Czech armies, borrowing the passes which had been famous in the wars of Frederick the Great, could arrive in the Silesian plain and, joining hands with the Poles above or below Breslau, open for them a safe passage of the Oder and a clear road to Berlin. In the same way, moving west along the valley of the Main, they could join hands with the French at Frankfort, opening for them the passage of the Rhine and isolating South Germany from North.

Finally, Czech troops descending the Elbe could reach Leipzig and Dresden, which were unfortified, and beyond them penetrate to the very heart of Germany, following the roads employed by Tilly and Wallenstein in the Thirty Years War. Berlin had thus become a frontier town and an equally vulnerable target for Polish and for Czech aircraft, which could easily be reinforced by French.

Given the new strategic situation of Germany, it was evident that her security could be assured only as she was allowed to maintain a military establishment of no inconsiderable dimensions.[1] Such possibility was denied her, however, and instead she was permitted a professional army of but 100,000 with which to oppose French, Polish, Czech, and Belgian forces together approximating a million. And while the reserves of her prospective opponents exceeded six millions, she was forbidden to train any. Finally, while the material of Germany's diminutive army was rigidly limited, France exhausted the resources of her industry and strained those of her finance upon the equipment of her own forces and those of her allies.[2]

By 1932, when the Disarmament Conference assembled in Geneva, it was not to be doubted that actually, if illegally, Germany had armed far beyond the limits pre-

[1] Rohde, Hans, *Franco-German Factors of Power*, 1932.
[2] Articles 160–180 of the Treaty of Versailles.

scribed by the Treaty of Versailles. Nevertheless the fact remained that the victorious nations, so far as lay within their power, had abolished German security and thereafter striven to keep her helpless. What she demanded as a matter of right, she had attained only by evasion. Nor, in her strategic position, did her demand for military parity with France[1] go beyond the limits of what was reasonable.

Since the Germans are a military people, they were acutely and even morbidly aware of their weakness as dictated by the Treaty of Versailles. The lessons of national history emphasized the significance of their present frontiers. The experiences of millions in the still recent war illustrated the meaning of invasion assured by the exiguity of their effectives. Continued denial of the demand for equality in means of self-defense, therefore, inevitably seemed the expression of a deliberate purpose to keep the German people forever helpless politically by holding over their heads the continuing menace of invasion. And on that issue Germany, in the autumn of 1933, quit the League of Nations.

At the end of 1934 Germany still found herself denied the right to security. How then did she stand in the matter of prosperity, the second objective of national policy? What was her situation in respect of economic self-sufficiency and of population pressure, the two determining factors? For her there could, of course, be no question of self-sufficiency on the American scale. Much less was there any possibility of autarky (note, page 84), despite the vain boasts of the extreme "Nazis." At most she could barely produce at home and sell abroad

[1] For text of German Arms Equality Memorandum, see *New York Times*, September 7, 1932; also Carnegie Endowment for International Peace, *International Conciliation*, No. 285, December, 1932.

enough to acquire the foodstuffs and raw materials necessary for national life and industrial activity.[1]

Here too, however, Germany suffered severely through the Peace Treaty. The enforced return of Alsace-Lorraine to France deprived her of the enormous reserves of iron which had been one of the foundations of her great industrial development after 1871. Actually, it had been the marriage of the coal of the Ruhr with the iron of Lorraine which had enabled the Germany of William II to outdistance the Great Britain of Edward VII in the field of heavy industry.

With the return of Lorraine to France, therefore, Germany was left disastrously crippled. Coal she still possessed in exportable quantities, but the cession of Upper Silesia to Poland cost her the Polish market and in addition forced her to face Polish competition in other European markets. In the same fashion the transfer of the Saar mines to French ownership, pending the plebiscite of January 13, 1935 (page 552), long deprived her of the chance to exchange coal for French iron.

Impressive, too, was German poverty in all of the essential raw materials of industry save coal. Iron, petroleum, copper, lead, cotton, rubber, manganese, nickel, wool, and tin, all had wholly or in large part to be purchased abroad. And of raw materials to sell, Germany had only coal, potash, and nitrates. As to coal, the competition was sharp and the market contracting.

[1] For general studies on the postwar economic position of Germany, see: Angell, J. W., *The Recovery of Germany*, 1932; Brady, R. A., *The Rationalization Movement in German Industry*, 1933; Carnegie Endowment for International Peace, "The Present Economic State of Germany," *International Conciliation No. 279*, 1932; Douglass, P. F., *The Economic Dilemma of Politics*, 1932; Foreign Policy Association, "Economic Structure of the Third Reich," *Foreign Policy Reports*, Vol. X, No. 15, 1934; Einzig, Paul, *Germany's Default: The Economics of Hitlerism*, 1934; National Industrial Conference Board, *Rationalization of German Industry*, 1931; Schmidt, C. T., *German Business Cycles*, 1934.

GERMANY

NATIONAL SELF-SUFFICIENCY IN FOODSTUFFS, ESSENTIAL INDUSTRIAL PRODUCTS, AND RAW MATERIALS

DOMESTIC PRODUCTION AND NET IMPORTS EXPRESSED AS PERCENTAGES OF
AVERAGE NATIONAL CONSUMPTION (1925-29)

—— GREAT ESSENTIALS ——

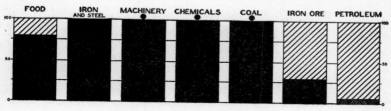

CRITICAL RAW MATERIALS

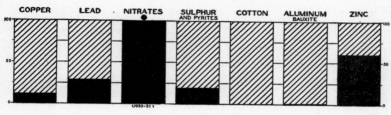

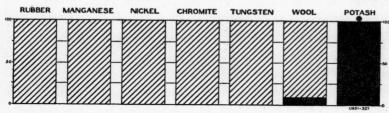

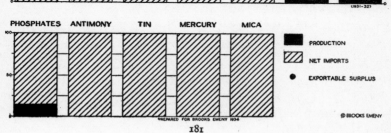

PRODUCTION

NET IMPORTS

EXPORTABLE SURPLUS

PREPARED FOR BROOKS EMENY 1934

© BROOKS EMENY

As to potash, with the loss of Alsace she had lost her monopoly, and French competition was keen. Finally, for nitrates the market was narrow and highly competitive.

There remained the great resources of chemicals and machinery. But the war had also broken German chemical monopoly by forcing her to part with her patent rights and by compelling other countries, deprived of German supplies during the war years, to develop their own manufactures. In machinery, too, postwar competition was keen, and by reason of political events the Russian market, by all odds the most important, was presently lost, at least temporarily.

In the field of foodstuffs, the Treaty of Paris had wrought further havoc in the German situation. In Alsace and Posen, the Reich had lost two of her most productive areas. Still able to raise 80 per cent of her food, postwar Germany nevertheless found herself short in fats, the want of which had been disastrous during the war. Coffee, tobacco, and many other things were similarly lacking. Finally, in stripping Germany of all of her colonies, the victors had deprived her of a precious if relatively small source of tropical oils and fruits and a growing market for German products.

With the spread of economic nationalism, moreover, the inherent weakness of the German situation became more and more apparent. That weakness, too, was aggravated by the Jewish boycott, which although in itself a slight affair, in the crisis of 1934 came near to constituting the last straw. In this year, foreign observers of German conditions agreed in comparing the situation in the Reich to that which had prevailed as a consequence of the blockade during the war.

Intact the German industrial machine still was. German technical skill, organization, and science were undiminished. The ship was seaworthy but the sea itself had gone dry and German prosperity visibly waited on the turn of the tide. And in this period of crisis, Germany for the first time disclosed clear if possibly only temporary evidence of population pressure, revealed by an unmistakable decline in the national standard of living.

In this respect, German statistics were illuminating. In 1910 the total population, living on an area of 212,000 square miles, had been 65,000,000. Twenty years later, despite the war, it was still the same, although the area had diminished by 30,000 square miles. In the forty years between 1871 and 1911 German numbers had expanded by not less than 25,000,000. That increase, almost exclusively urban, had been based not upon the expansion in the productivity of German soil, but upon the growth of German foreign trade. And now, under the influence of economic nationalism, that trade was drying up. At home the mouths remained to be fed, but abroad the work of the hands was unsalable.

By the German people both lack of security and loss of prosperity were charged to the character of the Treaty of Versailles. In their minds, their miseries and misfortunes had originated in the deliberate design of their conquerors, first to strip them of their well-being and then to keep them forever helpless and hapless. As they saw it, therefore, the German Revolution of 1933 was a rebellion against the consequences of the Peace Treaty. Actually, however, it was an instinctive uprising against, not a territorial, but an economic status quo, which was only in small part due to the decisions of Versailles.

The suppression of the Polish Corridor, the return of
Upper Silesia, even the union of the Reich and the Austrian Republic would not have provided considerable
supplies of the essential raw materials which were lacking or the additional markets that were needed. Not
even the return of the colonies, so passionately demanded, could do that. It was not lost provinces but
lost markets which were the secret of Germany's contemporary depression, and for this Austrian *Anschluss*
was of as little avail as Jewish pogroms, hot or cold.
But of one fact there could be no question: in 1934 Germany was as little prosperous as she was secure, and, on
both counts, her national policy was therefore dynamic.

There remains the question of unity.[1] Back of the
principle of self-determination, there had existed in
Wilson's mind the purpose to avoid the errors of the
Treaty of Frankfort in making that of Versailles. How
had it worked out? By the Treaty of Versailles something more than six and a half millions of people, ten
per cent of her total population, had been taken from
Germany. Of these, four millions had gone to Poland,
a million and three quarters to France, and the balance
had been distributed to Denmark, Belgium, and Lithuania. Germany's loss in 1919 was thus four times as
great as that of France in 1871.

Of the six and a half millions thus lost, however,
not less than two and a half were Polish and another
one and a half were the Alsatian and French survivors and
descendants of those who had protested against German
annexation after the Franco-Prussian War. In addition,
the population of Schleswig had by plebiscite voted

[1] For an ethnic map illustrating the distribution of the Germans in Europe, see
Chapter V, pages 102-103.

overwhelmingly for reunion with Denmark. By 1931, too, there remained of the one and a half millions of Germans who had been assigned to Poland in 1919 less than four hundred thousand living in the midst of four millions of Poles, the rest having taken the road to exile.

Actually, therefore, in 1934 the question of ethnic unity, for Germany, came down to the issue of the three hundred and fifty thousand Germans living in the Danzig Free State. Beyond that was the problem of security for two and a quarter millions more living across the Polish Corridor in East Prussia under German sovereignty. But here the issue was territorial and strategic rather than ethnic, for to suppress the Corridor and to recover Danzig as well, would liberate no more than half a million Germans at the price of re-establishing a Polish minority of far greater size. In fact, apart from the three hundred and fifty thousand Germans of Danzig, whose will to return to the Fatherland was not to be challenged, there was nowhere, east or west, on the Vistula or on the Rhine, a German minority in the true sense of the word, whose existence was to be charged against the Treaty of Versailles.[1]

By contrast, to the south, in the Austrian half of the old Hapsburg Monarchy there were now ten and a half millions of Germans—seven millions in Austria and three and a half in Czechoslovakia. These constituted the real German minority, and to join them to the Reich was the true problem of national and ethnic unity.

[1] Although by the recent Nonaggression Pact Poland and Germany have agreed to a temporary truce, the problem of the Corridor still remains unsettled and therefore dangerous. The following books dealing with various aspects of the question may be used for reference: Hamel, J. A. van, *Danzig and the Polish Problem*, 1933; Foreign Policy Association, "German-Polish Disputes: Danzig, the Polish Corridor and East Prussia," *Foreign Policy Reports*, Vol. IX, No. 9, 1933; Martel, René, *The Eastern Frontiers of Germany*, 1930; Smogorzewski, Casimir, *Poland, Germany and the Corridor*, 1930.

But these ten millions had not been German subjects
before 1914 nor had they, after 1919, been separated from
the Reich as a consequence of the Treaty of Versailles.
At most, that treaty had forbidden their union with the
German Republic.

What, then, was the actual situation of Germany at
the end of 1934? Strategically she had been deprived of
her old position, which gave her the priceless advantage
of the offensive in 1914. Thrown back behind the Rhine
and the Oder, all security was lacking precisely as long
as she was not permitted to arm up to the limits of
France and in addition to fortify her political frontiers
as France had done. To rid herself of the unilateral disarmament imposed by the Treaty of Versailles and to
abolish the demilitarized zones—these must be the primary objectives of Germany, seeking security.

These ends attained, however, the superiority of numbers and of industrial development would assure Germans of security east and west, and naval strength
sufficient to control the Baltic would protect her communications with East Prussia even in the unlikely
event that Polish armies could permanently hold the
Corridor. But these ends were, in 1934, already in
course of realization, for Germany was now arming with
impunity and would presently be able to fortify without
interference.

To recover Alsace-Lorraine and to achieve a new partition of Poland, the sole fashion in which she could
recover her old strategic situation of 1914, was, however,
beyond German military resources in any calculable
time. The British guarantee of Locarno still covered
France, and the French alliance protected Poland. And
beyond the Vistula and the Niemen, a new and formid-

able Soviet Russia was rising, openly resolved to defend the status quo in the east against all German attack.

For all present time, therefore, the limit of the possible in security for Germany, alike on her eastern and on her western frontier, was rearmament and reconstruction of her fortifications. In the west, Stresemann had recognized this fact in accepting the Locarno Pacts in October, 1925. Now Hitler repeated Stresemann's assurance of acceptance of the territorial status quo on the Rhine.[1] In addition, by a nonaggression pact[2] with Poland, he also established a ten-year truce on the east. Finally he had reached agreement with France as to the manner and time of the plebiscite in the Saar.[3] Only in the question of rearmament was he uncompromising, and there, although legal warrant was refused, prohibition by force was not attempted.

What, then, was left of the Treaty of Versailles, against which the German people had rebelled? The armies of occupation were gone, reparations were dead,[4] disarmament was in process of disappearance, the question of the Corridor had been adjourned on German proposal for ten years. That this last question might reappear

[1] Speeches of October 14, 1933, and January 30, 1934. In the latter address, after declaring that he proposed immediate settlement of the Saar question, the Chancellor went on to state that "as soon as this issue is settled, the German Government will be ready and resolved to assent truly and sincerely to the formal provisions of the Locarno Pact because then, in the German Government's opinion, there will be no territorial question left between France and Germany." (New York Times, January 31, 1934.)

[2] For text of the Polish-German Declaration, see Appendix F.

[3] The final plan for the settlement of the Saar question, approved by the Council of the League, provided for the plebiscite of January 13, 1935. For text of the Franco-German agreement, of December 3, 1934, see New York Times of December 6, 1934. For results of the plebiscite, see New York Times of January 14-16 1935.

[4] Carnegie Endowment for International Peace, "The Final Settlement of the Reparations Problems Growing out of the World War," International Conciliation, No. 262, September, 1930; Heinecke, Gunther-Erfrid, No More Reparations, 1932; McFadyean, Sir Andrew, Reparation Reviewed, 1930; Schacht, Hjalmar, The End of Reparations, 1931.

when Germany had rearmed was not to be denied. The truce with Poland was a truce of necessity and not of reconciliation. But it did constitute a recognition by Germany that the restoration of Poland was a permanent fact. The notion of the "season state" had disappeared. A new partition had become impossible. What remained was at most a boundary dispute.

Security by the revision of the armament clauses of the treaty was then the first objective of German policy. There remained, however, the two questions of prosperity and unity. But how was either to be obtained? As to prosperity, so far as it might be served by the recovery of old colonies or by the acquisition of new, the road was completely blocked. Nor was there brighter prospect of any reversal of the contemporary decision of all peoples, equally dominated by the spirit of economic nationalism, to seek domestic self-sufficiency at the cost of international trade. Here also the way was barred.

In one direction and in only one did there appear a way, and that way led to ethnic unity as well as to economic well-being. It was not an unknown pathway, for already in the prewar days Germany had heard with enthusiasm the slogan "Berlin-to-Bagdad." That dream, like so many others, had died with the war, but not until after German arms had, for a brief moment, opened this avenue of empire from end to end. Before the war, too, the necessity of maintaining the Hapsburg ally had put official restraint on the ambitions of the Pan-Germans. But now Hapsburg dynasty and empire had alike vanished and, at least in 1918, the ten millions of Germans of Austria had sought union with the Reich.

In southward expansion, also, there was clear promise of prosperity, for in the Danubian Basin the agrarian

states of Yugoslavia, Hungary, and Rumania were natural markets for German manufactures, while in the
Reich their foodstuffs and raw materials would find
ready sale. An economic Mittel-europa extending from
Hamburg to Istanbul would unmistakably have the
possibility of becoming a relatively self-sufficient and
materially prosperous unit. Here, too, was a region
undeveloped, possessing beyond the Danube and the
Drava resources as yet not even fully explored.

In that vast Danubian Basin political chaos and ethnic
feuds continued. French policy operating through the
Little Entente, and Italian policy working similarly
through Hungary, had prevented all progress. But
France, able to provide money but not markets, and
Italy, lacking money and having but a restricted market
to offer, had similarly failed to establish a new system
of order to replace that of the vanished Austro-Hungarian
Empire. Only Germany could offer the markets and
repay in manufactures necessary to all of these countries.

To include the ten millions of Germans beyond the
Bavarian, Saxon, and Silesian frontiers within the new
Third Reich would be to restore in large part the historic
German Empire — the "Holy Roman Empire" — the
memory of which had never disappeared from the German mind. It would be to bestow upon the most powerful of all the European peoples the blessing of ethnic
unity now enjoyed by nearly all other peoples, great and
small. For such an empire, having within its frontiers
not less than seventy-five millions of Germans, the question of security could hardly arise.

The keys to Vienna, moreover, were the keys to the
gateway of the Near East. To the realization of this
grandiose conception, union with Austria —*Anschluss*

ANSCHLUSS

—was the first step. Even before the National Socialist Revolution the Republic of Brüning, under the coercion of the rising tide of nationalism, had sought to take that first step by establishing an Austro-German Tariff Union, the agreement of which was made public on March 28, 1931. The attempt had been blocked, French money had compelled Austrian abandonment of the project, and in that campaign Italy had stood with France.[1]

But in 1934, as the events attending the murder of Dollfuss demonstrated conclusively, the Austrian-born dictator who ruled in Berlin in the place of the Empire and of the Republic was, in his turn, visibly looking eastward down the Danube to Vienna and beyond, where there was promise alike of power and of profit.

Manifestly the new orientation of German policy might not persist, and the failure of the July *Putsch* in Vienna, together with its repercussions in Rome, Paris, and London, foreshadowed at least a temporary pause. But if events in Berlin in June, and in Europe in August, suggested that the Hitler regime might prove transitory and that a new revolution within the Reich might paralyze national policy without,[2] nevertheless it remained true that, although regimes come and go and rulers change ceaselessly, the objectives of national policy endure. So also does the resolution of a great people.

[1] American Foundation, *The World Court's Advisory Opinion on the Austro-German Customs Union Case*, 1931; Argus, *pseud. The Economic Aspect of the Austro-German Customs Union*, 1931; Bitterman, M., *Austria and the Customs Union*, 1931; Einzig, Paul, *Behind the Scenes of International Finance*, 1931; Kleinwächter, F. F. G., *Self-Determination for Austria*, 1929.

[2] Although on the surface the vote of confidence which Hitler received at the polls on August 19, 1934, indicated an overwhelming majority of 89.9 per cent favorable to the regime, the increase in the number of negative votes over the November election of the previous year foreshadowed a rallying of opposition forces which might gather momentum with the continuance of acute economic distress. The following table

Three times, moreover, within a quarter of a century, under the Empire, the Republic, and the National Socialist Dictatorship, German policy had significantly turned to the south. National strategy had thus identified the Danubian front as the single point at which it might be possible to break through the circle within which Germany is restricted to circumstances incommensurate not merely with her aspirations but with her necessities as well. Since, however, Europe saw in the new German purpose the disclosure of the historic threat to the balance of power, and identified in the German program in the Danubian Basin the prospectus of a new hegemony, contemporary Austria became what Belgium had been in the far-off days of French greatness, the "cockpit of Europe."[1]

German national policy, then, a decade and a half after the Paris Peace Conference, was dynamic. The German people had overthrown a republican regime which, in their minds, was a symbol of defeat in war and of humiliation in peace, as the French, for the same reason, had dismissed the Bourbons fifteen years after Waterloo.

To understand German national policy, as indeed to comprehend that of any great people, it is essential to

which records the results of the August "plebiscite" as compared with the previous polls on November 12, 1933, is of interest:

	Aug. 19, 1934	Nov. 12, 1933 Reichstag	Nov. 12, 1933 Foreign Policy
Total votes	43,529,710	42,988,152	43,452,613
For	38,362,363	39,638,363	40,601,577
Against	4,295,654	....	2,100,756
Invalid	872,296	3,349,363	750,271

(For detailed account of the rise of the National Socialist Party to power, see Foreign Policy Association, "Hitler and the German Political Crisis," *Foreign Policy Reports*, Vol. VIII, No. 26, 1933.)

[1] Armstrong, H. F., *Europe Between Wars?*, 1934; Balla, V. de, *The New Balance of Power in Europe*, 1932; Simonds, F. H., *Can Europe Keep the Peace?*, 1934, rev. ed.

grasp the psychological factor. Otherwise that policy, viewed in the abstract, invariably appears inexplicable and even irrational. In the German situation this psychological factor is of dominating importance, for by 1933, when the National Socialist revolution intervened, the German problem had become pathological even more than political.[1]

During the four years of the World War, the Germans had been completely isolated from the world and insulated from the public opinion of the Allied nations. At the close of the war, although exhausted and defeated, they had identified in the intervention of Woodrow Wilson and in the language of his Fourteen Points and his later pronouncements[2] the promise both of reasonable peace terms and of rapid reconciliation with their recent foes. And at the moment of the Armistice, the German people were utterly unaware of the judgment their enemies had passed alike upon their mentality and upon their morals during their isolation.

When, however, the barriers were at last lifted, they suddenly discovered themselves to be counted a guilty people and commonly described as "Huns" and "Boches." At the Paris Conference they were denied any semblance of the treatment accorded to France at the Congress of Vienna. Instead, they were summoned to Versailles like criminals and there sentenced without ever having been permitted the ordinary justice of their day in court.[3]

[1] Armstrong, H. F., *Hitler's Reich*, 1933; Kosok, Paul, *Modern Germany; A Study of Conflicting Loyalties*, 1933; Moore, W. G., *France and Germany; A Study of National Character and Opinion*, 1932; Shuster, G. N., *The Germans; an Inquiry and an Estimate*, 1932; Spengler, Oswald, *The Hour of Decision*, 1934.

[2] Wilson's great principle of the self-determination of peoples, and of government resting on the consent of the governed, was set forth in many addresses.

[3] Schiff, Victor, *The Germans at Versailles*, 1930.

In the Treaty of Versailles, too, the German people discovered no equitable or fair fulfillment of the promise of Wilson's proposals. On the contrary, while professing the idealism of a New World, the Allies had reverted to the Roman example to make another Punic Peace. The reparations clauses of the treaty condemned the Germans to the condition of a tribute-paying nation. The provisions which imposed perpetual unilateral disarmament reduced them to the circumstances of a defenseless people. The territorial decisions definitively shattered their unity.

Germania delenda est—that, for the German people, was the meaning of the Treaty of Versailles, and against its terms they rebelled as Germans. Revision became henceforth the fixed, enduring, immutable purpose of the nation and the policy of the successive Governments. But since a disarmed and occupied Reich was too weak to challenge the "*Diktat*" of Versailles directly, these Governments resorted to indirection.

When, however, the Cuno Cabinet undertook to evade the reparations payments, France occupied the Ruhr.[1] When the Brüning Government endeavored to circumvent the prohibition of the *Anschluss* by framing an Austro-German Tariff Union Pact, French financial coercion swiftly brought Vienna to its knees and Berlin to terms. When the National Socialist Revolution swept Hitler to power in January of 1933 his demand for equality in the means of self-defense was repulsed as that of Brüning and of Papen had been before.

The occupation of the Ruhr had wrecked the German middle class and prepared the way for the Hitler Revolution. The French financial coercion of Austria set in

[1] January, 1923, to August, 1925.

motion the stream of events which produced the financial crash of 1931 in the Reich and made the revolution inevitable. But the revolution itself resulted in the moral isolation of the Reich and exposed it instantly to the peril of a war of prevention precipitated by France and her allies.

In 1925 the Germans had, with grave misgivings, followed Stresemann to Geneva. Because the League was the child of the Paris Conference, and because also it had sanctioned the partition of Silesia despite the results of the plebiscite, the Germans had suspected it as the Trojan Horse of Allied diplomatic strategy. But to Geneva they came, prepared to make the action of the League in the matter of treaty revision the test of its sincerity, the measure of its idealistic nature. And when even the right to self-defense was denied, the German people followed Hitler out of the League, disillusioned and disgusted.

Meantime the circumstances of the National Socialist Revolution, the persecution of the Jews, the revival by the "Nazis" of the most preposterous of the territorial pretensions of the Pan-Germans of the prewar era, the renewal by new voices of the most absurd of the old bellicosities of Potsdam, while they could present no problem to the alienist, threw European statesmen into a panic. Actually these manifestations were no more than the symptoms of violence inseparable from the delusion of persecution. But they armed France and her allies with obvious justification for denying to Hitler what, with dubious warrant, they had refused to Stresemann and Brüning.

Yet to refuse again could only serve to fortify the sense of injustice and feed the delusion of persecution which was the foundation of the appeal of the Fuehrer.[1] And while it was easy to explain that condition of collective madness which now existed in the Reich and no more difficult to fix the responsibility for it upon the authors and administrators of the Treaty of Versailles, nevertheless to bestow arms upon a people now driven to violence by a sense of despair would be an act of justice so tardy as to seem in itself irrational.

For sixteen years, moreover, sixty millions of people had, across their mutilated frontiers and in the midst of inflation, financial disaster, and economic depression, continued to repeat the single word "revision."[2] It had become the be-all and the end-all of popular appraisal of national policy. Such, then, was the psychological factor. And to ignore it is to reduce the German problem to limits which render it at once academic and unintelligible.[3]

For, at the end of everything, to understand the national policy of a Great Power it is necessary to see into the soul of its people. Deep in the German soul today is the corroding sense of wrongs remediable only by the force of German arms and constituting in themselves the enduring evidence of the relentless purpose of France and indeed of the whole world.

[1] Hitler, Adolf, *My Battle*, 1933. *Führer*, the German word for "Leader" (or *Reichsführer*, for "Realm Leader"), is the title popularly bestowed on Hitler. The equivalent English spelling is Fuehrer.

[2] Foreign Policy Association, "Revision of the Versailles Treaty," *Foreign Policy Reports*, Vol. V, No. 8, 1929.

[3] Banse, Ewald, *Germany Prepares for War*, 1934; Heiden, Konrad, *A History of National Socialism*, 1934; Hoover, C. B., *Germany Enters the Third Reich*, 1933; Huddleston, Sisley, *War Unless—*, 1933; King, Joseph, *The German Revolution; Its Meaning and Menace*, 1933; Stowe, Leland, *Nazi Means War*, 1934.

Chapter XI

FRANCE

IF Germany, even in defeat, was still potentially the first among European powers, France in victory was at least temporarily restored to her traditional primacy on the Continent; for when the British and American armies had been demobilized and the German army dissolved, French military superiority was, for the immediate present and in fact as long as the Treaty of Versailles lived, beyond possible challenge.

The power of France, moreover, constituted the decisive factor in European history throughout the decade and a half following upon the ratification of the Treaty of Versailles. The terms of that treaty were such that German recovery was contingent upon their revision, and all revision was impossible without French consent. Responsibility for the nature of the terms, British and American statesmen shared with French; but the Anglo-Saxon nations surrendered control of French action in the matter of the application of these terms when they withdrew their armies from the Continent.

Influence upon French policy was similarly lost when

the United States Senate declined to ratify the Treaty of Guarantee. That treaty had been proffered to Clemenceau by Woodrow Wilson and Lloyd George, in the names of their respective nations, in return for his consent to waive the French claim to permanent occupation of the left bank of the Rhine. With the repudiation of that pledge, therefore, German recovery took on in the eyes of all Frenchmen the color of a threat to the very existence of France.

To the understanding of French policy,[1] moreover, two facts are essential. In the first place the French is the oldest tradition of authority among the Great Powers of Europe. In the second place, French territorial unification antedated that of all other Continental Powers. And if French power was never fully restored after Waterloo, French prestige enjoyed a brilliant Indian summer during the Third Empire. Nor did the disasters of 1814 and 1815 bring any real impairment of French unity.

The rise of Germany, however, at one blow swept away French influence in Europe and shattered French national unity. The consequences of the loss of Alsace-Lorraine, moreover, were enduring; for what had been taken from France seemed in the eyes of her people not territory but a portion of her living flesh. And while the wound to the body was eventually healed by the restoration of the lost provinces in 1918, the injury to the spirit has never yet been undone.

[1] The following books dealing with the general aspects of French national policy will prove useful for reference: Council on Foreign Relations, *Permanent Bases of Foreign Policy*, Chapter on "France" by Jules Cambon, 1931; Gooch, G. P., *Franco-German Relations, 1871-1914*, 1923; Recouly, Raymond, *De Bismarck à Poincaré*, 1932; Schuman, F. L., *War and Diplomacy in the French Republic*, 1931; Soltau, R. H., *French Parties and Politics, 1871-1930*, 1930; same author, *French Political Thought in the Nineteenth Century*, 1931; Tilley, Arthur, *Modern France*, 1923.

Actually from that day in 1681 when Strasbourg opened its gates to Louis XIV, down to the making of the Treaty of Frankfort in 1871, the eastern frontiers of France had endured substantially unchanged. Lorraine had come peacefully into French possession in 1766, but Metz, Toul, and Verdun, the keys of that province, had already been French since 1552. Together with the rest of France, the people of Alsace and Lorraine had lived the great epic of the French Revolution and the Empire. Two centuries of common association, moreover, had established a unity of spirit to which the people of the annexed districts testified eloquently if fruitlessly in their protest against separation from France.

During the years between the Franco-Prussian War and the World War, the Third Republic had created a French colonial empire second only to the British.[1] In those years, too, the French people had definitively renounced all the traditional ambitions in Europe. Only the recovery of Metz and Strasbourg remained a fixed hope, and even that hope grew fainter year by year as Germany waxed ever more powerful. And when the victory of 1918 restored the historic unity, no other European territorial aspiration survived.

It is true that Marshal Foch, backed by Poincaré, President of the Republic, clamored for the permanent occupation of the left bank of the Rhine, but neither asked for the extension of French political frontiers to that limit. For France, too, Clemenceau accepted a plebiscite to determine the ultimate possession of the Saar Basin. As for the four millions of people of French

[1] Roberts, S. H., *History of French Colonial Policy, 1870-1925*, 1929, 2 vols.; Lyautey, Pierre, *L'Organisation de l'Empire Colonial Français*, 1931; Maurois, André, *Lyautey*, 1931; Southworth, Constant, *The French Colonial Adventure*, 1931; Worsfold, W. B., *France in Tunis and Algeria*, 1930.

speech in Belgium and Switzerland, neither Hainaut nor the Pays de Vaud constituted a French irredenta.

After 1918, then, France again had unity. She also possessed the basic elements of prosperity. Of all the Great Powers of Europe the most nearly self-contained, she was able on her homeland territory to feed her forty-two millions. If her coal reserves were inadequate, half the iron of Europe was within her frontiers. As a creditor nation, she was confronted by no such problem as faced Germany and Italy in the purchase of those essential raw materials which all three lacked.[1]

Again, while population pressure showed itself in the appalling totals of German, British, and Italian unemployed, it was largely absent in France. When German unemployed numbered more than six million, British three million, and Italian more than one and a half million despite vast Fascist relief programs, the *chomeurs* of France hardly exceeded three hundred and fifty thousand. Thus France was spared a social problem which in various forms and degrees confronted all three of her neighbors.

The reason for French immunity was simple. By comparison with all three, France was underpopulated. Whereas nearly forty millions of English and Welsh lived on little more than fifty thousand square miles of territory, the forty-two millions of France occupied two hundred and twelve thousand. By contrast, sixty-five millions of Germans were confined in no more than one hundred and eighty thousand, and forty-two millions of Italians in less than one hundred and twenty thousand square miles of land area.

[1] Einzig, Paul, *The Sterling-Dollar-Franc Tangle*, 1933; Haig, R. M., *The Public Finances of Post-War France*, 1929; Ogburn, W. F., and Jaffé, William, *The Economic Development of Post-War France*, 1929.

FRANCE

NATIONAL SELF-SUFFICIENCY IN FOODSTUFFS, ESSENTIAL INDUSTRIAL PRODUCTS, AND RAW MATERIALS

DOMESTIC PRODUCTION AND NET IMPORTS EXPRESSED AS PERCENTAGES OF
AVERAGE NATIONAL CONSUMPTION (1925—29)

—— GREAT ESSENTIALS ——

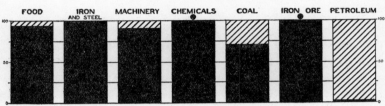

FOOD — IRON AND STEEL — MACHINERY — CHEMICALS — COAL — IRON ORE — PETROLEUM

CRITICAL RAW MATERIALS

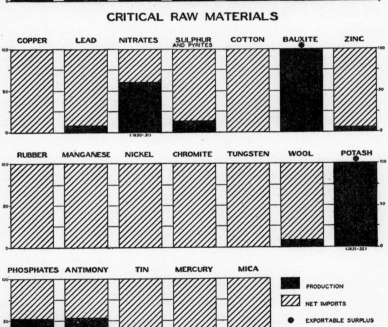

COPPER — LEAD — NITRATES — SULPHUR AND PYRITES — COTTON — BAUXITE — ZINC

(1930-31)

RUBBER — MANGANESE — NICKEL — CHROMITE — TUNGSTEN — WOOL — POTASH

(1931-32)

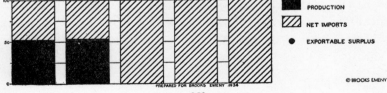

PHOSPHATES — ANTIMONY — TIN — MERCURY — MICA

PRODUCTION

NET IMPORTS

● EXPORTABLE SURPLUS

PREPARED FOR BROOKS EMENY 1934

© BROOKS EMENY

In the good years there had crowded into France nearly three millions of immigrants—Italian, Polish, Spanish, and Belgian.[1] When the depression came, these foreign laborers could be repatriated and became a problem in unemployment, not for France, but for the countries of their origin.

Furthermore, while German population annually increased by a third of a million and Italian by nearly half a million, French population substantially stood still. Finally, in North Africa, particularly in Morocco, opportunity beckoned to the adventurous and there was still a new frontier to be made good.

The colonial aspect of the French situation will be discussed elsewhere.[2] Here, however, it is necessary to consider it in its relation to the European problem. Thus viewed, it is clear that the possession of a vast colonial empire assured to the French not only a reservoir of recruitment[3] but also, in a period when economic nationalism was closing the doors of the world to German industry and Italian labor, a constant market, manifestly destined to grow and not to contract with the passing of time. And it also bestowed upon French shipping a steady employment in transporting manufactures in one direction and raw materials in the other.[4]

In the light of all of these circumstances, security was naturally the single concern of French national policy, since both economic prosperity and ethnic unity were possessed. But the problem of security presented two very different aspects, the first constituted by the ordi-

[1] Lambert, Charles, *La France et les Étrangers*, 1927.
[2] See Chapter XXII.
[3] Davis, S. C., *Reservoirs of Men*, 1934.
[4] Ferdinand-Lop, S., *Les Ressources du Domaine Colonial de la France*, 1924; Maestracci, Noël, *L'Empire Colonial Français Contemporain*, 1931.

nary problems of national defense determined by geographical circumstances,[1] and the second by the policies
of the neighbors of France considered in the light of
history and of their resources to pursue these policies.

As to the geographic aspect of security, the situation
is simply told. With the recovery of Alsace-Lorraine,
France regained Strasbourg and Metz. From Basel to the
mouth of the Lauter, the Rhine now covered her eastern
boundary. Between the Rhine and the old frontier west
of the Moselle, a new system of fortification presently
closed the routes of invasion by which the elder Moltke's
conquering hosts had marched to victory at Gravelotte
and Sedan in 1870. Behind the old frontier, also, were
the fortress cities of Verdun, Toul, Epinal, and Belfort,
which had survived German assault in 1914 and thereafter.

To man these fortresses, and to defend the open frontier toward Belgium, where the deluge had burst in 1914,
the French maintained an army whose numbers were
fixed by French appreciation of national necessity un-
restricted by treaty limitation, and whose equipment
had been fashioned in the light of the still recent lessons
of the World War. Since German military forces were
necessarily concentrated behind the Rhine, even though
in numbers and equipment these indubitably surpassed

[1] "The geographical position of a nation, indeed, is the principal factor condition-
ing its foreign policy—the principal reason why it must have a foreign policy at
all. . . .

"France, like England, has sought through the centuries to realize her destiny; but,
while England by reason of her special situation has put her trust in a preponderant
naval power, France, whose frontiers to the north and to the east were open to invasion, has put her trust in military power. And so these two powers, whose behavior
at first glance seems to have been so different, in reality obey the same instinct: both
look for security, each in the manner dictated by its geographical position." (Articles
by Jules Cambon, Council on Foreign Relations, *Permanent Bases of Foreign Policy*, 1931,
pp. 1-2, 4.)

the restricted limits of the Treaty of Versailles, French armies were assured of the ability to enter German territory and to seize the important coal mines of the Saar Basin at the outbreak of hostilities. Thus, for all present time, France had security on the north and east, facing Germany.

Nor was she less fortunately situated on the Italian frontier. There the Alps, reinforced by a new system of fortifications, constituted an impregnable barrier, which could be held by small forces if France were compelled to fight Germany and Italy simultaneously. In the Mediterranean, too, France had decisive naval superiority over Italy, a fact of utmost importance because, in case of war, large French forces would have to be moved from Tunisia, Algeria, and Morocco to the Continent. Thus in 1934 France had present security on land and sea, against Italy as well as Germany.

In addition, she had many armed allies:[1] Yugoslavia, ready to attack Italy in the east if Italian armies undertook an offensive against France in the west; Czechoslovakia, watching Germany from the Bohemian plateau; Rumania, prepared to hold both Hungary and Bulgaria in check if either undertook to assail the allies of France in the rear, at the behest of Italy. Between France and Belgium, too, a military alliance of sorts existed. Belgium, moreover, was busy constructing a new line of forts on her German frontier and could at least be depended upon to defend her own national territory, as she had striven to do in 1914.

With Poland, a military alliance had long existed,[2] and it had been renewed in 1934. To be sure, the Poles

[1] Balla, V. de, *The New Balance of Power in Europe*, 1932; Foreign Policy Association, "Political Realignments in Europe," *Foreign Policy Reports*, Vol. IX, No. 5, 1933.

[2] Smorgorzewski, Casimir, *La Politique Polonaise de la France*, 1926.

had in the same year executed a nonaggression pact with Germany,[1] and Polish policy was becoming obscure and even unfriendly. Beyond Poland, however, the Soviet Union was again rising to European importance, and Moscow and Paris had recently renewed the old association of St. Petersburg with Paris and, in addition, the Soviet Union had entered the League of Nations.[2] Roused by German prospectuses of Ukrainian conquests at their expense, the Russians had therefore broken the old bonds of Rapallo with Berlin and thrown all their weight on the French side. In the closing weeks of 1934, the French Chamber of Deputies had heard the confident assurance that in case of German aggression, Soviet military forces would march to the support of France.

Last of all there was Great Britain, bound by the Pacts of Locarno to defend the status quo of the Treaty of Versailles in so far as French and Belgian frontiers were concerned.[3] The commitment had been made reluctantly, it had been accepted by the British people without enthusiasm, it was a constant cause of anxiety and even of acute apprehension. Nevertheless, it existed and, at intervals, British statesmen had reaffirmed its validity.[4] Nor was it less evident that, however great the British irritation with French policy and however general the eagerness to keep out of another European conflict, British concern for the inviolability of Belgian territory endured, and the prospect of a German advance to the coast of Flanders would once more insure British intervention, as it had in 1914.

[1] For text see Appendix F.
[2] Foreign Policy Association, "The Soviet Union as a European Power," *Foreign Policy Reports*, Vol. IX, No. 11, 1933.
[3] See Chapter XXV.
[4] Speech of Baldwin delivered July 19, 1934, in the House of Commons.

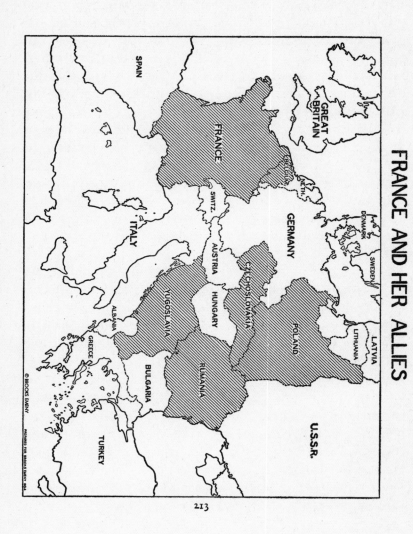

FRANCE AND HER ALLIES

SPAIN

GREAT BRITAIN

FRANCE

BELGIUM

NETH.

SWITZ.

GERMANY

DENMARK

SWEDEN

U.S.S.R.

LATVIA

LITHUANIA

AUSTRIA

CZECHOSLOVAKIA

POLAND

HUNGARY

YUGOSLAVIA

ITALY

ALBANIA

RUMANIA

BULGARIA

GREECE

TURKEY

Thus reviewed, the various elements which together made up the sum of French security on the morrow of the National Socialist triumph in Germany seemed impressive. Wherein, then, lay the cause of French apprehension? What further measure of security was to be attained by France within the limits of what might be considered humanly possible? This question goes to the very heart of the whole situation. To answer it is, moreover, to explain French national policy from the Armistice to the present hour.

Broadly speaking, France's demand for security beyond that measure which geographical situation, her own national resources, and her alliances bestowed upon her, was based upon the fact that there existed sixty-five millions of Germans and but forty-two millions of French. This obvious disparity in numbers was further increased by an even greater disparity between French and German industrial development. In machine power[1] even more than in man power, French inferiority was so manifest that there was no question of German victory in a new Franco-German conflict, if France stood alone.

If, in advance of the establishment of French security, Germany were to be permitted to rearm beyond the limits of the Treaty of Versailles and to unite with Austria, what assurance could there be that France and her allies would not be overwhelmed before Great Britain, faithful to the pledge of Locarno, could muster the forces necessary to restore the balance? In the World War, France had been compelled to carry the bulk of the burden for two years while Great Britain was arming, and the battle had been fought on French soil.

[1] See Self-Sufficiency Chart, Chapter IV, page 75.

What France sought, then, for herself, for her allies, for all countries, was the collective guarantee, by the nations of the world, of the security of each individual state. The machinery was at hand. The League of Nations was in existence. The peace treaties of the Paris Conference constituted the new public law of Europe. The League had been expressly designed to enforce the law. All that was lacking to the League was the means. Adequate means, too, could be supplied only when Great Britain and the United States should join their resources to those of France to act through the League in the name alike of the law and of world peace.

Meantime, without French consent no part of the Treaty of Versailles could be revised. Since Great Britain and the United States were obviously if unequally interested in seeing that law amended, their concern for French security should at least be equal to their interest in German recovery. The League of Nations at which Clemenceau had scoffed had now, thanks to Briand, become the ultimate instrument of French policy.

That policy, moreover, was crystal clear. The French objective was security, the instrument was the League of Nations, the strategy consisted in holding Germany to the letter of the law which was the Treaty of Versailles, until the Anglo-Saxon nations, which had forced the League upon France, were prepared to invest it with that authority which its founder had designed it should have. Nor was it less obvious, after the Manchurian episode, at least, that without authority backed by power Geneva was helpless.

After the Treaty of Versailles was made, however, the British and the American people had changed their minds about its terms. They had judged them to be too harsh and identified in them the promise of later German resentment and reprisal. In addition, the British had promptly found the reparations payments injurious to their own commercial interests, as the Americans later found them disastrous for their investments in the Reich. But when Germany, inspired by obvious Franco-British coolness, undertook to resist reparations payments, the French occupied the Ruhr.[1] And when, later, relying upon British and American investments in the Reich to insure Anglo-Saxon restraint of France, Germany had announced a tariff union with Austria, France had defeated the American attempt to save the German banking structure by the Hoover moratorium and had brought Austria to her knees by financial coercion.[2]

The third German rebellion against the Treaty of Versailles, disclosed in the demand for military parity with France, met a similar uncompromising resistance.[3] Once more the Anglo-Saxon powers, convinced of the essential reasonableness of German demands and alarmed by the prospects of violence that resistance to these demands forecast, sought compromise through French concession. And again they were met by the unvarying French response that concessions to Germany must be balanced by guarantees to France. As a result, Germany quit the League, the prestige of Geneva was at least temporarily shattered, and the European crisis became visibly more acute.[4]

[1] Stegemann, Hermann, *The Struggle for the Rhine*, 1927; Tuohy, Ferdinand, *Occupied, 1918-1930*, 1931.

[2] Einzig, Paul, *Finance and Politics*, 1932; Salter, Sir Arthur, *Recovery, The Second Effort*, 1932.

[3] See Chapter XXVIII; also, Foreign Policy Association, "The Disarmament Crisis," *Foreign Policy Reports*, Vol. IX, No. 17, 1933; Dulles, A. W., "Germany and the Crisis in Disarmament," *Foreign Affairs*, January, 1934.

[4] Armstrong, H. F., *Europe Between Wars?*, 1934.

Obviously, however, while French security would be enormously fortified by an Anglo-Saxon guarantee, extended through the machinery of the League, British and American safety would be correspondingly impaired. As a consequence, in both countries the idea of transforming the League into a superstate and underwriting its authority with British and American resources in men and money seemed preposterous. But in France it seemed not less preposterous that the Anglo-Saxon powers should demand of France that she allow Germany to rearm while refusing to give France solid guarantees not only of her own security but also of the permanence of the entire European edifice.[1]

The French saw the problem of Europe as integral. They were satisfied that if Germany were allowed to rearm she would one day be able to realize unity with Austria by force. Thereafter, Czechoslovakia would be helpless, almost encircled by German territory and having a large German minority. Afterwards Bucharest and Belgrade would be brought to heel. How then could Poland hope to retain the Corridor? Once treaty revision were accepted in principle, there would be no going backward: the old tragedy of 1866 and 1870 would be repeated.

When the Hitler Revolution arrived, the Anglo-Saxon peoples saw in it the justification of their worst fears and the confirmation of their constant forecast. French insistence upon the letter of the law of Versailles had led to German upheaval. But the French perceived in what had happened the ultimate proof of their conten-

[1] Potter, P. B., "Sanctions and Security; An Analysis of the French and American Views," *Geneva Special Studies*, Vol. III, No. 2, 1932; Wheeler-Bennett, J. W., and Longemann, F. E., *Information on the Problem of Security, 1917-1926*, 1927; Wheeler-Bennett, J. W., *Disarmament and Security since Locarno*, 1932.

tion that the Germans were always what Tacitus had described them to be nearly two thousand years earlier. In the extravagant violence of the "Nazi" prospectus of the Third Reich they identified the voice of the authentic German. And what they had refused to the Republic of Stresemann they were under no temptation to bestow upon the Third Reich of Hitler.

In French eyes, moreover, British and American pretensions were compromised by their performances. At the Paris Conference, Wilson and Lloyd George had persuaded Clemenceau to renounce the French claim to garrison the left bank of the Rhine forever. In return, in the name of their respective countries, they had pledged him the ratification of a Treaty of Guarantee. But the American Senate had repudiated the promise of the American President, and as the British promise had been contingent upon the American, both, therefore, fell together.

Five years later, Great Britain had made the Locarno Pact. But that was too late and too little. France had already been forced to negotiate her alliances with Poland and the Little Entente. The Rhine was only one of the rivers of controversy in Europe; and for a people living in the Continent, there was no safety in one corner when there was danger of conflagration in another.

At times the British and even the Americans had imagined that France could be coerced. But that was to forget the French tradition of authority. The original French Republic had successfully defied all Europe in defense of its rights. And postwar France had a great army, many allies, a diplomatic ascendancy in Geneva and in Europe which were unrivaled assets. When, too, Poincaré had restored the franc, the financial weapon was a resource not of Anglo-Saxon but of French diplomacy.

Ironically enough, the French had ended by taking Woodrow Wilson at his word, long after his fellow-countrymen had repudiated that word. The American President had said he would make a peace of justice. The French accepted as such the treaty which he had imposed upon them. He had created machinery to restrain nations seeking to violate that treaty. The French accepted that machinery and asked only that it be made stronger. Wilson and Lloyd George had forced the Treaty of Versailles upon the French; they had never liked it, but they had agreed to it on the precise assurance that Great Britain and the United States would help enforce it against Germany; and now both were trying to revise it in the interests of Germany.[1]

In law and in logic, the French position was impregnable. And back of law and logic was force. In British and American eyes, however, French policy seemed so shortsighted and suicidal that both London and Washington continued to expect that French Liberalism would conquer French Nationalism; but in fact it never did. From Clemenceau to Doumergue, France never budged an inch. In moments of crisis, Herriot spoke the language of Tardieu. For all Frenchmen of the Left and of the Right, there was only one question, and that was France; only one enemy, and that was Germany; only one policy, and that was security.

To understand French policy it is necessary to consider French psychology.[2] In Germany, as is well known,

---

[1] Schoonmaker, E. D., *Our Genial Enemy, France*, 1932; Tardieu, André, *France and America*, 1927.

[2] Carroll, E. M., *French Public Opinion and Foreign Affairs, 1870-1914*, 1931; Hayes, C. J. H., *France: A Nation of Patriots*, 1930; Hill, Helen, "The Spirit of Modern France," *World Affairs Pamphlets*, No. 5, Foreign Policy Association and World Peace Foundation, 1934: Lichtenberger, Henri, *Relations between France and Germany*, 1923; Madariaga, Salvador de, *Englishmen, Frenchmen, Spaniards*, 1931, rev. ed.; Moore, W. G.,

it is the Treaty of Versailles which is responsible for the existence of a national delusion of persecution. In France it is the Treaty of Frankfort which explains a state of mind otherwise unintelligible, for by that treaty Germany destroyed French unity. Even more, during the World War German statesmanship frequently and openly proclaimed German war aims to include the annexation of the Briey District and further "rectifications" of the French frontier which would add Belfort and Verdun to the lost cities of 1871. Finally, to the still unforgotten rigors of the invasion of 1870 there were added the tragic memories of the devastations of the incursion of 1914.

Victory in 1918, therefore, had meant but one thing to the French mind—could, in fact, mean but one thing— and that was security. Not approximate, relative, reasonable security, but *absolute* security. On that question the mood of France was the mood of the French poilu at Verdun. Petain's immortal phrase "They shall not pass" was the watchword of French national sentiment from the Armistice onward. And that phrase was addressed to the Briton and the American as well as to the German.

Unless France yielded, both Anglo-Saxon nations saw that there could be no peace or order in Europe. What they failed to see with equal clarity was that without at least British guarantees there would be no essential French concessions. For in the French mind, concessions unaccompanied by precise British guarantees would prove only the preface to a third invasion and a second mutilation of French unity. Clemenceau, Millerand,

France and Germany, 1932; Sieburg, Friedrick, *Who Are These French?*, 1932; Siegfried, André, *France: A Study in Nationality*, 1930.

Briand, Poincaré, Tardieu, Herriot, and Doumergue passed through the Quai d'Orsay in swift succession; but each in turn repeated the same phrase: "Security comes first." Always the France of the Treaty of Frankfort faced the Germany of the Treaty of Versailles.

There were moments of pause, such as the Truce of Locarno, but even then French concessions were prefaced by British commitments. And when compensating guarantees did not accompany demand for concession, as in the case of the Hoover moratorium, the response was inevitable.

Chapter XII

GREAT BRITAIN

UPON the British mind, the World War exerted an influence whose effects were still discoverable in British policy a decade and a half after the close of the conflict.[1] As Wellington had said of Waterloo, "the thing had been run to a fine point." In 1917 the ominous upward curve in submarine sinkings had seemed the certain preface to a surrender dictated by starvation. As late as April, 1918, the British army had been fighting with its back to the wall in Flanders. It was not until August 8, Ludendorff's "blackest day of all," that the tide changed.

Not even the dramatic suddenness of that change, however, could remove the enduring psychological consequences of the strain and agony of the four terrible years. Furthermore, British realization that their insular position could no longer serve as a bulwark against Continental attack by sea or air was to have a profound influence upon their future national strategy.[2]

[1] Hirst, F. W., *The Consequences of the War to Great Britain*, 1934.

[2] This new factor in the problem of British security has been clearly expressed by Sir Austen Chamberlain, as follows: "The development of aeronautics has further impaired our insular security and has given fresh force to the secular principle of British

Not even the surrender of the German battle fleet, the limitation of the German army to a strength little above that of the "Old Contemptibles" at Mons, or the fact that the bulk of the German colonies were on the way to becoming good British mandates, could compensate for the shock of her war experiences. Although the victory was by no means the least considerable of the many Great Britain had won in her long history of strife on the Continent, its cost had been the most formidable. Instinctively, therefore, the British turned toward what was for them the greatest possible gain of victory— enduring peace and the enjoyment of the material profits of trade and commerce.

Peace had long been the supreme objective of British Continental policy. Of the things which dictate national policies, security, prosperity, and unity, only the first was for the British Empire a European problem of primary importance; and both security and prosperity, in their European phase, turned upon peace. Since the real affair of the British was imperial and trade was the life-blood of empire, peace in Europe, as elsewhere, was essential to British prosperity.

The fact that a killing in an obscure Balkan city had not merely interrupted the business of empire but actually placed the very existence of England in jeopardy was at once incredible and final evidence of mistakes of policy which must not be repeated. The part of British instinct

policy that the independence of the Low Countries is a British interest, that their frontiers are in fact our frontiers, their independence the condition of our independence, their safety inseparable from our own. . . . Here, at any rate, we find a permanent basis of British policy, recognized and reaffirmed by the guarantee we have given in the Treaty of Locarno to the frontiers of Germany and her neighbors on the west." (Council on Foreign Relations, *Permanent Bases of Foreign Policy*, 1931, pp. 34-35.) See also, Cole, D. H., *Changing Conditions of Imperial Defence*, 1930; Turner, C. C., *Britain's Air Peril*, 1933; Richmond, Admiral Sir H. W., *Imperial Defence and Capture at Sea in War*, 1932.

GREAT BRITAIN
STRATEGIC NAVAL POSITION

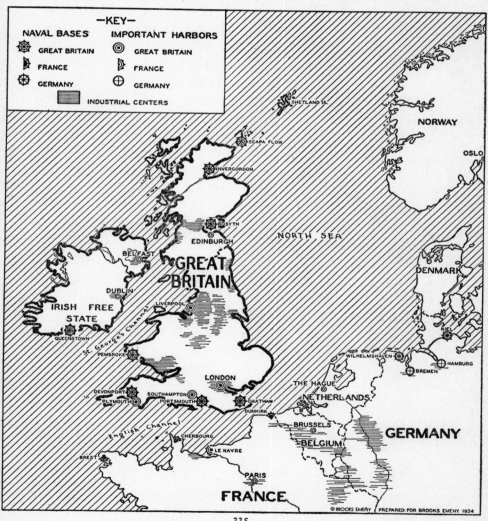

-KEY-

NAVAL BASES · IMPORTANT HARBORS

GREAT BRITAIN — GREAT BRITAIN

FRANCE — FRANCE

GERMANY — GERMANY

INDUSTRIAL CENTERS

SHETLAND IS.

NORWAY

OSLO

SCAPA FLOW

HNVERGORDON

NORTH SEA

ROSYTH
EDINBURGH

BELFAST

DENMARK

GREAT BRITAIN

DUBLIN

KIEL

IRISH FREE STATE

LIVERPOOL

QUEENSTOWN

WILHELMSHAVEN
HAMBURG

PEMBROKE

BREMEN

St. George's Channel

THE HAGUE

LONDON

NETHERLANDS

GERMANY

DEVONPORT
PLYMOUTH
SOUTHAMPTON
PORTSMOUTH
CHATHAM
DUNKIRK

English Channel

CHERBOURG

BRUSSELS
BELGIUM

BREST

LE HAVRE

PARIS

FRANCE

© BROOKS EMENY   PREPARED FOR BROOKS EMENY 1934

which was imperial and that which was insular imposed the same conclusion. The British people at the close of their terrible war years demanded of their government not merely that it should get them out of the present Continental mess but also that it should keep them out of all future Continental follies. And the Dominions, whose sacrifices had been only less considerable than those of the mother country, were not less insistent that they should not have to come again as before.

Discussion of the broader aspects of Imperial Policy belongs to another chapter; but here at least passing notice must be taken of the importance of the Dominions. Although Great Britain ranks next to Germany in industrial development, her domestic poverty in all essential raw materials save coal and iron renders her dependent upon the British Empire for these. To maintain the security of imperial communications is therefore the primary concern of national policy. Hence British insistence upon the two-power naval standard in Europe, which carries with it supremacy in the Mediterranean, through which runs the chief highway both to India and to Australia.

Of equal significance, also, is the political influence exerted by the Dominions upon British policy.[1] While the prestige of Great Britain in European councils is immeasurably enhanced when backed by the united Commonwealth, yet insistence by the Dominions that the mother country assume no new responsibilities on the Continent enormously accentuates British desire for permanent peace; for it is by no means beyond the limit of possibility that if events like those of 1914 should again

[1] Toynbee, A. J., *The Conduct of British Empire Foreign Relations Since the Peace Settlement*, 1928. (For further discussion of this problem, see Chapter XXII.)

expose the British Empire to the hazards of a European war, refusal of the Dominions to repeat the services and sacrifices of the World War might lead to the parting of the ties that bind them to Great Britain.

Since the Armistice, therefore, peace has been the primary objective of British policy in Europe, as it has constituted the single sufficing prescription alike for the security of the British Isles and for the survival of the British Empire. If peace could be established on a permanent basis, British policy in the Old World could safely be limited to retention of naval supremacy in European waters and possession of the further strength necessary to police the vital lines of communication with the Empire.

As to the nature of the peace to be made with Germany, Castlereagh and Wellington had shown the way a century before.[1] Thus, at the close of the World War, the first consideration of Lloyd George and Balfour was to see to it that Germany's power to renew the challenge of 1914 was abolished; next, Germany had to be made to pay for her war; but, finally, extreme care had also to be taken to curb the ambition of France. To that end, the balance of power was to be restored on the Continent, as it had been re-established after the Napoleonic downfall.

Balance of power on the Continent was the tradition of British policy. It was, in fact, the oldest and soundest tradition.[2] The business of British statesmanship was to see that parity existed not only among the Great Powers individually but also between any two coalitions

[1] Webster, C. K., *The Foreign Policy of Castlereagh, 1812-1815*, 1931.

[2] Edwards, William, *British Foreign Policy from 1815 to 1933*, 1934; Flournoy, F. R., *Parliament and War*, 1927; Fuller, J. F. C., *Imperial Defence, 1588-1914*, 1926; Muir, Ramsay, *A Short History of the British Commonwealth*, 1922-23, 2 vols.; Pargiter, R. B., and Eady, H. G., *The Army and Sea Power*, 1927; Ward, Sir A. W., and Gooch, G. P., eds., *The Cambridge History of British Foreign Policy*, 1922-23, 3 vols.

GREAT BRITAIN
NATIONAL SELF-SUFFICIENCY IN FOODSTUFFS, ESSENTIAL INDUSTRIAL PRODUCTS, AND RAW MATERIALS

DOMESTIC PRODUCTION AND NET IMPORTS EXPRESSED AS PERCENTAGES OF AVERAGE NATIONAL CONSUMPTION (1925-29)

——— GREAT ESSENTIALS ———

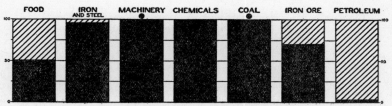

CRITICAL RAW MATERIALS

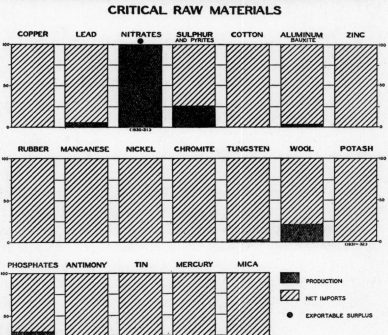

PREPARED FOR BROOKS EMENY 1934

© BROOKS EMENY.

229

into which these powers might divide, in order that the danger of any pursuit of hegemony by an individual state should be abolished.[1] Substantially that situation of balance, which was the surest and cheapest method of providing security, had existed from Waterloo to the decade before the Marne. As a consequence, Great Britain had been able to travel the pathways of empire with only occasional backward glances at Europe.

After 1900, however, the rise of Germany to disproportionate power and the disclosure by German leaders of disruptive tendencies, and primarily of a purpose to challenge British supremacy upon the sea, had forced the British to quit the "Splendid Isolation" of the Victorian Age for the Triple Entente of the Edwardian Era.[2] And that change eventually had involved them in war. Now that war was over, however, and German challenge to British naval supremacy abolished, it was time to go back to the old system which in the very nature of things necessitated the establishment of something like a state of balance between Germany and France.

Obviously, such a state of balance could not be restored over night. First came the problem of making peace. Nevertheless the strategy of the balance of power could be employed at Paris,[3] for the entrance of the United States into the European equation had placed Great Britain in the fortunate position of being able to

[1] The traditional British policy of balance of power has been succinctly expressed by Sir Austen Chamberlain as follows: "All our greatest wars have been fought to prevent one great military power dominating Europe, and at the same time dominating the coasts of the Channel and the ports of the Low Countries." (Speech before the House of Commons, March 24, 1925.)

[2] Kantorowicz, H. U., *The Spirit of British Policy and the Myth of the Encirclement of Germany*, 1932; Pribram, A. F., *England and the International Policy of the European Great Powers, 1871-1914*, 1931; Schmitt, B. E., *England and Germany*, 1918.

[3] Fabre-Luce, Alfred, *La Crise des Alliances*, 1922; Vrieslander, Wismann, *Lloyd George*, 1923.

act between France and America. In the main, that
would mean standing with Wilson against Clemenceau.
On most questions, the Wilsonian formula coincided
admirably with British interest and judgment. There
was, too, in the immediate postwar England, a marked
conviction that co-operation in a common struggle in
1918 had abolished the last resentments surviving from
the conflict of 1776.

Against the rising clamor of the French press for possession of the left bank of the Rhine and the demands of
Foch for permanent military occupation of that barrier,
Wilson and his peace program presented Lloyd George
with a potent ally and with a convenient principle. By
contrast, on the two questions of the freedom of the seas
and of the reparations to be demanded of the Germans,
Clemenceau could be counted upon to stand with Great
Britain and against the United States. For the time being, at least, the strategy of the balance of power was
therefore applicable to the Paris situation in which the
United States and France were to be the dominating and
opposed powers. By means of the American support,
Germany could be saved. Later, even if the United
States ultimately retired from Europe, the British position between France and Germany would be com-
manding.

At the Paris Peace Conference, events on the whole
moved according to British calculation. The French
ambitions in the matter of the Rhine were blocked. The
American ideas about the freedom of the seas and reparations were put aside. In return for the French concession as to the Rhine, however, Wilson and Lloyd George
were compelled, in the names of their respective countries, to pledge Clemenceau a Treaty of Guarantee assur-

ing to France Anglo-Saxon aid in case of German aggression. And since the objective of France at the Rhine was security and not territory, Clemenceau was temporarily able to silence the opposition both of Foch and of Poincaré.

In the matter of reparations, the problem was more intricate. Lloyd George had gone to the people before the Paris Conference pledging himself to make Germany pay. French sentiment on the same question was dictated by the still unreconstructed devastated area. Both Lloyd George and Clemenceau might therefore be compelled to insert in the treaty provisions which the British prime minister, at least, perceived were impossible; for already in British circles the truth was just beginning to be whispered, not only that it was beyond German capacity to pay the costs of the war, but also that it was contrary to British interest to compel her to make the effort.[1]

To escape that danger, Lloyd George proposed to leave it to a Commission to decide the sum which Germany was to pay and, meantime, to satisfy British and French public opinion by writing into the treaty the most drastic regulations covering the manner in which Germany should be made to pay and the penalties which were to be exacted of her if she attempted evasion. His calculation was that, in the Reparations Commission, Great Britain and America would have the controlling influence and could make the sums to be exacted correspond with reason and therefore divest these punitive provisions of all relevance.[2] Since the United States and Great Britain were the guarantors of French security, more-

[1] Keynes, J. M., *Economic Consequences of the Peace*, 1920.
[2] Baruch, B. M., *The Making of the Reparation and Economic Sections of the Treaty*, 1920; Lloyd George, David, *The Truth about Reparations and War Debts*, 1932.

over, their authority over French policy would be inevitable.

Thus, by the territorial clauses of the Treaty of Versailles, Lloyd George, with the aid of Wilson, saved the Rhineland for Germany. He was less successful in the east, because Wilson stood with the French for Poland. Lloyd George, however, was interested not merely in saving Germany territorially but also in insuring her economic recovery. It was to British interest, to European advantage, to world profit, that the great German people should be brought back into the economic and financial life of the world as soon and as completely as possible. It was, moreover, the single prescription for peace, because only a prosperous Germany could be a contented nation.

British policy at Paris, then, was sane, at least enlightened in its selfishness, and it was in the main successful. But it had necessarily given two hazards to fortune. Unless the United States now stood by the bargain of Wilson in the matter of French security and also joined the British in reducing reparations figures from astronomical to reasonable proportions, what had been accomplished would be of no lasting importance. And that was the case because if Great Britain and the United States should go back on the security pledge, and if the United States should absent itself from the Reparations Commission, the French would have a grievance of unmistakable authenticity and, in addition, a power for destruction of almost limitless extent.

When, therefore, the United States Senate did reject the Treaty of Versailles and repudiate the double pledge of Wilson and Lloyd George to Clemenceau in the matter of French security, the British were confronted by the fact that provisions written into the treaty to compel German payment could be employed to accomplish German ruin. The absence of America in the Reparations Commission placed control in French hands. The primary objective of British policy was still to accomplish German recovery, both for material considerations and to re-establish the balance of power. But as long as French security remained doubtful, prevention of that recovery was sure to be the controlling purpose of French policy.

In simple terms, the Treaty of Versailles had lodged in French hands the power to postpone or even to prevent German recovery by insistence that reparation defaults which were inevitable should be punished by the infliction of penalties which were legal. And from this impasse there was no peaceful escape; for the British public opinion, reinforced by that of the Dominions, was unanimously opposed to assuming single-handed responsibilities which might have been tolerable if shared with the United States.

Whatever the British government may have conjectured, the mass of the British people did not believe that France was either sufficiently unwise or strong enough to undertake a new occupation of German territory contrary to American wish and in the face of determined British opposition. On the contrary, there still lingered in British minds the convenient conviction that the war had weakened France to the point where authority rested with Great Britain. On all counts, too, a fresh invasion of Germany seemed so contrary to reason and even to sanity as to be beyond the realms of possibility.

Unfortunately for British calculation, however, British military resources were no longer adequate to restrain France if she did decide to march. In addition, British public opinion was not ready to sanction naval coercion of the French. On the military side, Great Britain, like the United States, had demobilized her forces. Since the German army had also been forcibly disbanded, French military supremacy on the Continent was beyond British challenge. And the withdrawal of the United States from Europe had eliminated the one nation whose support could enable Great Britain to employ her old strategy of the balance of power against France.

In Europe, no possible ally was left. Russia had fallen away to Bolshevism, and in 1920 the defeat of the Red armies before Warsaw as a result of French military intervention had raised French prestige to almost unimaginable heights. In place of the Austrian Empire were the Succession States, ready, like Poland, to cast their lot in with France in return for the protection of French arms. Italy was sinking to the impotence which preceded the Fascist Revolution. Germany was out of the calculation. Last of all, Belgium was looking to Paris, not to London.

It was France and not Great Britain, therefore, which could play the balance of power game. She could choose between two policies: either she might associate herself with Great Britain in a policy of salvaging Germany, or she might draw to herself the smaller states which had replaced the old Great Powers, for the purpose of coercing Germany. So far from being isolated, if she turned her back on the old Entente Cordiale, her military supremacy would be reinforced by a diplomatic ascendancy at Geneva, assured to her by the support of the representatives of the states which were her military allies.

When the British declined to meet the French views on security, the French turned to the double task of creating a new political system to control the Continent and of exploiting the Treaty of Versailles to postpone German recovery. As a consequence, in due course, French armies occupied the Ruhr, and thereafter, when the inflation which resulted from attempted German resistance produced in the Reich an economic and financial disaster more complete than that of the war itself, the complete bankruptcy of British policy was exposed. The power of France to prevent German recovery could no longer be questioned, once the British had suffered the occupation of the Ruhr to proceed without an ultimatum.

Postwar British policy then falls naturally into three periods.[1] The first extends from the Paris Conference to the close of the London Conference of 1924 which made the Dawes Plan. Its culminating detail was the occupation of the Ruhr.[2] The second phase lasts from 1924 to the Labor victory of 1929. Its dominating feature was the Pact of Locarno.[3] The third phase extends from 1929 to the final collapse of the Disarmament Conference, and its distinguishing feature is the German Revolution, with its bloody aftermath both in the Reich and in the Austrian Republic in the summer of 1934.

During the first phase, the British resisted the French demands for security and the French ended by marching into the Ruhr. In the second phase, the British met French demands partially, consenting to guarantee the status quo in the Rhineland against aggression coming

[1] Chamberlain, Sir Austen, *Peace in Our Time*, 1928; Sipple, C. E., *British Foreign Policy Since the World War*, 1932; Toynbee, A. J., ed., *Survey of International Affairs*, annual; Willert, Sir Arthur, *Aspects of British Foreign Policy*, 1928.

[2] D'Abernon, E. V., Viscount, *The Diary of an Ambassador*, 1929-1931, 3 vols.

[3] See Chapter XXV.

either from France or from Germany. Germany, for her part, formally renounced all design to recover Alsace-Lorraine, and on that basis was welcomed into the League of Nations. During the following years a Concert of Europe was established; and Stresemann, Chamberlain, and Briand, acting for Germany, Great Britain, and France respectively, organized European peace from Geneva and through the League.

These latter were the years of recovery and of relative tranquillity, but the Truce of Locarno was broken by British Labor when it came to power in 1929. Already British public opinion was becoming restive over the apparent subordination of Great Britain to France and the corresponding penalizing of the British taxpayer to the profit of the French. The success of Briand at Geneva had bestowed upon France an ascendancy which was not too pleasing to British pride; and in addition French demands on the British seemed limitless. In the Labor calculation, therefore, the time had come to get back to the traditional policy of the balance of power. The true role of Great Britain was not to play the part of a "shining second" to France but that of an impartial arbiter between France and Germany. In a word, British Labor demanded that Great Britain should henceforth occupy the center of the "teeter" and not always sit heavily on the French end.

Labor's return to power, therefore, was marked by a rude attack by Philip Snowden upon a French Finance Minister at the Hague.[1] With that attack, too, Europe recognized at once that the Truce of Locarno had come to an end. What followed constitutes the third stage in

[1] Andreades, A. M., *Philip Snowden*, 1930; Maddox, W. P., *Foreign Relations in British Labour Politics*, 1934.

British postwar policy and lasts to the definitive failure
of the Disarmament Conference in the summer of 1934,
when the British Parliament was put on notice by the
British ministry that the moment for rearmament had
arrived.[1]

The decisive events in this third period are the actions
of the French: first, in the London Naval Conference;
second, in the matter of the Austro-German tariff union;
and, finally, in the Disarmament Conference. In the
Naval Conference of 1930, the French blocked the way
to any Five-Power treaty whatsoever and made even a
Three-Power agreement conditional, by insisting that
they should have a naval strength which upset all the
Anglo-American-Japanese figures.

French action at the London Naval Conference, however, was only a demonstration. There France struck
back directly at the Labor Government which had broken the Truce of Locarno, and thus deprived Ramsay
MacDonald of the prestige of a successful conference.
That conference, moreover, did not touch the main question, which for the British was always peace through
German recovery. When, however, the Germans, counting on the lapse in Anglo-French association, undertook
to make a tariff union with Austria, the French struck
swiftly and fatally. Employing financial coercion, they
forced Vienna to its knees, and, using their political
weapon, they procured from the World Court a decision
pronouncing the tariff union illegal. Finally, by their
pressure upon Austria they forced Germany publicly and
under conditions of extreme humiliation to abandon the
Austrian project.

The financial dislocations in Vienna, moreover, proved

[1] Baldwin's speech before the House of Commons, July 19, 1934.

to be the starting point for the great banking crisis of the summer of 1931 in Germany. When this crisis became acute, President Hoover, on British urging and German appeal, made his proposal for a moratorium. By this time, too, British and American investors had risked billions in the Reich. But since there was no reference to French rights and interests in the Hoover proposal, the French held it up until whatever usefulness it might have had, had disappeared. Consequently the German crisis continued and presently extended to England, and the British were forced off the gold standard.[1]

Last of all, in February, 1932, a despairing Republican regime came from Berlin to Geneva asking of the Disarmament Conference recognition of the German right to equality with France in armaments. Already the shadow of Hitler loomed large on the horizon and the fate of the Republic seemed to turn on success at Geneva. But even before the Conference assembled, Tardieu announced that nothing could be done in the direction of German parity until French security was assured. Thereafter the Conference fell to deadlock and Germany to revolution. For the British were still unready to meet French views on the question of security.

With the arrival of the German Revolution, German economic recovery was adjourned indefinitely, while the domestic conditions in the Reich had by 1934 taken on the aspect of those which existed during the blockade at the time of the war. Default on private and public debts, moreover, had ruined German credit, while open but illegal German rearmament had proved the signal for a general race to arms, which spread over the Continent and produced repercussions even in the United States.

[1] Salter, Sir Arthur, *Recovery, The Second Effort*, 1932.

Sixteen years after the Armistice, therefore, Great Britain had failed to establish peace in Europe, and the moral and material plight of Germany was actually far worse than it had been at the moment of the Paris Conference. For the student of international affairs, nothing in postwar history can be more interesting or more illuminating than this Anglo-French battle of policy, fought over the prostrate body of Germany; for in this conflict, triangular at least in its implications, there is presented an accurate picture of postwar Europe.

Looking backward, it seems clear that the British policy was sound. If selfish interests dictated the desire to see Germany re-established both economically and politically, nevertheless British interests coincided with those of most of the rest of the world. Lasting peace in Europe was impossible unless there was a prosperous and contented Reich. French policy, therefore, was bound in the end to produce despair and create a condition of collective madness which would make the German people a peril for the whole of Europe; and all that happened in 1933 and 1934 has but furnished confirmation for British forecast in this respect.

British postwar policy in Europe, however, failed completely to accomplish its purpose. That failure was due, first, to the war, which destroyed the old system of order in Europe and, secondly, to the refusal of the United States to remain a participant in European affairs. The war eliminated the European powers, other than Great Britain and France, from immediate reckoning. In their place it raised up a number of lesser states whose collective power was great and whose common interests were identical with those of France. Finally the departure of the United States left Great Britain isolated in the face of France, which possessed a supreme army and was supported militarily and diplomatically by the smaller states.

If, however, the policy pursued by France after 1919 was responsible for the fall of the German Republic and the triumph of violence in the Reich, this policy — or impolicy—had its origin in a French desperation not less dominating than the German. The events of the Franco-Prussian War and the World War had combined to establish in French minds the conviction that the existence of France must always be in jeopardy if the two nations were left to face each other alone. Instinctively, therefore, the French people identified German recovery, unaccompanied by British guarantees of French security, as a deadly threat to their country and to themselves.

The British people, however, saw the effects of French policy plainly. They also saw with utmost clarity the possible consequences for themselves of new involvement in Continental affairs. At the close of the war and during the years before the occupation of the Ruhr, they did permit their government to return to the Continent and to make the Pact of Locarno. But they promptly discovered that this pact was not enough to satisfy the French, who were determined that the British should guarantee, not merely the French frontiers at the Rhine, but a system of order in Europe.

In this respect, however, the French thesis, in its turn, was also sound; for if Germany were left free to absorb Austria, crush Poland, and rescue the German minority of Czechoslovakia through partitioning that country, there would not be peace in Europe but war. Both the Poles and the Czechs were bound to resist, and to conquer them the Germans would have to create a military establishment which would enable them to dominate the Continent even if the British stood with the French at the Rhine. The fact that the British and French armies, even with that of Russia, had not sufficed to defeat Germany in the World War, made this clear.

Because they were an insular people the British saw Europe only as far as their own immediate security was involved, and therefore their concern did not pass the Rhine. The French, as a Continental people, saw Europe as a whole. They were aware that although the World War had begun in an obscure corner of the Balkans it had swiftly spread over most of the Continent between the Urals and the Pyrenees. When, however, they sought to persuade the British to extend the commitment of Locarno to cover the Continent, the British, far from consenting, instinctively sought to limit rather than to extend the responsibilities imposed by Chamberlain's pledge. And that instinctive drawing back, which found expression in the victory of the Labor Party in 1929, was disastrous for the German Republic.

In the earlier postwar years, British public opinion had been profoundly affected by the ideas of Woodrow Wilson, and in particular by his League of Nations program. Like the Americans, the British were vague rather than realistic in their conceptions of the Geneva body. They saw all nations uniting to make peace, but they were very far from agreeing that Great Britain should assume any general responsibility for enforcing that peace. And the realization that, in the business of keeping the peace, the British fleet would be expected to play a decisive part and that this obligation foreshadowed collision with the United States, was not slow in arriving or slight in its effects upon British policy.

As a consequence, the French attempt to turn the League into an instrument for the enforcement of the Treaty of Versailles, and the parallel effort to establish a collective guarantee for the security of all member nations, disclosed in the Protocol of 1924, promptly awakened British suspicion and insured Parliamentary rejection of that proposal. At Geneva, British policy was, thereafter, always paradoxical, since it sought at the same time to strengthen the League morally and to weaken the practical effect of the sections of the Covenant prescribing coercion by all states in the case of aggression by one.

When Austen Chamberlain told the League Assembly that in addition to the Geneva association of nations there was an older if smaller society, the British Commonwealth of Nations, and that if compelled to choose between the two he would select the latter, he only repeated the authentic voice of Great Britain. As an instrument of conciliation, the British endorsed Geneva; as a means of coercion controlled by other hands than British, they shrank from it. But as a consequence of this equivocal attitude, British influence in the League was slight, for France could always rally the European neutrals as well as her own allies to the principles of the Protocol and to the doctrine of collective responsibility.

At Geneva, as in European councils elsewhere, Great Britain was therefore usually isolated, commonly impotent, and generally unpopular. Among the British people, the League steadily lost in popular favor and confidence as it came increasingly to be identified as an instrument of French policy rather than a means of international accommodation. And, since they lacked both the material and the moral resources to pursue national policy successfully to its goal, which was European peace, the British were, in the end, compelled to stand aside and see French policy prevail.

In 1934, then, as at all times since the Armistice, British public opinion resisted all proposals of direct involvement in European disputes. On the other hand, the excesses and violences of the German Revolution, particularly the "Blood Bath" of June and the Austrian *Putsch* of July, inevitably silenced British appeals for concessions to Germany. At the end, if British public opinion was still unconvinced as to the wisdom of past French policy, it was no longer inspired with any burning desire further to champion the nation in whose interests—as well as its own—it had quarreled with France for half a generation.

Neither, however, was British opinion convinced of the immediate necessity to renew the old Entente of the prewar days with France. On the contrary, rearmament on the sea and in the air was the first British reaction to the rise of German nationalism and the fall of the Disarmament Conference. Beyond that, British policy would follow the once derided but always familiar Asquithian prescription of "wait and see."

But although Great Britain still remained firm in her resolution to make no further commitments on the Continent and to that extent was indifferent to the fate of Austria, the Succession States, and Poland, nevertheless the murder of Dollfuss led to a formal joint declaration with Italy and France endorsing Austrian independence. Her concern for the Rhineland frontiers of France and Belgium also increased, and presently found expression in Stanley Baldwin's phrase describing the Rhine and not the cliffs of Dover as the British military frontier.

Unmistakably, then, conviction of the existence of a new German danger was developing in the British mind; and if that danger seemed at the moment remote, its implications for the future could not be ignored. Thus, at the end of a decade and a half of uninterrupted pursuit of security through peace, Great Britain perceived that she might presently be compelled to seek that security by the sole alternative method, the traditional method of Continental coalition and of increased armaments.

In a word, in 1934, as the British still held to the historical conception of an unwritten constitution, they also remained faithful to the tradition of a pragmatic national policy. Nevertheless the experience alike of the recent and the distant past foreshadowed the direction that policy would take, once a new challenge to British security appeared on the Continent. The fact, too, was made evident by the unconcealed conferences which took place between British and French military experts.

The American student of British national policy, therefore, is confronted by the double fact that such policy inevitably appears in Continental eyes to be the result of deliberate design, and in British eyes to be the unpredictable consequence of accidents which could not be foreseen. Time, nevertheless, has invested these accidents with the appearance of habit, and frequent repetition has endowed the unpredictable with the color of the inevitable.

Thus, while it is never possible to forecast why or when the British will make up their minds, it can always be calculated in advance that certain Continental circumstances will invariably produce the same well-defined British repercussions. Failure to realize that fact was perhaps the most considerable of all of the many

German blunders in July, 1914, and not the least of those
of the period twenty years later, when the expansion of
German air forces reawakened the same apprehensions
that had been aroused by the growth of the German fleet
between 1905 and 1914, and in December, 1934, provoked
an announcement in Parliament of a program of expansion in air forces without parallel in postwar history.

Chapter XIII

ITALY

OF the Great Powers of Europe, Italy was the last to arrive[1] and still remains the least in material resources. Italian unification preceded the founding of the German Empire, but Prussia was a Great Power while Italy was still "a geographical expression." Today, moreover, although Italian population is as great as the French numerically, the inferiority of Italy in material circumstances robs her numbers of equal value. And although Italy has overseas possessions,[2] Libya, Eritrea, and Somaliland are of such slight economic worth that in effect she is essentially a Continental state.

Even within the European region, Italy had little real influence before the war, notwithstanding her membership in the Triple Alliance. Her refusal to march with her Austro-German allies in 1914, however, was for them a great disappointment and for France an inestimable

---

[1] Croce, Benedetto, *A History of Italy, 1871–1915*, 1929; Marriott, Sir J. A. R., *The Makers of Modern Italy*, 1931; Whyte, A. J. B., *The Political Life and Letters of Cavour, 1848–1861*, 1930.

[2] Booth, C. D., and Bridge, Isabelle, *Italy's Aegean Possessions*, 1928; Tittoni, T., *Italy's Foreign and Colonial Policy*, 1914; Villari, Luigi, *The Expansion of Italy*, 1930.

advantage, since troops which would otherwise have been held in the Alps fought at the Battle of the Marne. Again, Italian entrance into the war on the Allied side, in 1915, was ultimately responsible for the collapse of the Austro-Hungarian Monarchy. Nevertheless, at the Paris Conference the Italian role was inconspicuous and Italian claims were treated cavalierly by Clemenceau and Lloyd George, and contemptuously by Woodrow Wilson.[1]

Resentment aroused by this treatment at Paris was, moreover, one of the causes of the domestic revolution which established the Fascist regime[2] and placed Italian fortunes in the capable hands of Benito Mussolini. But even the coming of the Duce[3] did not immediately improve the Italian situation in European councils. On the contrary, during the Locarno years, in which Great Britain, France, and Germany, through Chamberlain, Briand, and Stresemann, co-operated at Geneva, Italy was isolated and ignored.

With the rupture of the Truce of Locarno and the rise of National Socialism in Germany, however, the Italian situation was transformed. The fresh outbreak of hostility between France and Germany, together with the obvious retreat of Great Britain from the Continent, bestowed upon Italian support an evident value, alike for

[1] Lémonon, E., *L'Italie d'apres Guerre, 1914–1921*, 1922.; Villari, Luigi, *The Awakening of Italy*, 1924.

[2] The following books dealing with the background and history of Italian Fascism will be useful for reference: Goad, H. E., *The Making of the Corporate State*, 1932; King, Bolton, *Fascism in Italy*, 1931; Munro, I. S., *Through Fascism to World Power; a History of the Revolution in Italy*, 1933; Pitigliani, Fausto, *The Italian Corporative State*, 1933; Salvemini, Gaetano, *The Fascist Dictatorship in Italy*, 1927; Schneider, H. W., *Making the Fascist State*, 1928; Schneider, H. W., and Clough, S. B., *Making Fascists*, 1929; Spencer, H. R., *Government and Politics of Italy*, 1932.

[3] *Duce*, the Italian word for "Leader," is the title popularly bestowed on Mussolini.

IMPERIAL ITALY

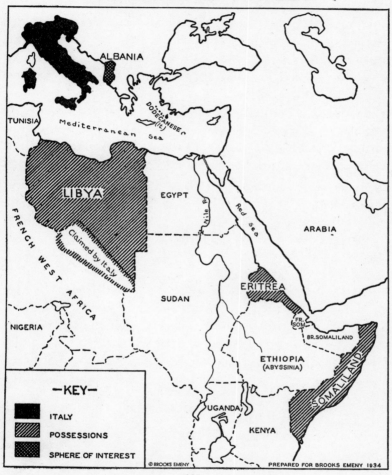

ALBANIA

TUNISIA

Mediterranean Sea

DODECANESE (It.)

LIBYA

EGYPT

FRENCH WEST AFRICA

Claimed by Italy

Nile R.

Red Sea

ARABIA

SUDAN

ERITREA

FR. SOM.

BR. SOMALILAND

NIGERIA

ETHIOPIA (ABYSSINIA)

SOMALILAND

UGANDA

KENYA

-KEY-

ITALY

POSSESSIONS

SPHERE OF INTEREST

© BROOKS EMENY

PREPARED FOR BROOKS EMENY 1934

251

the Germans and for the French. Thus, almost over night, Rome acquired an importance in European affairs which it had not had previously since the far-off days of the medieval Papacy. This change is significant, too, because it supplies a key to the problem of Italian policy generally.[1]

Looking backward, it is evident that, alone of the contemporary Great Powers, Italy has risen to her present rank only partly by her own efforts. The Congress of Vienna, in bestowing Sardinia and Genoa on the Savoy kingdom in its effort to block the French pathway to the plains of northern Italy, created a state sufficiently strong to dream of liberating and uniting the whole peninsula. War between France and Austria in 1859 made possible the next long step toward Italian unity, while the Seven Weeks War between Prussia and Austria brought about the addition of Venetia in 1866, and the Franco-Prussian War of 1870 made possible the occupation of Rome. Finally, the World War enabled Italy to complete her unification by the redemption of Trieste and the Trentino.

In all these various struggles, the role of Italy was subordinate and her rewards were due in no small part to the arms of other powers. This is not to say that Italian contribution was not in proportion to Italian resources or to seek to minimize the brilliance and gallantry of the Risorgimento. On the contrary, it is merely to emphasize the fact that Italian strength was limited and Italian statesmanship was therefore bound, in the very nature

[1] Benoist, Charles, *La Question Méditerranéenne*, 1928; Cippico, Antonio, Conte, *Italy, the Central Problem of the Mediterranean*, 1926; Currey, M. I., *Italian Foreign Policy, 1918-1932*, 1932; Foreign Policy Association, "Italian Foreign and Colonial Policy," *Information Service*, Vol. III, No. 1, 1927; Migot, Robert, and Gusthal, Comte, *La Guerre Est Là*, 1932; Salvemini, Gaetano, *Mussolini Diplomate*, 1932.

of things, to exploit European discord to Italian profit. Single-handed, Italy was not a match for Austria or for France, and, as a consequence, aspiration had always to wait upon opportunity.

The course pursued by Italian statesmanship in the opening stage of the World War is therefore typical. With the issues at stake between the two contending coalitions, Italy was not directly concerned. Her single immediate objective was the redemption of Trieste and the Trentino. To fight as the ally of Germany against the British was out of the question, given the Italian geographical situation. Her neutrality, however, might have been secured by the Central Powers in return for Austrian cession of Italia Irredenta.[1] When Vienna, despite the urgings of Berlin, declined to pay that price, Italy joined the Allies.

The tradition of Italian national policy, then, is opportunist. When, moreover, one turns to the problem of security, it is evident that in so far as land frontiers are concerned the geographical position of Italy is more favorable than that of any other Great Power of Europe. The Alps, extending in a broad half-circle from Ventimiglia on the French frontier to Fiume on the Yugoslav, constitute a formidable rampart. They are, moreover, covered on the north from the St. Bernard Pass to the Stelvio Pass by Switzerland, and from the Stelvio to the Karawanken by Austria.

Since, for all practical purposes, the Franco-Italian frontier from Mont Blanc to Menton is impassable for invading armies, and, in addition, French policy has no purpose fundamentally inimical to Italy, the frontier in the west, like that on the north, is secure. On the east,

[1] Bülow, B., Fürst von, *Memoirs*, 1931–32, 4 vols.

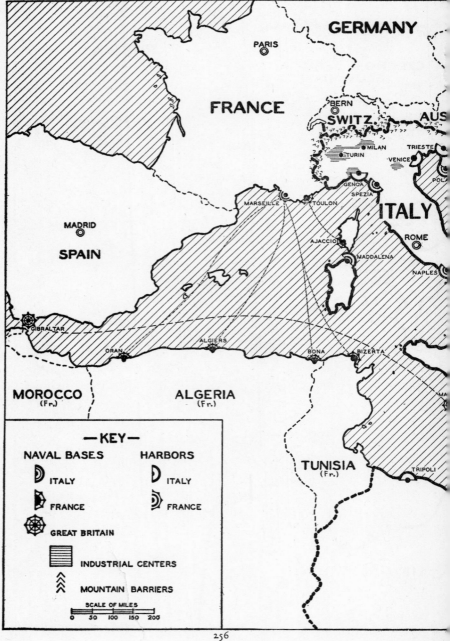

ITA

STRATEGIC MILITARY

GERMANY

PARIS

FRANCE

BERN
SWITZ.
AUS

MILAN
TURIN
TRIESTE
VENICE
POL

GENOA
SPEZIA

MARSEILLE
TOULON

ITALY

MADRID

AJACCIO
ROME

SPAIN

MADDALENA

NAPLES

GIBRALTAR

ORAN
ALGIERS
BONA
BIZERTA

MOROCCO
(Fr.)

ALGERIA
(Fr.)

MA

TUNISIA
(Fr.)

TRIPOLI

—KEY—

NAVAL BASES   HARBORS

ITALY   ITALY

FRANCE   FRANCE

GREAT BRITAIN

INDUSTRIAL CENTERS

MOUNTAIN BARRIERS

SCALE OF MILES
0   50   100   150   200

LY
AND NAVAL POSITION

POLAND

RUSSIA

PRAGUE

CZECHO-
SLOVAKIA

VIENNA

TRIA

BUDAPEST

HUNGARY

RUMANIA

BELGRADE

BUCHAREST

YUGOSLAVIA

BLACK SEA

ADRIATIC SEA

SOFIA

BULGARIA

BRINDISI

TIRANË

ALBANIA

ANGORA

GREECE

AEGEAN SEA

TURKEY

MESSINA

ATHENS

DODECANESE
(ITALY)

(Rhodes
Is.)

CYPRUS
(BR.)

LTA

PORT SAID

LIBYA
(Italy)

EGYPT

the situation is less satisfactory; for the creation of Yugoslavia was as grave a check to Italian ambitions[1] as the renascence of Poland was to German prospects. Nevertheless, the Italians were permitted to draw their own frontier at the Paris Conference and they made it well-nigh impregnable.

Actually, then, Italy has succeeded where France failed. She has reached her natural frontier at the Alps, whereas the French have been unable to acquire theirs at the Rhine. Again, although the dissolution of the Yugoslav monarchy and the establishment of an independent Croatia would doubtless be of advantage to the Italians, no extension of their land frontiers could give them greater security than they now possess, and in this respect the contrast between their situation and that of the Germans is impressive.

On the sea and in the air, however, the Italian situation is less satisfactory. Dependent upon the outside world for her raw materials, which must be imported by sea, Italy is confronted by the fact that the approach to her shores is commanded both by British naval bases at Gibraltar, Malta, and Aden, and by French bases at Toulon, Corsica, and Bizerta.[2] And all of her great cities,

---

[1] Adriacus (*pseud.*), *From Triesta to Valona*, 1919; MacDonald, J. N., *A Political Escapade*, 1921; Woodhouse, E. J., and Woodhouse, C. G., *Italy and the Jugoslavs*, 1920.

[2] "Ours is a vital problem that involves our very existence and our future, a future of peace, tranquillity, and work for a population of 42 million souls, which will number 50 million in another fifteen years. Can this population live and prosper in a territory half the size of that of Spain and Germany and lacking raw materials and natural resources to meet its vital needs, pent up in a closed sea beyond which its commerce lies, a sea the outlets of which are owned by other nations, while yet others control the means of access—the Caudine Forks of her liberty, safety, and means of livelihood —and while all the nations of the world are raising barriers against the development of trade, the movement of capital, and emigration, denationalizing whoever crosses their frontiers to enter, I do not say their own homes, but even their protectorates and colonies?" (Article by Dino Grandi, "The Foreign Policy of the Duce," *Foreign Affairs*, Vol. 12, No. 4, 1934, p. 566.)

Turin, Milan, Genoa, Florence, Rome, Naples, and Palermo, are within easy range of French air attack, while Trieste, Venice, and Bologna are similarly exposed to Yugoslav attack from the air.

Territorial security for Italy is therefore a question of ships and aircraft. Since naval parity with the British is beyond Italian financial resources, Italian national policy must definitely accept the necessity of avoiding war with Great Britain. Even to arm up to the level of France at sea would be possible for Italy only if France consented both to Italian parity and to a limitation of naval strength fixed at a low level; for the limitations imposed by Italian financial resources makes competition out of the question. As long as France refuses such parity, Italian inferiority is inescapable.

In the air, the situation is more satisfactory, for the Italians possess approximate parity with the French. Unfortunately for them, however, the advantages of geography all lie with France. Of the larger French cities, only Nice, Marseille, and Lyons are vulnerable to Italian air raids, while all Italian cities are exposed to French air attacks, supplemented as these might be by the operations of the Yugoslav ally of France.

On land, then, Italy does possess security, but on the sea she lacks it, while in the air her safety is at least open to grave doubt.

Turning to the question of national unity, it is evident that no ethnic problem, such as confronts the Germans, faces the Italians. Aside from a handful of Italians in the Swiss canton of Ticino, there is no Italian minority on the mainland of Europe, and although the inhabitants of Corsica speak Italian, they are as French in sentiment as were the Alsatians before 1871. In point of fact,

Italy has not only attained but passed her ethnic limits. In the upper Adige, she holds a quarter of a million Germans,[1] and in the hinterland of Trieste half a million Slavs.[2] There is, then, no Italian irredenta left. With the World War the unification of Italy was completed.

By contrast, on the economic side Italy is the weakest of all the Great Powers.[3] Like France, to be sure, she is largely able to feed her population, but unlike France she has only a limited supply of iron, and unlike Germany she is without coal. In addition, she is completely destitute of most of the other essential raw materials of industry. To supply her own national industrial establishment she has to draw heavily upon the outside world, and to pay for her imports she has neither resources in raw materials nor, like Germany, the capacity to export machinery or chemicals.

Before the war, however, Italy was able to maintain a balance in her economy by the export of labor. Every year hundreds of thousands of her people left home for the United States, South America, and France.[4] The larger part of these emigrants settled abroad, although a fraction returned each year in the slack periods. Many, however, continued to remit a portion of their earnings, and thus supplied their mother country with considerable resources in foreign exchange.

Even before the war, however, the United States, by its immigration laws, began shutting out Italians like all other aliens. In South America and France, too, the postwar depression led to a similar course. Thus, just

[1] Reut-Nicolussi, E., *Tyrol Under the Axe of Italian Fascism*, 1930.
[2] Jaquin, Pierre, *La Question des Minorités entre l'Italie et la Yugoslavie*, 1929.
[3] Einzig, Paul, *The Economic Foundations of Fascism*, 1933; McGuire, C. E., *Italy's International Economic Position*, 1926.
[4] Foerster, R. F., *The Italian Emigration of Our Times*, 1919.

as Germany after 1933 could not sell her manufactures, Italy presently found herself unable to dispose of her surplus labor.[1] But reduction in the foreign markets brought with it no corresponding diminution of the domestic requirements, and since economic self-sufficiency no longer existed, Italian necessity had outrun Italian resources.

At that point population pressure began to operate inevitably, because on an area only a little more than half as large as that of France and far less productive, Italy supported an equal population. And whereas French population was stationary, Italian population increased by above four hundred thousand annually and emigration no longer served as a safety valve. To expand or to suffocate[2] was the Italian alternative, if the increase in population were not artificially restricted.

Restriction, however, which for France was possible, because she had already attained her desired situation in Europe and in addition had secured a vast empire beyond the seas, in the Italian case could only mean acceptance of the present narrow territorial limits, and in effect the eventual surrender of the rank of a Great Power. For Poland, Rumania, and Spain already surpassed Italy both in extent of their territories and in the wealth of their resources, and their populations were steadily growing.

For Italy, therefore, acceptance of a policy of artificial limitation of population must impose renunciation of the single means by which she can hope to escape from a territorial status quo which insures a progressive decline in international importance. France, Great Britain, and Soviet Russia have laid the foundations of a future as promising materially as the present, in their lands be-

[1] Woog, Claude, *La Politique d'Emigration de l'Italie*, 1931.
[2] Guyot, Georges, *L'Italie devant le Problème Colonial*, 1927; Villari, Luigi, *The Expansion of Italy*, 1930.

ITALY

NATIONAL SELF-SUFFICIENCY IN FOODSTUFFS, ESSENTIAL INDUSTRIAL PRODUCTS, AND RAW MATERIALS

DOMESTIC PRODUCTION AND NET IMPORTS EXPRESSED AS PERCENTAGES OF
AVERAGE NATIONAL CONSUMPTION (1925 - 29)

—— GREAT ESSENTIALS ——

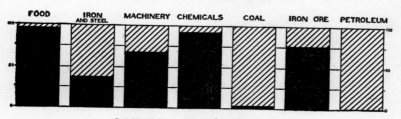

FOOD   IRON AND STEEL   MACHINERY   CHEMICALS   COAL   IRON ORE   PETROLEUM

CRITICAL RAW MATERIALS

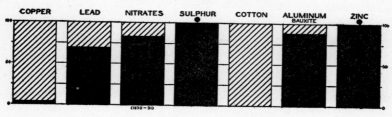

COPPER   LEAD   NITRATES   SULPHUR   COTTON   ALUMINUM BAUXITE   ZINC

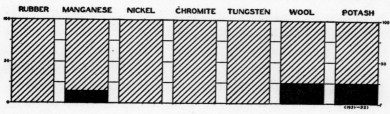

RUBBER   MANGANESE   NICKEL   CHROMITE   TUNGSTEN   WOOL   POTASH

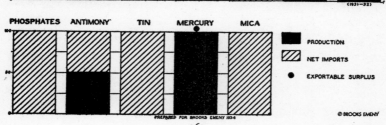

PHOSPHATES   ANTIMONY   TIN   MERCURY   MICA

■ PRODUCTION
▨ NET IMPORTS
● EXPORTABLE SURPLUS

PREPARED FOR BROOKS EMENY 1934

© BROOKS EMENY

263

yond the European region. Within the European region,
Germany is instinctively reaching out for an ethnic unity
which carries with it economic implications that are unmistakable.

For France, the future is visibly in Africa, for Russia in
Asia, for Great Britain all around the Seven Seas, and,
last of all, for Germany in Central Europe. But where
does the Italian future lie? With the rise of Fascism,
Italy presented to the world the spectacle of an amazing
paradox. The poorest of the Great Powers, she was
dominated not only by the most ambitious of national
policies but also by the most determined of national dictators. Since Napoleon, no state had possessed a master
of the capacity and quality of Benito Mussolini; and for
his country he dreamed of a population of sixty millions
and a place in the sun assured by the force of these numbers.

To support such a population, Italy would need land,
and to acquire land she would have to despoil a present
possessor. Obviously, however, it was beyond Italian
power to seize British or French territory, and it was beyond British or French purpose voluntarily to surrender land. Moreover, the dream of territorial compensations in the colonial field, which Italy had cherished at
the Paris Conference, had been roughly shattered. To be
sure, her prewar bargains, the "secret treaties" of which
so much was once heard, had marked with Italian color
the southern half of Asia Minor above the Gulf of Adalia.
But Kemal Pasha in revitalizing Turkey had demolished
that hope.

In Central and Southeastern Europe, too, the Italian
road was blocked. In the Danubian Basin, French guarantees covered the nations of the Little Entente, whose

collective strength was formidable. In the Balkan region Mussolini's first adventure at Corfu had disclosed to the Duce the insuperable obstacle of the British fleet defending the status quo in the Mediterranean. Everywhere the pathway to an Italian place in the sun was, at least temporarily, closed.

What then remained for Italian policy? Obviously the only recourse for Mussolini was a return to the national strategy of maneuver, in accordance with the tradition of Cavour. The European situation in 1933, when the triumph of Hitler and National Socialism in Germany visibly carried Europe from a postwar period to a prewar era, was like the situation which had existed in 1914 and 1915, when Italy had bargained with both the Central Powers and the Allies. It was also like the situation of 1859, of 1866, and of 1870 as well, when Italian unity was in the making.

On the Continent, two conflicting purposes were squarely in shock, the status quo policy of France, supported by Poland, the Little Entente, and more recently by Soviet Russia, and the revisionist policy advocated by Germany and, on her own independent course, by mutilated and irreconcilable Hungary. On the side lines, too, was Great Britain, equally disturbed by the spectacle of the German Revolution and by the fact of French political supremacy on the Continent.

What then was the natural and immediate objective of Italian policy in this confused and incoherent situation? Obviously, to prevent a German union with Austria, which would bring the military frontier of the Reich to the Brenner Pass and the hinterland of Trieste and not impossibly might also prove the preface to the construction of a Mittel-europa which would automatically put a term to Italian influence in Europe. So far, Italian policy was manifestly on all fours with French. And that fact had been demonstrated as far back as 1931, when Brüning had tried to achieve an Austro-German tariff union.

On the other hand, Italian interest dictated the destruction of French political influence in the Danubian area by the dissolution of the Little Entente and the substitution therefor of a combination directed from Rome. And as German advance was to be blocked only by the maintenance of Austrian independence, Italian combination in the Danubian area could similarly be based only upon Austria and Hungary. As Italy backed France against Germany in the matter of Austro-German tariff union, moreover, she had also stood with Germany, even before the coming of Hitler, against French plans for reconstruction in the Danubian region.

In the matter of disarmament, Italy supported Germany against France, claiming for the Reich the right to parity with France, because were such equality to exist, the Italian army would retain the balance of power on the Continent.[1] In the matter of naval establishments, Italy stood with Great Britain for a reduction of the French navy to limits which would satisfy the requirements of the Anglo-American agreement of London, because such reduction would insure Italian naval equality with France. Finally, in the case of the League of Na-

---

[1] Concerning the function of Italy in the balance of power in Europe the following paragraph taken from an article by Dino Grandi ("The Foreign Policy of the Duce," *Foreign Affairs*, Vol. 12, No. 4, 1934, p. 561) is of interest:

"This function is dictated to Italy by her geographical position and her Mediterranean interests. With her natural frontiers, Italy has no dreams of continental conquests; but she must be safe in the continent to which she is attached and on the seas that surround her. This security can only be guaranteed by the equilibrium of European forces. Italy's freedom is compromised the moment this balance is disturbed. Thus Italy cannot be other than adverse to the formation of military alliances, political blocs, and closed systems. . . ."

tions, Italy stood with Germany against both France and Great Britain,[1] because at the bottom of the League conception was the idea of stabilizing the world situation, and for Italy such stabilization involved the loss of its present position as a Great Power and its later prospect of eventual expansion.

In the place of the League, Italy on the morrow of Hitler's triumph had advocated the restoration of the Concert of Europe, limited to Great Britain, France, Germany, and herself, because in such a *partie-carrée* with the smaller allies of France excluded, Italian influence would always be considerable, and in the matter of armaments Rome might count upon the support of both Great Britain and Germany, where French military or naval strength was in question. Always, too, in such a combination, French assistance against Germany seemed certain, where the fate of Austria was in play.

When, however, following the meeting between the Duce and the Fuehrer, in Venice in June, 1934, Hitler failed to make good his promise and end "Nazi" interference in Austria, and instead the bloody revolt of July 25 culminated in the murder of Mussolini's ally, Chancellor Dollfuss, the Italian dictator was forced to abandon his program of German-Italian co-operation and to mobilize his military forces to defend Austrian independence against National Socialist attack.

Thereafter, convinced not perhaps of the impossibility of eventual German-Italian association but at least of the utter irreconcilability of his own program with that of Hitler, Mussolini moved rapidly toward a combination with France based upon the necessity of opposing a

---

[1] Reale, Egidio, *La Politique Fasciste et la Société des Nations*, 1932; Silvio, Trentin, *Le Fascisme à Genève*, 1932.

united front to a common peril. And in order further
to facilitate the effectiveness of this Franco-Italian rapprochement, the purpose of the two countries to resolve
the differences which had long been outstanding between them seemed definitely established by December,
1934, when the French Foreign Minister, M. Laval, in
a public speech disclosed the progress toward agreement
already made.[1]

Although Italian policy, intricate, involved, ever
shifting in its immediate objective, is manifestly beyond
the resources of a democracy, it is fully within those of
a state whose action is completely dictated by a single
mind, particularly by a mind as acute and agile as that
of Mussolini. But it must be clearly apparent that such
a policy has nothing in common with the ideas and
ideals which had been professed by all the world in the
immediate postwar years.

On the contrary, Italian policy, as it has progressively
disclosed itself, is *Realpolitik* in its least disguised form.
It is a deliberate and calculated pursuit of power and
prestige by the exploitation of the divisions existing between other powers. Beyond these immediate objectives, too, lies the larger possibility that, as Italy has
acquired Milan, Venice, Rome, and Trieste as a consequence of wars between other powers, similar conflict
may in the future bring equally shining prizes. The very
essence of Italian policy, then, is the prevention of the establishment of a system of ordered and permanent peace.

While the Italian national policy is dynamic, like the
German, nevertheless the distinction between the two is
significant, for it opens new vistas—or, more exactly, re-
vives old—in the field of international relations.

[1] *New York Times*, December 3 and 4, 1934.

At bottom, the German challenge to the existing order constitutes a revolt against a system of inequality imposed as a consequence of military defeat. The rights which Germany demands shall be recognized in her own case, those of self-defense and of self-determination, do not, moreover, conflict directly with the similar rights which all other great peoples possess and have exercised. On the contrary, it is only the implications of German policy, as they affect the security of France and of the other powers adjoining the Reich, which explain their resistance to German rights. As for the French, territorially they want nothing in Europe. Since, however, there are sixty-five millions of Germans and but forty millions of French and no Alps guard the northern or eastern frontiers of France, security is the dominating concern of French policy.

Contemporary Italy, by contrast, possesses the largest measure of physical security national frontiers can conceivably bestow. Again, unlike the Germans, who see, just beyond their frontiers, not less than ten millions of people who speak their language and have expressed their desire to be united with the Reich, the Italians can discover no ethnic minority. They have, in fact, not only achieved but overpassed their ethnic limits.

Psychologically, then, what is the explanation for the Italian intransigency? No Treaty of Versailles of as recent date as 1919 inspires contemporary revolt. No Treaty of Frankfort of ancient date but enduring memory explains their unrest. In fact, every treaty of peace Italy has signed, during the past three quarters of a century, has expanded her frontiers and increased her population. Yet she is today manifestly in rebellion against the status quo. Why?

The answer to this question must be sought in the ideology of Fascism itself. In its international outlook Fascism starts with the assumption that the rights of peoples, territorial and otherwise, have their origin in force. French title to Tunisia, British to Malta, Yugoslav to Dalmatia, that is, to lands the possession of which Italy covets, have no other validity than the force which lies behind them.

Fascism does not approach the world with the claim that, because Italian territory today hardly suffices to contain and support Italian numbers and tomorrow must prove insufficient, Italy should be allotted new colonies or a fresh mandate. On the contrary, Fascism teaches the Italian people that the single means of escape from their present circumstances is force. As for the outside world, Fascism meets its proposals for a peace of stabilization with an uncompromising negative.

The alleged idealism of these proposals Fascism rejects with scorn. For it, they are no more than the disclosure of Hypocrisy endeavoring to masquerade as Virtue. And at this point Italian policy does revert to Italian experience. Before she entered the World War on the Allied side in 1915, Italy made certain bargains with her prospective Allies. Territories and compensations were promised her, not only European, but also Asiatic and African. Dalmatia was one prospective prize, Libyan hinterlands another, Adalian Anatolia a third.

But at Paris the British and French partners produced American principles to justify them for the repudiation of their Italian bargain. The principle of self-determination which was invoked against Italian acquisition of Dalmatia was not, however, invoked to prevent France from obtaining a mandate for Syria, or Great Britain for

German East Africa. If geographical circumstances and
economic considerations dictated that Fiume, despite its
ethnic character, should go to Yugoslavia, what then
hindered the return of Malta to Italy or of Cyprus to
Greece?

What Frederick the Great said about Maria Theresa in
the time of the Partition of Poland—"She weeps but she
takes her share"—the Italians say of the postwar idealism of the Anglo-Saxons. The Fascists might perhaps be
prepared to accept the principle of self-determination as
applied to Italian aspirations, but only after it has also
been applied to British possessions. Since it is not likely
to be applied, however, they regard it as an instrument
of policy, not an expression of spiritual elevation. If
D'Annunzio's seizure of Fiume or Mussolini's occupation of Corfu was a crime, how, Fascism inquires, shall
one defend the course of Theodore Roosevelt, who, in
his own phrase, "took" Panama, or Woodrow Wilson's
action in Vera Cruz?

It is, in a word, the example and not the precept of the
British and the Americans which the Italians accept.
And with neither do they quarrel in principle. They believe that Italy was excessively badly treated at the Paris
Peace Conference, particularly because, unlike Great
Britain, France, Japan, and Belgium, she was denied a
mandate. But they also believe that the cause of her
misfortunes was primarily the ineptitude of the Liberal
regime which they have abolished. Apart from that
fact, too, they believe Italy can never expect better treatment save as Italian strength commands greater consideration. They continue to press a legal claim against
France for unfulfilled promises but they do not invoke
any moral issue to support their claim.

Internationally the strong nation takes what it needs
and keeps what it has taken; that is the Fascist philoso-
phy in a nutshell. And because it expects that Italy will
one day be as strong in body as it now is in spirit, Fascism raises no protest to what other nations have done
in the past but only to what they now say about their
deeds. In Fascist estimation, however, the League of
Nations was merely the product of American naiveté,
which was skillfully exploited by the British and French
as an instrument of their respective national policies.

"The Golden Age of Reason and Peace has now arrived," say the British from Malta, the French from
Bizerta, the Americans from Panama.

"How fortunate to be able to afford the Gold Standard
in morals!" Fascist Italy replies. "For ourselves, however, unhappily we have not yet been able to accumulate
sufficient capital to indulge in that measure of virtue.
Not being able to imitate your present pretensions, therefore, we must be forgiven if we continue to model our
policy upon your past performance."

That, simply, cynically, but clearly is the Fascist
"Credo." In the contemporary Italian conception internationalism is the last resort of the valetudinarian; by
contrast, nationalism, undisguised and uncompromising, is the inherent virtue of peoples which are young
like the Italy of Benito Mussolini. As a matter of expediency Italy can temporarily work with Germany against
France or with France against Germany; it can similarly condemn or exploit Geneva; but a change in material interest will invariably bring a change in partners. Always it seeks profit by force; occasionally it
must advocate peace to preserve its force; but such peace
is not an end but a means.

One weak point there was at all times in Italian policy, however, and that was the quarrel with Yugoslavia. In its origin this quarrel dated back to the Paris Conference, where Italy, on the strength of her "secret treaties" with her allies of the war, claimed Dalmatia. Bitterness thus provoked was heightened when D'Annunzio seized Fiume, in defiance of Europe. The treatment of the Slav minority of nearly half a million included within Italian frontiers, further exacerbated Yugoslav feelings, while Italian resentment was similarly aroused by Yugoslav claims to Fiume, Trieste, and Gorizia.

The postwar years were therefore marked by a long series of incidents which disturbed the relations of the two Adriatic states and at times even threatened the tranquillity of Europe. Always, therefore, Italian action was limited by the knowledge that while Yugoslavia was too weak to undertake a war single-handed, any opponent of Italy would find a ready ally beyond the Adriatic. When, after the triumph of Fascism, relations between Paris and Rome became bad, an alliance between Yugoslavia and France was speedily made and thereafter Italy was confronted by the possibility of a war on two fronts if she came to grips with France.

By contrast, when the killing of the Austrian Chancellor in the summer of 1934 forced Mussolini to renounce his cherished plan for an anti-French partnership with Germany and, instead, to look to Paris for support in his defense of Austrian independence, the prospect of Franco-Italian partnership instantly awakened Yugoslav resentment and led Belgrade to turn towards Berlin. The Duce's threat to occupy Austrian territory, too, although backed by British and French approval, evoked a sensational challenge from the Yugoslav capital.

It was largely in the hope of finding some solution for this Italian-Yugoslav quarrel that the French Foreign Minister, Louis Barthou, invited King Alexander to visit France in October, 1934. But when monarch and minister both perished at an assassin's hand in Marseille, the promise of adjustment seemed dissipated. And by this time the possibility of war between Italy and Yugoslavia was evident, while the probability of an eventual if not an immediate understanding between Berlin and Belgrade seemed equally plain.

Both for France and for Italy the desertion of Yugoslavia to the German camp would be very unwelcome. For France it would mean the collapse of the entire system of alliances upon which her supremacy on the Continent and security at home have been based. And for Italy the menace would be even more direct and serious, since if she undertook to move troops to defend Austrian independence, her army would be confronted by the double danger of German attack in front and Yugoslav in flank and rear.

It was equally evident, too, that should Yugoslavia turn from Paris to Berlin, Rumania might follow suit. For Yugoslavia and Rumania, as for Hungary also, association with Germany promised a market for their agricultural production which neither Italy nor France could offer. Nor did German territorial aspirations menace any one of the three. Italy had, then, to recognize the possibility that as France might lose Yugoslavia, she might, herself, lose Hungary. Nor was it less unmistakable that beneath the surface "Nazi" sympathies in Austria had not been destroyed even by the fiasco of July, 1934.

Since Poland and Germany have by their Nonaggression Pact adjourned the question of the Corridor for a decade, it is then plain that the danger point on the Continent has been shifted from the Vistula to the Danube, and from the Baltic to the Adriatic. For ten years France and Italy had successfully blocked each other's efforts to establish a stable political and economic situation in the Danubian Basin, but in the first days of 1935 they were both confronted by the fact that the profit of their performances might fall to the Germans.

Tardy recognition of this fact was disclosed in the pacts signed by the Duce and the French Foreign Minister in Rome on January 7, 1935. On the one hand these pacts constituted a liquidation of the colonial disputes between France and Italy, and on the other hand they bound both to consultation and, by implication, to common action to preserve the independence of Austria. Less clear in other details, these pacts nevertheless seemed to foreshadow united opposition to German claims for parity in armaments and to promise Italy's renunciation of her plans for territorial revision in the Danubian region.

Aside from all details, however, the importance of the Rome Agreements was accepted as inherent in the evidence they constituted of a reconciliation between France and Italy. Precisely as, nearly a generation before, Great Britain and France had in 1904 liquidated their colonial disputes and laid the foundations for the Entente Cordiale which insured united action a decade later when Belgium was invaded, the two Latin nations had in 1935 cleared the way for identical action in case of the violation of Austrian neutrality. Twice within a single generation, therefore, German statesmanship had performed the miracle of reconciling traditional rivals to its own lasting disadvantage.

Chapter XIV

SOVIET RUSSIA

ANY attempt to draw a rigid distinction between European and Asiatic Russia must be largely without justification in fact. Not only does the territory of the Union of Soviet Socialist Republics extend in vast unbroken continuity from Archangel to Vladivostok and from the Crimea to Kamchatka, but also the size of its population and the development of its industries, transportation system, and military strength all make it an important factor alike in Europe and in Asia.

Strategically, the Soviet Union, like the United States, is vulnerable only at its eastern and western extremities. But whereas in both the east and the west the United States has only to reckon with naval attack, the U. S. S. R. is in direct contact with Japan in Manchuria in the east, and is separated from Germany on the west only by new frontiers of doubtful permanence. As a consequence, Russian security is incomparably less complete than American, and this fact has necessarily a decisive influence upon Russian national policy.

Although Russia's vast domain makes possible the

attainment of a degree of economic self-sufficiency approximating that of the United States,[1] she lacks the further advantage that assured access to regional sources of raw materials bestows upon the latter. Food, petroleum, and lumber she has in exportable quantities. Iron, steel, and coal she possesses in amounts adequate for domestic needs, while her cotton production seems destined to keep pace with her home demands. Gold, manganese, and platinum also constitute resources to balance her present imports of machinery.

Today, of course, the Soviet Union is notoriously in a process of transformation. From the largely agricultural empire of the Romanoffs[2] it has already expanded into one of the most considerable industrial countries of the world.[3] Although it is true that, in comparison with the American industry, the Russian is still small, yet the Soviet production of iron and steel is rapidly overtaking that of the other industrial nations and in this field the Soviet Union has already decisively outdistanced both Japan and Italy.

Measured by her own domestic requirements, however, Russia's progress toward industrialization has as yet been relatively slight and she still has far to go before she can even provide the agricultural machinery necessary for her farms or the clothing required by her

[1] Gubkin, I. M., *The Natural Wealth of the Soviet Union and Its Exploitation*, 1932; Wood, J. B., *Incredible Siberia*, 1928.

[2] For general books on the political, social, and economic history of Czarist Russia, the student should refer to the following: Mavor, James, *An Economic History of Russia*, 1925, 2 vols.; Miller, M. S., *The Economic Development of Russia*, *1905-1914*, 1926; Pares, Sir Bernard, *History of Russia*, 1930; Robinson, G. T., *Rural Russia under the Old Regime*, 1932; Vernadsky, A. G., *A History of Russia*, 1929.

[3] Chamberlin, W. H., *Russia's Iron Age*, 1934; Dobb, M. H., and Stevens, H. C., *Russian Economic Development Since the Revolution*, 1928; Dobbert, Gerhard, *ed.*, *Red Economics*, 1932; Fischer, Louis, *Machines and Men in Russia*, 1932; Friedman, E. M., *Russia in Transition*, 1932; Hoover, C. B., *The Economic Life of Soviet Russia*, 1931; Lawton, Lancelot, *An Economic History of Soviet Russia*, 1932.

RUSSIA

NATIONAL SELF-SUFFICIENCY IN FOODSTUFFS, ESSENTIAL INDUSTRIAL PRODUCTS, AND RAW MATERIALS

DOMESTIC PRODUCTION AND NET IMPORTS EXPRESSED AS PERCENTAGES OF
AVERAGE NATIONAL CONSUMPTION (1929-32)

—— GREAT ESSENTIALS ——

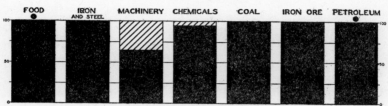

CRITICAL RAW MATERIALS

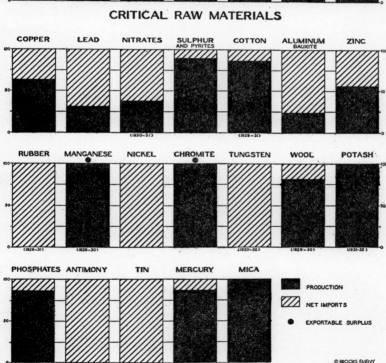

PREPARED FOR BROOKS EMENY 1934

© BROOKS EMENY

279

people. In fact, the distance still to be traversed before she can insure to her people even a decent standard of living is enormous.

It is easy, too, in the light of Red propaganda, to exaggerate not merely the present progress but also the future possibilities of Russian industrialization. Foodstuffs there are in quantities which, with modern farm machinery, will adequately supply the growing population.[1] Iron and coal exist in many regions but rarely in the same happy proximity as in the United States. No new Pittsburgh or Cleveland seems likely to rise beside the headwaters of the Yenesei or on the shores of Lake Baikal. Today the coal of the Kuznetsk Basin has to be moved fifteen hundred miles to meet the iron of the Urals at Magnitogorsk, although in the Donetz Basin in Europe the corresponding distance is less.

Provided Russia is spared domestic upheaval or foreign interference, however, it is hard to set any limit to her possible expansion in numbers and power. More than three millions are annually added to the population of the Soviet Union, now estimated at one hundred sixty-five million, and that means a gain of one hundred million in a single generation. Of cultivable land there still remains a considerable area as yet unoccupied, although the "covered wagon" era is over in Russia as in the American Far West. However, of the whole Siberian area, which seems so imposing on the map, the larger portion is tundra and desert and therefore has small exploitable value.

So far as one can see today, then, Russia will never be industrially a considerable or serious competitor in the

[1] Beauchamp, Joan, *Agriculture in Soviet Russia*, 1931; Timoshenko, V. P., *Agricultural Russia and the Wheat Problem*, 1932.

world markets, although she will continue to be a large exporter of certain raw materials.[1] Meantime, having determined to concentrate its energies upon industrialization rather than upon communizing the rest of the world,[2] the Soviet regime stands squarely for peace.[3]

But although the basis of Soviet national policy may be that of peace, the potentialities of Russian power in war are such that her recent return to the councils of Europe, particularly following the overthrow of the German Republic, has profound significance. That such a return was bound, sooner or later, to take place was evident, in view of the size of the population and the extent of the resources of the great Slav state. Indeed, it had already been foreshadowed in the early sessions of the Disarmament Conference in Geneva, during 1932, where the words of Litvinov attracted world-wide attention even if they failed to produce proportionate results.[4]

Nevertheless, in 1932 and even in 1933, when the German Revolution was just beginning to make itself felt, the Soviet Union was still separated from the western world by that barrier of mutual suspicion which the

---

[1] Budish, J. M., and Shipman, S. S., *Soviet Foreign Trade: Menace or Promise*, 1931; Campbell, T. D., *Russia, Market or Menace?*, 1932; Luboff, Edouard, *Soviet Dumping*, 1931.

[2] Fairburn, W. A., *The International Goal of Russian Communism*, 1931; Florinsky, M. T., *World Revolution and the U.S.S.R.*, 1933; Rosenberg, Arthur, *A History of Bolshevism*, 1934.

[3] "The object of the Soviet Government is to save the soil of the first proletariat state from the criminal folly of a new war. To this end the Soviet Union has struggled with the greatest determination and consistency for sixteen years. The defense of peace and of the neutrality of the Soviet Union against all attempts to drag it into the whirlwind of a world war is the central problem of Soviet foreign policy." (Radek, Karl, "The Bases of Soviet Foreign Policy," *Foreign Affairs*, January, 1934, p. 206.)

[4] Carnegie Endowment for International Peace, "The U.S.S.R. and Disarmament," *International Conciliation*, No. 292, 1933; Foreign Policy Association, "The Soviet Union as a European Power," *Foreign Policy Reports*, Vol. IX, No. 11, 1933; Litvinov, Maksim, *The Soviet's Fight for Disarmament*, 1932.

RUSSIA

POTENTIAL NATIONAL SELF-SUFFICIENCY IN FOODSTUFFS, ESSENTIAL INDUSTRIAL PRODUCTS, AND RAW MATERIALS

EXPRESSED IN PERCENTAGES OF ALL AVAILABLE DOMESTIC SOURCES
OF SUPPLY TO CONSUMPTION

—— GREAT ESSENTIALS ——

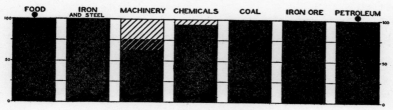

FOOD · IRON AND STEEL · MACHINERY · CHEMICALS · COAL · IRON ORE · PETROLEUM

CRITICAL RAW MATERIALS

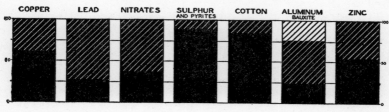

COPPER · LEAD · NITRATES · SULPHUR AND PYRITES · COTTON · ALUMINUM BAUXITE · ZINC

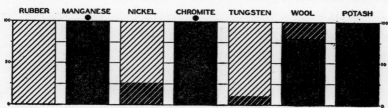

RUBBER · MANGANESE · NICKEL · CHROMITE · TUNGSTEN · WOOL · POTASH

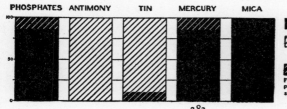

PHOSPHATES · ANTIMONY · TIN · MERCURY · MICA

AVERAGE DOMESTIC PRODUCTION.

NECESSARY NET IMPORTS.

● EXPORTABLE SURPLUS

ADDITIONAL SUPPLIES POTENTIALLY AVAILABLE FROM INCREASED DOMESTIC OUTPUT. (SUBSTITUTES, STOCK-PILING, AND SECONDARY RECOVERY NOT CONSIDERED.)

© BROOKS EMENY

283

early stages of the Red Revolution had established. On the Russian side, this suspicion dated back to the numerous White offensives, inspired and financed by Allied governments,[1] which had marked the first years of the Russian Revolution.[2] Even as late as 1932 there still lingered in the Russian mind the dominating suspicion that the capitalistic states were plotting a new attack calculated to abolish the threat for them always resident in the Red regime.

The western states likewise were still under the empire of fears born in 1917.[3] At the Peace Conference in 1919, when Bela Kun had briefly ruled at Budapest, Paris had foreseen Bolshevism sweeping over Central Europe at least to the Rhine. In 1920, the approach of the Red armies to Warsaw had produced new apprehension. Even when the defeat at the Vistula had broken the thrusting power of Bolshevism and the Treaty of Riga had stabilized the consequences of that defeat on the map, apprehension still endured.

After 1920, fear of a Russian military offensive disappeared, but it was replaced by the expectation of domestic disturbances engineered from Moscow. That new fear was based upon the obvious fact that the Kremlin was slow to recognize that for a long time to come the conceptions of the Third International and the expectations of a World Revolution must be put aside. As a result the agents of Moscow continued to work

[1] Denikin, A. I., *The White Army*, 1930; Goode, W. T., *Is Intervention in Russia a Myth?*, 1931; Graves, W. S., *America's Siberian Adventure 1918-1920*, 1931; Stewart, George, *The White Armies of Russia*, 1933.

[2] Florinsky, M. T., *The End of the Russian Empire*, 1931; Mavor, James, *An Economic History of Russia*, 1925, 2 vols.; Ross, E. A., *The Russian Soviet Republic, 1918-1922*, 1923; Trotsky, Leon, *The History of the Russian Revolution*, 1932, 3 vols.

[3] Arnot, R. P., *Soviet Russia and her Neighbors*, 1927; Fletcher, J. G., *Two Frontiers*, 1930.

secretly if fruitlessly in many countries, and Red scares, in the main little justified, were frequent alike in Great Britain and even in the United States.

It was only gradually that, on the one hand, Stalin turned the attention of the Revolution inward and, on the other, the western nations became less apprehensive of domestic disturbance due to Communistic activities. Whatever Lenin had believed[1]—and the point was long debated—Stalin did see clearly that the Revolution, after 1920, had lost its expansive force and that, in the military jargon, the moment had come to "dig in" and to consolidate the gains already made, which amounted only to the capture of Russia itself.

When, therefore, Stalin had won his victory over Trotsky and the Soviets had turned from a program of promoting revolution abroad to a plan for organizing a Marxian state at home, the chief obstacle to the resumption of normal intercourse between Russia and the outside world disappeared. The Five-Year Plan,[2] moreover, excited the curiosity of western peoples, set in motion a column of tourists journeying to Moscow, and presently not only stimulated the hope of vast trade but actually produced a small trickle of commerce, as well. Thus Russia ceased to be at once a mystery and a menace and became the best-publicized of all nations.[3]

---

[1] Trotsky, Leon, *L'Internationale Communiste après Lénine*, 1930; same author, *The Real Situation in Russia*, 1928.

[2] Chamberlin, W. H., *The Soviet Planned Economic Order*, 1931; Dobb, M. H., *Soviet Russia and the World*, 1932; Dobbert, Gerhard, ed., *Soviet Economics, a Symposium*, 1933; Knickerbocker, H. R., *The Red Trade Menace; Progress of the Soviet Five-Year Plan*, 1931.

[3] Batsell, W. R., *Soviet Rule in Russia*, 1929; Chamberlin, W. H., *Soviet Russia*, 1931, rev. ed.; Duranty, Walter, *Duranty Reports Russia*, 1934; Eckardt, Hans von, *Russia*, 1932; Foreign Policy Association, "The Political Structure of the Soviet State," *Foreign Policy Reports*, Vol. VIII, Nos. 1 and 2, 1932; Gurian, Waldemar, *Bolshevism: Theory and Practice*, 1932; Harper, S. N., *Civic Training in Soviet Russia*, 1929; same author, *Making Bolsheviks*, 1931.

In the Anglo-Saxon countries people argued, discussed, and described the Soviet experiment until familiarity robbed it of most of its sinister implications and curiosity almost everywhere conquered fear. Naturally the change was not complete. The threat to all western states inherent in the Soviet experiment, and the scare the Red Revolution in its earlier stages had given even the democracies of Great Britain, the United States, and France, were in the nature of things bound to have enduring consequences. Yet by 1934, when the Brown Peril of German reaction had captured the columns of the newspapers to the exclusion of the once familiar Red Revolution, the Soviet Union had escaped from its isolated eminence as the major peril to world order, and its entrance into the League of Nations was easily achieved.

In these postwar years, too, a parallel change had taken place in the national policy of the Soviet Union.[1] At Rapallo, in 1922, the Russians and the Germans, at that moment the two pariah peoples of the world, had made a treaty whose immediate effects were enormous. At that time, the Allied peoples were still dominated by their wartime emotions in respect of Germany and their even more recent feelings toward the Red Revolution. As a consequence, when at the Genoa Conference Rathenau produced a pact between Moscow and Berlin, the conference collapsed, Lloyd George's political fortunes were fatally compromised, and the preface to the occupation of the Ruhr was written.

[1] Besiedovskiĭ, G. Z., *Revelations of a Soviet Diplomat*, 1931; Dean, V. M., "Soviet Russia, 1917–1933," *World Affairs Pamphlets*, No. 2, Foreign Policy Association and World Peace Foundation, 1933; Dennis, A. L. P., *The Foreign Policies of Soviet Russia*, 1924; Fischer, Louis, *The Soviets in World Affairs*, 1930, 2 vols.; Foreign Policy Association, "Developments in Russia's Foreign Relations," *Information Service*, Vol. III, No. 10, 1927, and "The Soviet Union as a European Power," *Foreign Policy Reports*, Vol. IX, No. 11, 1933; Scheffer, Paul, *Seven Years in Soviet Russia*, 1932.

In point of fact, however, while Rapallo made a tremendous sensation in the world, it had little lasting effect. The fact that Germany had thus undertaken to make a bargain with the Reds, the simple text of which was endowed with every sort of secret and sinister implication, damaged her case alike in the United States and in Great Britain and strengthened the hand of Poincaré correspondingly. Since Rapallo was followed by a period of close co-operation between German generals and the Red Army, many alarmist reports were launched. But three years after Rapallo, German policy abruptly changed cars.

The change followed Stresemann's decision to abandon the effort to evade the Treaty of Versailles, a course which had invited the disaster of a new French invasion; to put aside the eastern orientation, which had outraged western public opinion; and to come to terms with all the wartime foes of the Reich, beginning with France. That decision, which found its expression in the accords of Locarno, made Geneva instead of Moscow the goal of German policy, and progressively from 1925 to 1929, when Stresemann died, the ties between the Soviet Union and the German Republic were loosened. There was no actual break—on the contrary, right down to the Hitler uprising the commercial relations continued close; but the older idea of a Russo-German war of vengeance upon the western nations vanished.

With the arrival of the Hitler Revolution, however, the relations between Moscow and Berlin underwent a swift and far-reaching change. The reasons for that change were various. Hitler and his followers justified the severity and violence of their performances by the allegation that they were saving Germany from the real and immediate danger of a Communist upheaval. Germany, so the legend went, was on the very point of sinking into Bolshevist control, and the National Socialist Revolution which had saved it had also protected all the world from this calamity. On this assumption, too, the "Nazis" justified a persecution of the domestic Communists as vigorous as that directed at the Jews. But naturally Moscow resented a violence whose victims were those of its own political faith.

The offense to Moscow, however, was even more direct; for Hitler and his followers promptly proclaimed their purpose to supplement the suppression of Communism in the Reich by the invasion and partition of the Soviet Union itself. Thus the Ukraine was marked down as a field for German conquest and colonization, and the program outlined by the terms of the Treaty of Brest-Litovsk, which the victorious Germans had forced upon Red Russia early in 1918, was reaffirmed.

The result of such a performance was inevitable. In the face of a German danger which had been frankly foreshadowed by the National Socialists themselves, the single resource left to the Soviet Union was to seek friends among peoples similarly threatened by National Socialist designs. Thus, in an odd fashion, history repeated itself. Forty years before, when William II dropped Bismarck, the Treaty of Russo-German Reinsurance awaited renewal. Bismarck had planned to renew it; but when he fell the treaty lapsed. As a consequence, St. Petersburg turned to Paris and in no long time made the Franco-Russian Treaty of Alliance which was to prove the first long step toward the Treaty of Versailles.[1] In 1933 still another change of regime in

[1] Korf, Baron S. A., *Russia's Foreign Relations During the Last Half Century*, 1922.

Germany had been followed by another shift in German attitude toward Russia. And once more the result was to bring Russia and France together.

At Geneva, during the sessions of the moribund Disarmament Conference in the spring of 1934, Litvinov no longer indicted all of the capitalistic nations for their common failure to make honest effort to bring about reduction of armaments. On the contrary, he significantly took up the French thesis that security must precede reduction of armaments, and that the completion of regional pacts and mutual agreements, constituting Eastern and Mediterranean Locarnos, must come before the settlement of the question of military parity for Germany. Thus the League and Europe were presently treated to the spectacle of Litvinov and Barthou reviving the tradition of co-operation established by Isvolsky and Poincaré which was so roundly condemned by the Bolshevists in their earlier days.

France, to be sure, approached this new association slowly and with evident hesitation. None of the enthusiasm which had welcomed the old Russian alliance greeted the new. Nevertheless, at long last, the French turned to Moscow because government and people alike had finally abandoned all hope of effective Anglo-Saxon support or of solid British guarantee. Even in the face of the rising storm in Germany, Great Britain remained immovable in her resistance to new guarantees, although abandoning her support of the Reich in the attempt to secure military parity with France. And, after fifteen years, the French felt that they could wait no longer.

On the Soviet side, the attractions of the French association were obvious. Red Russia, like republican France

and democratic England, desired only peace. The ultimate success of the great Communist experiment depended upon the maintenance of peace over a period of years. But not only was Germany now threatening a war of aggression in the West, but also Japan, in the East, was disclosing similar disturbing purposes. And there were even reports that Tokyo and Berlin had already joined hands in a common program of Russian spoliation. Germany, so the rumor ran, was to attract Russian attention in the Ukraine while Japan concentrated its efforts upon Siberia.

To insure French action at the Rhine in order to balance any German action at the Niemen had thus become a prerequisite of Soviet security. Nor was it less useful now for the Soviets to associate themselves with that League of Nations on which they had for nearly a decade and a half poured out the vials of their wrath; for in the face of German and Japanese aggression, there would be assured the moral if not the material advantage incident to the pronouncement of Geneva against the guilty nations. At Geneva, too, there remained whatever was still left of the machinery designed to preserve world peace.

Peace was the dominating desire of Moscow as it was of London; for security, prosperity, unity, all would manifestly be called into question in case of war. Military defeat, too, would involve not merely territorial mutilation but possibly the collapse of the Communist experiment as well. Like France, therefore, the Soviet Union was dedicated to the gospel of the status quo. For the Kremlin, like the Quai d'Orsay, nourished no imperialistic aspirations. It had long ago accepted as definitive the frontiers of the Treaty of Riga which had liquidated the defeat in Poland.[1] It was now ready to make similar concession in regard to Bessarabia, which had been transferred to Rumania after the World War.

Once Paris and Moscow had reached a preliminary basis of agreement, at least two of the nations of the Little Entente, Czechoslovakia and Rumania, hastened to give their approval. Even Turkey and Bulgaria did not disguise their satisfaction. In Prague, in Bucharest, and even in Sofia, the effect of the evident return of Russia to European councils was a matter of more than passing interest because of the ethnic tie. Pan-Slavism might be dead, but Pan-Germanism, which carried an obvious threat to all the smaller Slav states, was again threatening. And in Russian policy they detected, or at least dreamed, the evidence that once more Slav and Teuton were coming to grips as they had in the years preceding the World War.

The implications of the Russian move were not lost on Berlin. On the contrary, the memory of the consequences of the former lapse of Russo-German friendship were revived and the sense of German isolation heightened. The old mistake had been repeated and the old consequences were reappearing—that was what Berlin whispered when the German ambassador in Moscow resigned in protest over a policy which foreshadowed disaster. Germany was again becoming walled about by a circle of steel. To break this circle on the east, Hitler had purchased Polish passivity by a treaty of nonaggression perpetuating the hated Corridor for another decade at least. But now, beyond Poland, Russia was taking a position of hostility.

[1] Carnegie Endowment for International Peace, "The Soviet Security System," *International Conciliation*, No. 252, 1929.

Hitler had dreamed of friendship with Great Britain; his own book testified to that. But after the "Nazi" persecution of the Jews, the Liberals, and the Democrats, following the "cold" pogroms of March, 1933, and the even colder proscription of June, 1934, there was no longer left anything but horror of the Hitler regime in the British mind. In the same fashion, the Fuehrer had dreamed of an Italian alliance; but at Venice the Duce had made Austrian independence the price of his support of German claims to military parity with France, and Hitler refused to pay that price. Last of all, the western world, with its eyes fixed upon the bloody second stage of the German Revolution, evinced little enthusiasm for the vision of "Nazi" Germany, as the soldier of western civilization, leading a crusade against the Red Peril of Communism.

The return of Russia to European councils had further implications. It had been the disintegration of Austria and the disappearance of Russia which had led to the collapse of the balance of power and the vanishing of the Concert of Europe. These two things, taken together with the enforced disarmament of Germany, had bestowed upon France her new period of Continental hegemony. But they had not abolished the danger of the eventual dominance of a rearmed and restored Germany. Even with her smaller allies, France could hardly get rid of that peril permanently.

If Russia were back in her old place, however, and if in addition she returned as an ally of France, then, in a restored Concert of Europe, Germany could hope for little effective gain, and on the battlefield of the future she would still be outnumbered as she had been in 1914. Even with Italian aid, Germany could accomplish little in councils in which France was assured of the backing of Soviet Russia. Nor was there any prospect that Great Britain would lend her support to either Fascist or National Socialist programs for revising the map of Europe by violence.

Meantime, with the financial aid of France, the Soviet Union could push its program of industrialization which must every year make it more formidable alike economically and militarily.[1] By the end of the century the Russian population would probably exceed a quarter of a billion, while the German population was at last tending downward under the influence of a birthrate lower than that of France. Nor was it likely that even a Red regime in Russia would permit the extinction of the independence and ethnic unity of the smaller Slav peoples which dwelt in the pathway of German advance up the Elbe and down the Danube.

To the German mind, the World War, at least in the early days, had seemed primarily a struggle between Teuton and Slav. The fact that the Anglo-Saxon nations, as well as the Latin, had stood with Russia had been denounced as a betrayal of Europe for Asia, a championship of the barbarian against the civilized state. The result of the war had been the enormous decline of Germanism in Central Europe and a striking gain for Slavism. Now, in German eyes the old peril was arising in a new form and once more the Slav had been assured of French backing.

Fantastic as German interpretations of the Russian phenomenon seemed, it was nevertheless difficult to deny them a certain measure of basis in fact. The primary objective of Russian policy being peace, and national

[1] Charques, R. D., *The Soviets and the Next War; the Present Case for Disarmament*, 1932.

security, prosperity, and unity being for the Soviet Union conditioned upon Continental tranquillity based on the status quo, a collision between Soviet and German interests was inevitable. Since, in addition, the Franco-German quarrel had survived the war unmodified, a Franco-Russian alliance was similarly assured. To that alliance also the smaller states of Central Europe, menaced by German plans for Mittel-europa, were bound to turn. Against such a coalition there was available for Germany only an Italian partner, who in turn was sure to change sides if German union with Austria were in question.

National Socialist Germany, like Nationalist Germany before it, had calculated upon Russia as a free field for German expansion economically and territorially. It had counted upon the distrust and hatred of Communism in the western nations to insure it unrestrained freedom of action. The program sketched at Brest-Litovsk was to be fulfilled by Hitler after the interruption of two decades. Now, however, Germany saw Capitalistic France and Communistic Russia repeating the policies of the earlier regimes which were respectively Republican and Czarist.

Obviously, the return of Russia to the European field is of too recent date and the implications of that dramatic episode too complex and too numerous to permit of any appraisal of policy as clear and definite as is possible in the case of France or Great Britain. One thing, however, seems fairly certain. Precisely as long as Germany is controlled by a regime which has made war upon its own domestic Communists and has also proclaimed the purpose to seize Russian territory, Soviet policy must be anti-German.

For the student of international relations there can be no more illuminating detail than that supplied by the development of Soviet national policy in the postwar period. In that time a great revolution has swept over the face of Russia, producing changes as vast and as far-reaching as those of the French upheaval of 1792. An imperial regime has been overthrown, its masters and servants scattered. A social as well as a political system has been abolished. A new order has replaced an old, and not one of the ancient landmarks has been left unmoved.

Twenty years after the historic moment, on the very eve of the World War, when Poincaré, President of the French Republic, took leave of the last of the Romanoffs in St. Petersburg, shortly to become Petrograd and eventually Leningrad, the world was called upon to witness at Geneva a hardly less impressive demonstration of Franco-Russian solidarity by Barthou and Litvinov. And once more it was the perception of a common danger that united two governments, as divided in economic ideas and political ideals in 1934 as those which entered the World War as allies in August, 1914.

Less than a decade and a half after Clemenceau undertook to construct an impassable *cordon sanitaire* about Soviet frontiers to protect the whole world from the infection of Red doctrines proclaimed by Lenin, Doumergue and Stalin were paving the way for the erection not of a *cordon sanitaire* but of a *cordon militaire*, this time restraining not a Red Russia but a reactionary Germany within a wall of steel. What better illustration could there be of the fashion in which the policies of European countries, dictated by their basic interests, survive all the changes of regimes and of governments as they also

survive the shock of new principles and new instrumen-
talities such as Woodrow Wilson set forth in his Fourteen Points and other pronouncements and established
by his League of Nations?

When, moreover, in the midsummer of 1934, London
gave its unequivocal endorsement of the proposal for an
Eastern Locarno, designed to bind Russia, Poland, and
Czechoslovakia as well as Germany to respect the status
quo and to join in action against any power seeking
to destroy it by violence, and when, in addition, the
approval of Rome was also forthcoming, the extent of
impending German isolation was made clear. Nor was
the embarrassment of Berlin in rejecting that proposal
lessened by the perception that the alternative might be
a definitive Franco-Russian alliance sanctified by regis-
tration at Geneva as a pact of mutual assistance against
aggression. Finally, in December of the same year the
French Chamber of Deputies was told that Soviet armies
would march if France were attacked, and at Geneva
Litvinov and Laval agreed to make no new political
engagements until Paris and Moscow had consulted.

Such, then, is the European aspect of Russia's circumstances and policy. Her relation to the Far Eastern
Question will be discussed in later chapters.[1]

[1] See Chapters XXI and XXII.

Chapter XV

THE SMALLER STATES

To complete the European picture, it is necessary to consider briefly the situation of the lesser Continental countries,[1] for upon certain of these the World War bestowed an importance which was lacking throughout the preceding century. That importance had its origin not merely in the military forces of the so-called "Succession States," but also in their right to speak and vote in the Assembly of the League of Nations, a right unprecedented in the past, when the smaller countries had been condemned to wait, powerless and justly apprehensive, upon the decisions of the Concert of Europe.

In postwar Europe, however, the influence of the lesser states was by no means always equally important. On the contrary, where the interests of the Great Powers were concerned, the smaller were by choice or necessity frequently excluded from the debate. Where the question of the organization of peace was involved, particularly in the League of Nations, the voices of these

[1] For a brief general survey of each of the lesser states, see: Cole, G. D. H., and Cole, Margaret, *The Intelligent Man's Review of Europe Today*, 1933; Macartney, C. A., *National States and National Minorities*, 1934.

smaller countries were, however, both audible and not
without weight.

Of the nations which by their own decision or by
special circumstances are removed from the field of
controversy, Spain is the most considerable. To this
category also belong the Netherlands, Switzerland,
Denmark, Norway, Sweden, and Finland.[1] Relative insignificance, too, excludes Estonia, Latvia, and Lithuania in the north, and Albania in the south, from other
than purely local concerns.[2] Portugal, the perpetual ally
of Great Britain, is physically removed from all contact
with Continental problems. Finally, following the conflict of 1922, Turkey and Greece found a mutually satisfactory adjustment for their quarrels[3] and thus cleared
the way for regional agreements and understandings
among the Balkan states, which presently bestowed
upon them a peace and stability not before enjoyed
since the overthrow of Turkish rule.[4]

In reality, therefore, the smaller nations which
counted and continue to count in European controversies
are Poland, Czechoslovakia, Yugoslavia, Rumania, Belgium, Austria, Hungary, and Bulgaria. As to the last
three, it is to be recalled that, like Germany, they were
disarmed by the Paris Settlement and still remain, on
the military side, practically helpless. By contrast, the

---

[1] Atchley, W. W., *Finland*, 1931; Bellquist, E. C., *Some Aspects of the Recent Foreign Policy of Sweden*, 1929; Meuvret, J., *Histoire des Pays Baltiques*, 1934.

[2] Benn, Sir E. J. P., *About Russia*, 1930; Bihlmans, Alfred, *Latvia in the Making, 1918-1928*, 1928; Graham, Stephen, *The Dividing Line of Europe*, 1925; Mousset, Albert, *L'Albanie devant l'Europe*, 1930; Rutter, Owen, *The New Baltic States and their Future*, 1926; Sobolevitch, E., *Les États Baltes et la Russie Soviétique*, 1930.

[3] Ladas, S. P., *The Exchange of Minorities*, 1932.

[4] Armstrong, H. F., *The New Balkans*, 1926; Buell, R. L., ed., *New Governments in Europe*, 1934; Foreign Policy Association, "The Balkans in the World Crisis," Vol. IX, No. 20, 1933, "Recent Balkan Alignments," *Foreign Policy Reports*, Vol. VII, No. 1, 1931; Papanastassiou, A. P., *Vers l'Union Balkanique*, 1934; Schevill, Ferdinand, and Gewehr, W. M., *The History of the Balkan Peninsula*, 1933, rev. ed.

POSTWAR EUROPE
REVISIONIST AND STATUS QUO STATES

REVISIONIST   STATUS QUO

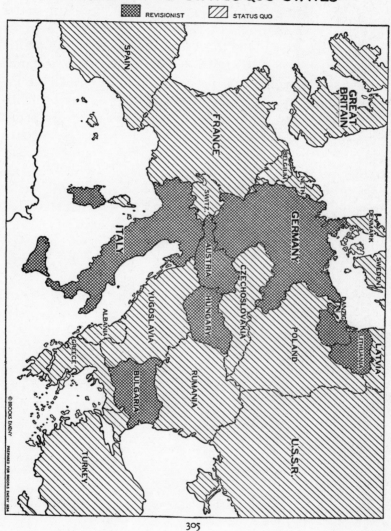

305

other four eastern states today maintain standing armies amounting in the aggregate to approximately three quarters of a million men and are in possession of trained reserves at least four times as numerous.

When one turns to the consideration of the interests which determine the character of the national policies of these four states, it becomes evident at once that, for them as for France, security is the major and all-embracing objective. For all are confronted by unmistakable dangers. Poland faces the eventual if temporarily postponed purpose of Germany to recover the Polish Corridor and Upper Silesia. Czechoslovakia is confronted by the resolution of the Reich to reclaim the German minorities in Bohemia and Moravia and the determination of the Hungarians to recapture their ethnic minorities in Slovakia. Yugoslavia is face to face with Magyar irredentism in the Bachka and Italian imperialism in Dalmatia. Finally, although Rumania has acquired recognition by Soviet Russia of her title to Bessarabia, she has always to consider Hungarian resolution to recover the lands and people taken by the Treaty of Trianon in 1919,[1] and Bulgarian determination to recover Silistria taken by the Treaty of Bucharest in 1913.

It follows naturally, therefore, that in the face of perils which are unmistakable all four of these eastern states must seek security alike by armaments and by alliances.[2]

[1] For the lands transferred from Hungary to Rumania in 1919, compare the boundaries shown in the maps on pages 143 and 305. The location of Magyar ethnic minorities in Slovakia, Yugoslavia, and Rumania is shown in the map on page 103—excepting several very small areas and one area of considerable size in Rumania. That one important area not shown on page 103 is the home of the Szeckler branch of the Magyars, in the easternmost corner of the land taken from Hungary, now almost in the center of Rumania.

[2] Balla, V. de, *The New Balance of Power in Europe*, 1932; Foreign Policy Association, "Political Realignments in Europe," *Foreign Policy Reports*, Vol. IX, No. 5, 1933; Malynski, Emmanuel, Count, *Les Problèmes de l'Est et la Petite Entente*, 1931.

Since, too, each has an identical concern for the preservation of the status quo of the Paris Conference, there has existed from the very beginning of the postwar period a community of interest between all four of these states and France. Among the three Danubian states (Czechoslovakia, Yugoslavia, and Rumania), furthermore, there has been an enduring basis for accord in the threat, to all, of Hungarian irredentism, which explains the existence of the Little Entente and similarly explains the outspoken championship of the Yugoslav cause by the Czech and Rumanian Foreign Ministers during the crisis of December, 1934.

When, therefore, in 1919, following the rejection by the United States Senate of the Treaty of Versailles and the parallel failure of the Treaty of Guarantee to France, Great Britain declined to bestow her own guarantee upon French security, there was thus waiting at the hand of French statesmanship an alternative means to establish national safety. That method was the creation of a system of alliances. Beginning in 1921, Paris swiftly made partnerships with Warsaw, Prague, Belgrade, and Bucharest. The bases of agreement were obvious: France binding herself to support with her arms and wealth the territorial integrity of each of her allies, and they in turn pledging themselves to support France with their armies if she were attacked.

The system of alliances thus created bestowed upon France not only transient security but temporary hegemony as well. In the face of a German attack at the Saar, she was assured of the prompt intervention of Polish armies in Silesia and Czech armies in Saxony. In the event of Italian support of a German offensive, French defense in the Maritime Alps would be supported by a

Yugoslav offensive in the Julian Alps. Each of the allies, too, was assured of the double aid of French arms and French finance.

The price for France of such benefits as her Continental system assured her was, however, quite evident. She assumed responsibility for the permanence of the Polish Corridor and thereby compromised the chance of permanent reconciliation with Germany, assuming that such chance had ever existed. She undertook to guarantee the Yugoslav title to Dalmatia and therefore encountered continuing Italian resentment. Finally, she accepted responsibility alike for the independence of Austria, which constituted a further cause of quarrel with Germany, and for the permanence of the status quo of the Treaty of Trianon, which inevitably insured that Hungary would enter either the German or the Italian camp.

In effect, France therefore undertook the colossal task of guaranteeing the status quo upon the whole European Continent. In return, she acquired for herself military and diplomatic support insuring a position which had not been hers since the overthrow of Napoleon and had not been German even after Sadowa and Sedan. Having undertaken that task, however, it was inevitable that France should appear in every international meeting, whether at Geneva or elsewhere, demanding that the military superiority which belonged to her through her alliances should not be compromised until the status quo, of which she alone among the Great Powers was now the guarantor, should become the equal responsibility of all. And in that policy she was, of course, heartily supported by all of her allies.

On the other hand, France encountered British and

American opposition, because both Anglo-Saxon states were satisfied that world order was contingent upon a viable settlement with Germany and that such a settlement was obtainable only at the price of treaty revision in respect both of frontiers and of armaments at the expense of the allies of France. Italian resistance, too, was inevitable because Italy was equally incensed by the guarantee bestowed upon Yugoslav frontiers by France and by the predominant position in Europe insured to France by her alliances.

In the Danubian region, moreover, France, Italy, and Germany thus stood opposed. Czechoslovakia, Yugoslavia, and Rumania, the allies of France, presently united in the famous Little Entente, designed to preserve the status quo in Central Europe against all outside interference, whether German or Italian, and against Magyar purposes as well.[1] Thus allied, these states undertook to establish some economic system of order. But no such system was possible without Austrian and Hungarian participation and German and Italian approval, and both were unattainable.

When, however, Germany undertook to achieve tariff union with Austria, not only France and the Little Entente but Italy as well rallied to oppose it. Finally, when Italy, in her turn, strove to establish a rival system in the Danubian region by understandings with Vienna and Budapest, she encountered the fatal opposition of Bucharest, Prague, and Belgrade.

Thus, on the one hand, the peace treaties had "Balkanized" Middle Europe from the Bavarian frontier to the Black Sea, and on the other hand, the Great Powers

---

[1] Codresco, Florin, *La Petite Entente*, 1930; Crane, J. O., *The Little Entente*, 1931; Machray, Robert, *The Little Entente*, 1930.

henceforth acted in the new Balkans as they had in the old. The triangular conflict in the Danubian region also insured that the economic and financial dislocations incident to the war and the treaties of peace would be enormously extended. For the material existence of the Austrians and the enjoyment of any degree of prosperity by the Hungarians depended upon the restoration of their old markets in the territories which had become Czech, Serb, and Rumanian, while tolerable existence for the states of the Little Entente was similarly contingent upon a return to old economic relations in the valley of the Danube.

To her allies, France could make loans and give military guarantees against the destruction of their territorial unity, but she could not offer them adequate markets for their agricultural and industrial surpluses. To her Austrian and Magyar associates, Italy could give similar military guarantees against aggression and a small though precious market, but she could not restore lost provinces, provide adequate loans, or supply sufficient commercial outlets. As for Germany, she alone could offer adequate markets, but her purpose to bring Austria within her frontiers constituted a threat of varying proportions for the Danubian states and a danger for Italy as well.

When, with the rise of Hitler, the fate of Austria came to be more and more in the balance, there was an open *détente* in Franco-Italian relations as there was a strengthening of the ties between Rome on the one hand and Budapest and Vienna on the other. Nevertheless, the Little Entente continued to block all the aspirations of Italy to establish a Danubian bloc under its control, and Hungarian irredentism, supported by Italian influence, closed the door to the expansion of the Little Entente to include Hungary and thus to the creation of a viable economic system on the ruins of the Hapsburg Monarchy.

After Hitler came to complete control in March, 1933, Mussolini, in conference with MacDonald, launched from Rome a proposal for a renewal of the Concert of Europe to be constituted by Great Britain, Germany, France, and Italy.[1] Instantly, however, that proposal aroused violent protest in Warsaw, Prague, Belgrade, and Bucharest, for Poland and the nations of the Little Entente clearly perceived that in such a Concert they would be sacrificed to German and Italian ambitions; and despite the fact that France signed the treaty embodying this plan, it was never ratified.

When Hitler, subordinating all else to his desperate attempt to bring about a triumph of the National Socialists of Austria and thus insure actual if not legal union between the Reich and the Republic, proposed a ten-year truce with Poland, Warsaw, angered by French hesitation in the matter of Mussolini's Four-Power Concert and resenting French treatment of her greatest ally as a satellite, welcomed the proposal. But although the relations between Paris and Warsaw became visibly less intimate, the Franco-Polish alliance was not immediately dissolved. And while the Hitler regime, on the surface at least, scored a diplomatic success over France at Warsaw, it paid a high price, measured by the perpetuation of the Corridor for another decade.

The relations of the Great Powers to the smaller states of Central and Eastern Europe in the postwar period are then unmistakable. France, to insure her own security

[1] Grandi, Dino, "The Foreign Policy of the Duce," *Foreign Affairs*, Vol. XII, No. 4, 1934; Foreign Policy Association, "Political Realignments in Europe," *Foreign Policy Reports*, Vol. IX, No. 5, 1933.

and to restrain Germany within the limits of the Treaty of Versailles, joined to herself, by a system of military alliances, the nations of the Little Entente and Poland. To break up the French system and thus to put an end to French Continental supremacy and French protection of Yugoslavia as well, Italy sought to press the question of territorial revision in the interests of Germany in the east and Hungary in the south. In addition, she supported the project of parity in armaments for Germany as a means of reducing French military superiority. As for Germany, she accepted Italian aid but, in open opposition to Mussolini, continued to press for union with Austria.

When Hitler first came to power, Europe and the world were seized by the greatest war scare of the postwar period because, in the first weeks, there seemed a clear possibility that an alliance, including Germany and Italy among the Great Powers, and Austria and Hungary among the smaller, might be consummated and thereafter challenge the French system. When, however, Hitler chose to make his offensive in the south instead of the east, and against Austria rather than Poland, Mussolini was driven to treat the Fuehrer as a prospective enemy rather than as a possible ally.

In the same fashion, at long last, the British having striven both within and without the League of Nations to bring about a peaceful revision of the territorial and the military clauses of the Treaty of Versailles in the hope of placating Germany, were finally driven by the implications of violence of the National Socialist regime to abandon a course which had involved them in controversy with France, intermittently, ever since the Paris Conference in 1919. And the complete *volte face* in British policy was disclosed when, after the German massacre of June 30, 1934, British approval of the Franco-Russian policy of regional pacts was forthcoming.

Fifteen years after the close of the Peace Conference, therefore, it was beyond question that a French policy of alliances which had resulted from the refusal of the British and Americans to give their guarantees to France, although visibly weakening, was as yet unbroken, and French hegemony in Europe was still beyond challenge. If Poland had made a truce with Germany, the Soviet Union had appeared in the Polish place both at Geneva and elsewhere, while the Little Entente still maintained its military predominance in the Danubian area. Finally, after the Austrian *Putsch* of July, 1934, Italy had been compelled unwillingly to mount guard on the Danube against German invasion instead of making use of Franco-German disputes elsewhere to overthrow French influence in Central Europe.

The isolation of Germany, which had been the constant objective of French policy, had now become well nigh complete. Great Britain had frankly abandoned her pursuit of peace by means of concessions to Germany, and Italy had put aside even the pretense of co-operation with the Reich. The status quo which had seemed so precarious at the close of the Peace Conference had already survived for nearly half a generation and appeared less fragile in the summer of 1934 than at any previous moment since Woodrow Wilson had taken ship for America.

Meantime, as Hitlerian proposals for Ukrainian annexation had brought the Soviet Union back to European councils as a guarantor of the status quo in the east and south, National Socialist programs of aerial armament had recalled the British to similar concern for the security of the frontiers of the Netherlands and Belgium in the west. For the latter country, too, the menace of Hitler had served as a spur to drive a reluctant parliament to appropriate the moneys necessary to restore the old forts of Liège and Namur, to construct a new Hindenburg line from the Netherlands to the French frontier, and finally to return to the shelter of that alliance with France which had all but lapsed in later years.

Looking to the future, too, it is evident that the role of the smaller states in European affairs may well prove to be more considerable than it has been even in the immediate past. Poland, which has already a population of more than 33,000,000 and adds nearly half a million to its numbers annually, is larger in area than Italy, and in addition is comparatively rich in coal, iron, and foodstuffs. Already this newly restored state claims for itself the rank of a Great Power.[1] And having made a nonaggression pact with the Soviets and a ten-year truce with Germany, it would seem to have insured for itself a period of security during which the completion of its national consolidation can be achieved. Furthermore, by rejecting and thereby destroying the Eastern Locarno, so strongly urged alike by France and Russia, Poland at the same time disclosed her escape from French leadership and her resolution to play a balance of power game between Russia and the Reich.

Like Poland, Rumania is also both larger in area and richer in natural resources than Italy. The fact that in recent times it has at last obtained Russian recognition of its title to Bessarabia has removed the single serious

[1] Dyboski, Roman, *Outlines of Polish History*, 1931, 2d ed.; Machray, Robert, *Poland, 1914-1931*, 1932; Martel, René, *The Eastern Frontiers of Germany*, 1930; Smogorzewski, Casimir, *Poland, Germany and the Corridor*, 1930.

contemporary challenge to its territorial integrity. To
the south, Bulgaria still remains resentful of the loss of
the Silistrian region, but if there be danger in that direction, it is remote. On the other hand, Hungarian resolution to recover Transylvania and the Banat endures unmodified and must long constitute a potential menace.[1]

As for Yugoslavia, if she has made at least a temporary
truce with Bulgaria, as a result of the agreements of the
summer of 1934, she nevertheless finds herself always at
grips with Italy over the Adriatic question and threatened
in the rear by Hungarian irredentism. Hers, however, is
a rich territory, as large as the mainland of Italy, endowed with mineral as well as agricultural resources,
and as yet troubled by no problem of population pressure. Like Rumania, too, she could contemplate the
possibility of German possession of Austria with relative equanimity, since Germany is a potential market
and an equally possible ally against Italy.[2] As a consequence, Italian mobilization at the moment of the Dollfuss murder aroused sharp protest in Belgrade, and the
possibility that Yugoslavia might turn from the French
to a German orientation had henceforth to be recognized,
with all its disturbing implications. Finally, the assassination of King Alexander in Marseille (in October,
1934) lent emphasis to the Italian and Hungarian issues.
Two months later, too, the Yugoslav threat to Hungary
and the stout resistance of the Magyars to Yugoslav
violence, produced a fresh crisis or at least a new phase

[1] Cabot, J. M., *The Racial Conflict in Transylvania*, 1926; Popovici, Andrei, *The Political Status of Bessarabia*, 1931; Rouček, J. S., *Contemporary Roumania and her Problems*, 1932.

[2] Ancel, Jacques, *Les Balkans Face à l'Italie*, 1928; Aranitović, Relja, *Les Ressources et l'Activité Économique de la Yougoslavie*, 1930; Beard, C. A., and Radin, George, *The Balkan Pivot: Jugoslavia*, 1929; Pezet, Ernest, and Simondet, H., *La Yougoslavie en Peril?*, 1933.

in the crisis precipitated by the crime of Marseille.

The three states, therefore, Poland, Rumania, and Yugoslavia, all with relatively large armies, considerable natural resources, and rapidly increasing populations, are, it would seem, destined to have an importance in the future which none but Great Powers possessed before 1914. Having survived the dangers of the immediate postwar years and the uncertainties of "season states," they have now become accepted as enduring forces.

Far less clear, however, is the outlook for Czechoslovakia, Austria, and Hungary.

Czechoslovakia, although industrially the most considerable and economically the soundest of the three, finds itself threatened within by problems arising from the fact that among its many races there is none constituting a majority.[1] Beyond question, the events in Germany culminating in the proscription of June 30, 1934, have temporarily, at least, silenced the aspirations of the German-speaking minority of Czechoslovakia for union with the Reich; but at best this would seem a postponement.

As for Austria, after as before the murder of Dollfuss and the revolt of the domestic "Nazis," its ultimate fate remained obscure and its material circumstances unmistakably desperate. Unlike all of the other states of the Danubian region, it is incapable of self-support. Nor does its present dependence upon Italy bring any prospect of material advantage. Only inclusion within the tariff limits of Germany or restoration of its fiscal unity with the portions of the old Hapsburg Monarchy now consti-

---

[1] Borovička, J., *Ten Years of Czechoslovak Politics*, 1929; Crane, J. O., *The Little Entente*, 1931.

tuting Hungary and Czechoslovakia, would seem calculated to give it any hope of tolerable existence. But political obstacles today bar the way to economic relief in either direction.

The situation of Hungary in Southeastern Europe recalls that of Germany in Central Europe. Precisely as viable peace on the Continent is out of the question while the great German people stand unreconciled and uncompromising, so any system of order in the Danubian region is impossible as long as the Magyars continue to preserve a similarly irreconcilable attitude. Their grievances are manifestly great, and the least tolerable might be remedied by Rumanian, Czech, and Serb surrender of solid blocks of Hungarian populations in their frontier provinces. Failing such concessions, there is small hope that Hungary can be brought to any change in her present policy of passive but passionate resistance.[1]

It was, moreover, the consciousness of the evil implications for the future of this unconquerable spirit of the Magyars, already illustrated in successful resistances to Turk and Austrian, which prompted both the Yugoslavs and the Czechs to launch their campaign of coercion against Hungary, in December, 1934. What was, however, well nigh incredible was the assumption of the Serbs and the Czechs, both of which peoples had for centuries struggled against the attempts of alien masters to crush their aspirations for independence and unity, that they could by brutal force extinguish the similar aspirations of a race numerically larger and possessed of a far more splendid tradition than either Slav state.

Thus there seems destined to endure in the very heart

[1] Apponyi, A., Gróf, et al., *Justice for Hungary*, 1928; Eckhart, Ferenc, *A Short History of the Hungarian People*, 1931.

of Europe precisely the conditions out of which the World War arose; for in the Danubian region the policies of three Great Powers—France, Germany, and Italy— are as entangled as were those of Russia and Austria in the old Balkans in 1914. Only if the Great Powers could agree would it be possible to establish any system of order even temporarily acceptable to the smaller states. And of such agreement there was in 1934 slight prospect. On the contrary in December of that year it taxed the utmost resources of statesmanship, not to organize peace but to postpone conflict.

In contemporary Europe, moreover, it is necessary to recognize that predominant influence today belongs not as before 1914 to a Concert of Europe made up of the six Great Powers—divided, to be sure, into the Triple Alliance and the Triple Entente,—but to a system of alliances in which there is but one Great Power and at least four smaller. And if the desertion of Poland to Germany should become a fact, her place in the French system would be filled by Soviet Russia. Against such a combination Germany and Italy, as long as they are divided by the question of Austria, can, despite Mussolini's efforts, make no common cause. Nor is Great Britain, increasingly apprehensive over the menace of the Hitlerian phenomenon, likely to make further effort to diminish the military superiority of France, which may tomorrow be an ally against Germany, once more a prospective opponent.

Finally, however, as the successive murders of Duca, Dollfuss, and King Alexander and the several crises these crimes precipitated—above all, the crisis of December, 1934—plainly demonstrated, Balkan conditions remain fundamentally unstable. And as the World

War was precipitated by the event of Serajevo, another general conflict could be similarly produced by some new act of violence destroying the precarious peace which today exists in the regions between Innsbruck and Salonika.

The fact that the Yugoslav threats to Hungary in December, 1934, did not have more serious consequences than those revealed in the temporary crisis at Geneva, was due to the resolution of France and Italy not to permit themselves to be drawn into collision with each other by the clash between their smaller allies. And the intervention of both Britain and the Soviet Union fortified that resolution.

For the moment a Concert of Europe was thus reestablished, and Germany, occupied with the Saar plebiscite, was under no temptation to challenge it. Nevertheless, during and after this December crisis, Europe continued to reflect upon what might have happened had Italy supported Hungary then as Russia had backed Serbia in 1914.

Chapter XVI

THE PROBLEM OF EUROPEAN PEACE

IT remains now to summarize briefly the results of the foregoing survey of the causes and character of the national policies of the Great Powers and lesser states of the European region. For it is self-evident that it is from the collective consequences of these policies that the problem of peace in contemporary Europe actually arises.

At the very outset, it was noted that during the three centuries preceding the World War the doctrine of the balance of power had exercised a controlling influence upon European statesmanship. In the same fashion, between Waterloo and the Marne, the Concert of Europe constituted the nearest approach to international authority in the Old World. At the Paris Conference and on the initiative of Woodrow Wilson, however, it was proposed to substitute the principle of self-determination for the balance of power, and the League of Nations for the Concert of Europe.

But when confronted by the consequences of the application of the principle of self-determination to the situation of the Germans, the statesmen of the Paris Conference reverted to the doctrine of the balance of power. They did this because to have permitted the seventy-five millions of German-speaking people of the former Hohenzollern and Hapsburg empires to unite would have established a state potentially as dangerous to European independence as the France of Louis XIV or of Napoleon Bonaparte.

In thus reverting to the doctrine of the balance of power, however, the statesmen of Paris fatally compromised their projected League of Nations. For at the bottom of the Wilsonian project was the double assumption that all peoples were prepared to pledge themselves to respect the frontiers of their neighbors and that each nation was ready to assume its share of the costs of restraining a country which violated this pledge. When, however, the German people, outraged by the terms of the Paris Settlement and identifying the denial of their right to the benefits of the principle of self-determination as a breach of faith, refused to accept as definitive the territorial decisions of the Treaty of Versailles and thus disclosed their purpose not to respect the frontiers of other countries, the first of the Wilsonian assumptions broke down. When, too, the United States and Great Britain, in turn, declined to lend their forces to protect the frontiers of nations menaced by German and other revisionary projects, the second collapsed as well.

Thenceforth, the European stage was dominated by the clash of rival policies. The Germans subordinated all else to the demand for treaty revision. The French set security above everything. The British sought profitable and inexpensive peace through an attempt to establish a balance of power between Germany and France. The Italians strove to profit alike in prestige and in more material things by exploiting Franco-German disputes. The smaller states ranged themselves about the great, as their interests dictated.

Inescapably, therefore, the League of Nations, which had become the meeting place of the statesmen of Europe, also became the battleground of conflicting policies. Each nation sought to exploit the League machinery to serve its own policy, although Italy, finding the League itself an obstacle to her ambitions, carried on a campaign of sabotage against it.

When, however, Germany in despair and desperation flung herself into the arms of Hitler and thus accepted the National Socialist prescription of violence as the method to achieve treaty revision, Europe as a whole took alarm. After the murder of Dollfuss in July, 1934, Germany was surrounded by a circle of steel; Italy mounted guard at Vienna diplomatically, while Great Britain officially, though without success, urged the Reich to accept the Franco-Russian project for regional pacts which would commit her to the recognition of the territorial decisions of the Treaty of Versailles as immutable.

Confronted by the rise of another common peril, Europe therefore followed its traditional course. On the one hand, it moved instinctively toward coalition against the nation which was universally identified as constituting a danger to European liberty, and on the other it hastened to multiply its armaments and extend its fortifications. Differences between Paris and London were laid aside, animosities between Rome and Paris softened. Moscow forgot its quarrel with capitalistic countries, and these countries put behind them their fears of the Red Peril.

The German "Blood Bath" of June, 1934, like the invasion of Belgium twenty years earlier, rallied public sentiment the world over against Germany. The Austrian *Putsch* of July completed the achievement. Thereafter, Great Britain lost interest in German demands for equality in armaments, and Italy abandoned hope of extracting profit from the Franco-German deadlock. After a decade and a half, the territorial decisions of the Treaty of Versailles still stood, and Germany was again as isolated as she had been when the Paris Settlement was made.

Nevertheless, the student of international affairs must perceive that, if for the moment adjourned, the major problem of peace in Europe remains intact and unsolved, and that it is primarily the problem of finding a basis of adjustment between the right of the German people to unity and prosperity and the right of Europe to security. Austria has become the focal point in that problem. Today the German people are as unwilling as ever to accept the status quo of Versailles, and while France and her allies were as resolved in 1934 as in 1919 not to permit German rearmament without Anglo-Saxon guarantees which would insure their own security, Italy stood with them in opposition to German designs on Austria and the Danubian area.

The Germany of self-determination seemed at the Paris Conference a potential threat to European independence. The Germany of the Paris Settlement—that is, a Germany consonant with the principle of the balance of power—continues to appear in German eyes intolerable. The rise of Hitler and the reversion of Germany to doctrines of violence has momentarily united most of Europe in opposition to German policy, and that unity may well endure as long as the present National Socialist regime survives in the Reich, as it will certainly last as long as that regime adheres to its original program. But a change in regime might well be followed by a change alike in British and in Italian policy.

Had Hitler chosen to look east instead of south for the realization of his dream of expansion, a German-Italian alliance to counterbalance that of France and the Little Entente might have come into being. Had Goering not repeated the blunder of Tirpitz, this time in aerial instead of naval armaments, Great Britain might have watched with outward protest but inward satisfaction the division of Europe into two systems of alliances. Had the National Socialists not proposed to seize the Ukraine, as the prewar rulers undertook to control at Constantinople, Soviet Russia might not have followed the example of Czarist Russia in striking hands with France. Thus the present European situation was quite literally "made in Germany."

Fundamentally, moreover, not only solution but even accommodation of the crisis which has endured in the European region ever since the close of the World War still waits upon the decision of the German people in the face of familiar alternatives. Either they must accept a status quo which, as the victors of 1918 designed, leaves the future of the Reich hopelessly restricted in respect both of economic prosperity and of ethnic unity, or they must concentrate their efforts upon preparation to overthrow that status quo by force.

Change of regime in the Reich, civil disorder involving the substitution of one form of dictatorship for another, restoration of the Throne or collapse to Communism, these by producing prostration and paralysis within the nation can compel Germany to accept another truce of exhaustion like that which followed the occupation of the Ruhr. But, as the recent past has demonstrated, domestic collapse cannot permanently abolish the purpose of the German people to establish in Central Europe an economic and political unit, vaguely recalling the Holy Roman Empire of the long past and more definitely the Mittel-europa of the World War.

Only co-ordination of policy among the European nations great and small, resulting in the creation of a system of political order and of economic prosperity in the Danubian region, could extinguish either the hope or the possibility of German success in this enterprise. Even such co-operation would be doomed to eventual failure unless the German people themselves ultimately became reconciled to their territorial circumstances. For while recent events have demonstrated that European powers can unite to restrain a Reich which has become a common peril, European history demonstrates that such coalitions are foredoomed to dissolution, once the immediate emergency which called them into existence has passed.

After 1815, there did survive among the nations which had overthrown Napoleon a sufficient degree of unity, dictated by common fear of France, to guarantee the permanence of the structure of Vienna during the first critical years. When that unity was destroyed following the Revolution of 1848, France was no longer strong enough to resume her struggle for Continental hegemony. After 1918, however, the successful coalition broke up almost at once, because victory had abolished any further fear of Germany in the Anglo-Saxon powers. As a consequence of Anglo-Saxon policy, the League of Nations, unlike the Concert of Europe a century before, was unable to exercise authority, because it lacked force. In French eyes, however, German recovery was irreconcilable with French security, precisely as long as that security lacked an Anglo-Saxon guarantee. To establish any basis of order in Europe between 1918 and 1935 the Anglo-Saxon nations had either to satisfy or to coerce France; for French power was at all times adequate to prevent German recovery, as was demonstrated alike in the Ruhr in 1923 and in Vienna in 1931, at the time of the projected Austro-German tariff union.

The attempts of the Anglo-Saxon countries to promote the economic recovery of Germany without concern for French security, since the former was a vital concern to them and the latter of less importance, have so far only contributed to the eventual ruin of the Reich because they have encouraged a resistance to France which was foredoomed to failure and brought economic ruin and political upheaval in its train.

The World War, the Paris Conference, and the postwar diplomacy have, each in its turn, failed to accomplish any material transformation in the traditional political circumstances of the Old World. On the contrary, the doctrine of the balance of power still continues to be the sole means of assuring European independence, and a coalition of endangered states the only means of upholding that doctrine. Now, as in the past, however, while such a coalition may avail temporarily to restrain an aggressor, it cannot provide any permanent system of order. Such transitory truce as it furnishes is based upon force and guaranteed by armaments. As a consequence, any real or even apparent shift in the resources of force inevitably serves as an invitation to a new adventure.

Fundamentally, therefore, the political situation in the European region remains today what it has been for approximately three centuries. Now, as ever since the Thirty Years War, there is a tradition of unity, which invariably finds expression in coalition in the face of common danger. But there is no basis or capacity for the continuation of such co-operation beyond the period of actual danger. Thus, seemingly at least, a United States of Europe is still as far removed from actuality as it has been at any time since the nation states system took definitive form and European history assumed its familiar pattern.

In the foregoing chapters, moreover, emphasis has been laid upon the fact that while the political circumstances of the Old World have been little altered as a consequence of the World War and the postwar developments, the economic circumstances have been revolutionized. Wholly aside from the old issues which divided states, such as the questions of national security and ethnic unity, there have arisen economic problems, whose gravity has been accentuated by the Great Depression.

Thus, for at least two of the Great Powers of the European region, Germany and Italy, the absence of economic self-sufficiency and the operation of population pressure have dictated the adoption of dynamic policies envisaging the revision of the territorial status quo. And on the economic side these policies are in no sense the exclusive consequence of the nature of the Paris Settlement; for while Germany was defeated and diminished, Italy was victorious and expanded.

On the contrary, in both cases it is the present lack of most of the chief essentials of industry, together with the growing inadequacy of domestic food supplies, that explains the expansionist policies of the two countries, quite as much as any hunger for power or for prestige. To buy abroad the foodstuffs and raw materials necessary to support national life and industry, these nations must sell their manufactures or their labor, and against both practices the more fortunate states are progressively closing their doors. The result is that both the German and the Italian people are confronted by the prospect of a growing disparity between their own standard of living and that of their neighbors.

Revision of the territorial decisions of the Paris Peace Conference to satisfy the strategic or ethnic claims of Germany and Italy would not bestow upon either country the requisite resources in raw materials and foodstuffs or the necessary additional markets. Both nations, therefore, have turned their attention toward the Danubian Basin as a sphere of economic as well as political influence. But this development has in turn led to the collision in interests of the two Great Powers whose policies are dynamic.

If, then, the problem of peace in Europe is primarily the problem of finding a basis of adjustment between the right of the German people to unity and that of Europe to security, it manifestly is also, to an extent hardly secondary, a question of discovering some method of establishing equality in economic opportunity among the peoples of the Continent. For it must be self-evident that no great people will without violent reaction permanently endure such disparity in national well-being as under present circumstances must exist between the Germans and the Italians on the one hand and the British and the French on the other. But it is today equally unmistakable that none of the more fortunate powers is prepared to share its superior resources with the less fortunate nations.

In Asia, the Japanese people, in the same circumstances as the German and the Italian, have undertaken by violence to escape from their economic handicaps. In Europe, however, such escape is impossible because the doctrine of the balance of power, although invoked to support the territorial status quo, operates in an identical fashion to preserve the economic status quo. Were the Soviet Union and Turkey as helpless as is China, it is clear that German and Italian imperialism would, as they long ago planned to do, repeat the achievement of the Japanese by making Ukraine and Anatolia the fields of expansion. Under existing circumstances, however, both regions are defended by armies sufficiently strong to discourage aggression.

The problem of peace in the European region therefore remains intact and it has its origin in the fact that, politically and economically, the interests of the Great Powers of the Old World are irreconcilable on any terms consonant with the principle of absolute sovereignty, which is the basic conception of the nation states system. For any viable system of order that might be established under existing conditions would necessarily demand a sacrifice on the part of the more fortunate peoples or a surrender on the part of the less, equally incompatible with the present conception of sovereignty.

The crisis of December, 1934, precipitated by Yugoslav demands both upon the League and upon Hungary, served, too, to reveal with startling clarity the fashion in which the contemporary situation in the Danubian region resembled the conditions of 1914 in the Balkans, out of which the World War had arisen. In the earlier year, it had been the quarrel between Russia and Austria over Serbia which led to the catastrophe. In the later year, French support of Yugoslavia and Italian support of Hungary made the clash of interests between Budapest and Belgrade a similar menace to the peace of Europe.

After the murder of the Archduke in Serajevo, the Austro-Hungarian government decided to seize upon the issue thus created to dispose of the Serbian threat to the unity of the Hapsburg Monarchy, and it was the ultimatum dispatched by Vienna to Belgrade which led to conflict. After the assassination of King Alexander in Marseille, the Yugoslav government adopted a similar course and with an identical objective in view. Magyar irredentism, like Serb, constituted a standing menace. The brutal crime of Marseille provided the same pretext as that of Serajevo.

In 1934 all of the nations of the Little Entente,— Rumania and Czechoslovakia as well as Yugoslavia,— feeling the same threat, stood together against the Hungarians. Their real purpose, however, was to force Italy to renounce her support of Hungary and compel the Magyars to come to terms with the Little Entente. And, of course, the Austrian purpose in 1914 had been to compel Russia to abandon her support of Serbia and force the latter to come to terms with the Hapsburg Monarchy.

Like the Austrian policy in 1914, that of the Little Entente twenty years later was a policy of desperation. It deliberately risked the peace of Europe in the pursuit of security. It presented a pistol at the head of the League of Nations and it confronted both France and Italy with unwelcome alternatives. If France declined to support the Little Entente, her diplomatic position in

Europe was at an end. If Italy abandoned Hungary, her prestige in Central Europe would disappear. But if both countries supported their respective allies, then they were bound to come into collision. Such a collision, however, both desired to avoid, because conflict in such circumstances could only prove disastrous to each.

Much the same situation in a less acute form had existed at the close of the two Balkan Wars of 1912–13, when Austria had supported Bulgaria and Russia had championed Serbia. Fortunately at that time Germany had acted to restrain her Austrian ally and France and Great Britain to hold back their Russian partner, and the Council of Ambassadors had been able to reach a peaceful solution of the immediate issue. No solution, however, was to be discovered for the major problem, which arose from the resolution of the Serbs to liberate the Southern Slavs of the Dual Monarchy. As a consequence, when the crime of Serajevo lent new emphasis to that issue, Austria embarked upon her fatal policy designed to deal with the Serb danger once and for all.

Once Austria had acted, moreover, it was inevitable that Russia should defend Serbia, that Germany should stand with Austria, and that France and Britain should support Russia. So the World War came. What, then, was of first interest in December, 1934, was whether the League could succeed as the Council of Ambassadors had succeeded in 1913. But what was also plain was that while it might, as it actually did, repeat the achievement of old-fashioned diplomacy two decades earlier, that success would be of little permanent value unless it were followed by some solution of the larger problem.

In a word, war might be postponed again as before, because once more all the interested Great Powers shared the same desire for peace. But as long as the Hungarians were determined to rescue their subject minorities, as the Serbs had been resolved to liberate their fellow Slavs, the peril would remain and a new incident could provoke a fresh crisis. To establish real peace in the Danubian region, Hungary would either have to be destroyed or her wholly legitimate demand for the return of at least one and a half million of the three millions of Magyars taken by the Treaty of Trianon would have to be honored. And since the Great Powers had once more involved themselves in the quarrels of the smaller powers, European peace was also contingent upon such an adjustment.

Primarily this latest crisis had its origin in ethnic issues created by the Treaty of Trianon. Hungary had been sacrificed to the appetites of the three Succession States—Yugoslavia, Czechoslovakia, and Rumania. And in the same fashion Austria had been denied the exercise of the right of self-determination in the name of security. Fundamentally, however, the political anarchy in the Danubian region had its cause in the failure to substitute any economic order for that which had existed before 1918, while the Hapsburg Monarchy still endured.

It was material misery which invested the "Nazi" movement with vitality in Austria, and economic prostration which accentuated the ethnic wrongs of Hungary. The clash of policy between France and Italy had steadily from 1919 to 1934 prevented any solution of either the ethnic or the economic problem, since the French supported the nations of the Little Entente in their insistence upon the maintenance of the status quo, while the Italians encouraged the Hungarians in their demand for treaty revision.

When, in 1934, the disclosure of German purposes in
Austria alarmed both Rome and Paris, and the two
Latin nations which had long been at odds over Danubian questions were driven by German events to come to
agreement in the face of a common peril, then the
repercussions in Central Europe were immediate. The
nations of the Little Entente by their violent and provocative treatment of Hungary sought to force the French
hand, while the Magyars turned to Italy as their single
friend. Alarmed by the implications of the crisis,
Britain and the Soviet Union strove to restore a common
front between the Great Powers. As for the Germans,
they were able to sit back and watch the progress of an
episode predestined, so it at least appeared, to be profitable for them alone.

Nor was it less plain that catastrophe would be at
most only postponed if the crisis were not followed by
adjustment of the economic as well as the ethnic problem. For otherwise the pressure of material misery was
bound to drive governments to provocative moves
abroad to avoid fatal disorders at home. Thus, although
the Council of the League was able to resolve the
Hungarian-Yugoslav crisis, since the solution of the
problems responsible for that crisis was beyond its
capacity, peace in the Danubian region continued to be
precarious.

Chapter XVII

THE AMERICAN REGION

BETWEEN the conditions of the American region and those of the European region the difference is impressive. Whereas in the Old World rival powers have for centuries struggled for mastery, in the New World the disproportionate strength of the United States has long assured it an unquestioned supremacy. Possession of irresistible strength has not, however, at least in the present century, tempted the United States to attempt military conquest, even where it has been moved to undertake temporary intervention. Accordingly, while these transitory interferences have aroused passing apprehensions among the smaller states, they have never driven those states to unite to establish a balance of power.

Again, while the Americas, like Asia, are the seat of but one Great Power, the two regions differ in all other essential respects. In the former there is no clash of rival imperialisms such as constitutes the significant detail of the latter. On the contrary, between the Dominion of Canada and the United States peace has become a tradition and the status quo is mutually satisfactory. And while anarchy is not an unfamiliar detail in various Latin-American areas, notably in the Caribbean, there is nothing anywhere to parallel Chinese conditions.

In fact, what constitutes the unique characteristic of the American region is the total absence of any problem having its origin in the clash of the domestic interests of Great Powers or in the collision of their imperial enterprises. Sufficiently strong itself to forbid any European or Asiatic power to engage in imperialistic adventure within the Americas, the United States has today no purpose which could constitute even a remote threat to the sovereignty or security of any other American state, large or small.

While, too, the United States stands ready to protect the states of Latin America against invasive imperialism, whether European or Asiatic, the rapid expansion of many of the larger of these nations in population and in resources has already brought them to the point where they are capable of defending their own liberty and unity unaided,[1] and are even openly resentful of any pretension on the part of the United States to play the unnecessary role of protector. Finally, so far as any question of peace or war can arise within the American region itself, that can hardly go beyond the limits of a minor dispute over boundaries such as the war between Bolivia and Paraguay about the Gran Chaco.[2]

Within the relatively enormous area of the two Americas, moreover, there are lacking economic as well as political conditions like those which are responsible for European and Asiatic turmoil. Everywhere, save in a

[1] Haring, C. H., *South America Looks at the United States*, 1928; Rippy, J. F., *Latin America in World Politics*, 1931.

[2] Foreign Policy Association, "Unsettled Boundary Disputes in Latin America," *Information Service*, Vol. V, No. 26, 1930.

few insignificant islands, the population is sparse, and the land fertile and easily available. Nowhere does the population pressure exert its disruptive influence as in Italy and Japan. In all states prosperity is still a problem of national development and not of territorial expansion. Finally, disputes having their origin in ethnic issues are totally lacking, and consequently psychological conditions do not, as in Europe and Asia, constitute barriers to international accord.

Precisely as the disproportionate strength of the United States has failed to produce any resort to the European balance of power technique by the lesser American states, the development of the larger of the Latin American nations has likewise been unattended by any menacing rivalries having their origin in questions of prestige or sentiments of jealousy.[1] Already Brazil has outdistanced both France and Italy and become the largest of the Latin nations. While there is actual rivalry between Brazil and Argentina, for example, yet, since it is a competition in progress rather than in power, there is in their relations nothing to suggest the bitterness which characterizes the relations of Italy and France.

In dealing with the two Americas, Nature has been unequally lavish, bestowing upon both vast agricultural resources but limiting to North America the abundant essentials of industry;[2] and it follows naturally that, with the exception of Brazil and the smaller states of the Caribbean and Pacific coasts, the economic relations of Latin America with Europe are at least as important as those with the United States. It is in Great Britain, France, and Germany rather than in the great North

[1] Robertson, W. S., *History of the Latin-American Nations*, rev. ed., 1932.
[2] Emeny, Brooks, *The Strategy of Raw Materials; A Study of America in Peace and War*, 1934; Rouma, Georges, *Les Ressources Economiques de l'Amérique Latine*, 1923.

American republic that many South American peoples find markets for their foodstuffs and raw materials. And it is from their European customers rather than their American competitor that they buy more considerably.[1]

Culturally, too, the face of Latin America is turned toward Europe and not toward the United States. Paris and Madrid, rather than New York and Washington, attract its leisure classes. In art, literature, and music, France and not the greatest of the American republics comes first. For Canada, by contrast, economic relations with the United States are far more considerable than with Europe, and the influence of New York upon the press and thought of the great Dominion is also much greater than that of London.

Politically, however, the attention of all of the states of both Americas is directed toward the United States and not toward Europe. On the part of Latin America, it is true that this attention has in the past been marked by at least as much suspicion as sympathy, and the continued membership of most of these states in the League of Nations has been influenced considerably by this fact.[2] In the case of Canada, on the other hand, there is happily absent any element of distrust, and while the two English-speaking neighbors quarrel over business and dispute about tariffs, their frontiers remain unfortified. The presence of Canada in the League of Nations is explained by British imperial consideration rather than by any de-

[1] Cooper, C. S., *Latin America: Men and Markets*, 1927; Jones, C. F., *Commerce of South America*, 1928; Lee, T. F., *Latin American Problems*, 1932; Normano, J. F., *The Struggle for South America*, 1931; *South American Handbook*, Annual since 1924.

[2] Every Latin-American Republic is or has been a member of the League, Ecuador having been admitted in 1934. At the end of 1934 the only American non-members were the United States, Costa Rica, and Brazil; Costa Rica having resigned in 1927 and Brazil the following year. For general survey of the policies of Latin American states toward the League, see: Kelchner, W. H., *Latin American Relations with the League of Nations*, 1930.

sire to counterbalance the influence of the United States.

In reality, then, the Americas constitute not merely a region but almost a world within themselves. Such regional problems and provincial rivalries as exist within their limits are without concern for the outside world, while for the nations of North and South America alike, disturbances in Europe or Asia are primarily of importance because of their effect upon domestic trade and commerce. Of all of the American nations, none save the United States can exert real influence beyond the Atlantic or the Pacific; and within the American region, foreign nations have, in recent years at least, invariably respected the wishes of the United States.

Were the United States at some future time to set forth on a career of imperialism in Latin America, it is far from impossible that it might one day have to face the resistance of a coalition of the southern republics united to establish some form of balance of power. Under such circumstances, too, European powers might conceivably undertake to fish in troubled waters as Napoleon III intervened in Mexico while the United States was paralyzed by Civil War. Similarly, were there to be a revival of the once familiar annexationist policy in respect of Canada, Anglo-American relations might take on a different aspect and Great Britain might strive to repeat in the Americas the policy of balance of power she has pursued in Europe.

Such speculations, however, are without present basis. Today in the American region only two things are important: first, the fact that, because of its strength, the United States has asserted and all other powers have in the end accepted the Monroe Doctrine which insures the preservation of the status quo in both Americas; second, the equally significant fact that the United States has attained the continental limits and acquired the advantages of an insular position which respectively satisfy its own standards of prosperity and of security. And, together, these deprive its policy of all threat to any other American state, large or small.

Supremacy in the Western Hemisphere the United States undeniably possesses. It is, moreover, difficult to see what limits could be set to its imperialism, if it should undertake to follow the traditional pattern of foreign expansion. But although from time to time such an enterprise has seemed possible and even probable, on every occasion it has ultimately been rejected by the conscience and common sense of its own people. Nor is it less unmistakable that at the present time the direction of public opinion in the United States is away from economic as well as territorial imperialism and toward the "Good Neighbor" ideal of Franklin D. Roosevelt.

It is, of course, geographic isolation and economic good fortune which together explain the difference between the political conditions in the American region and those in the European and Asiatic regions. Looking to the distant future, it is possible to conjecture that the Americas may in their turn presently be assailed by those evils which attend the economic and political maturity of continents as well as of countries. The student of international relations must therefore recognize that differences in the physical circumstances and historical background of Europe and America, and not in ethical or intellectual details, explain the fact that the tradition of the American region is peace whereas that of the Asiatic and the European regions is war.

The fact that the American region has no concern for

"natural frontiers," no problem of ethnic minorities, no curse of "lost provinces," the circumstance that no state, large or small, is confronted by the consequences of population pressure, and the further detail that as a result of these conditions the policies of all American countries are static and not dynamic, certainly explain the comparatively fortunate condition of the Western Hemisphere. But all these things are in their turn simply explicable in terms of physical geography, economic circumstance, and historical development.

It is natural, therefore, that such inter-American problems as exist should find adjustment either through normal diplomatic channels or within so loosely knit an association as the Pan-American Union.[1] For not only are circumstances absent from the American region which would necessitate a complicated organization like the League of Nations, but also European conceptions of sanctions and balance of power, arising from the eternal conflict between status quo and revisionist states, are alien to American thought and action.

The essential fact about the American region today, then, is that, unlike the European and Asiatic regions, it is confronted by no problem of power from within its own area and directly affected by none originating beyond its limits. Only the national policy of the United States among all the states of both Americas has importance for international relations, and for the American

[1] Carnegie Endowment for International Peace, "The Sixth International Conference of American States," *International Conciliation*, No. 241, 1928; also "The Montevideo Conference, Antecedents and Accomplishments," *International Conciliation*, No. 300, 1934; Foreign Policy Association, "The Seventh Pan-American Conference," *Foreign Policy Reports*, Vol. X, No. 7, 1934; also "The Pan-American Arbitration Treaty," Vol. V, No. 18, 1929; Inman, S. G., *Problems in Pan Americanism*, 1925; Lockey, J. B., *Pan-Americanism; Its Beginnings*, 1920; Scott, J. B., *ed.*, *The International Conferences of American States, 1889-1928*, 1931; Urrutia, F. J., *Le Continent Américain et le Droit International*, 1928.

346   REGIONAL AND WORLD POLITICS

region the policies of European and Asiatic powers are without real significance.

Even the consequences for the Americas of Canadian participation in another European conflict, or involvement in future Asiatic conflicts of the British Empire, would be relatively minor. On the other hand, if the United States were to participate either in a European or in an Asiatic war, the American region as a whole would be involved directly or indirectly and many of the states might again, as in 1917,[1] find it to their advantage to ally themselves with the great North American republic.

It is, therefore, as the American region constitutes a setting for the national policy of the United States that it has world importance. Even in this respect, also, its influence is negative rather than positive; for it is the absence from the Americas of precisely those regional circumstances which are characteristic of Europe and Asia that bestows upon the United States a freedom to act elsewhere, unhampered by concern over conditions of security within its own region.

British policy, wherever in the world the British Empire has interests, is always handicapped by the perils incident to the proximity of the British Isles to the European Continent. French action in Asia or in Africa is likewise invariably conditioned upon the existing situation beyond the Rhine and the Alps. Soviet Russia, like Czarist Russia before it, whether facing west in Europe or east in Asia, must always reckon with the possibility of attack in the rear. Finally, Japan, even when she is able to control the seas which have importance for her, is confronted by circumstances on the Asiatic mainland at once beyond her control and perilous to her security.

[1] Martin, P. A., *Latin America and the War*, 1925.

By contrast, two broad oceans give the United States identical security against attack whether coming from Europe or from Asia. In addition, her control of the Caribbean gateway to the Panama Canal is far more complete than the British hold upon the Mediterranean approach to Suez can ever be, and her land frontiers alike at the Rio Grande and at the St. Lawrence River constitute no danger. As a consequence, she is free to adventure in Europe or in Asia as she may choose, ever tranquil as to her own domestic security. That, after all, is the significance of the regional situation of the United States, and that regional situation itself is important to the world only in its relation to the one and only Great Power of the Americas.

Chapter XVIII

THE UNITED STATES[1]

THE years which separate the administrations of the two Roosevelts have witnessed an almost incredible transformation in the circumstances of the United States.[2] Thus, in the brief span of a single generation, the practice of intervention has been substituted for the tradition of regional isolation. Simultaneously, the role of a debtor nation has been exchanged for that of a creditor nation, and a predominantly agricultural position for that of the most extensively industrialized state in the world. And, finally, from the strategic point of view, the United

[1] In the study of American foreign policy the student should have available for general reference the following: Howland, C. P., *ed.*, *Survey of American Foreign Relations*, 1928–31, 4 vols.; Lippmann, Walter, and Scroggs, W. O., *The United States in World Affairs*, annual since 1931; Toynbee, A. J., *Survey of International Affairs*, annual; Wheeler-Bennett, J. W., *ed.*, *Documents on International Affairs*, annual since 1930; Foreign Policy Association, *Foreign Policy Reports*, fortnightly; *Foreign Affairs*, quarterly; Carnegie Endowment for International Peace, *International Conciliation*, monthly; World Peace Foundation publications.

[2] Adams, J. T., *The Epic of America*, 1931; Beard, C. A., and Beard, Mary, *The Rise of American Civilization*, Vols. 2, 1927; Malin, J. C., *The United States after the World War*, 1930; National Bureau of Economic Research, *Recent Economic Changes in the United States*, 1929, 2 vols.; Patterson, E. M., *America: World Leader or World Led?*, 1932; Slosson, P. W., *The Great Crusade and After, 1914-1928*, 1930; Williams, B. H., *Economic Foreign Policy of the United States*, 1929.

States has, through the construction of the Panama Canal and the establishment of a fleet equal to the British, attained absolute regional and territorial security.

What has, however, constituted and still constitutes the most striking detail in the contemporary situation is that public opinion in the United States has not kept pace with the physical change in the circumstances of the nation. Confronted by a wholly new international situation, the American people have, as yet, decided upon no viable compromise between tradition and actuality.[1] On the contrary, they, like the British, continue to cherish an apparently ineradicable instinct for "muddling through." Inevitably, the result has been an endless series of contradictions and a long-protracted period of confusion. Thus while the national policies of many other powers have seemed clear and their objectives unmistakable, it has always been and still remains a matter of conjecture what ends the people of the United States actually seek.

To explain these contradictions of policy, it is necessary first to examine the circumstances of the United States and particularly its situation in respect of security, prosperity, and unity. As to unity, that may be dismissed at once, for no ethnic problem such as confronts various European nations, great and small alike, exists anywhere in the American region. Security and prosperity, therefore, are the sole objectives of the national policy of the United States.

Once, however, the question of security is considered, it becomes evident how completely different is the situation of the United States in this respect from that of any

---

[1] Madariaga, S. de, *I Americans*, 1931; Simonds, F. H., *Can America Stay at Home?*, 1932; Whitton, J. B., *Isolation: An Obsolete Principle of the Monroe Doctrine*, 1933.

other Great Power. While for all others there exist perils which are real and in many cases immediate as well, such dangers as it is possible to conjure up for the United States appear by comparison remote and even shadowy. In fact, the fears of foreign attack which still lurk in the American mind seem based upon traditions coming down to us from the Revolution and the War of 1812 rather than founded on contemporary realities.

Actually, the geographic situation of the United States, separated as it is by broad oceans alike from Europe and from Asia, bestows upon it an immunity from foreign danger enjoyed by no other Great Power. When, moreover, that safety, due to distance, was doubled by an assured naval supremacy in the waters of the American region, the security of the United States became, at least in the eyes of the peoples of all other Great Powers, little short of absolute.

With the withdrawal of the soldiers of Napoleon III from Mexico, a withdrawal which itself represented inescapable surrender to the demands of the United States when released from the restraints of the Civil War, the era of military intervention by Europe in the Americas came to an end. The equally complete surrender of Germany in the Venezuelan affair nearly four decades later put a similar term to foreign naval adventure in American waters. When, too, following the extinction of Spanish rule in the New World in 1898, the British voluntarily withdrew their fleet from the Caribbean Sea, the last potential challenge to American supremacy in the waters of the western Atlantic disappeared. The construction of the Panama Canal, together with the earlier annexation of Hawaii, presently bestowed similar supremacy in the eastern Pacific Ocean.

With the annexation of the Philippines, the proclamation of the doctrine of the Open Door, and the participation of American troops in the suppression of the Boxer revolt, the United States renounced isolation for intervention in the Far East and resumed a course which had been momentarily adopted half a century earlier, when Perry entered Japanese waters. Similar intervention was foreshadowed in respect of Europe when American representatives attended the Algeciras Conference, and was consummated when the United States became a belligerent during the World War.

National policy has therefore outrun national tradition. Between 1898 and 1918 the United States in practice renounced isolation for intervention, with the appearance of its armies alike in China and Siberia and in France and Germany; but at the Washington Naval Conference in 1921–22 it also claimed for itself naval parity with Great Britain and superiority over Japan which would insure for it supremacy in the American region. That claim, partly realized in the American capital in 1922, was fully recognized in London in 1930. But when Japan denounced the Treaty of Washington in December, 1934, the naval issue again came to the fore.[1]

Security for the United States, however, no longer constitutes a problem of policy nor can it become a question of national concern as long as the people of the country are prepared to support a navy of present relative proportions. For all practical purposes, the Monroe and Caribbean doctrines, the former seeking to exclude European imperialism from American shores and the latter to establish American naval supremacy in waters which constitute the approaches to the Panama Canal,

[1] *Cf.* Chapter XXVII.

have become past history because both have been universally and voluntarily accepted by those countries which might formerly have challenged them.

Henceforth, both European and Asiatic powers are hardly more likely to attempt imperialistic adventures in the Americas than in the moon. For any calculable future only an admiralty which is an annex of Bedlam could think of challenging the American fleet in its own waters. Once Great Britain, in the Conferences of Washington and London, had recognized the right of the United States to naval parity and an American administration had come to power ready to translate that right into reality, the question of security became academic since that security itself had in fact been attained.

By sea, by air, and even by land, the United States is today immune from attack. London, Paris, Berlin, Rome, and Tokyo are easily accessible targets for air raids launched from the territories of prospective or potential enemies. Washington, by contrast, is almost as safe from aerial threat in 1934 as it was a century ago. And in the same fashion, while all the European Continental powers are condemned to face the dangers of invasion by land, the United States can consider with equal tranquillity the situation at its boundaries on the north and on the south.

Distance from possible enemies and decisive naval superiority in its home waters, however, are only the façades of the security of the United States. Behind these is an industrial strength not merely unrivaled but actually unapproached by any other power. And that industrial strength rests not only upon a vast amount of machine power but also upon the largest measure of economic self-sufficiency of any nation, great or small. Security against direct attack by sea, by air, and by land is thus reinforced by immunity from the indirect menace of blockade in war or embargo in peace.[1]

Not only is half the machine power of the world concentrated in the territory of the United States, but in addition, inside its own frontiers (page 359) or within that American region dominated by its fleets (page 363), are practically all of the raw materials and sources of motive power necessary to support national industry in peace or war, together with resources in foodstuffs sufficient to sustain the national population. Even in the case of the few essentials which are lacking, such as rubber and tin, for example, stocks kept on hand and secondary recovery would remove any danger of defeat in war due to shortage in economic necessities.[2]

National prosperity, moreover, has the same foundation as national security. Neither need of additional resources in foodstuffs or raw materials, nor want of fresh reserves in the supplies of motive power, drives American statesmanship to expansion and therefore to dynamic policies. Since, too, the national lands which are rich in all forms of natural wealth are also as yet sparsely settled, no population pressure disturbs American calculations. On the contrary, satiety in the economic field completely reconciles the people of the United States to their status quo.

The very uniqueness of the situation of this country economically, however, poses problems which have no counterpart in the case of any other power. Great Brit-

[1] Beard, C. A., *The Navy: Defense or Portent?*, 1932; Moore, Frederick, *America's Naval Challenge*, 1929; Phelps, Phelps, *Our Defenses Within and Without*, 1932; Williams, B. H., *The United States and Disarmament*, 1931.
[2] Emeny, Brooks, *The Strategy of Raw Materials; A Study of America in Peace and War*, 1934.

UNITED STATES
NATIONAL SELF-SUFFICIENCY IN FOODSTUFFS, ESSENTIAL INDUSTRIAL PRODUCTS, AND RAW MATERIALS
DOMESTIC PRODUCTION AND NET IMPORTS EXPRESSED AS PERCENTAGES OF AVERAGE NATIONAL CONSUMPTION (1925-29)

—— **GREAT ESSENTIALS** ——

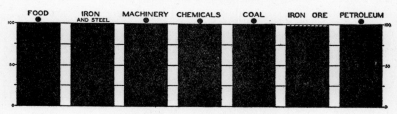

FOOD   IRON AND STEEL   MACHINERY   CHEMICALS   COAL   IRON ORE   PETROLEUM

CRITICAL RAW MATERIALS

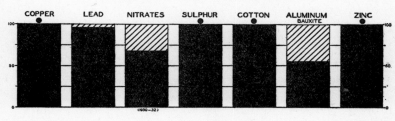

COPPER   LEAD   NITRATES   SULPHUR   COTTON   ALUMINUM BAUXITE   ZINC

(1930-32)

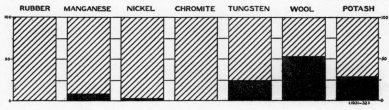

RUBBER   MANGANESE   NICKEL   CHROMITE   TUNGSTEN   WOOL   POTASH

(1931-32)

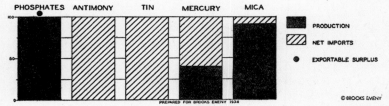

PHOSPHATES   ANTIMONY   TIN   MERCURY   MICA

■ PRODUCTION

▨ NET IMPORTS

● EXPORTABLE SURPLUS

PREPARED FOR BROOKS EMENY 1934

© BROOKS EMENY

ain and Germany, deficient as they are both in foodstuffs and in raw materials, are able to exchange the products of their factories for those of the fields and mines of other countries. Even Japan, as she has risen to the rank of an industrial nation, has come to rely upon foreign sources for iron, food, and cotton. The United States, by contrast, appears on the markets of the world able and eager to sell her manufactures, minerals, meats, and cereals; but what shall she buy? That question is vital, for the student of international relations must accept as axiomatic the fact that nations can, in the larger view, sell abroad only to the extent to which they buy or lend. Small incidental differences between exports and imports, to be sure, can be balanced by gold payments, but the supply of this precious metal is too limited to permit it to serve in the case of constant and considerable annual disparities.

Before the World War, this problem did not exist for the United States, for although even then it annually sold more abroad than it bought, it was still a debtor nation since the holdings of American securities by foreign investors were in excess of American investments abroad. As a consequence, the annual difference between exports and imports sufficed to meet the interest charges on what this country owed to Europe.

The World War, however, changed all that, for, while the United States was still neutral, it sold abroad so much more than it bought that the European nations were compelled to balance the account by turning back to American investors their own holdings in American securities. Even before the United States entered the conflict, therefore, it had already increased its lendings to Europe by billions, not by shipping money to Europe, but by sending great quantities of munitions, food, and other supplies and accepting in exchange the notes of the Allied nations.

Once the war had ended, however, and conditions had become normal again, the United States was faced by a problem of incalculable complexity. European nations owed it upwards of $12,000,000,000 in governmental debts, and private investments abroad exceeded foreign holdings in the United States by some $3,000,000,000. At the same time, the United States was still selling abroad more than it bought.[1] How, then, was it to be paid on the interest and principal of the $15,000,000,000 lent abroad, as well as on the surplus of its foreign sales over its foreign purchases?

For that problem there were but two practical solutions: the United States could either cancel the foreign debts or open its markets to foreign goods by the reduction of its own tariffs. Both solutions, however, were politically out of the question, the first because it involved the transfer of the burden of the $12,000,000,000 owed by the foreign governments to the backs of the domestic taxpayers, and the second because it necessitated letting American workmen stand idle while foreign products crowded the American market.

Since these solutions were politically impossible, the United States rejected both. By contrast, although it insisted upon the payment of the war debts, it also proceeded to raise the duties it levied upon foreign goods.[2] Under these circumstances, a crisis which otherwise

[1] National Industrial Conference Board, *Trends in the Foreign Trade of the United States*, 1930.

[2] Academy of Political Science, "Tariffs and Trade Barriers," *Proceedings*, Vol. XV, No. 3, 1933; Boucke, O. F., *Europe and the American Tariff*, 1933; Wright, P. G., *The American Tariff and Oriental Trade*, 1931.

UNITED STATES

POTENTIAL REGIONAL SELF-SUFFICIENCY IN FOODSTUFFS, ESSENTIAL INDUSTRIAL PRODUCTS, AND RAW MATERIALS

EXPRESSED IN PERCENTAGES OF ALL AVAILABLE SOURCES OF SUPPLY (NATIONAL AND REGIONAL) TO DOMESTIC CONSUMPTION

—— GREAT ESSENTIALS ——

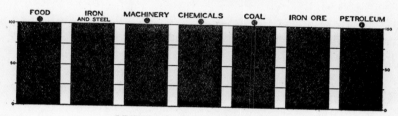

FOOD · IRON AND STEEL · MACHINERY · CHEMICALS · COAL · IRON ORE · PETROLEUM

CRITICAL RAW MATERIALS

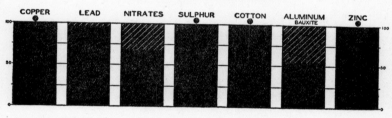

COPPER · LEAD · NITRATES · SULPHUR · COTTON · ALUMINUM BAUXITE · ZINC

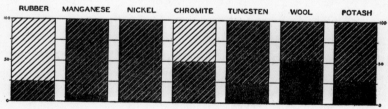

RUBBER · MANGANESE · NICKEL · CHROMITE · TUNGSTEN · WOOL · POTASH

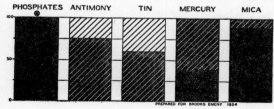

PHOSPHATES · ANTIMONY · TIN · MERCURY · MICA

■ AVERAGE DOMESTIC PRODUCTION

▨ NECESSARY EXTRA-AMERICAN IMPORTS

● EXPORTABLE SURPLUS

▨ ADDITIONAL SUPPLIES POTENTIALLY AVAILABLE FROM INCREASED DOMESTIC OUTPUT AND AMERICAN REGIONAL SOURCES. (SUBSTITUTES, STOCK-PILING, AND SECONDARY RECOVERY NOT CONSIDERED)

© BROOKS EMENY

PREPARED FOR BROOKS EMENY 1934

would have been immediate was temporarily adjourned by an expedient which for the moment escaped general notice. In effect, the investors of the United States proceeded to lend European debtors and customers annually a sum sufficient to cover the interest charges on debts and also the surplus arising from the excess of foreign purchases in America over domestic buying abroad. Thus, between 1920 and 1929, while on the one hand the government debts were but slightly reduced, on the other, American holdings of foreign securities in Europe increased from $3,000,000,000 to $10,000,000,000. As a result, by the end of 1929 the United States was on balance a creditor nation to the tune of $22,000,000,000 instead of $15,000,000,000 as in 1919.[1]

Then in 1929, following the boom and crash in Wall Street, the United States stopped lending. Thereupon, inevitably, the foreign debtors ceased paying and the foreign customers quit buying. As a consequence, the American government and investors were confronted by the default of foreign debtors, and American exporters by a decline of two thirds in their sales abroad.[2] By 1934 foreign interest paying had almost completely stopped and foreign purchase of American goods was limited to amounts covered by American buying of foreign goods and services.

Inevitable as was this outcome of the attempt of the United States to combine the role of a creditor nation with that of a debtor country, the collapse of the experiment produced a popular resentment as general as it was

[1] Angell, J. W., *Financial Foreign Policy of the United States*, 1933; Moulton, H. G., and Pasvolsky, L., *War Debts and World Prosperity*, 1932; Southard, F. A., Jr., *American Industry in Europe*, 1931; Stern, S., *Fourteen Years of European Investments, 1914-1928*, 1929; Stoddard, Lothrop, *Europe and Our Money*, 1932.

[2] Rogers, J. H., *America Weighs Her Gold*, 1931; Simonds, F. H., *The A B C of War Debts*, 1933; Winkler, Max, *Foreign Bonds, an Autopsy*, 1933.

unreasonable. To the minds of the masses, the simple truth that a nation can sell only to the amount that it buys or lends internationally was wholly incomprehensible. The fact that international money does not exist and foreign trade is a process of barter rather than of sale was not to be grasped, and the easier if fallacious explanation based upon moral offending was readily accepted.

American passions, however, were awakened without practical results. To pass legislation forbidding American investors to purchase the securities of defaulting governments, as Congress did, could afford a measure of moral satisfaction, but materially it could not contribute to the collection of a single dollar of all the billions lent abroad or to the sale of an additional bushel of wheat. Nor could a contemporary agitation adequately described by the slogan "Buy American" have any other effect than further to restrict sales as it reduced purchases. And in the same fashion, when American Jews undertook to boycott German goods in reprisal for "Nazi" persecutions, it was American exporters who paid the first costs in reduced sales.

Such, then, is the background of national policy alike in respect of territorial security and in respect of the basic elements of prosperity. In both instances it is manifest that the situation of the United States is without parallel. What, then, must be the objectives of national policy? Obviously, since no direct dangers exist, it must be to remove perils which are at once indirect and relatively remote.

Thus in the matter of security it is clear that the only menace for the United States is not invasion at home but involvement abroad. Peace in Europe is therefore a proper objective of national policy.[1] Again, the similar possibility of involvement in an Asiatic conflict imposes similar aims in the Far East. In the latter field, also, the desire to preserve equality in opportunity in the Chinese market dictates further concern for the status quo in the Orient.[2]

If peace in Europe and the preservation of the status quo in Asia are concerns of American policy, it must, however, be perceived that they are relatively minor interests. They have not for the United States the importance that peace and the status quo in Europe have for the British or the French, for example, or that peace and the status quo in Asia have for the Soviet Union. As a consequence, while the United States has, in the postwar period, consistently sought to promote peace in Europe, it has also steadily refused to assume responsibility for the maintenance of that peace. In the same fashion, while striving to insure the territorial integrity of China, it has always refused to resort to force to insure respect for Chinese sovereignty.

To assist in the prevention of war in Europe and the perpetuation of the status quo in Asia, the United States is prepared to do everything but incur the risk of fighting. It was, moreover, because the Treaty of Versailles and membership in the League of Nations carried the risk of conflict incident to the duties of the Covenant that the United States Senate rejected the treaty. On the other hand, because the Pact of Paris purported to establish peace without engaging responsibility, it was wel-

[1] Simonds, F. H., *America Faces the Next War*, 1933. Also *cf.* Chapters XXII, XXIV, XXVI, XXVII, and XXVIII.

[2] American Academy of Political and Social Science, "American Policy in the Pacific," *Annals*, Vol. 168, 1933; Bau, M. J., *The Open Door Doctrine in Relation to China*, 1923; Clark, Grover, *Economic Rivalries in China*, 1932; also *cf.* Chapters XIX, XXI, and XXII.

comed in Washington. But to the Washington Treaties designed to insure the status quo in Asia, as to the Pact of Paris, the Senate, with the approval of the country, attached reservations excluding all responsibilities for upholding by force what was established by phrase.

This apparent confusion between word and deed, this evident unreadiness to back enthusiasm for principle by effective promise of action, have been responsible for endless criticism both at home and abroad, and for no little confusion of thought, as well. Such confusion in thought, however, has originated in a failure rightly to appraise the true objectives of the policy of the United States. In Europe, that objective is to prevent a war in which the United States might become involved. In Asia it is both to prevent war and also to preclude territorial changes or the establishment of an economic and political hegemony by another Great Power, which might be costly to our national interests.

Clearly, however, to risk war to avoid war would be absurd, while to risk war for trade would be an unprofitable undertaking. And the people of the United States in the postwar period have remained unshaken in their conviction that the extent of the risks incident to guaranteeing peace in Europe would be out of all proportion to the chances that such guarantees might preclude conflict.

To persuade the American people to join the League of Nations, to subscribe to any system of collective responsibility for preserving peace in either Europe or Asia, or to bestow an individual guarantee upon any power in order to promote disarmament, it would be necessary to prove to their satisfaction, first, that only such action would insure their own security or prosperity, and, secondly, that these are directly and gravely endangered by the prospect of conflict. And to make such proof, of course, is today utterly out of the question.

As a consequence, while the people of the United States are at all times prepared to permit their government to participate in international conferences and councils and to sign all forms of self-denying ordinances, they are resolutely opposed to every form of international commitment. "Intervention in words, isolation in action," sums up the proper policy for the country in the eyes of the American people. To disarm the armed nations of Europe is an objective worth seeking alike for moral and for material reasons, but attainment of that objective at the price of involvement is an unattractive project.

In the light of their own present circumstances in respect of security and prosperity, therefore, the people of the United States are satisfied that the risks of foreign responsibilities for the maintenance of peace by force are out of proportion to the possible benefits. This being the case, there is nothing left for administrations which for moral or material reasons are moved to participate in international discussions, but to propose pacts without sanctions, advocate disarmament without security guarantees, and endorse international order uninsured by international policies.

But in the present posture of the world, at least, it is self-evident that all such proposals are foredoomed to failure, and the collapse of the various American projects based on this general principle of peace by consent and not by authority, serves to demonstrate this fact. It is, moreover, open to question whether in thus pressing projects which in the very nature of things cannot suc-

ceed, the United States does not risk entanglements it is
desperately seeking to escape. That conclusion, too, in
recent times has been responsible for a growing impatience with the practice of participation in futile conferences. But it has not prompted any serious proposal
for a change in national policy.

What is, perhaps, worthy at least of passing note is
the extent to which the people of the United States, in
their international relations, have fallen in with the cus-
tom of the British and readily justify as a matter of conscience what is primarily a question of convenience.
Thus, because they are resolved not to give guarantees of
force to maintain world order, the American people pro-
nounce the proposal itself unethical and its supporters
responsive to inspirations which are, as the case may be,
undemocratic, militaristic, or imperialistic.

At bottom, however, the conceptions of the American
people, like their national policy, have their origin in
physical circumstances which are unique.[1] That fact explains the misconceptions of European realities which
are general on this side of the Atlantic. The same emphasis should also be laid upon the tendency of European
people to assume that the conclusions which they have
reached on the basis of their own physical circumstances
hold good for America.

Actually, the question which is still pending in respect to the national policy of the United States is
whether, in view of the extent of its security and the character of the bases of its prosperity, the visible risks of
sharing in a collective system to insure world peace and
order exceed the possible profits. To say that the United
States cannot usefully promote world peace by its present

[1] Semple, E. C., *American History and Its Geographic Conditions*, 1931, rev.

course is to say what is demonstrably true. To insist that, as a consequence, the wise course would be to abstain from futile effort is, at least, not illogical. But to assert that in the world of today, and specifically in Europe and Asia under existing circumstances, the United States could by assuming responsibilities realize profit out of proportion to the risks run is to proclaim what has neither been proved as yet nor is at present susceptible of proof.

Looking back over a century and a half of national existence, it is clear that the policy of the United States has passed through various stages.[1] In the earliest period, the great convulsion of the French Revolution and the Napoleonic epoch, followed by the European Reaction after Waterloo, served to consolidate American resolution to keep out of Europe and to keep Europe out of America. The acquisition of Louisiana from France and of Florida from Spain, followed by the extension of the frontiers of the United States to include Texas and later the conquests of the Mexican War, bestowed upon the nation a territorial estate of satisfying proportions.

As the Napoleonic and post-Napoleonic events in Europe were responsible for the Monroe Doctrine, the Mexican War, in its turn, was the signal for an outburst of American imperialism. Even the strain of the Civil War upon American resources did not arrest this eagerness for expansion, which found expression in the purchase of Alaska and various proposals for the acquisition of Cuba, Santo Domingo, and even Canada. In the

[1] Bemis, S. F., ed., The American Secretaries of State and Their Diplomacy, 1927-29, 10 vols.; Johnson, W. F., America's Foreign Relations, 1921, 2 vols.; Jones, R. L., History of the Foreign Policy of the United States, 1933; Latané, J. H., A History of American Foreign Policy, 1927; Mathews, J. M., American Foreign Relations, 1928; Moore, J. B., A Digest of International Law, 1906; Sears, L. M., A History of American Foreign Relations, 1927.

Pacific, too, possession of California proved the preface to that expedition of Perry which opened Japan to the western world.

With the Spanish War, a new wave of imperialism swept the country, finding its inspirations in the British model of which Kipling was both the poet and the prophet. Possessor of the Philippines, the United States seemed for a moment launched upon a career of conquest and expansion such as, at that moment, was being followed by all the European Great Powers. Nevertheless, even in the Far East where it was most frankly imperialistic, American policy sought expression in the championship of abstract principles such as that of the Open Door, rather than in the customary processes of territorial aggrandizement.

Before the coming of the World War, the second explosion of American imperialism, which had followed the Spanish-American War, had died away. In 1918 there was no American demand for a share in the territorial spoils of victory, and the notion of mandates in Armenia or at Constantinople found no support on this side of the Atlantic. On the contrary, in still more recent times, the desire to be rid of the responsibility and competition of the Philippines has led to an ultimate surrender of sovereignty there.

Within the American region, the opening of the twentieth century saw the rapid development of a policy which seemed to foreshadow the assertion of the right to organize regimes which could provide peace and order in the islands and Central American states about the Caribbean Sea. By the Platt Amendment, the United States asserted rights of supervision over both the foreign relations and the domestic circumstances of Cuba, while its intervention in Haiti, Santo Domingo, and Nicaragua and its actions in respect of Mexico aroused apprehension in Latin America and expectation in Europe that the United States was entering upon a policy in the regions to the south of it identical with that pursued by European powers in Africa.[1]

Actually, however, apart from the role played by the United States in the revolution which produced the separation of Panama from Colombia and made possible the construction of the Canal, and the acquisition by the United States of the territories and islands necessary to defend it, American imperialism in the Caribbean area had had only transitory consequences and by 1934 was in full retreat. Thus the power of reoccupation reserved by the Platt Amendment in the case of Cuba had been renounced, the withdrawal of American forces from occupied countries had taken place. And, in the Pan-American Conference at Montevideo (1933), the United States formally renounced the right and practice of occupation of foreign territory in the interests of order and thus for the benefit of American creditors.[2]

With the inauguration of the administration of Franklin D. Roosevelt, the United States sought on the one hand to win and deserve the confidence of its Latin American neighbors, and on the other to expand the commercial relations between North and South America. "Dollar Diplomacy" was then frankly renounced, and

[1] Howland, C. P., ed., American Foreign Relations, 1929; Jones, C. L., Caribbean Backgrounds and Prospects, 1931; Latané, J. H., The United States and Latin America, 1926; Lee, T. F., Latin American Problems; Their Relation to Our Investors' Billions, 1932; Miller, H. G., The Isthmian Highway; a Review of the Problems of the Caribbean, 1929; Munro, D. G., The United States and the Caribbean Area, 1934.

[2] Carnegie Endowment for International Peace, "The Montevideo Conference, Antecedents and Accomplishments," International Conciliation, No. 300, 1934; Foreign Policy Association, "Seventh Pan-American Conference," Foreign Policy Reports, Vol. X, No. 7, 1934.

"Good Neighbor" methods formally substituted. As a result, there is at least a promise that the doubts and suspicions, if not the jealousies, which in recent years have poisoned the relations between the United States and Latin America, will presently disappear.

Within the American region, therefore, national policy in recent times has been made to square with long-standing pretension. Of imperialistic purposes, whether territorial, economic, or financial, nothing is left. So far from seeking to act as the single policeman of the American region, the United States has clearly predicated all future intervention upon association with the other American states. In respect of the American region, then, national policy has today become clear and consistent.

In respect of Europe and Asia, by contrast, the policy of the United States is lacking in definition. So far, the American people are equally eager to promote world peace, both for moral and material reasons, and to avoid foreign involvements, for considerations which are at least comprehensible. Thus American action continues to respond alternately to the inspiration of Wilson's Fourteen Points and to the admonition of Washington's Farewell Address, invariably reverting to the latter, however, when the question of assuming foreign responsibilities is raised.

Although the United States enjoys the maximum of security from attack, either European or Asiatic, failure to clarify national policy in its relations with both regions carries obvious dangers. Thus, in respect of Europe, since the issue which was responsible for our involvement in the World War, namely that of Freedom of the Seas, found no determination either during or at the close of that conflict, it is clear that another European struggle might lead to new perils of entanglement.

At the outset of the last great struggle, President Wilson undertook to establish the legally imprescriptible rights of his country as a neutral. But inasmuch as he was unprepared to employ an embargo against the Allies or to resort to arms against the Germans, American notes, unsupported by force, were without practical effect.[1] Since Great Britain would certainly undertake in any future war to employ the means which proved most effective in the last, fresh collisions between American rights and British acts on the high seas would be inevitable. Similar collision might also take place were the Japanese and the Soviet Union to engage in war.

Unless we decide either to maintain our neutral rights by arms or to waive them, save in the matter of damages, we may presently be faced by the same problem as between 1914 and 1917. If, moreover, the United States is to maintain its neutral rights by force beyond American waters, then our present fleet is inadequate to meet the British in Europe or the Japanese in Asia.[2] Save in the case of the British and the Japanese, too, the question of neutral rights could hardly become acute for us today.

Even more necessary, it would seem, is decision in respect to the policy of the United States in the Far East. If this country is determined to uphold the territorial integrity of China against Japan and as a corollary to preserve the ratio of the Washington Treaty, then it must envisage the probability of conflict with Japan. If, on the other hand, it is unready or unwilling to carry its

[1] Seymour, Charles, *American Diplomacy During the World War*, 1934.
[2] Grison, Philippe, *La Liberté des Mers et la Rivalité Anglo-Américaine de 1920 à 1930*, 1930; Kenworthy, J. M., and Young, G., *Freedom of the Seas*, 1929; Percy, Lord Eustace, *Maritime Trade in War*, 1930; Rutherford, V. H., *War or Peace?*, 1930.

protests against Japanese aggression to their logical conclusion, it must abandon all efforts to attain by indirection, and by such devices as the application of the
Stimson Doctrine of non-recognition to the Manchukuo
situation, an objective which can be reached only by
force and therefore by war.

For in the Far East the Japanese policy is fixed, and
while the Stimson Doctrine can, by the denial of American recognition of Manchukuo, hamper that policy by
encouraging Chinese resistance, the result is far more
likely to be an involvement of the United States in war
than a withdrawal from Manchuria by the Japanese.
Thus whatever may be said of the American attempt to
promote peace in Europe by pacts without sanctions, it
must be perceived that the effort to arrest Japanese imperialism in Asia by paper protests adds the risk of war
to the certainty of failure.

In sum, while the United States can perhaps indefinitely use words to cover its resolution to avoid action
in Europe, too frequent resort to words in Asia may in
the end make undesirable action inevitable.

Chapter XIX

THE ASIATIC REGION[1]

BETWEEN the European and Asiatic regions, the contrasts are striking. In the former, not less than five of the seven Great Powers of the world have their seats of administration and wealth; in the latter, but one, as in the case of the American region. Again, while four of the five considerable European states are continental, Japan, the single Great Power which is exclusively Asiatic, is insular. For all five of the Great Powers directly or indirectly concerned with the Asiatic region

[1] In the study of the Asiatic Region, the student should have available for reference the publications of the Institute of Pacific Relations, particularly *Problems of the Pacific*, 1925, 1927, 1929, 1931, 1933, published by the University of Chicago Press. The quarterly magazine, *Pacific Affairs*, edited by Owen Lattimore, and the fortnightly information service published by the American Council on Pacific Relations, New York, entitled *Memoranda of the American Council*, will also prove useful. An indispensable reference book on the economic aspects of Asia is *Economic Handbook of the Pacific Area*, by Field, F. V., *ed.* (New York, Doubleday Doran, 1934). In addition reference should be made to the *Foreign Policy Reports* (Foreign Policy Association), *Foreign Affairs* (Council on Foreign Relations), *International Conciliation* (Carnegie Endowment for International Peace), and the publications of the World Peace Foundation. For general history of the Asiatic Region, the student should refer to Gowen, H. H., *Asia, A Short History from the Earliest Times to the Present Day*, 1926; Treat, P. J., *The Far East*, 1928; Vinacke, H. M., *A History of the Far East in Modern Times*, 1928. One of the best general texts on international relations in Asia is Morse, H. B., and MacNair, H. F., *Far Eastern International Relations*, 1931.

—Japan, Great Britain, the Soviet Union, France, and the United States—the Asiatic mainland is, therefore, primarily a field of exploitation, and for the Soviet Union, alone, it is a land of extensive colonization as well.

As a consequence, whereas the European problem has its origin in the clash of national policies which are questions of life and death for all of the Continental states, since their security is directly at stake, the Asiatic problem arises from the collision of rival imperialisms, and only for Japan are the issues vital. Nevertheless, for Great Britain, since two thirds of the population of the British Empire lives between Aden and Singapore, and for the Soviet Union, three quarters of whose territory is located between the Urals and the Pacific, Asia is actually the field of largest importance so far as imperial policy is concerned.

By contrast, the interest of France is subordinate. Indo-China, to be sure, is reckoned one of the most profitable as it is also one of the most considerable of French colonial possessions, but whereas British and Russian imperial interests are primarily Asiatic, the French imperial interests are essentially African. Thus the French people are always aware that they are encamped rather than established in Asia and, like the Dutch in their far more valuable East Indies, they recognize the impossibility of defending their colonies against any serious challenge.

Last of all, the United States, since it has decided to relinquish possession of the Philippines, will shortly have no territorial stake in the Far East. Its concern, therefore, is largely commercial, and its interest confined to the preservation of the status quo of treaties which

THE POWERS IN ASIA

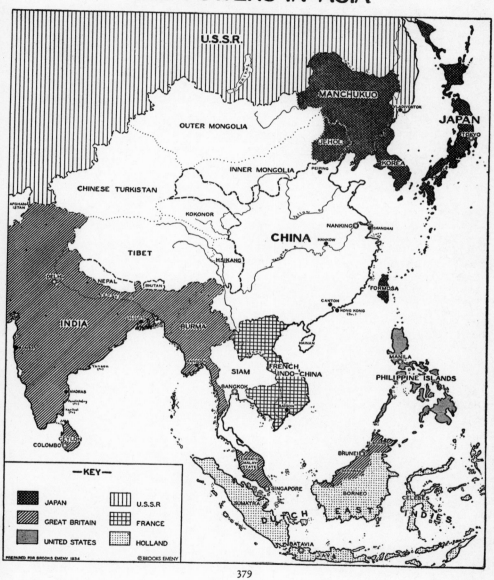

U.S.S.R.

MANCHUKUO

JAPAN

OUTER MONGOLIA

VLADIVOSTOK

JEHOL

TOKYO

KOREA

INNER MONGOLIA

PEIPING

CHINESE TURKISTAN

AFGHAN-
ISTAN

KOKONOR

NANKING

SHANGHAI

CHINA

HANKOW

TIBET

HSIKANG

DELHI

NEPAL

BHUTAN

FORMOSA

CANTON

INDIA

BURMA

HONG KONG
(Br.)

HAINAN

MADRAS

Pondichery
(Fr.)

Yangon
(Fr.)

SIAM

FRENCH
INDO-CHINA

MANILA

PHILIPPINE ISLANDS

BANGKOK

SAIGON

CEYLON

COLOMBO

FEDERATED
MALAY
STATE

SINGAPORE

BRUNEI

BORNEO

CELEBES

SUMATRA

DUTCH

EAST

INDIES

BATAVIA

JAVA

—KEY—

▓	JAPAN	‖‖‖	U.S.S.R
▨	GREAT BRITAIN	⊞	FRANCE
▤	UNITED STATES	⠿	HOLLAND

PREPARED FOR BROOKS EMENY 1934

© BROOKS EMENY

insure it equality of opportunity in the Chinese markets. This detached position, moreover, invests American policy with a totally different character from that of all of the other states whose policies are based upon territorial possessions.[1]

In larger view, then, the Asiatic problem, at least in its present phase, has its origin, not in the direct clashes among the three imperial powers, Japan, Great Britain, and the Soviet Union, growing out of their present territorial holdings, but in the collision of the rival interests of all the powers in China.[2] And in fact the Far Eastern problem is actually the question of China, which has today become a vast area of political anarchy and economic disintegration almost wholly surrounded by British, French, Soviet, and Japanese territories and spheres of influence.[3]

Within the land area of China, which is half again as large as the United States and contains a population of from a third to a half of a billion, there are conditions which have no counterpart elsewhere in the world. To begin with, all semblance of central administration has disappeared, and the national territory is divided among bandit generals and provincial juntas. Such gov-

[1] American Council, Institute of Pacific Relations, *Conflict in the Far East, 1931-1932*, 1932; Dennett, Tyler, *Americans in Eastern Asia*, 1922; Dulles, F. R., *America in the Pacific*, 1932; Field, F. V., *American Participation in the China Consortiums*, 1931; Howland, C. P., ed., *American Foreign Relations*, 1930; Moncado, H. C., *America, the Philippines and the Orient*, 1932.

[2] Blakeslee, G. H., *The Pacific Area*, 1929; Blakeslee, G. H., "Conflicts of Policy in the Far East," *World Affairs Pamphlets*, No. 6, 1934; Golovin, N. N., *The Problem of the Pacific in the Twentieth Century*, 1922; Pollard, R. T., *China's Foreign Relations, 1917-1931*, 1933; Remer, C. F., and Palmer, W. B., *A Study of Chinese Boycotts with Special Reference to Their Economic Effectiveness*, 1933; Roosevelt, Nicholas, *The Restless Pacific*, 1928; Thompson, H. C., *The Case for China*, 1933; Whyte, Sir A. F., *China and the Foreign Powers*, 1928, rev.; Young, C. W., *The International Relations of Manchuria*, 1929.

[3] American Council, Institute of Pacific Relations, *Behind the Far Eastern Conflict*, 1933; Barnes, Joseph, ed., *Empire in the East*, 1934; Foreign Policy Association, "The Dismemberment of China," *Foreign Policy Reports*, Vol. X, No. 4, 1934.

ernment as exists, moreover, is supported at least as much by the familiar devices of violence, pillage, and extortion as by the orderly collection of customs and taxes.

What is unique about the Chinese situation, too, distinguishing it from the circumstances of all other states, is the absence of any effective national spirit. Beyond all question, the well-nigh innumerable millions of this colossal nation are united by ethnic and cultural ties as unmistakable as those which bind Germans or French in Europe. Yet Chinese nationalism, so far as it exists, discloses none of the characteristics of nationalism in Western states and peoples.[1]

On the contrary, for untold centuries this huge mass, constituting the largest ethnic group in the world, has resisted invasion not so much by arms as by absorption.[2] In turn, the Mongols and the Manchus have descended from the north beyond the Great Wall to conquer and control, only to disappear after a few centuries as rivers vanish in the ocean. Hatred of the foreigner, the "barbarian" of Chinese phrase, constitutes the dominant emotion of this great people and not infrequently finds expression either in the violent explosion of a Boxer uprising or in the passive resistance of an economic boycott.

Nevertheless, in the face of foreign perils the Chinese throughout history have shown themselves destitute of that capacity for unity which discloses itself in all the great Western peoples. Instead of presenting a united front and a common resolution to the foreign foe, the

[1] Bland, J. O. P., *China: The Pity of It*, 1932; Holcombe, A. N., *The Chinese Revolution*, 1931; Hsü, L. S., *Sun Yat-Sen, His Political and Social Ideals*, 1933; MacNair, H. F., *China in Revolution*, 1931; Peffer, Nathaniel, *China, the Collapse of a Civilization*, 1930; T'ang Leang Li, *The Inner History of the Chinese Revolution*, 1930.

[2] Latourette, K. S., *The Chinese, Their History and Culture*, 1934, 2 vols.; Williams, E. T., *A Short History of China*, 1928.

Chinese have invariably yielded and submitted, relying upon the double strategy of numbers which absorb and of intrigue which divides the barbarians.

All Chinese history, too, is marked by ever-recurring periods of strength and weakness, periods in which internal anarchy invites invasion, and eras of domestic resurgence which follow the disappearance of the invaders in the sea of Chinese numbers. So far as one may judge, the world is at present witnessing one more of the epochs of weakness, which in the past have not infrequently lasted over centuries. Today, however, the role formerly played by the Mongols and Manchus beyond the Great Wall is being filled by the Western nations and particularly by Japan.

The contemporary problem of China, then, takes its rise from the double fact of political weakness and economic desirability. For, despite all the present circumstances of anarchy, political and economic, China is still conceived by the trading nations to constitute one of the most considerable of the few surviving fields for exploitation. Today, Africa has been apportioned among the several imperialisms, the United States has made good its Monroe Doctrine closing the Americas to further European annexations, and even Asia, outside the vague limits of the so-called Chinese Republic, is apportioned and closed.

Only China, therefore, remains. And for at least three centuries there has existed in the West a profound faith in the fabulous wealth of this Celestial Kingdom, a faith surviving from the remoter days of the Age of Discovery. It is true that, little by little, this faith has been dissipated. Anciently that wealth seemed to be expressed in gold and jewels; in our own time it was discovered in the promise of vast mineral resources suitable to the development of industry.

Today, however, the poverty of the Chinese people has become proverbial; and scientific exploration has destroyed the conviction as to industrial resources. The fact that China lacks large available reserves of high-grade iron, although relatively rich in coal, probably precludes all possibility of the development of a national heavy industry commensurate with national needs. And this fact, in turn, would seem to close the door to all prospect that China will ever become a World Power. But although resources of China have been demonstrated to be far inferior to early expectations, yet in certain industrial fields, in the manufacture of textiles, for example, she has demonstrated her potential capacity not only to satisfy her own domestic needs, but also to become a competitor in the world market.[1]

In fact, within a time which is still recent, the world has been witnessing a striking phenomenon in the Far East. In the area which, in the imperialistic calculations of the West, there was to be found the ultimate and most considerable market for the products of European and American factories, the actual demand has been increasingly for foodstuffs and raw materials; and under the pressure of Chinese, Indian, and Japanese competition, the Western nations in the all-important field of textiles are in full retreat. Only in the case of the heavy industries, in the products of iron and steel, does the poverty of the East in raw materials seem to promise the existence of a continuing market for Western production.

[1] Bain, H. F., *Ores and Industry in the Far East*, 1933, rev. ed.; Condliffe, J. B., *China Today: Economic*, 1932; Cressey, G. B., *China's Geographic Foundations*, 1934; Field, F. V., *Economic Handbook of the Pacific Area*, 1934; Vinacke, H. M., *Problems of Industrial Development in China*, 1926.

In the postwar years, too, there is no mistaking the fact that in the West the old imperialistic ardor is cooling. If the American withdrawal from the Philippines is the most significant indication of the change, others are not lacking. Everywhere, conquered peoples have disclosed an odd capacity to confound their masters. Today nations which sought to acquire wider markets by expanding their frontiers are finding their own domestic situation rendered difficult by the competition of their colonial possessions in the home market. Thus Philippine sugar has caused a revision in the program of American imperialism, and Indian textile competition has roused emotions not wholly dissimilar in Lancashire.[1]

As far as Great Britain, the United States, and France are concerned, therefore, Asiatic policy is a question rather of preserving than of extending. British and French policies are thus static even in the matter of territory, while in the field of trade they are identical with American policies. Actually, only Russia and Japan today adhere still to the old conceptions of expanding imperialism. But even upon the Soviet Union, present weakness temporarily imposes a static policy.

For the moment at least, therefore, all four of the Western Powers—Great Britain, France, Soviet Russia, and the United States—are agreed upon a common policy, which is to preserve the territorial integrity of China. This purpose, despite convenient propaganda, has about it little of idealism or even of respect for the sanctity of treaties. In America there may be a certain sentimental sympathy with the Chinese, but in all the

---

[1] Ray, Parimal, *India's Foreign Trade Since 1870*, 1934; Utley, F., *Lancashire and the Far East*, 1931.

European peoples that sympathy is certainly lacking. Actually the same motives which explained British concern for the inviolability of Belgian territory and the sacredness of the treaty which established it, underlie the concern of the Western nations for Chinese independence. And these motives are, of course, purely selfish.

At a moment when the old-fashioned form of imperialism is visibly losing favor in the West, not for moral but for material reasons, Japan has suddenly taken the field, affirming the once familiar principles and employing the ancient practices. On the other hand, having become satisfied that these former practices are no longer profitable for themselves, the Western nations are now moved to common condemnation of the Japanese course. This Japanese action must, however, be identified as simple if belated fidelity to principles which once found complete Western acceptance.

Actually the Japanese have crowded into the brief span of four decades imperialistic operations which in British history have consumed at least three centuries. Not until the Sino-Japanese War of 1895 did Japan take the first step toward continental lodgment. European intervention then robbed her victory over China of its calculated fruits. Only ten years later, therefore, after the triumph of the Russo-Japanese War, did the capture of Port Arthur and the occupation of Korea clear the way. A decade later, the World War permitted the eviction of Germany from Shantung. Another ten years, and the descent of Europe into new political anarchy, and the whole world into the depths of the Great Depression, permitted the Japanese to consolidate their position in Manchuria by the creation of the puppet Empire of Manchukuo.

Meantime, the Washington Naval Conference, on the one hand, threw Great Britain and the United States back strategically upon Singapore and Hawaii, and on the other established a ratio of naval strength between the two great maritime powers and Japan which assured Japanese naval supremacy in all the waters of the western Pacific from Indo-China to the Aleutian Islands. Last of all, relying upon the accomplished facts of military occupation of Manchuria and naval supremacy in all waters of national interest, Japan has, by indirection, to be sure, begun to arrogate to herself the authority inherent in a new Monroe Doctrine investing her with the same rights in Chinese territory that the United States has claimed over Latin America.

Diplomatic, military, and naval activity, moreover, has been accompanied by economic. That economic activity, too, has had the heaviest consequences for the British, consequences measured by the ever-declining share of Lancashire in the textile field. While, therefore, British naval power still suffices to halt Japanese imperialism at Singapore, and American naval power is adequate to check it at Hawaii, economically Japan has with success invaded all of Asia and made startling inroads upon South American and East African markets.

In the Asiatic region, all other problems are subordinate to the Japanese phenomenon, as in the European region all others are less serious than the German. The essential difference, however, lies in the fact that while in Europe the German challenge to the existing order is immanent rather than actual, in Asia Japan has already put the world face to face with a *fait accompli*. With her triumph over Russia, in 1905, Japan became in fact a Great Power. Since that time she has followed an

imperialistic policy in no sense different from that of all
the other Great Powers in the nineteenth century.

What has invested the Japanese action with the air
of novelty, however, is the fact that it is identified as an
anachronism because either satiety or disillusionment
has led the other imperialist powers to renounce their
old policies and practices. What has bestowed upon it the
character of a menace is the further fact that the powers
which no longer dream of expanding their territorial
holdings see in it an eventual threat to the lands they
once seized and still desire to retain. Thus Russia in
Siberia, Great Britain in India, and France in Indo-
China identify in Japanese policy an ultimate danger to
their possessions.

In point of fact, the student of history cannot fail to
find striking and illuminating parallels between the Far
Eastern question of today and the Near Eastern question
in all of the years between the fall of Napoleon and the
outbreak of the World War. About a helpless China
the Great Powers have long been gathering, as they
assembled about the Turkish Empire in the nineteenth
century. In the present instance, Japan is playing the
role of Russia in the earlier case, while the present attitude of the Soviet Union toward China is vaguely that
of the old Hapsburg Monarchy toward Turkey, and
British concern in the Far East now is little different
from what it once manifested in the Near East.

At the moment, none of the four Western Great
Powers—Great Britain, Russia, France, and the United
States—is prepared to fight to prevent that extension of
Japanese power in China which all (save perhaps the
British) desire, for obvious reasons, to prohibit. In
this respect, the situation differs from the circumstances

of the crisis which led to the Congress of Berlin in 1878. Being unwilling or unable to resort to war in the pursuit of their national policies, the Western nations have sought by invoking the Covenant of the League of Nations, the Treaty of Washington, and the Pact of Paris to restrain actions clearly illegal by sanctions which were purely moral.

Without permanently escaping from the possibility of war, however, Great Britain, the United States, and Russia have so far completely failed in their undertakings. The reasons for failure must be sought in the circumstances of Japan itself, explaining as they do a national policy that has made Asia potentially a field for a new war and actually the graveyard of all the postwar program of world peace based upon the Covenant of the League of Nations and the Pact of Paris.

Chapter XX

JAPAN

A VERY slight study of the map suffices to demonstrate how striking is the resemblance between the position of Japan in relation to the Asiatic continent and that of Great Britain in relation to the European. The Korea Strait replaces that of Dover, the Sea of Japan takes the place of the North Sea, Korea measurably takes the place of Belgium, and Hokkaido and Sakhalin command the Russian outlet to the open sea on the north as Scotland and the Orkneys control that of Germany.

During past centuries, the British position has imposed two wholly different directions upon national policy. Until the close of the Hundred Years War, the proximity of the English shores to those of the Continent bound the fortunes of England closely to those of the mainland. Caesar conquered Britain for Rome. Angles and Saxons from the mainland founded the English nation: William the Conqueror made England a part of his Norman kingdom. Under the Plantagenets the order was reversed and English sovereigns ruled over the larger part of France.

Not until the middle of the fifteenth century did the feeble Charles VII, thanks to Joan of Arc, succeed in freeing French soil, and even in the sixteenth Calais still remained in English hands. With Elizabeth, however, England turned her back upon the Continent definitively and launched herself upon that imperial career which was to end by the creation of a great empire scattered about the Seven Seas.

From the Age of Louis XIV to the present hour, moreover, British policy in Europe has been defensive. The narrow seas which separate England from France have been primarily a barrier and not a bridge of empire. On the Continent of Europe, the British have fought neither to acquire territory directly nor to establish protectorates. On the contrary, their dominating interest has always been national security, which, to be sure, they have ever sought to defend on foreign soil.

In Japanese history something of the British experience is reproduced. In the thirteenth century the Japanese defeat of the Mongols recalls the English destruction of the Spanish Armada; in the sixteenth, Japanese invasion of Korea is vaguely reminiscent of English action in France. Then for three centuries the Island Kingdom retired into that complete isolation which was broken by the famous mission of Commodore Perry only eight decades ago.

Since that time it has been the example of Plantagenet England and not of Tudor England which Japan has followed.[1] And the reason is obvious: while the Japanese position, like the British, dictated overseas expan-

[1] Hara, Katsuro, *Introduction to the History of Japan*, 1920; Latourette, K. S., *The Development of Japan*, 1926, 2d ed.; Murdoch, James, *A History of Japan*, 1926; Sansom, G. B., *Japan: A Short Cultural History*, 1931; Takekoshi, Yosaburo, *The Economic Aspects of the History of the Civilization of Japan*, 1930, 3 vols.

sion, it was only in the middle of the last century that Japan emerged from her long isolation, and then not only the Americas but northern, western, and southern Asia as well were barred against her. Actually there was left open to her only those Asiatic shores facing her own coast.

Strategically, too, the Japanese problem was identical with the British.[1] Naval supremacy in all the waters surrounding her islands was the prerequisite of security.[2] To be sure, the problem was simpler. For Great Britain there is the double necessity of mastery in the near-by Atlantic, Channel, and North Sea, and in the Mediterranean as well, to insure safety at home and security of the lines of communication with India and Australasia. For Japan, by contrast, supremacy in domestic waters alone insures safety for all the maritime lines of communication in which she has strategic interest.

To be secure at home, however, Japan must dominate all the waters which extend from the Aleutian Islands to the broad strait separating Formosa (Taiwan) from the Philippines. But it was not until the Washington Conference of 1921-22 that the Western powers, particularly the United States and Great Britain, were finally put on notice of Japanese policy in this respect.

[1] "Japan is an island nation. But her distance from the continent of Asia is so small that she cannot be indifferent to what happens in Korea, Manchuria, China, and Siberia, any more than England can keep aloof from developments in the Low Countries across the Channel and along the North Sea. Particularly in Korea and Manchuria, we have consistently followed a policy dictated by the sole motive of establishing our own security. We have looked upon their frontiers as our own frontiers, even as England looks upon the frontiers of the Low Countries as her own." ("The Permanent Bases of Japanese Foreign Policy," by Viscount Kikujiro Ishii, in Foreign Affairs, Vol. 11, No. 2, 1933.)

[2] Ballard, G. A., The Influence of the Sea on the Political History of Japan, 1921; Bywater, H. C., Sea-Power in the Pacific, 1921; Davis, Col. W. J., Japan: The Air Menace of the Pacific, 1928; Etherton, P. T., and Tiltman, H. H., Japan: Mistress of the Pacific?, 1933; Kennedy, Capt. M. D., Some Aspects of Japan and Her Defence Forces, 1929.

At Washington, Japanese ends were served, first, by persuading the Anglo-Saxon powers to renounce all plans for extending the fortifications of their establishments in Alaska, the Philippines, Guam, and Hong Kong; and, second, by also acquiring their approval of a relative naval strength for the Japanese fleet which insured to it actual supremacy in all the seas washing the Asiatic littoral from Kamchatka to Indo-China. And, no doubt, in future naval conferences Japanese representatives will continue to reject that ratio of the Washington Conference which guaranteed Japanese naval supremacy where her interests are vitally concerned, and continue to demand parity.

Japanese security, then, demands Japanese naval supremacy in the Far East. That supremacy, however, constitutes the basis not merely of security but of hegemony as well. For not only does her naval superiority enable Japan to defend her own shores from both military and naval attack, but it also insures the same freedom of communication with the adjoining coasts of Asia which the British fleet bestowed upon British armies during the World War. At will, Japan can move her military forces by sea against any point from Vladivostok to Shanghai.

For Japan, therefore, the East China, Yellow, and Japan seas are, at present, as secure as are the North and Irish Seas and the English Channel for Great Britain. Neither on her homeland territory nor in domestic waters can she be attacked. Such challenge as can threaten her must come by way of the Asiatic mainland and be directed at her position there. Thus in practice the two possible perils for Japan are discoverable in China and in Soviet Siberia.

To abolish these dangers, the Japanese have already fought two wars: the Sino-Japanese, which gave them Formosa and brought about the separation of Korea from China; and the Russo-Japanese War, which gave them both Korea and Port Arthur. In addition, her participation in the World War enabled Japan to evict Germany from the Shantung Peninsula and thus to dispose of another potential rival. Finally, the disarray of the other Great Powers in the postwar period has permitted the Japanese, by creating the shadowy state of Manchukuo, to establish themselves as firmly in Manchuria as the British in India or the French in Indo-China.

Looking back over the four decades which mark the rise of imperialism in Japan, it is obvious that she has proceeded logically and almost ineluctably to the situation in which she now finds herself. China, Russia, and Germany have, in turn, been removed from her pathway by war; the Anglo-Saxon powers, by the less expensive method of conference. Her present situation, however, imposes three concerns. In respect of China, she has to guard against attacks which might be inspired and financed by foreign states unable themselves to strike directly. In respect of the Soviet Union, she has always to be on guard against a military challenge to her whole position on the Asiatic mainland. Finally, in respect of the Anglo-Saxon powers, and the United States in particular, she has always to maintain an adequate degree of naval strength.

From the first of these concerns of national policy flows the Japanese insistence in recent times upon what has already been described as a Far Eastern Monroe Doctrine. That doctrine in fact constitutes the assertion by the Japanese of a right to supervise Chinese financial and political relations with the outside world in such fashion as to insure her own immunity from a Chinese attack sustained by foreign loans or material supplies.[1]

From the second concern is derived the ever-recurring rumor of a new Russo-Japanese War, a war of prevention designed to throw Russian frontiers back to the Baikal, while Soviet military power is still inadequate to defend eastern Siberia.[2]

Last of all, from the third concern arises the constant insistence of the Japanese upon a larger relative naval strength vis-à-vis both Anglo-Saxon powers.[3] From the 10–6 ratio of Washington, raised to the 10–7 of London in respect of cruisers, Japan would now ascend to full parity, as she made clear at London in the illuminating conversations of December, 1934. And obviously her demand is based upon the fear that at some future time the British and American fleets may be united in common challenge of Japanese imperialism, and under such

[1] The famous Amau "restatement and clarification" of Japanese policy toward China (*New York Times*, April 18, 1934) reads in part as follows:

"We regard Japan as principally responsible for the maintenance of peace in Eastern Asia and we are determined to fulfill this mission. In order to do so, Japan must share China's responsibility for the maintenance of peace.

"Japan sincerely desires the integrity, unification, and restoration of order in China. History teaches that that is achievable only through China's own self-awakening and China's own endeavors. . . .

"In the situation which has arisen since the Manchurian and Shanghai incidents, if other powers attempt to co-operate in assistance to China, whether under the guise of financial or technical assistance, ultimately such efforts almost inevitably produce political results. The outcome for China may be calamitous, endangering her integrity and producing a division of spheres of influence.

"Japan does not object to other powers individually negotiating with China for assistance in the fields of economics and commerce, provided this does not disturb peace and maintenance of order in Eastern Asia.

"But if such efforts lead to a disturbance of the peace, Japan must object.

"Japan must object to the supplying of military airplanes, the establishment of airdromes, the furnishing of military advisers and instructors, and the granting of political loans."

[2] Betts, T. J., "The Strategy of Another Russo-Japanese War," *Foreign Affairs*, Vol. 12, No. 4; also Lattimore, Owen, *Manchuria, Cradle of Conflict*, 1932.

[3] See statement of Premier Okada, *New York Times*, August 1, 1934.

circumstances, parity would mean only a 10–5 ratio in the face of the combined Anglo-Saxon naval forces. Sufficient as even that ratio seems in the eyes of foreign naval experts, to Japan it appears inadequate.

If the geographical position of Japan is responsible for her pursuit of security by methods which insure her supremacy in Eastern Asiatic waters, it is nevertheless to economic rather than strategic circumstances that it is necessary to turn to discover the explanation of that Manchurian adventure which has at last brought her into sharp controversy with the Western world. For it is in search, not of prosperity measured by American or even European standards, but of the means of bare existence that Japanese imperialism has invaded northern China beyond the Great Wall.

To understand the Japanese situation it is necessary to keep in mind a few statistics. On an area three fourths as great as that of Germany, Japan maintains an equal population. But while more than half of German lands are arable, less than one fifth of Japanese are available for agriculture. Whereas German coal production annually exceeds 250,000,000 tons, the Japanese rarely exceeds 30,000,000. Iron resources are even more inadequate. Water power, by contrast, is considerable but insufficient for industrialization on any great scale.[1]

In the matter of foodstuffs, Japan might conceivably support herself at an excessively low standard of living from her own production. Annually, however, a million mouths are added to the number to be fed as contrasted with a quarter of a million for Germany and four hundred thousand for Italy. Save for Great Britain, too, Japan has the highest density of population of any Great

[1] See Coal, Iron Ore and Water Power map, Chapter III, pages 46-47.

Power, and that population is established on the poorest of all homeland areas.[1]

Until the late sixties of the last century, Japanese population had remained fairly stationary at the figure of twenty-five millions. To have added forty millions to the population of an area materially smaller than that of the state of California, and inferior in natural resources as well, and to have permitted this transformation to take place in less than three generations, is obviously to have created a problem of the first magnitude.[2]

Nor have the Japanese, like the Italians before the World War, succeeded in sending any considerable portion of their growing population abroad. On the contrary, in the Anglo-Saxon countries of North America and Australia, immigration laws have closed the door to Japanese immigrants. And in Korea and Manchuria, climate and domestic standards of living have proved fatal obstacles to Japanese settlement.

Of necessity, therefore, the Japanese have been driven to meet the ever-growing problem of population pressure by domestic devices rather than by means of emigration. Like the Italians and Germans, too, they have turned to the double method of increasing domestic agricultural production and expanding national industry.

As to the first method, however, there can be little question that the limit of possible extension has been reached. Actually, in recent years Australian and Manchurian foodstuffs have annually become a more

[1] For books dealing with various aspects of the economic position of Japan, see: Field, F. V., ed., *Economic Handbook of the Pacific Area*, 1934; Moulton, H. G., and Ko, Junichi, *Japan; An Economic and Financial Appraisal*, 1931; Orchard, J. E., *Japan's Economic Position*, 1930; Penrose, E. F., *Food Supply and Raw Materials in Japan*, 1930.

[2] Crocker, W. R., *The Japanese Population Problem; the Coming Crisis*, 1931; Dennery, Étienne, *Asia's Teeming Millions;* 1931; Thompson, W. S., *Danger Spots in World Population*, 1929.

JAPAN

NATIONAL SELF-SUFFICIENCY IN FOODSTUFFS, ESSENTIAL INDUSTRIAL PRODUCTS, AND RAW MATERIALS

DOMESTIC PRODUCTION AND NET IMPORTS EXPRESSED AS PERCENTAGES OF
AVERAGE NATIONAL CONSUMPTION (1925-29)

—— GREAT ESSENTIALS ——

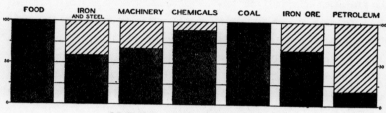

FOOD   IRON AND STEEL   MACHINERY   CHEMICALS   COAL   IRON ORE   PETROLEUM

CRITICAL RAW MATERIALS

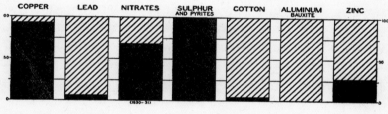

COPPER   LEAD   NITRATES   SULPHUR AND PYRITES   COTTON   ALUMINUM BAUXITE   ZINC

(1930-31)

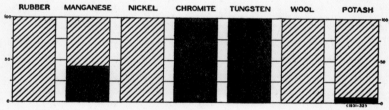

RUBBER   MANGANESE   NICKEL   CHROMITE   TUNGSTEN   WOOL   POTASH

(1931-32)

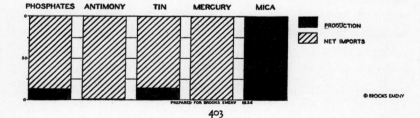

PHOSPHATES   ANTIMONY   TIN   MERCURY   MICA

■ PRODUCTION

▨ NET IMPORTS

PREPARED FOR BROOKS EMENY 1934

© BROOKS EMENY

considerable factor in national imports, although at the same time Japan has become an exporter of many types of canned goods.

In the field of industry, poverty in coal and relative destitution in iron have proved insuperable obstacles to the development of any large iron and steel production. When it is realized that the annual steel and iron output of Japan today falls far short of that of the small state of Belgium and amounts to less than half of that of the still smaller Grand Duchy of Luxemburg, the nature of the limitations Japan faces in this field can be properly appraised.

In fact, it is only in cotton, wool, and silk textiles that Japanese industrialization has made real progress. Here the growth has been remarkable, but it has imposed a far-reaching change in Japanese economy: cotton and wool have to be imported, and this rising dependence upon the outside world for raw materials is paralleled by what will be a similarly rising dependence in the matter of foodstuffs. Thus Japan is moving steadily toward the situation of Great Britain, without, however, making the smallest attempt to limit population by birth control as is now being done voluntarily and to an impressive extent in Great Britain.

Great as has been the progress of Japan in the field of textiles, moreover, there is here, too, an eventual if not an immediate limit. Today Japanese success at the expense of Great Britain is unmistakable. That success, however, has led the British government to seek to limit the ravages of Japanese competition in Lancashire by closing Crown colonies (where alone their political control is complete) to Japanese production. Even more serious, however, is the growing competition of China and of India, in both of which countries costs of production are lower owing alike to cheaper labor and larger domestic supplies of coal and cotton.

Nevertheless, for Japan, the Chinese market continues to have primary importance; not, to be sure, because of immediate sales, since in 1932, which was in this respect a typical year, Japan sold three times as much to the United States as to China, but because of future possibilities. Thus, the Chinese share in Japanese exports has steadily been rising, although even here the Japanese sell barely half as much as does the United States. On the other hand, the possibility of Japanese domination of the Chinese market is slight, for in the field of steel and iron, for example, Japan is out of the running, while she has neither foodstuffs nor raw materials to sell and cannot long meet the competition of the Chinese themselves in textiles.

As the situation stands today, despite an enormous expansion of industry Japan is still, as in the past, confronted by two facts of ominous import: a rising standard of living and a rapidly expanding population. For the moment it is still possible to foresee the preservation of that parity in progress and population. Doubtless there will be still further gains in foreign trade in textiles and in rubber goods, electric appliances, novelties, and certain other manufactures. An adequate supply of cheap labor is also assured, and costs of production may therefore for the present fall rather than rise.

Nevertheless, Japanese exports are already encountering constantly multiplying obstacles in the way of competition from India and China and of tariff barriers among the Western nations. The further advantage of the depreciated *yen*, to which no inconsiderable part of recent trade expansion has been due, is of course transitory. Thus, so far as Japan and her Korean and Formosan possessions are concerned, it is plain that these cannot long continue to support their growing population under existing conditions. Like Italians, therefore, the Japanese face the alternative of artificial restriction of population or the acquisition of new territory.

It is precisely at this point that one comes face to face with the Manchurian policy of Japan. Manchukuo is, in fact, the answer which Japanese statesmen and soldiers have undertaken to give to the problem of future national existence posed by the economic, demographic, and strategic circumstances of their homeland territory.[1] How far does the answer seem adequate? Obviously the question remains difficult to answer because the ultimate appraisal of Manchurian resources has yet to be made.

Nevertheless certain facts seem at least tentatively established. Thus, on an area more than three times as great as Japan proper, Manchuria possesses many resources which are complementary to the Japanese. There is considerable coal and some iron, although neither the quantity of the former nor the quality of the latter are such as to permit any large development.[2] Beyond these there are resources in foodstuffs which, in fact, constitute for Japan the chief importance of its new sphere of influence. Soya beans and wheat are raised in considerable and increasing quantities, and both are

[1] American Academy of Political and Social Science, "Prerequisites of Japanese Security," by Orchard, J. E., *The Annals*, July, 1933; Eldridge, F. R., *Dangerous Thoughts on the Orient*, 1933; Etherton, P. T., and Tiltman, H. H., *Manchuria, the Cockpit of Asia*, 1932; Foreign Policy Association, "Two Years of the Manchukuo Regime," *Foreign Policy Reports*, Vol. X, No. 14, 1934; Kawakami, K. K., *Manchoukuo, Child of Conflict*, 1933; Young, C. W., *Japan's Special Position in Manchuria*, 1931, 3 vols.

[2] Bain, H. F., *Ores and Industry in the Far East*, 1933, rev. ed.

precious additions to Japanese domestic food supplies.[1]

Although the density of population in Manchuria is relatively low, something like eighty per square mile as contrasted with four hundred and fifty for Japan, there is, however, small prospect that any considerable number of Japanese can be persuaded to settle there. The explanation of this fact is twofold. On the one hand, the thirty millions of Chinese already established can underlive and outlive the Japanese workers; on the other, the climate is such that the Japanese masses find it too rigorous. For Japan, therefore, Manchukuo seems destined to be always a land of exploitation, like Senegal for France, or Nigeria for Great Britain.

In this relatively vast territory, with a population of more than thirty millions, which is still mounting rapidly, and an area nearly four times that of Italy, it is manifest that Japan can, for a certain period of time, find a field for profitable development and exploitation. But she cannot find new fields for her surplus population or adequate markets for her industry. The answer to her supreme problem, that of population, is hardly discoverable in Eastern Asia.

Nevertheless, it is plain that, in the minds of the Japanese masses, the Manchurian adventure has been accepted as the direct consequence of national necessity. Manchuria is thus for the Japanese people what the Danubian Basin is for the German—the line of least resistance. Japanese national feeling, too, is exacerbated as is German by a sense of injustice, an injustice which for Japan arises, on the one hand, from the stigma of inferiority disclosed in the immigration laws of the

[1] Carnegie Endowment for International Peace, "The International Trade of Manchuria," *International Conciliation*, No. 269, 1931; *Manchuria Year Book*, annual since 1930; Field, F. V., *ed.*, *Economic Handbook of the Pacific Area*, 1934.

United States and, on the other, from the prohibition of Japanese settlement on the still vast empty spaces of the American and Australasian regions.

Psychologically, then, Japanese reaction to the protests and interferences of the West, growing out of her Chinese policy, has, like the German feelings about treaty revision, taken the form of intense and explosive nationalism in which the Soviet Union, Great Britain, and the United States have in turn been identified as the relentless enemy. As a consequence, military and naval leaders have found it easy to exercise decisive influence politically and Manchuria has come to occupy in Japanese eyes the character of Austria in German eyes.

It is idle to suppose that it is possible by any other means save that of war, to bring about any modification of Japanese policy in respect of Manchuria. The British, who have viewed it with the largest measure of calm, have recognized that the concentration of Japanese interest and energies upon Manchuria may, for a time at least, abolish for them the ever-present danger that, sooner or later, Japanese ambition will be turned toward the unsettled areas of Australia and New Zealand, which alone seem to offer climatically and otherwise a suitable field for colonization.

What is most important to note is the fact that geographical position plus existing naval strength have given Japan naval supremacy in the eastern Pacific. This supremacy is supplemented by military force sufficient to defend the Japanese position everywhere upon the Asiatic mainland against any present challenge, whether Chinese or Russian. In the nature of things, however, Japanese policy must also concern itself with the prospect of eventual challenge, and that explains its efforts on the one hand to assert a political and financial guardianship over China and on the other to achieve the isolation of Russia.

That there is any dream on the part of Japan of achieving a complete and continuing domination of China, or of organizing this vast empire as the British have undertaken to organize India, seems unlikely. Such a task all sensible Japanese plainly perceive is beyond national resources and might lead to disasters which are incalculable. On the other hand, it is far from unlikely that Japanese influence may be extended into Inner and even Outer Mongolia. Always, of course, the decisive factor must be the question of the persistence or disappearance of Chinese anarchy.

What the student of international affairs must perceive is that the World War and the Washington Conference together bestowed upon Japan power in the Far East, which is beyond challenge today, alike on the naval and military sides, save as the British and American peoples are prepared to undertake a war in which they would inevitably have to make use of the Soviet Union as an ally. He must also see that the economic circumstances of Japan, and the decision the Japanese people have reached upon the basis of those circumstances, render futile all attempts to restrict Japanese imperialism by such means as the Pact of Paris or the Stimson Doctrine, the former of which was evaded by the simple device of failing to declare war, while the latter was merely ignored.

To defend their present position in Manchuria, the Japanese people are prepared to fight. To retain their existing naval supremacy in the Far East, they are ready to build, even at the cost of new sacrifices measured in a reduction in the national standard of living. So far the steadily mounting population pressure has been met by an industrial expansion which has postponed a crisis that would otherwise have been inescapable in view of the fact that Japan can no longer hope to feed her population from domestic resources.

It is, however, self-evident that domestic social dangers having their origin in economic and demographic circumstances have been at best only temporarily exorcised. Manchuria is an expedient and not a solution. Eventually, Japanese policy must face the problem of seeking new lands for colonization or of restricting population increase by artificial means. So far the Japanese problem is on all fours with the Italian. The basic difference, however, lies in the fact that while the Italian pathway, barred by other Great Powers, is beyond the present strength of Italy to overcome, Japan, in the absence of such barriers, has been able to establish her supremacy in her own region.

Nevertheless, the position of Japan is precarious. She has to fear the possible resurgence of China, the eventual development of the Soviet Union, and the latent menace incident to future Anglo-Saxon co-operation either with China or with the Soviet Union. Her reliance, therefore, must be on force and her national policy dynamic, because any status quo in the Far East must constitute an eventual if not an immediate restriction upon an expansion dictated by the internal population pressure. For all present time, however, and until she is defeated in war by a coalition of Western powers, or paralyzed by social upheaval at home, her dominance in the eastern Pacific seems beyond effective challenge.

Chapter XXI

THE PROBLEM OF PEACE IN ASIA

BETWEEN the situation of the Germans in Europe and of the Japanese in Asia, the parallel is striking. It is the revolt of sixty-five millions of people within the Reich against the status quo of the Treaty of Versailles which constitutes the single serious challenge to peace and order upon the European Continent; and, in the same fashion, it is the attack of the sixty-five millions of Japanese upon the status quo guaranteed by the Treaty of Washington which renders peace in the Orient problematical.

At bottom, the driving impulse is the same. In both cases, a great people is in revolt against physical circumstances which in their eyes constitute permanent barriers to national prosperity and even to tolerable national existence. For Germany, ethnic considerations reinforce economic, but underneath all else is a corroding sense of injustice born of the conviction that the world is seeking by force to confine the German people within limits equally incommensurate with national needs and with national rights.

For Japan, there is no ethnic factor in its imperialism, since there are no Japanese minorities to be redeemed on the Amur as there are German minorities on the Danube. Physically, however, the resemblances between the circumstances of the two peoples are impressive. Within a smaller and poorer area the population of Japan approximates that of Germany, and the annual rate of increase is far greater. Driven by a dominating sense of domestic limitations, Japan has therefore already launched in Manchuria an imperialistic enterprise similar to that which Germany plans in the heart of Middle Europe.

Japanese imperialism, too, is of long standing. As far back as the Russo-Japanese War, three decades ago, the way was cleared for that undertaking, finally launched in the autumn of 1931, which led swiftly and successfully to the establishment of Manchukuo. This phantom state, even more completely under Japanese control than is India under British, having an area more than twice that of France and a population of over thirty millions, represents a Japanese attempt to escape from the ever-tightening grip of population pressure and economic poverty in her insular homeland.

In launching herself upon this career of imperialism, Japan has at once encountered the opposition of at least three of the Great Powers. As France, Italy, and the Little Entente have resisted German attempts to achieve Austro-German union, so Great Britain, the Soviet Union, and the United States have similarly, but with far less success, endeavored first to prevent Japanese seizure of Manchuria, and thereafter, by nonrecognition of Manchukuo, to deny this Japanese puppet state the appearance of permanence.

In addition, as the European powers invoked the

treaties of Versailles and of St. Germain to establish the illegality of the projected *Anschluss*, the nations concerned over Asiatic circumstances have appealed to the Nine-Power Treaty of Washington, the Pact of Paris, and the Covenant of the League of Nations to prove Japanese action at once unlawful and immoral.[1] Unable to use either the military or the financial power which the opponents of German purposes have been able to employ effectively, they have, however, failed ignominiously to arrest Japanese policy.[2]

What are the bases of the opposition of the British, Russians, and Americans to the Japanese action? In point of fact, they are so different as to make community of action difficult if not impossible. Of the three, it is plain that the British are the least disturbed, although their Asiatic interests are colossal. In the immediate Manchurian region, they have no territory and relatively small trade. Practically, their interests begin only at Shanghai, while Hong Kong is the nearest outpost of their empire. Even in China proper, their stake, measured by trade, is less than that of the United States.

For Great Britain, the implications of Japanese imperialism are twofold—economic and political. On the economic side, Japanese textiles have already largely driven the British from the Far East and the invasion has even reached India. Profoundly as this competition has disquieted Lancashire, however, British statesmanship is faced by the fact that what Japan is doing is also being done by the Indians and Chinese and that for all practical purposes the Far East has recovered control of

[1] "The League and Manchuria," *Geneva Special Studies*, Vol. II, Nos. 10, 11, and 12, 1931, also Vol. III, No. 5, and "The League and Manchukuo," Vol. V, No. 3, 1934.
[2] Foreign Policy Association, "The New Status in the Pacific," *Foreign Policy Reports*, Vol. IX, No. 23, 1934.

its own market in textiles. On the economic side, there-fore, however irritating Japanese competition may be, it does not constitute a cause for war.

On the political side, the British view the Manchurian affair with divided emotions. For them, the danger of Japanese expansion toward the south, toward the wide open spaces of Australia and New Zealand, is real. Only in that direction, too, is there any hope for the Japanese to find lands suitable for colonization, since Korea is already densely populated and Manchuria climatically unsuited to their needs. The spectacle of Japanese im-perialism turning west rather than south and com-mitting itself to an experiment which may well absorb its energies for many decades, is therefore by no means wholly distasteful to the British.

It is true, however, that speedy success in Manchuria and a rising tide of nationalism stimulated by success may presently lead the Japanese not merely to assert their control of China proper but also to begin their march southward. And that march must be equally threaten-ing for India and for Australia and New Zealand. Thus the British have already undertaken far-reaching exten-sions of the fortifications of Singapore and are obviously preparing to make this stronghold the advanced base of their empire, as Hawaii has become for the United States.

In Asia as in Europe, however, British national policy is dominated by the conception of the balance of power. On the one hand, British statesmanship is resolved at all costs to avoid actual war with Japan, unless the safety of the Empire is directly assailed. On the other, it is unmistakably seeking to encourage resistance to Japan by the United States and by the Soviet Union; for it is self-evident that if one or both of these states should come to conflict with Japan, British security would be inexpensively established for a long time to come.

Clearly, it would be contrary to British interests to permit Japan to defeat the United States in war. But of this there is no real danger. And while decisive defeat of Japan would hardly be possible, a long costly struggle would necessarily weaken the Japanese disproportionately. On the other hand, a new Russo-Japanese War, since it would be fought on land, would have slight interest for the British. Even if the Japanese were successful again as in 1905 and the frontiers of the Soviet Union were thrust back to Lake Baikal, the actual result would be to involve Japan still more deeply in northeastern Asia.

In Europe, Great Britain is inescapably entangled in German action because, as Stanley Baldwin declared in a memorable speech in July, 1934, her military frontier is at the Rhine. Since, to attack France, Germany must pass the Rhine she thus constitutes a potential menace to Great Britain. In Asia, however, a Japanese naval war with the United States or military collision with the Soviet Union would leave the British in the comfortable position of a neutral, observing from a safe vantage point the struggle between a prospective enemy and a present competitor. All British interest, therefore, would dictate neutrality in a war between Japan and the United States, or between Japan and Russia.

As for the Soviet Union, its interests are evidently best served by a long period of tranquillity.[1] The gigantic task of industrializing Russia can be accomplished only

[1] Foreign Policy Association, "The Soviet Union and Japan in the Far East," *Foreign Policy Reports*, Vol. VIII, No. 12, 1932; Connoly, Violet, *Soviet Economic Policy in the East*, 1933.

during peace. Japanese occupation of Manchuria constitutes no considerable injury to Soviet interests. For a long time to come, the status quo must and can satisfy Soviet interests. And recognition of the need for peace was plainly disclosed in the willingness of the present Russian regime to part with ownership of the Chinese Eastern Railway, although this route cuts two days from the journey between Vladivostok and Moscow.

On the other hand, there is no mistaking the fact that the Soviet Union will fight to preserve the status quo, so far as its own frontiers are concerned. To that end, it has already double-tracked the Trans-Siberian Railroad as far as Lake Baikal and is now extending that construction eastward to the Pacific. It has, moreover, concentrated a very large portion of its military and air forces between Lake Baikal and Vladivostok.

But time works for the Russians. Eventually they seem likely to be superior to the Japanese both in machine power and in man power. Nor is it to be questioned that each year a war of prevention, hazarded by the Japanese, would involve greater risks and impose larger costs. In fact, for the Soviet Union, the failure of Japan to precipitate such a conflict in 1933 appeared a cause of genuine surprise as it certainly was of enormous satisfaction. Actually, for Japan, the single real menace is the Russian air force, which from Vladivostok could reach the Japanese islands. And that menace would, of course, disappear if a successful war of prevention thrust the Russians back to Lake Baikal.

For Russia, then, the problem of peace in the Far East turns upon Japanese acceptance or rejection of the idea of a war of prevention. Even as late as the winter of 1934–1935 it still seemed within the realms of possibility, at least, that by a direct and smashing attack Japan could capture Vladivostok and thrust the Soviet frontier back to the region of Lake Baikal. Then, and only then, could the security and permanence of Manchukuo be fairly assured. In the mountain ranges which constitute the eastern border of the Baikal country, with both the Trans-Siberian and the Chinese Eastern railways to supply them, Japanese armies could stand permanently and relatively inexpensively, for these mountains constitute the strategic frontier of a Japanese empire on the Asiatic mainland.

There was, however, no blinking the fact that such a war would involve a grave risk. In the Russo-Japanese War a far shorter advance than it would now be necessary to make led to the exhaustion of Japanese resources; and at the moment when the Treaty of Portsmouth was signed, Linevitch was in a position to resume an offensive which would have had disastrous results for Japanese fortunes. Undoubtedly the Soviet forces would fight better than the Imperial armies in 1905, nor is there any question as to the superiority of their equipment, or as to the advantages to be derived from the recent construction of new industrial units in central and western Siberia. On the other hand, it is not less evident that present failure to resort to a war of prevention will leave Japan open to an eventual challenge, which will progressively become more difficult to deal with.

There remains the question of the policy of the United States. What, after all, has it at stake in this Far Eastern mess? Plainly no question of territory arises, for in that respect it is in full retreat from Asia. Nor is the problem of national security involved, because as Japanese armies advance into Manchuria they must turn their backs upon American shores. Not less unmistakable is the fact that such threat as Japanese policy may have for the United States, as for Great Britain, will be lessened as Japanese resources are absorbed in a continental struggle with the Soviet Union.

The American stake in the Far East, then, is exclusively trade. In the interests of that trade it has for a generation sought to uphold the principle of the "Open Door" and the doctrine of the inviolability of Chinese sovereignty. It was to protect this material interest, moreover, that the Harding administration sought and obtained Japanese participation in the Nine-Power Treaty of the Washington Conference, which pledged all signatory nations to respect the status quo in the Far East so far as China was concerned. For Japanese signature to that treaty, too, the United States paid by renouncing the right to extend its fortifications at Corregidor, Guam, and the Aleutian Islands.

It was, furthermore, on the basis of the Washington Treaty and of the Pact of Paris that the Hoover administration protested against Japanese action in Manchuria and associated itself with the League of Nations in an attempt to arrest it. And it was in the hope of exerting moral pressure, while renouncing all employment of physical sanctions, that the Stimson Doctrine was proclaimed, withholding American recognition from the state of Manchukuo because of the circumstances attending its creation.

Naturally the Stimson Doctrine of nonrecognition of the fruits of conquest, like the Kellogg Pact and the League Covenant, was without avail, for the Japanese were in deadly earnest. For them, the control of Manchukuo had become a question of life or death. As a consequence, while continuing to consolidate their situation in Manchuria they also withdrew from the League of Nations. Finally, their resentment was chiefly directed against the United States, because the immigration laws, which single out the Japanese among the peoples of the Great Powers for exclusion on racial grounds, were an affront to national pride, and also because the Japanese correctly perceived that the Chinese drew their chief inspiration for resistance to Japanese policy from the official attitude of the United States.

The relations between Japan and the United States therefore became dangerous and still remain so. That the Japanese will deliberately attack is wholly unlikely. On the other hand, there is just as little chance of their renouncing that policy upon which they are now completely embarked after more than a generation of sustained preparation. Furthermore, they are likely in the future, as in the recent past, to continue to put the American people in the presence of *faits accomplis* which do violence to the two policies of the "Open Door" and the status quo in China.

The latent menace of war resulting from some unforeseen incident, therefore, has always to be reckoned with. The precedent of the "Maine," too, must linger in many minds. What adds to the danger is the total failure of the American people to perceive that the course laid down by the Stimson Doctrine, without in the smallest measure restoring vitality to the shattered pacts of Paris and Washington, does constitute a continuing cause of irritation and injury to the Japanese. American policy cannot change the Japanese aims, but, by making their pursuit more difficult, it produces a state of mind out of which conflict can come.

In reality the American position constitutes a striking but by no means unfamiliar paradox. The people of the United States have not the smallest intention of going to war to support the "Open Door" or to defend the status quo in China. On the other hand, they have committed themselves, for reasons which are moral and material alike, to a course which constitutes a refusal to bestow formal recognition upon what has taken place. At the bottom of their minds is the rather naïve notion that they can obtain, without resort to arms, the results usually achieved only by armed intervention. The danger lies in the obvious possibility that they may have to face the consequences of armed intervention, while they are certainly unlikely to harvest any profits from their present course.

Japanese resentment has already disclosed itself in uncompromising rejection of a proposal to perpetuate at the Naval Conference of 1935 the ratios of Washington and London in 1922 and 1930. In those earlier gatherings, the three great naval powers, Great Britain, the United States, and Japan, agreed upon relative strengths expressed in the 5–5–3 ratio. That agreement expires in 1936 and since Japan has refused to renew it she will then be free to seek parity by construction, if she chooses. American and British resistance to any attempt to attain parity by such a course is assured, and official warning of American purpose was uttered at London in December, 1934.

The problem of peace in the Far East, therefore, is twofold. It turns primarily upon the decision of the Japanese in the matter of a war of prevention directed at the Soviet Union. In the second place, it is conditioned upon the decision of the United States to continue or to abandon its present policy, illustrated by the Stimson Doctrine, which undertakes to exercise the maximum of pressure upon the Japanese to compel their abandonment of their present course without actually resorting to war.

In the first case, war may come suddenly and with little warning, as it did in 1904, if the Japanese again attack Russia. In the second place, conflict seems likely to arrive, if at all, only after a long protraction of the present strained relations, culminating in some incident or accident which produces an explosion on one side of the Pacific or the other. But while the prospects of a Russo-Japanese War are likely to diminish with delay, those of a Japanese-American conflict seem destined to grow rather than decrease, as long as the present policies prevail in Washington and in Tokyo.

On the strategic side, war between the United States and Japan would necessarily take the form of a long-range conflict, carried on by cruisers and restricted to raids. For the agreements of Washington, which forbade further fortification of Corregidor and Guam and new works in the Aleutian Islands, deprived the United States of any advanced bases which would make serious naval operations in Japanese waters possible, while in American waters Japan has never possessed a base.

Of course, with the refusal of Japan to accept the ratios of Washington and London, the United States will recover freedom to fortify as she may choose in the Philippines and elsewhere, while similar liberty will revert to the British at Hong Kong. But, with the surrender of American sovereignty in the Philippines, military defense of any naval base in the islands would become difficult in the extreme. Hawaii is, therefore, the advanced base of the United States as Singapore is of Great Britain, and in persuading these two countries to abandon further fortification of Corregidor and Hong Kong respectively, the Japanese established a naval supremacy in the waters of immediate interest to them, which they now seek to increase, since they have made parity with the United States a question of power quite as much as of prestige. The assurances of the Japanese Ambassador in Washington, made in December, 1934, that in any event Japan would not begin any competition in construction before 1942, together with the fact that the earlier treaties remain in effect until the end of 1936, at least promise a period of pause accompanied by fresh negotiations to avert an eventual race in construction otherwise inevitable.

Chapter XXII

THE WORLD POWERS

OF THE seven states which, by reason of the size and importance of their homeland populations and territories, constitute the Great Powers, four are also reckoned World Powers because of the influence which they exert beyond their own continental regions. To this category belong the British Empire, France, the Soviet Union, and the United States.

Of the World Powers the British Empire is in size by far the greatest.[1] Alike in area and in population it is four times as large as the United States, and its population is also three times as great as that of the Soviet Union. More than half of this great mass of people, however, dwell in Asia. In addition almost a third of the white population of the Empire live in self-governing Dominions. The population and area of the Crown Colonies, in which alone the British government exercises complete authority, is not materially greater than that of the French colonial domain.

[1] Somervell, D. C., *The British Empire*, 1930; Williamson, J. A., *A Short History of British Expansion*, 1922.

In considering the British Empire, it is necessary to take note of the three divisions; for already the white Dominions have become nations in their own right, bound to the Mother Country and to each other only by the single tie of allegiance to a common Throne, and of late years not only has India been moving toward a dominion status but also agitation for complete independence has taken on formidable proportions. Thus, for the future, the unity of the Empire may fairly be considered a matter of speculation and conjecture.[1]

It is, moreover, plain beyond dispute that the present stage in imperial conditions is transitional. In fact, the British Empire today furnishes the most impressive example of the breakdown of nineteenth-century imperialism in the postwar period. While the Dominions still constitute a profitable field for the trade, commerce, and investment of the Mother Country, they themselves have all made marked progress in industrialization and have increasingly demonstrated their determination to dominate their home markets to the exclusion of British goods as well as those of other countries.

In theory, the British Empire could, like the United States and the Soviet Union, constitute a single and largely self-contained economic unit. In practice, however, it does not; nor is there any present prospect that it ever will. On the contrary, for the British Isles, Europe is at least as important a market as the Dominions; the United States sells three times as much to Canada normally as does the Mother Country, and,

[1] Baker, P. J. N., *The Present Juridical Status of the British Dominions in International Law*, 1929; Elliott, W. Y., *The New British Empire*, 1932; Keith, A. B., *The Sovereignty of the British Dominions*, 1929; same author, *Dominion Autonomy in Practice*, 1929; same author, *The Constitutional Law of the British Dominions*, 1933; Nathan, Manfred, *Empire Government*, 1929; Toynbee, A. J., ed., *British Commonwealth Relations*, 1934; Wheare, K. C., *The Statute of Westminster*, 1933.

finally, in the Far East the textiles of India compete successfully with those of Lancashire. Nevertheless, forty per cent of British exports still go to the other parts of the Empire and thirty per cent of the imports of the United Kingdom are of imperial origin.

With the still recent renunciation of free trade by the British, it is manifest that the whole question of the economic relations between the United Kingdom and the rest of the Empire has come up for review and not improbably for drastic revision. In the world, too, the great period of British industrial supremacy is over. Not only have Germany, France, and the United States outdistanced Great Britain in heavy industry, but with the development of water power and the growing use of oil, British coal, once the basis of British trade, has also steadily lost ground.

During the war and postwar periods, the whole world has embarked upon a process of industrialization which has inevitably led to a steady restriction of British trade. Currency chaos also has had disastrous consequences, while the shrinkage in value of the British investments abroad has automatically reduced British purchasing power. Even the agreements of the Ottawa Conference of 1932, designed to promote inter-imperial trade by preferential duties, while moderately advantageous for the Dominions, have been of little real profit for Great Britain itself.

Today, after permitting a brief domestic boom, reversion to tariffs is producing in Great Britain the consequences that it must inevitably have everywhere. Agriculture is now demanding for itself the same monopoly in the home market that industry has recently acquired. But all concessions made to domestic agrarian interests must be at the expense of the Dominions which have hitherto been the chief sources of British foodstuffs. And as the United Kingdom seeks to protect its farms, Canada and Australia, as well as India, will strive to guard their factories still further.

In sum, one phase of imperial history seems to be coming to an end. Economically, the Dominions have come of age and, as a consequence, the Mother Country has been forced to revert to that system which it abandoned with the repeal of the Corn Laws nearly a century ago. Instead of imperial self-sufficiency, there is developing everywhere in the Empire a parochial spirit of economic nationalism which is centrifugal and not centripetal. Distance, which sometimes lends enchantment, has served not to promote co-ordination but to produce competition within the British Empire.

Even today, there still remains within the regions over which George V reigns practically all the reserves in motive power and resources in raw materials and foodstuffs essential to self-sufficiency. The coal of Great Britain, the wheat of Canada, the wool of Australia, the rubber of Malaya, and the cotton of India, together with gold and diamonds of South Africa, are all available. The British merchant marine is still the largest on the Seven Seas. After a brief abdication, "the City" in London has replaced the Wall Street of New York as the financial center of the world. Yet, even before the Great Depression, Great Britain was losing ground in every field, and the process continues.

Politically, as well as economically, great changes have taken place since the war. Thus the self-governing status of the white Dominions has been so fully established that in Parliament British legislators have heard

IMPERIAL BRITAIN
POTENTIAL SELF-SUFFICIENCY IN FOODSTUFFS,
ESSENTIAL INDUSTRIAL PRODUCTS, AND RAW MATERIALS
EXPRESSED IN PERCENTAGES OF ALL AVAILABLE SOURCES
OF SUPPLY (NATIONAL AND IMPERIAL) TO BRITISH CONSUMPTION

—— GREAT ESSENTIALS ——

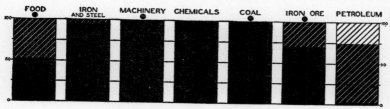

FOOD · IRON AND STEEL · MACHINERY · CHEMICALS · COAL · IRON ORE · PETROLEUM

CRITICAL RAW MATERIALS

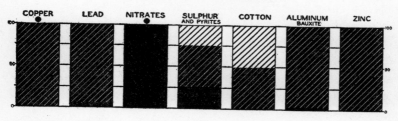

COPPER · LEAD · NITRATES · SULPHUR AND PYRITES · COTTON · ALUMINUM BAUXITE · ZINC

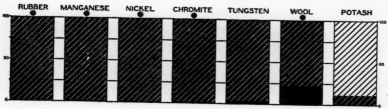

RUBBER · MANGANESE · NICKEL · CHROMITE · TUNGSTEN · WOOL · POTASH

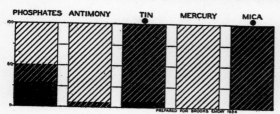

PHOSPHATES · ANTIMONY · TIN · MERCURY · MICA

AVERAGE DOMESTIC PRODUCTION.

NECESSARY EXTRA-IMPERIAL IMPORTS.

● EXPORTABLE SURPLUS.

ADDITIONAL SUPPLIES POTENTIALLY AVAILABLE FROM INCREASED DOMESTIC OUTPUT & FROM IMPERIAL SOURCES.

(SUBSTITUTES, STOCK-PILING, AND SECONDARY RECOVERY NOT CONSIDERED)

PREPARED FOR BROOKS EMENY 1934

© BROOKS EMENY

the Mother Country described as one of King George's Dominions. Again, on the military side at least, the traditional situation has been reversed, and in the last war it was the soldiers of the Dominions who fought for the Mother Country on French and Belgian battle-fields. That experience, too, has had a profound influence upon Dominion minds:[1] the imperial tie, which has so long seemed an inexpensive symbol of security and prestige, has come to have very definite implications of responsibility and risk.[2]

As a consequence, British policy in Europe has, in the postwar era, been subject to Dominion restraints. From beyond the seas there has come a constant protest against the assumption of Continental responsibilities. From the Locarno Pacts the Dominions significantly withheld their signature. In Ottawa, Canberra, and Cape Town, European conflicts awaken the same enthusiasm for isolation as in Kansas City, Omaha, or Denver. For Canada, too, the American fleet is at least as solid a guarantee of security as the British,[3] while even for Australia it is not without value.

Only a rash prophet would undertake to forecast early or even eventual dissolution of the British Empire polit-

[1] Cole, Capt. D. H., *Changing Conditions of Imperial Defence*, 1930; Dewey, A. G., *The Dominions and Diplomacy*, 1929; 2 vols.; Toynbee, A. J., *The Conduct of British Empire Foreign Relations Since the Peace Settlement*, 1928.

[2] Boycott, A. G., *The Elements of Imperial Defence*, 1931; Cole, Capt. D. H., *Imperial Military Geography*, 1930, 6th ed.; Fortescue, Sir John, *The Empire and the Army*, 1932; Fuller, Major-General J. F. C., *Empire Unity and Defence*, 1934.

[3] Canadian appreciation of this fact was recently given renewed emphasis in a letter written by Mr. G. H. Ferguson, High Commissioner for Canada in London, to a British correspondent and published in the New York *Herald Tribune*, August 7, 1934. In discussing the motives of loyalty to the Empire which prompted Canadian participation in the World War, Mr. Ferguson says: "A moment's thought, I think, will convince you that Canada has no selfish purpose in that action. She could have stayed out of the fight without the slightest fear of invasion of her own territory. The United States would have seen to it that no foreigner would be allowed to set foot on North American soil."

ically, although economic separation still proceeds apace. Not impossibly the Dominions would again fight for the Empire as they did in 1914–18. Nevertheless it is self-evident that the old relation between them and the Mother Country has largely disappeared and politically no substitute has as yet been established. As a consequence, the British Empire is today the largest question mark on the map of the world.

Within Great Britain, moreover, there has been unmistakably developing a state of mind which was first disclosed by the "Little Englanders" of the epoch of the Boer War. The imperial gospel of which Rudyard Kipling was the high priest has lost most of its disciples. The cost of empire has seemed increasingly to outweigh its value alike in profit and in prestige. Surrender of the mandate for Iraq was one evidence of this conviction, and continued protest against retention of that of Palestine, another. And as for ambition for new possessions, that has vanished utterly.

Like the Rome of Augustus, therefore, the Britain of George V is unmistakably seeking to restrict rather than to expand its frontiers, to discover defensible barriers, such as the older Empire found at the Rhine and the Danube, to maintain an imperial state which has definitively accepted the defensive. Even in India, British purpose has seemed to waver more than once in recent years, although the determination to hold on seems dominant again today.[1] And a similar uncertainty of purpose has been disclosed in Egypt.

In international conferences, the voice of Great Britain has lacked its ancient note of authority. In Europe,

[1] Cumming, Sir J. G., ed., *Political India, 1832-1932*, 1932; Krishnaswami, A., *The New Indian Constitution*, 1934; Thompson, E. J., and Garratt, G. T., *Rise and Fulfilment of British Rule in India*, 1934; Younghusband, Sir F. E., *Dawn in India*, 1931.

France and not England has exercised the predominant influence in the postwar era. In the Far East, Japan has enhanced her prestige at British expense. To the United States, Great Britain has voluntarily conceded a naval parity which could no longer be denied in the light of the superiority of the financial resources of the American republic. Yet a concession which disclosed wise statesmanship did not conceal a decline in world power. And, at bottom, all of these circumstances similarly reveal the fact that, imposing as the British Empire is in outward aspect, it does not possess that unity which once assured Great Britain her position of primacy in the world politically, financially, and industrially.

The postwar period has witnessed a sustained and gallant attempt on the British part to regain the old status; and it would be idle to deny that progress has actually been made. On the other hand, it is not less unmistakable that economically, financially, and politically the Empire of King George's Silver Anniversary will be far different from that of Victoria's Diamond Jubilee. And although the British Empire still remains one upon which the sun never sets, nowhere in that vast domain does that sun shine today with the same brilliance as in the closing years of the nineteenth century.

When one turns from the British to the French overseas empire, comparison is possible only between the Crown Colonies of the former and the Asiatic and African possessions of the latter. Here, however, the resemblances are striking and the comparison not unfavorable to the French. It is, moreover, worth at least passing note that as the uncertainties of the future in respect of the Dominions continue to mount, British attention is increasingly being directed to Kenya, Nigeria, and the

Gold Coast as French attention is similarly being concentrated upon Morocco and the regions of the Niger and the Congo.

In the main, the French colonial domain is the achievement of the Third Republic.[1] At the close of the Napoleonic era, there was left little of an empire which had once included the larger part of the North American continent and much of India. Martinique and Guadeloupe in the Caribbean area, Réunion in the Indian Ocean, Pondichéry in India, and Senegal in Africa—these were the chief remnants of that empire. Algeria was the later and final gift of the Bourbons at the very hour of their disappearance, although the conquest of this ancient stronghold of the Barbary corsairs was completed only under the Third Empire.

With the defeat of 1870, however, France turned abroad to seek in Africa and Asia colonies to replace the lost provinces of Alsace and Lorraine. Everywhere, too, success crowned her efforts. Faidherbe in Senegal, Galliéni in Madagascar, Joffre in the Sudan, De Brazza in the Congo, and last and greatest of all, Lyautey in Morocco, added new provinces and harvested fresh laurels. Diplomacy, too, played its role, and Waddington, with the somewhat cynical consent of Bismarck, brought Tunisia back from the Congress of Berlin, while Ferry, despite the thunders of Clemenceau, extended French rule in Indo-China.

By 1904, when France made her final settlement with Great Britain, her colonial empire was far larger than the United States, and today with Morocco and the Cameroons its population exceeds that of the Reich. The

[1] Roberts, S. H., *History of French Colonial Policy, 1870-1925*, 1929, 2 vols.; Southworth, Constant, *The French Colonial Adventure*, 1931.

FRENCH AFRICAN POSSESSIONS

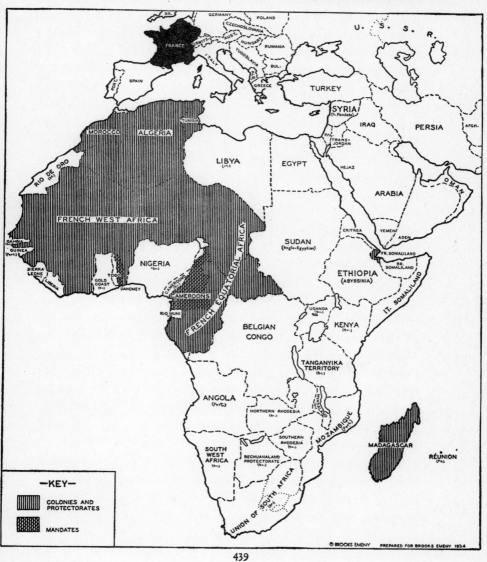

-KEY-

COLONIES AND PROTECTORATES

MANDATES

© BROOKS EMENY   PREPARED FOR BROOKS EMENY 1934

439

value of that empire as a source of man power was fully demonstrated during the World War, when, even as early as the Battle of Charleroi, African contingents fought with distinction in Belgium. In Champagne in 1915, Marchand, who had once defied Kitchener at Fashoda, led colonial troops to victorious assault. First and last, over half a million of overseas troops fought in French armies,[1] and another two hundred and twenty-five thousand were in the auxiliary services. After the war, German protests over the "Black Horror of the Rhine" signaled the presence of the Senegalese in Mainz.

France has therefore turned to her colonies to redress the balance between her numbers and those of Germany, and, since the war, the dream of Mangin in 1909 has found ever-increasing realization as the native battalions have been expanded. Primarily sources of recruitment, her colonies are only less valuable on the economic than on the military side. Even in the years of the Great Depression, her trade with her overseas possessions continued to grow. To them she now sends a third of her exports and from them draws a quarter of her imports.

Like the British Crown Colonies, these French possessions are fields of exploitation rather than of colonization. France, with an almost stationary population, sends few of her sons abroad. Nevertheless the European element in Algeria exceeds 900,000 and in all of North Africa numbers nearly a million and a quarter, in larger part French citizens. Algeria, too, is regarded rather as an extension of France than as a colony, and sends representatives to the French Parliament.

[1] "Thus, all together the French Colonies have furnished 545,000 native fighters, largely used in our shock troops; 115,400 have been killed under our flag."—*Comment Finit La Guerre*, by General Mangin, 1920, p. 259; see also Davis, S. C., *Reservoirs of Men*, 1934.

The proximity of the French North African territories to France proper—Algiers is as near to Marseille as Boston to Baltimore, and Tunisia closer to Paris than Kansas to Washington—is for France important both economically and strategically; economically, since French exports to Algeria alone exceed those of Great Britain to India; strategically, because the "Wet Triangle" of Toulon, Bizerta, and Oran enables France, with the consent of a friendly Great Britain, to dominate the western Mediterranean and thus to insure the transportation of colonial troops to homeland ports in war.

It is the territories in North, West, and Equatorial Africa which constitute by far the larger and more valuable portion of the French colonial empire. Greater in area than the United States, even with Alaska included, they extend uninterruptedly from the Mediterranean Sea to the Niger and the Congo. When the long-delayed Trans-Saharan railway is constructed, France will therefore be able to move her native troops from the heart of Africa to the Mediterranean without risk, and the security of Morocco, Tunisia, and Algeria will thus be assured.

From this empire, France draws many raw materials and foodstuffs: iron and phosphate as well as wine, cereals, and olive oil from North Africa; vegetable oils, cacao, and small quantities of rubber and cotton from the Congo and the Niger. In that empire, she finds a precious and growing market for her steel and iron as well as for her textiles. Year by year, her network of railways is expanding and in Morocco she has found a rich field for investment and development.

If, almost involuntarily, France in the prewar years became again a great colonial power, at least since the

FRANCE

POTENTIAL SELF-SUFFICIENCY IN FOODSTUFFS, ESSENTIAL INDUSTRIAL PRODUCTS, AND RAW MATERIALS

EXPRESSED IN PERCENTAGES OF ALL AVAILABLE SOURCES OF SUPPLY (NATIONAL AND COLONIAL) TO CONSUMPTION

—— GREAT ESSENTIALS ——

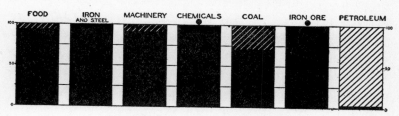

CRITICAL RAW MATERIALS

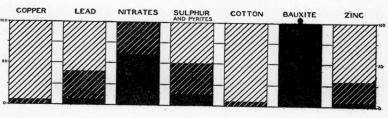

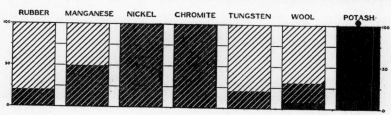

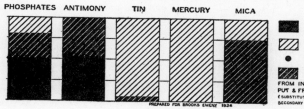

AVERAGE DOMESTIC PRODUCTION.

NECESSARY EXTRA-COLONIAL IMPORTS.

● EXPORTABLE SURPLUS.

ADDITIONAL SUPPLIES POTENTIALLY AVAILABLE FROM INCREASED DOMESTIC OUTPUT & FROM COLONIAL SOURCES. (SUBSTITUTES, STOCK-PILING, AND SECONDARY RECOVERY NOT CONSIDERED)

© BROOKS EMENY

PREPARED FOR BROOKS EMENY 1934

443

war her empire has acquired an ever greater importance in French eyes. Today with the extinction of all ambition for further territorial expansion in Europe, there is in France a growing conviction that the material future of the nation lies in Africa. By contrast, the rise of Japanese imperialism in Asia has reawakened those misgivings as to the permanence of French rule in Indo-China which Réclus voiced half a century ago.

The expanding importance of North Africa has also had a direct influence upon French national policy. Today France feels herself threatened in the Mediterranean by Italian ambition as she has long felt herself menaced by German purpose on the Rhine. As a consequence, she has rejected Italian claims to naval parity and has constantly sought British guarantees of the status quo in a Mediterranean Locarno. So far, however, Great Britain has refused to undertake such a responsibility, although her interests in the Mediterranean, like those of France, are best served by the maintenance of the status quo.

Modest by comparison with either the British Empire or the Soviet Union, nevertheless the French colonial empire, which entitles France to the rank of a World Power, provides an enormous reservoir of man power, supplies a large and growing market for French goods, and furnishes an invaluable source of raw materials and foodstuffs. In an era in which economic nationalism is steadily restricting the flow of goods across national frontiers, French Africa has acquired a new value for its possessor. Nor can its importance for the national merchant marine be ignored, for that enjoys a practical monopoly in the carrying trade between France and her colonies.

Unlike Great Britain and France, the United States and the Soviet Union are not in any real sense of the word imperial states, for Siberia, like our Pacific States, constitutes a contiguous portion of the national domain. As World Powers, their importance, which is, of course, unequal, has its origin not so much in the situation as in the extent and wealth in natural resources of their territories and in the size of their populations. Since all of these circumstances have been considered elsewhere they need no further comment here.

PART THREE

CAN PEACE BE PRESERVED?

Chapter XXIII

THE BACKGROUND

AT THE Paris Peace Conference in 1919, the first attempt
was made to establish a system of organized and administered peace which was designed to be universal in its
application. In Europe there was already a long-standing
tradition of co-operation through the medium of a
Concert of Powers. Before the World War the United
States had participated in the two Conferences of the
Hague and in the conclave at Algeciras summoned to
prevent war over Morocco. In the Old World, too, the
memories of the great Congresses of Vienna and Berlin
still survived.

Nevertheless the League of Nations, created by the
Paris Conference, was without precedent, at least in
modern history. It was the first clear evidence of reaction against the conceptions of the nation states system
which had been gaining ground steadily ever since the
Reformation had deprived Rome of the authority once
exercised by the medieval Papacy. Nor was the nature
of the grandiose experiment to be mistaken: it was publicly proclaimed by its author as designed to extend to

international relations that system of parliamentary democracy which, as a consequence of the World War, had become the accepted form of national governments in all of the Great Powers save Russia.

Throughout the century which had elapsed between the fall of Napoleon and the outbreak of the World War, European history had been dominated by two forces, democracy and nationalism. On the one hand, masses within national frontiers had sought political equality; on the other, nationalities, without regard to political frontiers, had striven to attain liberty and unity. As a consequence, parliaments had progressively absorbed the prerogatives of monarchs, and national states had replaced dynastic empires assembled without regard for ethnic circumstances.

With the victory of the Allied and Associated Nations in 1918, the triumph of the democratic doctrine seemed at last complete. That triumph, at various stages, had been attended by violence. The Revolutions of 1830 and 1848, while insignificant when compared with the mighty convulsion of 1792, had again shaken the European Continent. More permanently significant, however, had been the three great national wars, the Sardinian in 1859, the Austro-Prussian in 1866, and the Franco-Prussian in 1870. Nor had the pursuit of national unity been restricted to the Italian and German peoples. On the contrary, it had been common to all divided nationalities, great and small alike.

In fact, from Waterloo to the Marne, all the significant and considerable European wars had been due directly or indirectly to the aspirations of some people for unity. While Napoleon was still alive, the Greek War of Independence had opened the century-long series of national wars. The Belgians had risen successfully in 1830, the Poles vainly in 1833, and the Italians and Hungarians with equal futility in 1848–1849. The process had continued after the national wars of 1859–1870, and on the very eve of the World War the Bulgarians, Serbs, and Greeks had brought to a brief and brilliant close their five centuries of struggle with the Turk. Last of all, it was a Serb patriot who, in 1914, fired the train which produced world-wide explosion.

It was natural that the Allied democracies, having at last triumphed in 1918, should undertake to found their system of international order upon the two doctrines which asserted the right of majorities to rule within states and the right of peoples to national unity. It was even more natural that, since the pursuit of these goals had been the cause or the occasion of all of the considerable wars of the recent past, peoples should conclude that, now that these rights had been established, peace could also in its turn be insured.

Examination of the events of the past century, however, disclosed certain facts of more than passing challenge. Thus, although the two doctrines of democracy and nationalism had similarly been vitalized by the French Revolution and had later marched abreast for the first generation after Waterloo, with the failure of the Revolution of 1848 a subtle but very far-reaching change had taken place. Before that upheaval, peoples had with equal violence reacted against autocracy and against alien domination. To the minds of Metternich and those whom he served, moreover, the demands for political and racial rights seemed similarly subversive.

After 1848, however, the revolt of the masses against their monarchs had gradually ceased and the dynasties in their turn increasingly identified themselves with the national aspirations of their subjects. As a consequence, by 1914 the struggles between peoples and their princes, which had marked the first half of the nineteenth century, had largely been forgotten. Thanks to Cavour, the House of Savoy had become the symbol of the Risorgimento, and, through the genius of Bismarck, a Hohenzollern sovereign had forged a new German Empire in blood and iron. Thus, with the exception of the Romanoffs, still haunted by the ghosts of the Russian Revolution of 1905, thrones had recovered much of that prestige and popularity which had once seemed fatally compromised by the French Revolution.

This restoration of the *Einheitsfronte* between peoples and their kings, however, had been only a detail in the larger phenomenon of the spread of nationalism all over the European Continent. Originally that spirit had been born of the aspiration of peoples for unity, for a unity primarily based upon ethnic circumstances. After 1848, however, it had become colored by ambitions for national expansion. Acquisition of ethnic unity did not bring with it a sense of satiety either for the Italians or for the Germans. On the contrary, the Italians, having recovered Venice, now demanded the southern Tirol, where the population was German, and Dalmatia, where it was Slavic. And, in the same fashion, the Germans, having achieved their own unity, promptly shattered French unity by annexing Alsace-Lorraine.

Precisely the same spirit was disclosed by the smaller peoples. Thus, having liberated their own brethren from Turkish rule, the Greeks, the Bulgarians, and the Serbs promptly took up arms to enslave populations belonging to their recent allies. And similarly the Rumanians of the old kingdom, while proclaiming the right of their brethren of Transylvania and the Banat to political liberty and racial unity, forcibly annexed the Bulgarians of Silistria without concern for their rights.

Before 1815, European wars had resulted mainly from the rivalry of monarchs. Provinces and populations had been the pawns of such conflicts, and at the Congress of Vienna human beings had been parceled out by the head to insure parity in plunder for the victorious sovereigns. When, however, as the nineteenth century wore on, parliaments had largely replaced absolute sovereigns, the substitution of popular for royal authority had not been accompanied by any change in the character of national policies. On the contrary, democracy, rising to the seat of autocracy, instinctively and insensibly adopted the traditional aspirations of its predecessors. Peoples had acquired political power but they had displayed no inclination to exercise it peacefully. Europe had become progressively more democratic, but democracies showed themselves no more reasonable where national ambitions were concerned than had kings where royal appetites had been involved.

It is essential to perceive this paradox between the practice and the pretensions of democracies, because it constitutes a key to many occurrences in the postwar years which would otherwise be completely unintelligible. The basic assumption upon which the League of Nations was founded was that democracy itself was a prescription of peace. And that assumption, in turn, had its origin in the contemporary Liberal interpretation of the causes of the World War, an interpretation which found eloquent and authoritative expression in the speeches of Woodrow Wilson.

To the mind of the American President, responsibility for the great tragedy rested upon the shoulders of the monarchs and autocrats of prewar Europe. They had plunged their peace-loving subjects into war in pursuit of their own selfish and ignoble ends. To prevent a repetition of the catastrophe of 1914–1918, it was necessary to substitute for the Hapsburgs and Hohenzollerns and their military and naval servants that system of parliamentary democracy prevailing among the victorious Western Allies. The war had been fought to make the world safe for democracy, and it was now the mission of democracy to render the world secure for peace.

That was the first great assumption upon which the League of Nations was founded. There was a second, only less important, and that was that the transfer of political power to majorities would also insure the peaceful and permanent settlement of the disputes between nations over territories. The prewar world had been plagued by the problems of Alsace-Lorraine and of Trieste and the Trentino, by the claims of the Slavs of the Dual Monarchy, and by the wrongs of the Poles partitioned among three great empires. All of these problems, too, had their origin in the unmistakable denial to majorities of the right to determine their allegiance themselves.

Manifestly both of these major assumptions had their origin in the ideology of the American and French Revolutions. They were equally reminiscent of sentiments expressed in the Declaration of Independence and in the Proclamation of the Rights of Man. They had also found authentic echo in the Revolution of 1848. But, by contrast, they completely ignored the evidence supplied by the events of the years following Sedan. They dismissed the performance of the British democracy in South Africa, of the French in Tunisia, of the Italian in Libya, and of the American about the Caribbean. Above all, they turned a deaf ear and a blind eye to the unmistakable proofs of the extent to which democracies had succumbed to the subtle corruption of power and the extent to which peoples now demanded for themselves the prizes for which princes had once contended.

Unless the World War had brought with it a profound change in the point of view of peoples everywhere, there was no reason founded upon experience to justify these two assumptions. But at the moment of the Armistice, there were signs that such a change had taken place. The masses in every country had found the war to be an agony without parallel and without limit. They had borne the brunt of the fighting, they had carried the burdens of privation, they had now to shoulder the weight of the war debts. For the populations of the Great Powers, too, the fact was beyond challenge that their sufferings had been without reward; and for their countries the war had proved a tremendous disaster. In the furnace, the Dual Monarchy of Austria-Hungary had disappeared altogether, Russia had collapsed to Communism, and in Germany a poverty-stricken republic had been established amid the ruins of imperial splendor. Nor was the situation of the so-called victorious powers of Europe different, save in degree. For all, the conquerors and the conquered alike, the conflict had demonstrably proved a catastrophe.

Taught by their experience in the last war, was it not natural to believe that peoples everywhere would now exercise their political power to prevent a next war? If in their blindness majorities had, in the past, been the consenting victims of imperialistic policies and militaristic leaders, could they not be relied upon for all future time to follow men and support policies of peace? Everyone now knew what war meant. The masses who constituted the political majorities were fully aware of the fact that theirs would be the sacrifice in war and the suffering after it.

It is evident, however, that every assumption that democracy would henceforth insure peace rested upon the belief that the Paris Settlement could establish it. To the European map there was now to be supplied the principle of self-determination; but that principle could promise peace only as Paris was able to provide conditions nationally acceptable and economically tolerable. It was obvious, in advance, that various groups of people —fifty millions in all—who had been subject and divided were now to attain liberty and unity. Poland was to rise from the grave; Bohemia, rechristened Czecho-slovakia, was to reappear as an independent state after three centuries of servitude. Alsace-Lorraine and Italia Irredenta would henceforth cease to trouble European tranquillity.

But what about the circumstances of the hundred millions of Germans, Austrians, Hungarians, and Bulgarians, whose frontiers were mutilated, whose unity was destroyed, whose provinces were surrendered to permit the creation of the new Europe of self-determination? For, unhappily, Central and Eastern Europe are not divided into neat and convenient ethnic compartments. On the contrary, from Danzig to Salonika and from Bavaria to the Pripet Marshes, the Old World is a *macedoine* of races inextricably mingled and traditionally and irreconcilably hostile.

Would the inhabitants of those states whose territorial solidarity was destroyed and whose ethnic unity was abolished accept the decisions of the Peace Conference as just, even when sanctioned by the verdict of self-determination? Looking across their own mutilated frontiers to the territories once their own and now held by the Poles, the Czechs, the Rumanians, and the Serbs, would the Germans, the Magyars, and the Bulgarians reckon the miseries of another war more terrible than the permanence of the circumstances in which they found themselves? And for these circumstances war was clearly the only remedy.

Such temptation to war might be resisted if ethnic division were accompanied by economic well-being. Hitherto, the application of the principle of self-determination had resulted in the substitution of large states for small. The unification of Italy and the creation of the German Empire were familiar examples of this process, and both had brought prosperity. Now, however, it was proposed to reduce the Hapsburg Monarchy to its ethnic factors; and although it was a mosaic of nationalities it was an admirably balanced economic unit. Six states with as many frontiers were now to divide the territories of the old Dual Monarchy with its single fiscal frontier.

Could Europe collectively, could the Danubian area where this process of Balkanization was to be applied most rigorously, survive it? Would the Europe of self-determination be economically viable or would material misery accompanying political humiliation serve to fan into fresh flames the still smoldering fires of racial passions? And in such case would not the peoples who had been partitioned in the name of nationality and plundered on the ground of reparations, and thereby reduced from prewar prosperity to a permanent condition of poverty, confound the Peace Treaties and the League of Nations? Would they not see in the latter the instrument of tyranny to perpetuate the injustices of the former?

For the Settlement of Paris and the creation of the League of Nations were to be accomplished simultaneously. The inclusion of the Covenant of the League in the four Treaties of Paris severally named the treaties of Versailles, St. Germain, Trianon, and Neuilly, which imposed new frontiers and different conditions upon Germany, Austria, Hungary, and Bulgaria, was rendered inescapable by the terms of the Armistice which made Wilson's Proposals the basis of peace. These treaties were to become, thenceforth, the public law of Europe, and the League was constituted the executor of that law. Peace and the treaties of peace were henceforth inextricably entangled. But if the treaties proved in the eyes of the defeated inequitable and therefore intolerable, how was the League to escape sharing the evil consequence of that fact?

Such a question had been raised before in Europe. The settlement made at the Congress of Vienna had aroused resentment all over the Continent. But to perpetuate that settlement Alexander I of Russia had proposed his notorious Holy Alliance. Invoking the principle of legitimacy and appealing to the world in the name of peace, the Czar had sought to make permanent the status quo of 1815 by the collective guarantee of the victorious sovereigns. To the conception of Alexander, strangely compounded of religious mysticism and dynastic anxiety, neither Castlereagh nor Metternich had paid much heed, and as a consequence the Holy Alliance was never consummated.

Instead, the British and Austrian statesmen secretly made the Quadruple Alliance, which included Austria, Great Britain, Prussia, and Russia, and was rigidly restricted to the realistic purpose of preserving the status quo of Vienna. But in the popular mind the Holy Alliance and the Quadruple Alliance had been confused, and under the former name the association of the victors became the symbol of tyranny and reaction from Waterloo to the Revolution of 1848. And yet the underlying purpose of the partnership proposed in the name of religion, and of that alliance actually made in the name of practical politics, had been the preservation of peace.

At Paris, Woodrow Wilson appeared in the role of Alexander I. In his turn he proposed a new international association, at the outset, at least, to be composed of the victors. This new League of Nations was to be established upon the dogma of democracy, and not, like the Holy Alliance, upon the doctrine of legitimacy. It was to be a partnership of peoples and not of princes; but it was also designed to be the guarantor of a status quo established upon the foundations of a military victory and an imposed peace. And if in the eyes of conquered peoples the Settlement of Paris immediately or eventually assumed the character which the Settlement of Vienna had acquired in the eyes of the parceled and partitioned peoples a century before, was not the League bound to possess the ill repute of the Holy Alliance?

But the problem was not limited to the future attitude of the peoples that had been defeated in the World War. It was not merely the status quo in Europe established by the Settlement of Paris which was henceforth to be the basis of peace. What was now aimed at was not a European but a universal system of order. But would the Japanese, for example, find more tolerable that institution which forbade them the realization of their imperialistic purposes in eastern Asia, than the Germans would find the same institution which constituted a similar obstacle to their ambitions in Middle Europe?

Inherent in the whole League conception was the idea that the world had become static, that the age of expansion was over, that the moment had come when peoples everywhere were now prepared to accept as final the frontiers which existed in 1919, when the Treaties of Paris had been applied. And that conviction was vital to the whole idea of a League of Nations because all the territory of the world was now divided among the various nations and none could thereafter extend its own boundaries save through violence and at the expense of another. And it was to prevent such resort to violence that the League was called into being.

Consent and authority, these were to be pillars of the new structure: consent of peoples everywhere voluntarily to accept the territorial status quo of the moment as enduring; and authority delegated by the member nations to maintain that status quo against any future challenge by any single nation for the moment fallen into evil hands and dominated and directed by leaders inspired by the old doctrines of conquest and hegemony, by the ancient reliance upon force rather than by the new respect for law. Against such a regime there was to be mobilized through the League the public opinion of mankind. Against the force of that individual nation there was to be assembled the collective resources of all other states for coercion.

At the very bottom of the whole conception, moreover, was the belief that, internationally as nationally, the will of the majority could and would prevail, not by violence but naturally and inevitably as it did within democracies everywhere. Beyond all else, the League was to be an instrument to make effective the will of the peoples, as parliaments already served as the means to express the will of majorities within states. And this belief involved the supreme assumption that the moment had arrived when peoples could and would think internationally. It was, moreover, on the rock of that assumption that Wilson undertook to found the League of Nations.

In approaching the history of the postwar period, the student of international relations must therefore perceive at the very outset that all the experiments in peace have rested upon the basic assumption that the World War had not merely been a war but also a revolution; that as the French Revolution had launched a new gospel of nationalism, the later convulsion had set in motion a religion of internationalism; that as, after 1792, peoples had been dominated by the double resolution to possess political liberty and national unity, so, after 1919, they were destined to be inspired by a similar passion for peace.

If that world which was unmistakably nationalistic in 1914 had, after 1919, become—not momentarily, while the memories of the war still survived, but for all future time—international, then and only then could a League of Nations prove successful. It was beyond dispute an instrument exclusively designed to serve the ends of a new world. It could, in the very nature of things, have no validity in the prewar world. It was, in fact, a supreme testimonial to the conviction that the Age of Nationalism was over and that an Era of Internationalism had begun.

The test of the accuracy of the assumptions upon which the League rested must therefore be the fashion in which peoples themselves have thought and acted in the postwar years. Theirs was the power to use, abuse, or ignore the machinery of Geneva. It was for them to impose upon their governments and leaders policies in accord with the principles set forth in the Covenant. The price of a successful League was the subordination of national policies to international accord. These national policies were, in themselves, irreconcilable. To this fact had been due the World War. To continue to pursue these policies, and thus necessarily to attempt to impose them upon other countries, could only lead to fresh conflict.

Between the absolute sovereignty of the individual state and the supreme authority of the superstate there is no halfway station. The will of the majority must prevail internationally or the condition of anarchy which had existed before 1914 was bound to reappear after 1919. Either peoples were now prepared to modify their national policies to conform to international decision, or they were not. And if they were not, the circumstances of Geneva in the postwar period were condemned in advance to be no more fortunate than those of the Hague between 1907 and 1914, when the World War was coming on apace.

In the consideration of the history of the League of Nations, therefore, the student of international relations must not permit his attention to be drawn away from the main issue, which is the attitude of peoples as disclosed by their policies, and concentrated upon details concerning the nature and structure of the machinery set up at Geneva. The primary problem is not how that machinery was designed to operate, but why it did not function; and the key to that problem lies not in Geneva but in the policies of the several nations. Each in turn, beginning with the United States, was called upon to give a clear and unequivocal sign that it accepted or rejected the fundamental principle of the League, which was sacrifice of sovereignty either by delegation of national powers to an international institution, or by voluntary subordination of national interest to international decision.

Chapter XXIV

THE COVENANT OF THE LEAGUE

THE Covenant of the League of Nations,[1] which is in fact its charter, called into being, at the summons of the high contracting states that made the Settlement of Paris, an international congress consisting of two bodies, the Council and the Assembly. The Council includes representatives of all the Great Powers that are members, together with those of several of the smaller powers, while the Assembly is composed of delegates from all of the many member nations. Attached to the League is a Secretariat which fulfills the mission of a permanent civil service.[2] The Secretariat is housed at Geneva, Switzerland, which is also the meeting place of the Council and of the Assembly. Joined to the League also is a World Court, possessing a large degree of independence.

The functions of the League were designed to be threefold: to prevent war, to organize peace, and to promote

---

[1] For text of the Covenant, see Appendix A.

[2] For general studies on the origin and structure of the League, see: Howard-Ellis, Charles, *The Origin, Structure and Working of the League of Nations,* 1928; Mower, E. C., *International Government,* 1931; Walp, P. K., *Constitutional Development of the League of Nations,* 1931.

international co-operation in that vast field where the interests of nations are common or subject to amicable adjustment.[1] In addition, there were transferred to it by the Paris Conference many temporary and permanent tasks incident to the administration of the peace treaties, such as the supervision of mandates[2] and the government of the Saar Basin and the Danzig Free State.

Recalling in some measure the traditional Concert of Europe, the League was, nevertheless, to be of universal scope, and constituted a final testimony to the belief that the World War had demonstrated that conflict could no longer be localized in an integrated world. It was not an alliance, because eventually, if not immediately, it was to be open to all nations on similar terms. It was, furthermore, not provided with the resources of a super-state, and although it most closely resembled a national legislature, it was in fact able to proceed, in the main, only by unanimous consent. Thus, in practice, it became little more than an international conference having a permanent existence.

In becoming members of the League, states are, by virtue of the Covenant, required to take a variety of engagements, of which the most important are those con-

[1] For general studies on the functioning of the League, see: Conwell-Evans, T. P., *The League Council in Action*, 1929; Greaves, H. R. G., *The League Committees and World Order*, 1931; Hill, N. L., *International Administration*, 1931; Jackson, Judith, and King-Hall, Stephen, *The League Year-Book*, annual since 1932; League of Nations, *Ten Years of World Co-operation*, 1930; McClure, Wallace, *World Prosperity as Sought Through the Economic Work of the League of Nations*, 1933; Myers, D. P., *Handbook of the League of Nations Since 1920*, 1930.

For special reference in addition to the *Official Journal* and *Monthly Summary*, the publications released by the following Sections of the League of Nations will be useful: Administrative, Communications, Disarmament, Economic and Financial, Intellectual Co-operation, Legal, Mandates, Minorities, and Political.

[2] Bentwich, Norman De Mattos, *The Mandates System*, 1930; Gerig, Benjamin, *The Open Door and the Mandates System*, 1930; Maanen-Helmer, Elizabeth van, *The Mandates System in Relation to Africa and the Pacific Islands*, 1929; Margalith, A. M., *The International Mandates*, 1930; Wright, Quincy, *Mandates Under the League of Nations*, 1930.

tained in Articles X and XVI of that document. In accordance with the former, member nations "undertake to respect and to preserve as against external aggression the territorial integrity and existing political independence of all Members of the League." In conformity with the latter they agree that, should any member nation resort to war in violation of its various other commitments in the Covenant, that nation shall "be deemed to have committed an act of war against all other Members of the League."

With the nation guilty of such an act of war, member nations agree to sever all trade and financial relations and also to take steps calculated to insure the prevention of all financial, commercial, or personal intercourse. In such actions they also pledge themselves to support one another. It is the "friendly right" of each nation, moreover, to bring to the attention of the Council or the Assembly any question which threatens to disturb international peace,[1] and all agree that any war or threat of war is a matter of concern to the entire League, which is bound to take any action it deems wise and effectual to safeguard peace.[2]

All member nations are bound by the Covenant to submit any dispute, likely to lead to a rupture of relations with another state, to arbitration, to judicial settlement, or to inquiry by the Council, which in practice means to the Arbitration Tribunal at the Hague, to the World Court, or to the Council. Nor may any state resort to war until three months after decision has been had following such submission.[3] Member states also pledge themselves to submit issues

[1] Article XI, Paragraph 2.
[2] Article XI, Paragraph 1.
[3] Article XII.

to arbitration or judicial decision when they recognize them to be suitable for such procedure,[1] and to carry out in good faith any decision rendered. Nor may they resort to war against a member nation which complies with the terms of such a decision.[2]

When states do not deem issues suitable for arbitration or judicial settlement, they must submit them directly to the Council of the League for inquiry; and they may not go to war with a state which complies with the decision of the Council if that decision is unanimously agreed to by the members thereof other than the representatives of the parties to the dispute.[3] On the other hand, if the decision is not thus unanimous, the parties to a dispute reserve the right to act as they may choose.[4] But more important still to the machinery of peace is the provision in the Covenant which empowers the Assembly to "advise the reconsideration by Members of the League of treaties which have become inapplicable, and the consideration of international conditions whose continuance might endanger the peace of the world."[5]

In respect of armaments, member nations agree to accept such regulations of their military, naval, and air forces as the League may prescribe, and recognize that it is essential to peace that armaments shall be reduced to the lowest point consistent with national safety. The member states recognize, furthermore, that the private

[1] "Disputes as to the interpretation of a treaty, as to any question of international law, as to the existence of any fact which, if established, would constitute a breach of any international obligation, or as to the extent and nature of the reparation to be made for any such breach, are declared to be among those which are generally suitable for submission to arbitration or judicial settlement." (Article XIII, Paragraph 2.)

[2] Article XIII, Paragraph 4.

[3] Article XV, Paragraph 6.

[4] Article XV, Paragraph 7.

[5] Article XIX.

manufacture of munitions is open to grave objections, and the Covenant provides that "The Council shall advise how the evil effects attendant upon such manufacture can be prevented. . . ."[1]

Beyond these primary concerns of Geneva, the Covenant prescribes many other duties of the League, including due attention to slavery, opium traffic, and disease.[2] In reality, there is no fixed or discoverable limit to its possible field of activity in what may perhaps be described as the non-controversial questions having international importance, such for example as economic and transportation problems. Associated with the League, though not directly joined to it, is the International Bureau of Labor, which has its headquarters at Geneva and deals with all international issues affecting Labor.[3]

Here, then, is created an institution without close parallel in history, composed of a Council of fourteen members, of an Assembly in which sit three representatives of each member state, and of a Secretariat. The first meets four times a year; the second, annually in September; and the third is always in being. In addition there is a Labor Bureau at Geneva. The World Court at the Hague, whose judges are selected by the Council and Assembly together, can, in addition to rendering decisions, also give advisory opinions upon invitation of either the Council or the Assembly.[4]

---

[1] Article VIII, Paragraph 5.

[2] Articles XXIII and XXV.

[3] Cheyney, A. S., *ed.*, *The International Labor Organization*, 1933; Foreign Policy Association, "The International Labor Organization," *Foreign Policy Reports*, Vol. X, No. 9, 1934; Lorwin, L. L., *Labor and Internationalism*, 1929; World Peace Foundation, *The International Labour Organization*, 1931.

[4] Fachiri, A. P., *The Permanent Court of International Justice*, 1932, rev.; Hudson, M. O., *The World Court*, *1921-34*, 1934, 4th rev.; Jessup, P. C., *The United States and the World Court*, 1929; Lindsey, Edward, *The International Court*, 1931; World Peace Foundation, *Ten Years of International Jurisdiction*, 1932.

All of the members of this League are pledged in advance to respect the territorial integrity of one another and to defend it as well, and to submit their disputes to the Council, to the World Court, or to an Arbitration Tribunal. In the case of some incident endangering peace, a nation fearful of attack can appeal to the Council. The Council will then call upon parties to submit their dispute to the inquiry of a commission it will name. The disputants are pledged furthermore not to resort to arms until three months after the decision of the commission has been delivered, and not at all if that decision be unanimous.

At Geneva, most of the member nations maintain ministers as they do in national capitals. There the statesmen and diplomats of all countries are constantly in contact. With the passing of years, the League has developed a conference technique, and a machinery of international co-operation in non-controversial fields. It now possesses a splendid palace for its headquarters; and its reports, investigations, and activities generally continue to multiply.

Such, briefly summarized, is the machinery of the League. Nor could any summary, however brief, be fair or exact which did not lay emphasis upon the extent of the achievement of Geneva outside the area of high politics. In fact it would be impossible, even in a far greater space than the present study affords, merely to catalogue the various forms of activity of the League or to set down the value of the services which it renders. It must therefore suffice to note here that in the field of non-controversial international problems its success has been so unmistakable that its permanence is no longer open to doubt.

Nevertheless, there remains the larger field. Primarily the League was created to deal with those issues of peace and war which concern Great Powers directly or indirectly. It was to preserve and to organize world peace that this most grandiose of all experiments in internationalism was originally launched. It is, therefore, upon its achievement in these respects that its record must in the end be judged. And here the contemporary evidence of failure is not to be gainsaid.[1]

In 1934, fifteen years after the first Assembly of the League was convened, three of the seven Great Powers were absent from its sessions, and a fourth, the Soviet Union, had only just been admitted to membership. And while the United States had never belonged, and Germany and Japan had withdrawn in 1932, Italy from the beginning had attended only to proclaim hostility to the whole spirit of the Geneva experiment. Not less illuminating is the fact that the two Great Powers physically present and in principle still loyal—Great Britain and France—have in recent years met at Geneva only to disagree on most issues and, as a consequence of their disagreement, to precipitate deadlock.

Equally significant is the fact that during these fifteen years not one of the causes of dispute between Great Powers has found acceptable solution through the interposition of the League. On the contrary, all of the reasons for future conflict which existed when the League began, and notably those which have reduced the Danubian region to political anarchy and economic misery, still endure. In fact, many of them have become progressively more and more acute and dangerous.

[1] Beer, Max, *The League on Trial*, 1933; Morley, Felix, *The Society of Nations*, 1932; Williams, Sir J. F., *Some Aspects of the Covenant of the League of Nations*, 1934; Zimmern, L. A., *Must the League Fail?* 1932.

The fact of the persistence of disputes dangerous to peace was fully demonstrated by the clash between Yugoslavia and Hungary in December, 1934. Several weeks after the murder of King Alexander, the Yugoslavs, backed by their Rumanian and Czech partners of the Little Entente, assailed Hungary on the ground that she had harbored Croatian terrorists responsible for the crime. Danger of war, however, was very slight, because four Great Powers, France, Italy, Great Britain, and the Soviet Union, were united in the double determination not to be dragged into conflict themselves, and not to permit hostilities between the smaller states.

As a consequence these powers worked together in the Council of the League and elaborated a compromise which was accepted by both Hungary and Yugoslavia. The compromise, however, did nothing to remove the basic cause of the crisis, which was the demand of the Hungarians for treaty revision to abolish the grave wrongs done to them in the Treaty of the Trianon by the transfer of one and a half million Magyars to the nations of the Little Entente without any other grounds than those which were purely strategic.

The achievement of the League in bringing about a compromise in this dispute was identical with similar results achieved by the old Concert of Europe over and over again in the prewar years and notably in the winter of 1912–1913 at the close of the Balkan Wars. In that instance, as in the crisis of 1934, the Great Powers were similarly resolved not to be dragged into a general war because of the quarrels between Balkan states. As a result they co-operated in a council of ambassadors meeting at London and evolved the compromises which were embodied in the Treaty of Bucharest of 1913.

A year later, however, when, following the assassination of the Archduke, Austria issued first an ultimatum and then a declaration of war against Serbia, the operations of diplomacy were futile because there was no agreement of the Great Powers. On the contrary Austria was ready to risk war with Russia, so determined was she to abolish the Serbian menace. Russia, for her part, was prepared to fight rather than let Serbia be crushed. And Germany and France at all times stood with their Austrian and Russian allies. Under such circumstances nothing could be done; and, of course, the same results would have occurred in 1934 had the Great Powers been again divided.

In a word, when the Great Powers are united in their determination to prevent a war, then the machinery of the League or the older method of the council of ambassadors will suffice to serve the ends of these powers. In 1905 after the crisis of Tangier, in 1908 in the Bosnian episode, in 1911 in the Agadir affair, old-fashioned diplomacy functioned adequately because all the Great Powers were anxious to avoid actual conflict. The existence of an instrument such as the Council of the League, which is immediately available, patently permits action with greater celerity and ease.

The student of international affairs must not, however, confuse the situation of 1934 with that of 1914 and read into the success of Geneva in the later year a significance which it did not have. At no time in the more recent crisis was there any danger of collision between France and Italy, for example, although Yugoslavia was the ally of the former and Hungary of the latter. On the contrary the French and Italian statesmen and diplomats, always in close association with the British, worked together to restrain and not to encourage their respective allies. Had Austrian and Russian diplomats been in the same mood in 1914 there would have been no serious crisis or catastrophe then.

What happened in Geneva in December, 1934, was that the old Concert of Europe, composed of four of the five Great Powers—Germany being absent and unconcerned— employed the machinery of the League to avert a conflict the four nations were all equally concerned in preventing. No one would undertake to minimize the usefulness of the machinery thus used. But it must be plain that nothing then achieved constituted any promise that in case of an open clash between Great Powers such as occurred in July, 1914, the new method would be of more avail than the old had been. Nor can the fact be disguised that the basic cause of the crisis survived intact, to the enduring peril of peace in the Danubian region.

How is it possible to explain this situation? Obviously it is not a question merely of faults in machinery to be cured by amendments of the Covenant or by a modification of the methods of procedure. Nor would it be enough merely to bring the absent Great Powers to Geneva unless in advance some basis of agreement for common action by them were discovered. The fact that, of the seven Great Powers, one has always remained outside, two have entered and withdrawn, and still another has combined nominal association with actual opposition, is impressive evidence of fundamental weakness.

What, then, is wrong with the League? Primarily the fact that it was based upon a major assumption which has proved false. This assumption was that, as a consequence of the lessons of the World War, peoples everywhere had arrived at two revolutionary decisions: first, that a new conflict must bring common disaster to all mankind, and, second, that this disaster could be averted only by collective efforts of the several nations, all similarly ready and willing to sacrifice sovereign rights to insure the success of the international agency for peace to be established at Geneva.

As the original thirteen states of the American republic had been driven by common political dangers abroad and economic and social weaknesses at home to seek security in union, so it was assumed by the founders at the League of Nations that the peoples of the Great Powers, as well as of the smaller states, would, in the light of the supreme catastrophe of 1914–1918, be led to the delegation of sovereign powers to an international organization and to the acceptance of duties and responsibilities inherent in such a course. Vague and ill-defined as were the conceptions of the extent and limitations of the power of the new League of Nations, at bottom there was a clear conviction that peoples, even if they had in the prewar era thought nationally, were henceforth in the postwar years ready to think internationally and to give expression to their thought by collective action at Geneva.

That conviction found expression in Articles X and XVI of the Covenant. For what, after all, is the primary condition of any international association which is not foredoomed to futility? Obviously an agreement on the part of all nations, but primarily of the Great Powers, not merely to respect the territorial integrity and political independence of one another, but also to take common action against any nation, great or small, which violates this fundamental contract. That commitment

Woodrow Wilson himself correctly described as the very heart of the whole League conception. For if nations will not agree to obey the law, then the law has no moral validity; and if they will not agree to enforce it, then it can have no practical value.

In point of fact, however, all of the seven Great Powers have, from the very outset, evaded one or both of these essential engagements. The United States, while prepared to renounce any design to disturb the territorial integrity or to destroy the political independence of another country, rejected the Treaty of Versailles because it carried with it the responsibilities of the Covenant for the enforcement of peace. And by doing this, America gave the first clear proof of the inexactitude of one of the basic assumptions upon which the League had been established.

Like the Americans, the British were willing to obey the law because, also like their fellow Anglo-Saxons beyond the Atlantic, they were content with their own territorial possessions. Having by past aggression attained present satiety, they were now able, with complete sincerity, to renounce all purpose to disturb the status quo. But they, too, were not prepared to defend it, as they demonstrated by the rejection alike of the Cecil project for Mutual Defense (1923) and of the Protocol of Geneva (1924).

What the Americans and British were prepared to maintain was the status quo only in the regions in which their interests were vital. Thus the United States had long ago asserted the Monroe Doctrine, and in the post-war period the British, through the Pact of Locarno, undertook specific responsibility for the preservation of the status quo in the Rhineland. But in both instances responsibility had been based upon national interest and not primarily upon concern for international peace. And both peoples were at one in the rejection of responsibilities for the enforcement of the law on the Vistula, the Danube, or the Tisza.

Like the English-speaking nations, France and the Soviet Union—at least after the fall of Trotzky—were also quite ready to respect the territorial integrity and the political independence of other nations. For each of them, their present territorial circumstances were sufficient; for each, the period of imperialistic expansion was over. But whereas for the United States no problem of security arose outside of the American region, and for the British that problem in its European aspect was bounded by the Rhine, for France security was contingent upon the enforcement of the law and therefore the preservation of the status quo all over the European Continent. And the Soviet Union, sharing French circumstances in Europe, was similarly concerned with the status quo in the Far East as well.

In Europe, France was confronted by the double challenge inherent in the national policies of Germany and Italy, while Russia was threatened by German designs upon the Ukraine and in Asia by the Japanese upon Siberia. For these countries, therefore, it was not enough that the League should be the witness of the resolution of all nations to obey the law. On the contrary, it was for them even more important that Geneva should have the authority and the means to enforce the law. That, moreover, was the basis of French policy from the outset; but only much later, under the pressure of events in both Europe and Asia, did Russia come to the acceptance of the French basis.

Finally, Germany, Italy, and Japan in practice utterly refused to accept the law, which was the status quo established by several treaties of the Paris and Washington Conferences. For them that status quo was intolerable because, unlike the other four Great Powers, they found themselves restricted to limits incommensurate with present prosperity or future national development. While for the French the primary objective of an international organization was necessarily preservation of the status quo, which insured security, the primary objective for the Germans, Japanese, and Italians was a revision of the existing frontiers of the world, to permit national existence on terms which were nationally acceptable.

But it must be obvious that no effective co-operation by the Great Powers, either through the League or otherwise, is even conceivable while there is a complete disagreement in principle. The status quo of the world in 1919 and thereafter was based upon public international law embodied in treaties. Either the seven Great Powers had to accept that status quo or they had to agree voluntarily to a system of revision, if there was to be any true partnership. Failing that, at the very least, the four satisfied Powers had to undertake to defend the law, which meant in practice to guarantee the status quo, if there was to be any order in the world.

Agreement between the status quo powers and the revisionist powers was, however, always impossible. Consent of the Anglo-Saxon powers, which were at once satisfied and secure, to assume responsibility for the enforcement of the law was similarly unattainable. Thus the League began, based not upon a community of purposes but upon a collision of policies. The Americans outside of the League, and the British within, refused to assume responsibility for the enforcement of the existing law. The French and their allies within the League mobilized their resources to prevent a revision of the law. The Japanese and the Germans, when they found the law an obstacle to their pursuit of revision, quit Geneva altogether. And while the Italians lingered, they continued to demand the transformation of the League to permit revision. Finally the Russians, as their own security became endangered by German and Japanese programs of revision, moved toward the French and even entered the League. But if Dan thus came to Beersheba this dislocation was a question of expediency pure and simple.

It was assumed—and it still is, in quarters friendly to Geneva—that the desire of peoples everywhere for peace was a sufficient foundation for an international association to preserve peace. It was believed that the very existence of an institution such as was created at Paris would, in itself, mark a long step toward the abolition of war. What was not perceived was that unless there were agreements in advance, at least among the Great Powers, on the terms of such peace, controversies between the powers would inevitably be carried to Geneva and the League would become a place not for co-operation but for confrontation.[1]

---

[1] "Putting aside these theoretical arguments, we are faced at Geneva with the following reality: that the Powers—large and small—carry their difficulties and their conflicts of interests to the League of Nations. These conflicts do not shrink at Geneva: they expand. The Great Powers, in conflict with one another, seek for allies among the lesser Powers and form hostile groups which complicate and aggravate the situation; the small states court the support of the Great Powers, who in order to maintain their diplomatic combinations at once take sides. Thus all the disputes brought to Geneva finish sooner or later, either directly or indirectly, as conflicts between the Great Powers. During my stay in Geneva I never saw a dispute of any importance settled otherwise than by an agreement between the Great Powers. They alone are

That, too, was exactly what happened over the Manchurian affair, at the Economic Conference in London,
and at the Disarmament Conference in Geneva. The
same thing would have happened also over the Austrian
question had it been referred to the League in 1934, as
it did occur in the World Court when the legality of the
projected Austro-German tariff union was referred to
that tribunal, in 1931, for an advisory opinion.

American public opinion in respect of the League of
Nations has always been blinded by a failure to distinguish between actual peace and an absence of armed
conflict. And this failure has its origin in the fact that,
for the people of the United States, there is no distinction. But the situation which existed before 1866 was
for the Italians something quite different from peace,
because they found themselves divided and subject in
part to alien rule. For fifty millions of Poles, Serbs, and
Rumanians, too, the status quo of 1914 was not peace
but something only to be suffered while it could not be
challenged.

The Austrians, Prussians, and Russians who partitioned Poland thereafter described the existing situation
as peace and after two unsuccessful rebellions the Poles
submitted to it because they had no alternative; but they
did not renounce the purpose to regain their liberty and

responsible for the situations that arise. A few states that remain outside of fixed
diplomatic combinations and are therefore able to maintain an independent attitude,
have from time to time exercised a conciliatory influence at Geneva. But this only
happens in the case of secondary disputes, and, moreover, these lesser Powers, not
having at their disposal the forces that might become necessary to back their action,
are themselves compelled to have recourse to the Great Powers.

"The whole of the Geneva procedure is, in fact, a system of *detours*, all of which
lead to one or other of these two issues: agreement or disagreement between Great
Britain, Italy, France, and Germany—the latter now formally absent, but not yet
entirely detached from the League." ("The Foreign Policy of the Duce" by Dino
Grandi in *Foreign Affairs*, Vol. 12, No. 4, 1934, p. 558.)

unity. The Germans, Austrians, Hungarians, and Bulgarians accepted, in the same spirit, the Settlement of Paris, which shattered their national unity, because they were likewise without resources to resist; but they too did not abandon the purpose to change it by violence if no other means were discoverable.

Actual peace, as contrasted with a truce of exhaustion or necessity, must arise from the fact that peoples generally find their territorial circumstances satisfactory alike from the ethnic and from the economic point of view. Only then will they renounce the purpose to change those circumstances, a purpose which can be realized only by violence. No such situation existed in 1919 or in the following years. On the contrary, Europe was divided between peoples resolved to maintain the existing system, because it fulfilled national ambitions, and those determined to bring about a change in the status quo which they found intolerable.[1]

As a consequence, the existing system could be maintained only by force, and force sufficient to constitute a permanent guarantee was always lacking while the Anglo-Saxon Great Powers declined to assume responsibility for the Continental status quo.[2] The attempt of the French to transform the League into an instrument to maintain the status quo was successful in principle, because the status quo was the law and the League was naturally the executor of the law. It was, however, unsuccessful in practice, because, on the one hand, the Anglo-Saxon Great Powers refused to provide the police force necessary to enforce the law, and, on the other

[1] See map, page 305.
[2] Davies, D. D., Baron, *The Problem of the Twentieth Century*, 1931; Hindmarsh, A. E., *Force in Peace*, 1933; Mitrany, David, *The Problem of International Sanctions*, 1925; Wild, P. S., *Sanctions and Treaty Enforcement*, 1934.

hand, the revisionist states openly declared their purpose to challenge a law which thus lacked adequate police backing.

The League provides the means for making effective the agreements of powers, but it possesses no resources for compelling agreement and none for carrying into effect the will of a majority. It supplies a meeting place for nations, but if the national policies of the powers are irreconcilable they must meet as opponents and not as collaborators. Such encounters constitute a peril, not an aid, to peace, because Geneva becomes a sounding board for the conflicting theses and passions of peoples exacerbated by these clashes. The histories of the Manchurian affair and the Disarmament Conference constitute irrefutable evidence of this fact.

What the student of international affairs must perceive is that so far the League of Nations has failed to fulfill its larger mission, and that this failure has resulted from the fact that, contrary to the assumptions of the immediate postwar period, the World War produced no change in the spirit of peoples. The relations between the Great Powers were not basically different in 1934 from what they were in 1914. There was the same clash of interest and policy between the French and the Germans, and between the Germans and the Russians. Yugoslavia had replaced the old Hapsburg Monarchy on the Dalmatian coast and as a consequence the old bitterness between Rome and Vienna was reproduced in the new bitterness between Rome and Belgrade. Russo-Japanese relations had not improved, although the Soviets now occupied the seat of the Czars. The physical circumstances of the Magyars, Czechs, and Rumanians had been modified, but their secular hatreds remained.

As a consequence, the old struggles, which were formerly carried on between foreign offices directly, are now fought out upon the conference field of Geneva. Such battles, however, generally end in deadlock, because decision, that is to say, settlement, is usually out of the question. For a Japanese delegation at Geneva to agree to abandon Manchuria, for a French to consent to sacrifice security, for a German to renounce revision, for a British or American to accept responsibility for European frontiers, would only lead to another prompt domestic repudiation, as happened in the case of Woodrow Wilson and his Paris engagements. All of these peoples, the Japanese, French, German, British, and American, unmistakably desire peace, but none for a single moment conceives that the price of peace must be the sacrifice of national policy and the subordination of national interests to international accord.

In one word, although peoples originally welcomed the creation of the League of Nations as an instrument of world peace, they have without exception sought to employ it as an instrument of national policy, and the result has been the decline of the fortunes of Geneva to their present low estate.

Chapter XXV

LOCARNO

Six years after the dramatic scene in the Hall of Mirrors at Versailles, when the terms of peace were formally presented to the German delegates, there took place beside the waters of Lake Maggiore in the little Swiss town of Locarno a ceremony which at the moment seemed hardly less memorable. This was the signing of the Pacts of Locarno which were to bestow upon Europe five years of relative tranquillity. For, as a result of these agreements, France, Germany, and Great Britain were to co-operate in the task of removing the debris of the World War, and the League of Nations was at last to become the center of international relations.[1]

Although the subsequent arrival of the Economic Blizzard and the accompanying and at least measurably consequent rise of Hitler have, for the time being, dissipated the hopes of Locarno, it is difficult to escape the conviction that for a brief moment statesmanship took the true route and that sooner or later it is to that road

[1] For text of Locarno Treaty of Mutual Guarantee made by Germany, Belgium, France, Great Britain, and Italy, see Appendix C.

that Europe and the rest of the world, as well, must return if there is to be any escape from the chaos and conflict which have crowded the years since it was abandoned.

The Pacts of Locarno were an expression of the common weariness of the French, British, and German peoples with post-war struggles which had continued without interruption from the making of the Treaty of Versailles to the occupation of the Ruhr. In that time, British policy, incarnated by Lloyd George, had sought to restore a balance of power in Europe by re-establishing Germany as a counterweight to France. French policy, illustrated by Poincaré, had endeavored to hold Germany within the constricting limits of the Treaty of Versailles until such time as Great Britain was prepared to guarantee French security. Finally, German statesmanship, directed by a number of insignificant public men, had attempted to exploit Anglo-French quarrels to escape altogether from the chains of Versailles.

In this triangular struggle, however, France had triumphed. British policy had been everywhere unsuccessful and British prestige had sunk to the level it had known only in the age of the Stuarts. At the same time German resistance had provoked the occupation of the Ruhr, and that had brought about the financial and economic ruin of the Reich. But while French policy had prevailed and France was now supported by allies and dominant on the Continent by reason of her military force, she had neither collected reparations from Germany nor obtained guarantees from Great Britain.

By 1924, moreover, the French felt themselves dangerously isolated, the franc had begun to slump disastrously, the occupation of the Ruhr, while it had demonstrated French military power, had also awakened a sobering realization of the harvest of hatred which must inevitably be reaped from a policy of violence pursued indefinitely and directed against the most powerful of the peoples of the Continent. As for the Germans, their resistance to the treaty had led only to a ruin more complete than that of the war itself, and once more, as in November, 1918, they were exhausted.

Finally, the British had at last discovered that, unless they were prepared to make war to combat French policy, they must meet the French demand for security. All three peoples were thus in a mood for compromise for the first time since the making of the Paris Settlement. That mood was clearly indicated also when in the winter of 1923 Labor came to power in Great Britain and in the spring of 1924 the Left resumed a control of France which had lapsed with the war, while German affairs passed into the competent hands of Gustav Stresemann.

Before Locarno, however, there came a full year of preparation. The Dawes Plan was made in London, with decisive if unofficial American participation. At Geneva, Ramsay MacDonald and Herriot pledged their respective countries to make the League the basis of their international action. And it is with this Fifth Assembly of September, 1924, that the League of Nations at last emerged from the obscurity which had been its fate ever since the United States Senate rejected the Treaty of Versailles and repudiated the promises of the President who had been the chief architect of the Geneva institution.

At Geneva, however, one last battle had yet to be

fought between the British and French conceptions of organized peace. MacDonald called upon the Continental nations to disarm and to accept compulsory arbitration as the substitute for war. But the Continent riposted by demanding that Great Britain subscribe to the newly constructed Protocol,[1] the successor of the Cecil Pact of Mutual Assistance, which, by binding all nations to defend as well as to respect the territorial integrity of others, undertook to give reality to Articles X and XVI of the Covenant.

That Protocol the British Parliament rejected. The British people were no more ready in 1924 than they had been in 1919 to commit themselves to blanket responsibilities for the frontiers of Europe.[2] But the Tory Government which succeeded, headed by Stanley Baldwin and having Austen Chamberlain as Secretary of State for Foreign Affairs, was ready at last to face the fact that nothing affirmative could be accomplished in Europe until France felt herself secure.

From all of these several circumstances, there presently flowed the Pacts of Locarno.[3] By the terms of these agreements and by those of various written and unwritten understandings, three things were accomplished. To insure French security, Great Britain undertook to maintain the status quo in the Rhine area against

---

[1] Baker, P. J. N., *The Geneva Protocol*, 1925; Miller, D. H., *The Geneva Protocol*, 1925; Toynbee, A. J., *Survey of International Affairs, 1924*, 1926; World Peace Foundation, "Protocol of Arbitration, Security and Disarmament," *Publications*, Vol. 7, No. 7, 1924.

[2] Williams, Roth, *The League, the Protocol and the Empire*, 1925.

[3] Bonnamour, George, *Le Rapprochement Franco-Allemand*, 1927; Carnegie Endowment for International Peace, "Final Protocol of the Locarno Conference, 1925, and Treaties Between France and Belgium, and France and Czechoslovakia," *International Conciliation*, No. 216, 1926; Glasgow, George, *From Dawes to Locarno, 1924-1925*, 1925; Milenkovitch, V. M., *Le Problème de la Securité Européenne d'après les Accords de Locarno*, 1928; Toynbee, A. J., *ed.*, *Survey of International Affairs, 1925*, 1928, Vol. II, pp. 1-78.

all comers, a responsibility Italy likewise assumed; but neither accepted any responsibility for the frontiers in the east. In doing this, the British evaded all unilateral commitment. They did not renew the old Anglo-French Entente. On the contrary, they bound themselves to defend Germany against France, and France and Belgium against Germany, in case of violence originating on either side of the Rhine.

The Germans, on their side, accepted as final the return of Alsace-Lorraine to France and, at the same time, pledged themselves not to attempt by force to change the frontiers in the east and south, that is, the Austrian, Czech, and Polish boundaries. And they also agreed to enter the League, receiving in advance the assurance that they would at Geneva occupy the status of a Great Power with membership in the Council.

The French, on their side, consented to the early evacuation of the Rhineland as well as of the Ruhr, although they were entitled under the treaty to occupy the former until 1935. And already in London they had, by accepting the Dawes Plan, consented to a substantial modification of the reparations clauses. In effect, the Truce of Locarno temporarily closed the period of post-war strife, which had lasted from 1919 to 1924, as the Armistice of Rethondes had terminated the fighting which had continued from 1914 to 1918.

Actually this system of Locarno for the time being re-established the old Concert of Europe, but re-established it under the colors of the League of Nations. A year after the Pacts of Locarno were made, Briand welcomed Stresemann to Geneva, Chamberlain added his material contribution to this reconciliation of the recent foes, and there began a collaboration of this triumvirate of peace, which lasted until the death of the German statesman and the fall of the cabinet to which the British Foreign Secretary belonged, in 1929.

Between 1926 and 1929, Geneva was practically the capital of Europe. Its Assemblies were made memorable by the presence of all the considerable statesmen of the Old World. And the League itself quickly acquired the prestige which Wilson had dreamed for it. France, at last reassured as to her security, relaxed her hold upon Germany, and Anglo-French resentments died out. All over the Continent, a sense of tranquillity encouraged economic and financial reconstruction. By the arrival of 1929, it seemed at last that the World War was ended, that Europe was back to "normalcy," and that the League had become that instrument of international co-operation and collective effort which its author had designed it to be.

All of this promise, however, was swiftly blighted by the coming of the Great Depression, which in this and the following years swept first over Europe and then over the whole world. Germany, her middle class destroyed by inflation following the occupation of the Ruhr, progressively succumbed to the rising tide of explosive nationalism which was to culminate in the triumph of Adolf Hitler. France, correspondingly aroused by the march of German events, in her turn reverted to the state of mind of the pre-Locarno days. The British, alarmed by Continental events, strove to restrict their commitments and responsibilities, which seemed to be dragging them toward participation in a next war on the terms of the last.

As a consequence, Geneva, which had been the center of conciliation and co-operation in the years during which the sun of Locarno still shone, inevitably became the scene of conflict. British, French, and German policies came increasingly into collision until, with the meeting of the Disarmament Conference (1932), London, Paris, and Berlin, having drifted completely apart, arrived at a deadlock.

The Conference of Lausanne in 1932, which finally disposed of reparations,[1] was lighted by the last lingering afterglow of Locarno, but by that time it was too late. Stresemann and Briand were both dead and their common policy discredited in their own countries. Chamberlain, too, had given way to MacDonald, who significantly made Lausanne, and not the League, the scene of negotiations. A year later, with the deadlock over armaments unbroken, Germany left the League and in the subsequent crises following the arrival of Hitler, Geneva was pushed into the background completely.

The lasting significance of the whole episode of Locarno has so far found little appreciation, and yet it must supply by far the most illuminating testimony both to the strength and to the weakness of the League of Nations in the contemporary world. Before the Pacts of Locarno were made, Geneva had played no conspicuous role in international affairs. Its real history begins with 1924 when Herriot and MacDonald went there and laid the foundations for Anglo-French co-operation which were seized upon by Briand and Chamberlain as the bases of their Locarno agreements a year later.

The Assembly of 1926, which witnessed the entrance of Germany into the League, opens the pitifully brief period in which the Geneva institution actually func-

[1] Foreign Policy Association, "The Lausanne Reparation Settlement," *Foreign Policy Reports*, Vol. VIII, No. 19, 1932; Wheeler-Bennett, J. W., *The Wreck of Reparations*, 1933.

tioned as its author and his followers believed that it would. But all of the steps which led to this sudden blossoming were taken outside. Locarno was made with only a side glance at the League, and it was not until the Dawes plan had been formulated on the banks of the Thames, and Locarno on the shores of Lake Maggiore, that Geneva came into its own.

In effect, British, French, and German statesmanship, after having quarreled and fought for five years, with results equally unfortunate for all, finally made a truce. The terms of that truce included an agreement to employ the machinery of the League for carrying on that co-operation which they planned. But those terms also included an accommodation or adjournment of the political issues which had hitherto divided them. They came to Geneva with a bargain already struck, to the making of which the League had contributed nothing. And, precisely as long as they stuck to the terms of that bargain, they were able to make use of the machinery of Geneva profitably for themselves, and for the world in general.

When, however, the co-operation begun at Locarno broke down, then the consequences were immediately communicated to Geneva. And, just as the League had contributed nothing to producing the Truce of Locarno, so it could do nothing to prevent or even to postpone its rupture. When the French felt their security again imperiled, when the Germans saw their claims rejected, when the British felt their responsibilities mounting dangerously, all three immediately took separate routes once more. And the result was the conflict in the Disarmament Conference which paralyzed its operations and terminated in German secession from the League.

The importance of the Locarno episode lies in the fact that it clearly demonstrated the value of the League machinery for a world which actually desires to employ it and is ready to endure existing territorial conditions. Thus in 1925, when Great Britain, France, and Germany made the Locarno Pacts, all were equally eager to put a term to the chaos and conflict of the preceding years, and to that end Germany was also willing, temporarily at least, to accept the status quo, territorially and politically.

Stresemann[1] and Briand,[2] who were the moving spirits of the Locarno agreements, both envisaged a gradual evolution of the territorial situation. The German was not prepared for all future time to accept the Polish Corridor or to submit to the prohibition of Austro-German union. The Frenchman was aware that only at the cost of a new war could France forever sustain the status quo of the Treaty of Versailles on the Vistula and the Danube. Yet both saw that to raise the issue of territorial revision in 1925 or in the immediately succeeding years would only precipitate controversy and lead to ultimate conflict. Therefore they agreed to postpone discussion of what they could not settle.

When, however, in the fall of 1930, a year after Stresemann's death, the Brüning Cabinet—under the threat of Hitler, who was exploiting the nationalistic emotions of the German people—did reopen the question of the Polish Corridor and, in the spring of 1931, that of the Austro-German union, the Truce of Locarno automatically came to an end. After that European conditions rapidly reverted to the situation of 1919–1924, and

[1] Olden, Rudolf, *Stresemann*, 1930; Vallentin, Antonina, *Stresemann*, 1931.
[2] Thomson, Valentine, *Briand, Man of Peace*, 1930.

concomitantly the League relapsed to that impotence which had been its lot in the same years.

Had the policies of Stresemann, Briand, and Chamberlain continued to command the support of majorities within their own countries after 1929, as they had enlisted it in 1925, the League might have retained its importance, the settlement of the reparations question might have taken place at Geneva instead of Lausanne, and the Disarmament Conference in Geneva and the Economic Conference in London, which were held under the auspices of the League, might easily have had useful results.

Instead, first Germany, then France, and finally Great Britain were swept by nationalistic actions and reactions. The Germans, disappointed by the failure to obtain the national ends which they had looked for from the League, turned from the policy of Stresemann to the violence of Hitler. The French, confronted by this change in German policy, repudiated the idealism of Briand and returned to the logic of Poincaré. The British, in the face of growing Continental unrest, reverted from the policy of co-operation to that of isolation. Thereafter, Geneva was in permanent eclipse.

Such, too, had been the history of the Concert of Europe. From 1878 to 1914, it had, on the whole, worked efficiently and by virtue of its operation many wars had been prevented. As late as the winter of 1912–1913, a council of ambassadors, meeting in secret, had just managed to avert the general conflict which threatened as a result of Russian and Austrian disputes over Serbian boundaries. Before that, the old diplomatic machine had worked after Tangier in 1905 and during the Bosnian crisis of 1908 and the Agadir affair in 1911.

In July, 1914, however, the Concert broke down, because the nations at odds refused to employ it. All Sir Edward Grey's frantic and futile efforts in the tragic twelve days preceding the catastrophe were directed at the restoration of the Concert through the medium of a new council of ambassadors leading to a fresh conference like that of Algeciras which had prevented war in 1905. But these attempts of the British statesman failed, not because the machinery of the Concert was inadequate but because the previous willingness of statesmen to use that machinery was now nonexistent.

Twenty years later, at the moment of the assassination of Dollfuss in Vienna, the League machinery was as available as that of the Concert had been when Francis Ferdinand was murdered in Serajevo in 1914. But once more it was mobilization and not conference which was invoked, and the reason that mobilization did not lead to conflict in the later incident, as it had in the earlier, was solely that Germany was not prepared to meet the Italian challenge as she had met the Russian.

Wilson's theory of the League of Nations, which lingers in many quarters both in Great Britain and in the United States, was that of an international organization clothed with world-wide authority and able to invoke those moral sanctions which he believed would suffice to enforce its decisions. The conception of Geneva expressed in Locarno, on the other hand, was that of an instrument to be employed by Great Powers already in agreement in matters of high policy. It was, in fact, the conception of the old Concert functioning in a new and wider sphere.

Locarno, then, was in effect an attempt to bring Wilson's vision down to the limits of practical politics.

As such, after a brief period of brilliant success, it failed abysmally.   But success and failure are equally illuminating, because temporary success bestowed upon the League its only period of prosperity, and eventual failure brought it back to the level of the years before the Pacts of Locarno were made.

In Locarno there was embodied an idea which, after nearly a decade, is beginning to find fresh favor, and that is the idea of the regional pact. Originally the League was established to give the collective guarantee of its members to the security of each. That plan, however, broke down immediately when the United States rejected the League because it was unwilling to assume any responsibilities for European frontiers. Later, in rejecting the Protocol, Great Britain disclosed similar repugnance for responsibilities at the Vistula and the Danube that the United States had shown for all European commitments.

By the terms of Locarno, however, the British formally assumed responsibility for the status quo at the Rhine, as the United States had in the past continuously asserted responsibility for the American status quo through the Monroe Doctrine. Thus, for the universal responsibility, the British substituted the regional. After Locarno the French continuously, but without success, sought to persuade the British to extend their responsibilities to an eastern Locarno covering the Vistula, and also to a Mediterranean pact applying to the inland sea. In 1934, however, with the direct support of the Soviet Union and with the benevolent but nonparticipating approval of the British, they returned to the charge and sought to enlist the Germans in this eastern Locarno.

So far (1935) the attempt has failed and it may well continue to fail as long as the Hitler regime survives, for it obviously envisages renunciation by the Germans of their ambition to bring about the Austrian *Anschluss*, as in the original Locarno they renounced further claim to Alsace-Lorraine. By contrast, the National Socialist dictatorship did in 1933 consent to a nonaggression pact with Poland which for a ten-year period assured the status quo in respect of the Corridor and Upper Silesia. And the result was naturally a complete transformation in the economic as well as the political relations between the two countries.

Republican Germany and National Socialist Germany have in turn thus agreed to regional pacts covering the status quo on the Rhine and the Vistula, the former permanently, the latter for a ten-year period. The agreement on the Rhine brought a truce of five years in which Franco-German relations were more friendly than at any other period since the Treaty of Frankfort. The agreement on the Vistula has, at least momentarily, bestowed a character upon German-Polish relations without historical precedent. Both agreements, moreover, were voluntary, in contrast to the terms imposed by the Treaty of Versailles.

Without some similar regional agreement covering the Danube, it is self-evident that European tranquillity cannot now be restored, and such agreement, made in the name of Germany by the Hitler regime, would, in the light of its own professions and performances, be long in enlisting Continental confidence. On the other hand, it is equally clear that it is to Locarno and to the regional pact, rather than to Geneva and the collective system, that European statesmanship is today looking.

Evidence of this fact was supplied also by the activities of Barthou, the French minister of foreign affairs, up to the very day when a brutal crime deprived Europe of a statesman who had become in a very real sense the heir of Briand.

Chapter XXVI

THE PACT OF PARIS [1]

THE Pacts of Locarno had represented a deliberate and statesmanlike attempt to bring about at least a temporary adjustment between British, French, and German policies. Three years after these had been made there was signed at Paris still another of the formidable number of postwar pacts. This treaty, multilateral in form, since it was open to all nations to sign it, was known in Europe as the Pact of Paris and in the United States as the Kellogg Pact. [2]

In theory directed at the abolition of war, this treaty was actually designed to put an end to the confusion created by the rejection of the Treaty of Versailles by the United States Senate. For nearly a decade after the treaty fight the United States had stood aside and aloof from all the efforts of the League to organize world

[1] For text of the Pact of Paris, see Appendix D.

[2] The following are the most important books which have been written upon various aspects of the Pact of Paris: Butler, N. M., *The Path To Peace*, 1930; Miller, D. H., *The Peace Pact of Paris*, 1928; Myers, D. P., *Origin and Conclusion of the Paris Pact*, 1929; Shotwell, J. T., *War as an Instrument of National Policy*, 1929; Wehberg, Hans, *The Outlawry of War*, 1931; Wheeler-Bennett, J. W., *Information on the Renunciation of War, 1927-1928*, 1928.

peace, and in that time there had been no weakening of
the popular resolution to stay out of future European
political quarrels.

By 1928, however, American interest in the preservation of peace in Europe had been enormously increased
by reason of the recent and relatively huge expansion of
the holdings of the American investor in the securities
of Continental countries. To the war debts there had
been added private loans amounting to upwards of
$5,000,000,000. In addition, exports to Europe were
still maintained at huge figures. European peace had,
therefore, become an obvious and legitimate concern
of American national policy.

During the second Coolidge administration, too, the
passions awakened by the fight over the Treaty of Versailles had died down. Wilson was dead, the Democratic party had abandoned his international projects,
and the League had ceased to be an issue in domestic
politics. For all but a handful of devoted but politically
uninfluential champions of the League, the "solemn
referendum" of 1920 had been accepted as a definitive
verdict. In the eyes of the great mass of the American
people, Geneva had become the seat of an institution
whose importance was restricted to Europe.

As the League was no longer a cause for controversy
in the United States, the apprehension in administrative
circles which had moved Hughes to ignore communications from the League to the State Department had disappeared. The "overshadowing Senate," for the moment
at least, was no longer suspicious, and little by little
there was growing up between Geneva and Washington
a habit of co-operation which was destined to become
even more marked in the Hoover administration.

No leader of importance still urged that the United States should join the League, but, on the one hand, the considerable fraction of the population concerned over peace for moral reasons and, on the other, that smaller but not less influential fraction interested in European conditions for material considerations, advocated co-operation with Geneva. The new conception was that the United States reserving entire freedom of action, could safely and usefully participate in League conferences and activities where its own interests were affected.[1]

Naturally the League welcomed this change in American attitude, although it too easily interpreted the change as disclosing a reversal in public opinion on the larger question of membership. Co-operation of America, moreover, was an essential detail, because hitherto the problem of enforcing League decisions had been complicated by the possibility of collision between League sanctions and American policy in the matter of neutral rights. Thus even if the United States were still to refuse to join the League, much would be gained if its position in this respect were clearly defined and its passive, if not active, support assured.

But to bring about such a co-ordination between Washington and Geneva was by no means easy. The direct road to Geneva was still certainly closed. The door against specific commitments was still as evidently double-barred. If the United States was now willing to co-operate with Geneva, it was only on American

[1] Berdahl, C. A., *The Policy of the United States with Respect to the League of Nations*, 1932; Carnegie Endowment for International Peace, "The Cooperation of the United States with the League of Nations and with the International Labour Organization," *International Conciliation*, No. 274, 1931; Geneva Research Center, "The United States and the League," *Geneva Special Studies*, Vols. II, III, and IV, January of years 1931–32–33.

terms. To escape from this impasse, Frank B. Kellogg, when he succeeded Charles E. Hughes as Secretary of State, had recourse to a project which was at the moment attracting attention in the United States.

By the terms of this project, the nations of the world were to make a new and solemn compact pledging themselves not to employ war as an instrument of national policy, but henceforth to settle their disputes by arbitration. War, in the phrase of the moment, was thus to be "outlawed." For the League members such a pact would have value because it would close the famous "gap" in the Covenant[1] which still left a way to war open if the Council should be unable to reach unanimous decision when called upon to make inquiry in case of dispute between nations.[2]

As for the United States, by signing and ratifying the new contract it would establish a basis of common action with the League powers in a future crisis; for the nation which broke its faith pledged in the Covenant would similarly disregard its oath of the Pact. Inevitably, therefore, in moments of crisis the signatory powers of both treaties would come together to take counsel. Since war was thus made illegal, recourse to it became a crime and to the mind of the lawyer, as also to that of the moralist, this constituted a significant step toward the assurance of peace.

Unhappily the task of outlawing war was not as simple as it seemed to the lay and legal mind alike, for several reasons. First of all, while every nation signed

[1] Article XV, Paragraph 7.
[2] Carnegie Endowment for International Peace, "What Follows the Pact of Paris?", *International Conciliation*, No. 276, 1932; Clark, Evans, *ed.*, *Boycotts and Peace*, 1932; Geneva Research Center, "The Covenant and the Pact," *Geneva Special Studies*, Vol. I, No. 9, 1930; also "Sanctions and Security; An Analysis of the French and American Views," *Geneva Special Studies*, Vol. III, No. 2, 1932.

and ratified the new Pact of Paris, many attached to it reservations of immense significance. Thus the United States expressly stipulated that it undertook no responsibility for the enforcement of the new law.[1] Great Britain, in turn, announced that there were certain regions in which it would be inconvenient to permit the Pact to operate.[2] All nations, too, reserved the right to make war in self-defense.

But how was this question of self-defense to be decided? What was to constitute an aggression warranting resort to war, and who was to decide that such an aggression had in fact taken place? As to these details, the Pact was silent. Thus it lay within the right of every state to decide when considerations of self-defense dictated resort to war, and its decision was not subject to any international review.

Inevitably, therefore, the French demanded that the Pact of Paris be provided with teeth. To be effective at all, they argued, it must be amended, first, to provide a method for establishing the fact of aggression, and, second to supply the means for proceeding against the aggressor. For the French, the Pact of Paris was worthless as mere law without court to interpret and police to enforce. But for the Americans its chief merit lay in the fact that, unlike the Covenant, it imposed no responsibility and involved no commitment.

[1] In the report of the Senate Committee on Foreign Relations, upon the basis of which the Kellogg-Briand Treaty was ratified, is the following significant paragraph:

"The committee further understands that the treaty does not provide sanctions, express or implied. Should any signatory to the treaty or any nation adhering to the treaty violate the terms of the same, there is no obligation or commitment, express or implied, upon the part of any of the other signers of the treaty to engage in punitive or coercive measures as against the nation violating the treaty. The effect of the violation of the treaty is to relieve the other signers of the treaty from any obligation under it with the nation thus violating the same."

[2] See Chapter I, page 25, footnote.

Signed with great ceremony in Paris in 1928, celebrated briefly thereafter as a significant American contribution to the cause of world peace, the Kellogg Pact
three years later shared with the Covenant the evil consequences of the Japanese adventure in Manchuria. In
the crisis precipitated by that adventure, the Pact did,
as it had been designed to do, furnish a basis for co-
operation between Washington and Geneva, but the
co-operation produced no useful result, because, where
only force could avail, none was provided.

On the contrary, the whole effect of the Pact was
evaded by a simple procedure. It had imposed upon all
signatories the duty of refraining from employing war
as an instrument of policy. The Japanese, while using
their military forces both in Manchuria and before
Shanghai, omitted to declare war; and the Chinese, in
their turn, also refrained because they had submitted
their case to the League and were thereby bound under
the Covenant to wait until three months after the decision of the League, which did not come until nearly a
year and a half after the actual aggression.

In effect, therefore, the Pact of Paris did not restrain
Japan from an action as clearly aggressive as Frederick
the Great's invasion and annexation of Silesia. Nor did
it protect the Chinese against wanton aggression. Thus
it resembled a law making murder a crime only when
the killer obligingly warns his victim of his purpose in
advance. For the traditional declaration of war which
preserved the courtesy of the duel and the challenge,
the Pact in effect, although of course not by design,
substituted a new style of attack borrowed from the
gangster.

That style, too, was followed by the National Socialist dictatorship in Germany in the summer of 1934 when it undertook to destroy Austrian independence. Hitler did not declare war, he did not actually resort to armed invasion, but by every other conceivable means he undertook to destroy Austrian independence. Rebellion was preached from German soil, rebels were armed with German guns. In the struggle, the Austrian Chancellor was murdered, but technically war was not employed as an instrument of national policy, because it was not declared.

These two episodes, the Manchurian and the Austrian, constitute excellent examples of the fallacy underlying such international compacts as the Pact of Paris, which undertake to abolish war by resolution. Such undertakings could succeed only if, in fact, all of the nations which share in them do it in an identical spirit. To abolish crime in a community by a plebiscite in which all citizens renounced illegal practices and thereafter to dismiss the police as unnecessary would hardly seem a sound proceeding. But in effect that was like what the Pact set out to do.

The Pact of Paris failed because, although the Japanese and Germans signed it, they did not renounce their Manchurian and Austrian policies. And it was these policies which constituted the true peril to world peace. It was not the intention to employ war as an instrument of policy but the purpose to seize a Chinese province and to destroy the liberty of the Austrian state, which had to be renounced if there was to be peace in the world.

Again, while the Japanese and German peoples supported their respective governments in accepting the Pact of Paris, they also endorsed the actions in Manchuria and in Austria. But when the public opinion of the world protested against these aggressions, the Japanese and German people should in theory have turned against their governments. That was how the sanction of world opinion, the only sanction claimed for the Pact of Paris, was assumed to act. In practice, however, the Japanese and German peoples did nothing of the sort. On the contrary, both peoples were flamed into fury over foreign opposition to their national policies.

There was, then, only one way in which the Japanese aggression in Manchuria could have been halted and that was by the collective force of the nations which had ratified either the Covenant or the Pact of Paris. They had to stand ready to enforce the law they had together established. Although the machinery of Geneva was invoked and the Council and the Assembly functioned with the co-operation of the United States, the judgment which was finally passed by the League upon Japanese action was denied all sanction, since the powers declined to act. Thus China lost a province larger than France and Italy combined and containing thirty millions of Chinese.

What the student of international relations must perceive is that, in the contemporary world, the value of public international law is in direct ratio to the physical force which can be mobilized to apply it. The collapse of all the postwar machinery for preventing violence has been due to the fact that it has been long on law, both moral and judicial, but short on police.

The Pact of Locarno, unlike that of Paris, was a realistic contribution to the cause of peace because it provided force to maintain what it undertook to establish.

The British engaged their military and naval resources to defend the status quo in the Rhine area, and so did the Italians; and from that day to this there has been no attempt on the part of the Germans or French to disturb that status quo. The Pact of Paris undertook to do the same thing on a far wider scale, but since it made no provision for force to insure application, it fell to the ground three years after it had been ratified.

At the moment when the Manchurian affair was still in an acute state, Henry L. Stimson, Mr. Kellogg's successor as Secretary of State, undertook to implement the Pact of Paris by interpretation.[1] He asserted that, in signing the Pact, the United States had surrendered its traditional policy in the matter of neutrality. His reasoning was this: The Pact had outlawed war. Resort to it therefore must be a crime. In the presence of a crime, there could be no neutrals. The United States as a signatory to the Pact was bound therefore to come to council with all other signatories, and thereafter, if it concurred in the decision reached, not to insist upon its rights as a neutral when such insistence might benefit the aggressor.

This ingenious interpretation, however, found little general acceptance. The United States was willing enough to come to conference, but it was utterly unwilling to do more than that. And it was very far from having reached a point where it was ready to scrap its historic policy in the matter of neutral rights. Accord-

[1] "War is no longer to be the source and subject of rights. It is no longer to be the principle around which the duties, the conduct, and the rights of nations revolve. It is an illegal thing. Hereafter when two nations engage in armed conflict, either one or both of them must be wrongdoers—violators of the general treaty. We no longer draw a circle about them and treat them with the punctilios of the duelist's code. Instead we denounce them as lawbreakers.

"By that very act we have made obsolete many legal precedents and have given the legal profession the task of re-examining many of its codes and treaties."
(Secretary Stimson's speech of August 8, 1932.)

ingly, Mr. Stimson, with the support of President Hoover, presently produced a new project henceforth to be known as the Stimson Doctrine.[1] In conformity with it, the United States was never again to recognize territorial changes resulting from acts of violence, and this course was to be illustrated by a refusal to recognize the state of Manchukuo.

The object of this Stimson Doctrine was obvious. It was one more of the innumerable efforts of Americans, official and unofficial, to find some means of enforcing international law without the sanction of force. It was a new effort to set up a moral sanction in the place of the familiar military and naval means of enforcement. It was still another attempt to get around the national resolution neither to fight to maintain peace nor to act to enforce international law anywhere, save in those regions in which American interests were directly at stake.

But the trouble with the Stimson Doctrine is twofold. It does not lead to any renunciation of the fruits of aggression by a guilty nation, and it does not guarantee that the nation invoking it may not in the end become involved in actual conflict. Thus in 1932-1934, while

[1] In Secretary Stimson's note to China and Japan, dated January 8, 1933, the following significant paragraph appears:

"But in view of the present situation and of its own rights and obligations therein, the American Government deems it to be its duty to notify both the Imperial Japanese Government and the Government of the Chinese Republic that it cannot admit the legality of any situation de facto, nor does it intend to recognize any treaty or agreement entered into between those governments, or agents thereof, which may impair the treaty rights of the United States or its citizens in China, including those which relate to the sovereignty, the independence, or the territorial and administrative integrity of the Republic of China, or to the international policy relative to China, commonly known as the Open Door policy; and that it does not intend to recognize any situation, treaty, or agreement which may be brought about by means contrary to the covenants and obligations of the Pact of Paris of August 27, 1928, to which treaty both China and Japan, as well as the United States, are parties."

no nation of importance recognized Manchukuo, the Japanese proceeded steadily to consolidate their position, and no one imagines now that they can be expelled by any other means than that of armed force.

American refusal to recognize Manchukuo, and American condemnation of Japanese policy which this refusal indicates, have served to encourage Chinese resistance and thus to render the Japanese task at once more difficult and more costly. As a consequence, Japanese resentment directed at America has become increasingly bitter, relations between the United States and Japan have worsened, and the danger of an explosion following some accident or incident has always been present. American policy, therefore, has been equally unsuccessful in changing Japanese purposes in Manchuria and in avoiding the risk of war. The United States has not promoted peace, protected China, or escaped political involvement.

Of itself, the Pact of Paris had little actual importance. No European nation was naïve enough to imagine that it was possible to abolish war by resolution. The French and the British, however, did correctly foresee the Pact as a bridge over which the United States might travel from Washington to Geneva. Thus they signed, ratified, and otherwise ignored it. For Europe, the main disappointment was that the collapse of the League's Manchurian intervention came so swiftly after the appearance of the United States at Geneva, that American presence was without lasting importance.

Actually, the Pact was the latest in the long series of American prescriptions for peace which have with complete uniformity renounced force and instead have relied upon the sanction of world opinion to prevent war. It was brought forward at a moment when the sun of Locarno was still shining brilliantly, but it had hardly been ratified when Europe plunged into that crisis which has lasted ever since and proved similarly fatal to hopes centered in the Covenant and those centered in the Pact.

Chapter XXVII

NAVAL DISARMAMENT [1]

APART from the League activities and aside from the various pacts, of which that of Paris was the most ambitious and that of Locarno the most realistic, postwar efforts to promote peace have largely taken the form of endeavors to bring about so-called disarmament. The term "disarmament," however, is misleading, for what has been sought has at most been no more than the limitation or reduction of existing military and naval forces. Since, too, neither of these objectives has been attained, nothing has been possible in the larger field.

In the consideration of the postwar attempts to bring about the limitation and reduction of armaments, a clear distinction must be drawn between land and naval armaments. While permanent achievement has been lacking in both respects, in the matter of naval forces

---

[1] In the study of naval and land disarmament, the following will prove useful for general reference: Howland, C. P., *ed.*, *American Foreign Relations*, 1928–31; League of Nations, Disarmament Section, *Armaments Year Book;* same Section, *Preparatory Commission for the Disarmament Conference*, 1925–1934; Myers, D. P., *World Disarmament*, 1932; Toynbee, A. J., *Survey of International Affairs*, annual. *The Annotated Bibliography on Disarmament and Military Questions*, published by the League of Nations Library in 1931, is particularly valuable for extended bibliographical references.

certain interesting if impermanent agreements were made, notably at the Washington Conference in 1921–1922 and at the London Conference in 1930. And in the explanation of such progress as was achieved in respect of fleets at these two gatherings lies the key to the failure in respect of land armaments, which has been absolute.

At the very outset of the consideration of the question of armaments, it is essential to emphasize again the familiar fact that fleets and armies are merely the means by which nations seek to give effect to their national policies. They are, therefore, of but secondary importance and comparable with other instruments of policy such as money, tariffs, and embargoes. What is of primary importance is the policy of a state. If that is dynamic and therefore aggressive, then the armaments which it possesses, whether military or naval, are obviously a matter of concern for all nations menaced by that policy.

In 1921, when the Washington Conference was convoked, the policies of the three great maritime powers, Great Britain, Japan, and the United States, were not in direct collision. Since none of these states coveted the lands of another, the question of security was not at issue. Each nation naturally asserted the right to maintain a fleet adequate to insure its control of the waters vital to its own security and prosperity. But each could concede that right to the others without sacrifice of national interest.

This fact is of transcendant importance because it alone explains why any agreement was possible at Washington.[1] And not only did it find no parallel in the

---

[1] Archimbaud, Léon, *La Conférence de Washington*, 1923; Buell, R. L., *The Washington Conference*, 1922; Kawakami, K. K., *Japan's Pacific Policy*, 1922; Willoughby, W. W., *China at the Conference*, 1922.

circumstances of the military powers of Europe, but it was also not duplicated by the relations of France and Italy among the maritime states. On the contrary, since the policies of these latter countries were in collision in the Mediterranean, the consideration of security was invoked by both. It was, however, in the London Conference (1930) and not in Washington (1921-1922) that Franco-Italian relations played an important role, for in the Washington Conference both countries were similarly ignored.

What was considered in Washington was the question of the relative strength of British, Japanese, and American fleets, actual and prospective. And this question arose because during the later stage of the World War the United States had undertaken a building program which by 1921 was nearing fulfillment and was bound in no long time to bestow actual supremacy in the battle line upon the American fleet. In this situation the British had to do one of three things: embark upon a huge building program of their own, or resign that naval supremacy which had been theirs for three centuries, or come to an agreement with the United States.

As to the first possibility, the state of British finances in the first years following the war made such a venture difficult if not in fact impossible. As to the second, the British Government and public were equally unwilling to see their fleet fall to second rank and the United States replace Great Britain as the supreme naval power of the world, with all that this must involve. For the British, therefore, the single way of escape from the dilemma was to come to terms with the Americans.

Nor was there any insuperable obstacle to an Anglo-American agreement. While the United States now possessed prospective superiority, the cost of the completion of its naval program was bound to be enormous and the further expense of the upkeep of a supreme fleet sure to be staggering. And no practical advantage could flow from such expenditure, for the British and the Americans were both sated and therefore status quo powers, and neither, at the moment, was menaced by attack by a third power or by a coalition of powers.

Common sense therefore dictated that the two English-speaking nations should come to terms, and the obvious basis of agreement was equality. In battleships and battle cruisers the United States had a prospective superiority, in the second line the British possessed an actual advantage except for destroyers. Between the two nations, the problem was one of mathematics. The only conceivable political issue had its origin in the desire of the American administration to do away with the Anglo-Japanese alliance, which was a cause of more or less annoyance but in no sense constituted an actual danger.

The British, on their part, were ready to scrap this alliance because for them it had lost practical value.[1] Originally made as an insurance against Russia, it had been of great use during the war with Germany. But in 1921 Russia had fallen away to Bolshevism and Germany had ceased to be a naval or colonial power. In addition, the Dominions, Canada and Australia in particular, were, like the United States, insistent that the Anglo-Japanese Alliance should be terminated.

A bargain between Great Britain and the United States

[1] Chang, Chung Fu, *The Anglo-Japanese Alliance*, 1931; Dennis, A. L. P., *The Anglo-Japanese Alliance*, 1923; Weale, Putnam, *pseud.*, *An Indiscreet Chronicle From the Pacific*, 1922; Wood, Ge Zay, *China, the United States and the Anglo-Japanese Alliance*, 1921, 2 vols.

was therefore obviously possible. As between Great Britain and Japan, too, there was no question of policy whatever at stake. For the United States, on the other hand, not merely was the question of the Anglo-Japanese alliance of importance but, in addition, American policy had long ago adopted the double thesis of the "Open Door" and of the territorial integrity of China. Because President Wilson had failed to insure the return of Shantung to China by the Japanese, his work at Paris had been effectively attacked in America. His Republican successor, therefore, was anxious to succeed where the Democratic President had failed; and, as yet, despite the "Twenty-one Demands" served upon China by Japan during the World War, no direct clash between American and Japanese policy had arrived.

In contrast to Great Britain, and like the United States, Japan had certain political issues to serve. Ever since the Sino-Japanese War a generation earlier, Japanese policy had been directed toward the establishment of hegemony in Eastern Asia. The Russo-Japanese War had bestowed Korea and Port Arthur upon Japan and thrust Russia far back in Manchuria. The World War had resulted in the eviction of Germany from her Chinese possessions in Shantung. There remained only Great Britain and the United States as possible obstacles to Japanese dominance, the former seated at Hong Kong and the latter at Guam and in the Philippines.

To establish her own situation impregnably in the regions she purposed to control, it was necessary for Japan to eliminate the possibility of interference by either or both of the Anglo-Saxon powers. To do that, she had to remove the chance of the use of Corregidor and Hong Kong as naval bases by these powers in case of war. At Washington, therefore, the stake for which Japan played was absolute naval mastery in all Asiatic waters between the Aleutian Islands and Indo-China. In effect, she sought to throw the United States back upon Hawaii and Great Britain back upon Singapore.

In all respects the Washington Conference was a complete Japanese triumph. On the one hand, she successfully asserted her claim to a ratio of 3–5–5 vis-à-vis the two Anglo-Saxon powers, and on the other, she obtained from them a pledge not to add to the existing fortifications in Guam, the Philippines, and Hong Kong. The ratio thus established insured her actual supremacy in the waters in which she was interested, because distance more than counterbalanced the numerical advantage of the other fleets. In case of war with the United States, Corregidor and Guam were henceforth at her mercy, as was Hong Kong in the event of a war with Great Britain.

In return for these substantial benefits, the Japanese abandoned the alliance with Great Britain, consented to transfer Shantung to China, and accepted the Nine-Power Treaty of Washington, which guaranteed the territorial integrity of China. How Japan purposed to interpret that treaty was only disclosed a decade later in the Manchurian affair. Actually she exploited the so-called Disarmament Conference of Washington to insure for herself a clear field for a national policy which aimed at the attainment of hegemony in Eastern Asia. After that conference, power to interfere with that policy was lacking both to the British and to the Americas. But in 1922 the real purpose of the Japanese was disguised and their acceptance of the Nine-Power Treaty was taken at its face value.

As to the Anglo-Saxon nations, at Washington they reached an agreement which established a state of parity between them in the battle line. The agreement was not extended to cover other categories, because the French declined to accept any limitation in the matter of submarines and the British therefore refused to set any limit to their cruiser and destroyer forces. The United States, as a consequence, sacrificed prospective superiority in capital ships without obtaining any commensurate return in other categories. Since it consented in advance to scrap its excess tonnage in capital ships, the United States thus surrendered the most effective means of obtaining British consent to parity in all categories.

The Washington Conference was, then, a double defeat for the United States. It had been compelled to surrender its power to act in the Far East to preserve the "Open Door" and the territorial integrity of China in order to obtain Japanese adherence to the naval agreement. Because of his anxiety for a successful conference, the Secretary of State, Mr. Hughes, was manoeuvred into giving up prospective supremacy in the battle line without obtaining parity in other categories. Nor had actual progress in limitation or reduction of naval armaments been achieved, because competition was now transferred from capital ships, which had been limited, to big cruisers; and in this category competition took on fresh acuteness. As a result, the Washington Conference acquired in American eyes much the same character which that of Paris already possessed.

After the Washington Conference, the Harding, Coolidge, and Hoover administrations were caught between two conflicting currents of public opinion. The

American people desired parity with Great Britain in total naval strength, believing they had paid for it at Washington by scrapping their excess tonnage in battleships. But they were also averse to achieving that parity by the only means possible, which was matching the British fleet by new construction of their own. As a consequence, Washington continued to call upon London to reduce, and neglected to build itself.

In point of fact, however, there was still no clash in vital interests. What was at stake was prestige, not security. Accordingly, when after the failure of the Geneva Conference of 1927[1] the Coolidge administration presently indicated its resolution to achieve parity by building, if no agreement were to be had, and the superiority of American financial resources demonstrated that such tactics must win, the way was still open for amicable adjustment. That adjustment, too, was reached at London in the Naval Conference of 1930, during the Hoover Administration.[2]

At London, the British finally recognized the fact that the United States was resolved to have parity and that it was useless to attempt to prevent such parity by insisting upon tonnage totals which were prohibitively high. The Americans for their part perceived that they would not be able to get equality cheaply and must undertake a huge building program. Actually, the tonnage agreements reached at London imposed upon the American treasury an expenditure of approximately a

[1] Baker, P. J. N., *Disarmament and the Coolidge Conference*, 1927; Toynbee, A. J., *Survey of International Affairs*, 1927, 1929; United States, *Limitation of Naval Armaments, Records of the Conference at Geneva, June 20 to August 4, 1927*, 1928.

[2] Bouy, Raymond, *Le Désarmement Naval*, 1931; Foreign Policy Association, "The London Naval Conference January 21–April 22, 1930," *Foreign Policy Reports*, Vol. VI, No. 6, 1930; Howland, C. P., *ed.*, *American Foreign Relations, 1931*, 1931; Toynbee, A.J., *Survey of International Affairs 1931*, 1932.

billion dollars in new construction. Since the Roosevelt administration, moreover, presently undertook to endow the United States with a Treaty navy, the question of parity with Great Britain was at last settled.

By contrast, at London the Japanese, with their Manchurian adventure now clearly in mind, showed significant signs of impatience with the existing ratio of strength which they had accepted at Washington. They demanded and obtained a slightly higher ratio in cruisers, and parity in submarines. And, what was far more disturbing, they served notice that five years thereafter, when the naval powers met in conference again, they might demand parity in all categories.

All results actually achieved at London, moreover, were rendered purely conditional because, on the one hand, the British insisted upon retaining a two-power standard of naval strength vis-à-vis Europe and, on the other, the French declined to accept tonnage totals consonant with such British strength, unless the Anglo-Saxon powers consented to make fresh engagements in respect of French security. Since Italy, on her part, insisted upon parity with France, the prospective strength of the two Latin states was in excess of the totals accepted by the British, Americans, and Japanese.

Save as the United States was willing to agree to a consultative pact, Great Britain was resolved not to concede to France the Mediterranean Locarno which she sought. And, although the American delegation momentarily played with the idea of such a pact, public sentiment in the United States was obviously hostile. As a consequence, no satisfactory five-power treaty could be made. France and Italy stood aside. Great Britain, the United States, and Japan signed a treaty, but in that treaty the notorious "Escalator Clause"[1] reserved to Great Britain the right to exceed the tonnage totals agreed upon when they were insufficient to insure the existence of a two-power standard in Europe.

The result of the three naval conferences at Washington, Geneva, and London was, therefore, agreement upon temporary and conditional limitation on the three larger naval powers at maximum figures. Four years after London, too, with the prospects of another conference in 1935 plainly in mind, authoritative voices both in London and Tokyo urged the abandonment of all reliance upon ratios. On the one hand, the Japanese admiralty demanded parity with Great Britain and the United States, and on the other, the British urged that nations be left free to build as they chose. In addition the French and Italian fleets were now growing beyond the limits of the two-power standard.[2]

Nor had it been possible before 1935 to bring about any agreement between France and Italy such as had been sought at London and hoped for in the succeeding years. As the United States had claimed parity with Great Britain, Italy had demanded equality with France. But, unlike the United States, Italy was too poor to

[1] Article 16, Part III of the London Naval Treaty, which was not signed by France or Italy, contains the so-called "escalator clause":

"If, during the term of the present treaty, the requirements of the national security of any High Contracting Party in respect of vessels of war limited by Part III of the present Treaty are in the opinion of that Party materially affected by new construction of any Power other than those who have joined in Part III of this Treaty, that High Contracting Party will notify the other Parties to Part III as to the increase required to be made in its own tonnages within one or more of the categories of such vessels of war, specifying particularly the proposed increases and the reasons therefor, and shall be entitled to make such increase. Thereupon the other Parties to Part III of this Treaty shall be entitled to make a proportionate increase in the category or categories specified; and the said other Parties shall promptly advise with each other through diplomatic channels as to the situation thus presented."

[2] Foreign Policy Association, "The Franco-Italian Naval Dispute," *Foreign Policy Reports*, Vol. VII, No. 8, 1931.

match ship for ship with her rival. Thus, for her, parity
was attainable only as France consented to reduce. But
France, as long as she was faced by the possibility of a
German-Italian alliance, also insisted upon a two-power
standard. To all British urgings to come to an agreement with Italy, she responded by a demand for a new
British political commitment. And, failing this, she
continued to construct without regard for the effect of
such construction upon the terms of the London Treaty.

Twelve years after the Washington Conference it was
plain that only two concrete results had flowed from
that meeting for which so much was claimed at the
moment. Eventually and at the cost of a billion dollars
in new construction, the United States was certain in no
long time to acquire parity with the British in naval
forces. In return for abandoning the alliance with Great
Britain and accepting the ratio of Washington, Japan had
achieved complete naval mastery in the waters which interest her. Moreover, having repudiated the engagements
of the Nine-Power Treaty, shattered the territorial integrity of China, and proclaimed a Monroe Doctrine in the
Far East, which in American eyes seemed a clear challenge
to the doctrine of the "Open Door," Japan was now
demanding parity as the price of any future agreement.

In effect, as a result of the Washington and London
Conferences, the three larger naval powers, Great
Britain, the United States, and Japan, divided control of
the seas among themselves. They asserted and made
good claims which insured that they would each possess absolute superiority in the regions of primary interest to them, the British in Europe and Southeastern
Asia, the United States in the Americas,[1] and Japan in

[1] Map, pages 354-355.

the Far East. Each thus demanded and obtained absolute security for itself and at the same time abolished all
possibility of interference with its national policy.

Between the United States and Great Britain there
was no clash of policy, and therefore agreement on parity
has had no political consequences. When, however, the
British and Americans protested against Japanese action
in Manchuria, both were confronted by the fact that
they lacked the means to make such protest effective,
because at Washington they had not only surrendered
the right to maintain adequate naval bases at Corregidor
and Hong Kong but also consented to a Japanese ratio
rendering intervention impossible. Ironically enough,
therefore, the Washington Conference, called in the name
of disarmament and celebrated as a contribution to
peace, proved only a preface to aggression.

Thus, so far as anything practical has been achieved
in the matter of the limitation of naval armaments during the period 1920–1934, it has been achieved by the
British and Americans. Nor has agreement between
these two peoples gone beyond the elimination of a
competition in construction at once costly and futile.
This modest attainment, too, has been possible merely
because there is now no clash in national policy between
the two nations, and in addition there is a record of
unbroken peace extending over more than a century.

If American policy envisaged the annexation of Canada or of the corridor separating Alaska from the United
States, or if British policy contemplated the seizure of
Alaska to anticipate such annexation, there could be no
possibility of Anglo-American agreement in the matter
of naval strength. For parity would confer such decisive
superiority upon the United States in American waters

that Canada would be completely cut off from British aid, while the superiority Great Britain would demand for the defense of Canada would constitute a threat to the security of the United States.

It is because France and Italy are rivals in the Mediterranean and Italian policy envisages the acquisition of French territories in North Africa that no agreement has been achieved between them as to naval strength. If France consented to surrender her present superiority in naval strength while Italy declined to modify her purpose in the matter of Tunisia, parity would serve Italian interests at the expense of French, as British and American abandonment of the right to fortify Corregidor and Hong Kong has served Japanese interests. Since France means to maintain her territorial situation in North Africa and Italy to challenge it, only naval superiority can insure French security.

Adjustment between the United States and Great Britain in the matter of fleets having been predicated upon prior agreement in questions of territory, disarmament in national policy has already taken place in so far as the Anglo-Saxon peoples are concerned. In their relations with each other, therefore, armaments are not an instrument of national policy, because national policies already have been adjusted amicably and the adjustment accepted voluntarily. Between the two nations, therefore, the question of fleets is academic.

Likewise, in the case of Anglo-French relations no basic reason for rivalry exists. For years the British have suffered the French to maintain air forces vastly superior to their own because they were satisfied that French policy constitutes no threat to British security. On the other hand, at the first sign of German expansion in air forces the British took alarm because they saw in German policy a threat to their security.

Between the Italians and the French, on the other hand, the question of naval superiority is subordinate to the larger issue of territorial distribution. And as long as that issue remains unsettled, adjustment alike in the matter of land and sea forces cannot be achieved. Were Italy and France, however, to arrive at some measure of agreement in their national policies, as now seems likely under the common threat of recent developments in Germany, they could come to accord with the same facility as the British and Americans over the question of naval ratios.

In a word, if the policies of states do not clash, agreement in the matter of armaments is possible. But if their policies are in collision, no progress can be made in the adjustment of armaments until there has been previous accommodation in the matter of policy.[1]

In setting out to promote disarmament in Europe while political issues remained unadjusted, American administrations have, therefore, put the cart before the horse, and as a result have invariably met only with disappointment. They have also uniformly encountered demands that the United States give its guarantees to replace the armaments it would eliminate, and that has, in turn, aroused American resentment.

Such resentment, however, has no justification. Nations that feel themselves threatened by the policies of their neighbors will not reduce their armaments save as they see these neighbors abandon their menacing policies

[1] Bywater, H. C., *Navies and Nations*, 1927; Engely, Giovanni, *The Politics of Naval Disarmament*, 1932; Madariaga, Salvador de, *Disarmament*, 1929; Richmond, Admiral Sir H. W., *Economy and Naval Security*, 1931; Williams, B. H., *The United States and Disarmament*, 1931.

or can persuade other countries to underwrite their security. And although the United States could arrive at an agreement with Great Britain over naval armaments, it has never been able to persuade the British to abandon the two-power standard in Europe, because, while American equality had no menace for Great Britain, only decisive superiority in Europe seemed consonant with British security.

In all cases, political agreement must precede armament adjustments, whether these involve limitation or reduction; and where such agreement has been impossible, armament conferences have promptly bogged down into deadlock. By contrast, if political agreement is reached, the question of armaments loses most of its importance, because the danger of collision has been removed.

Final proof of this fact is disclosed in Japanese policy after 1931. Having embarked upon her Manchurian policy and being confronted not only by American opposition thereto but also by the clear purpose of the United States to establish a common front with Great Britain in the Far East, Japan denounced the Treaty of Washington with its ratios and demanded parity with both Anglo-Saxon powers. For only on such terms could she hope to retain naval control of the waters in which her interests are vital, if Great Britain and the United States should combine to halt her program in China.

Chapter XXVIII

LAND DISARMAMENT[1]

INTO the Treaty of Versailles the victors wrote their double assurance that the disarmament of Germany was "to render possible the initiation of a general limitation of the armaments of all nations" and also that the members of the League of Nations must subscribe to the principle "that the maintenance of peace requires the reduction of national armaments to the lowest point consistent with national safety and the enforcement by common action of international obligations."

Even more specific was the language of Clemenceau in his letter to Brockdorff-Rantzau. On June 16, 1919, the French Premier wrote to the head of the German delegation at Versailles: "The Allied and Associated Powers wish to make it clear that their requirements in regard to German armaments were not made solely with the object of rendering it impossible for Germany to resume her policy of military aggression. They are also the first steps toward that general reduction and limitation of

[1] For general bibliography on Disarmament, see Chapter XXVII, "Naval Disarmament."

armaments which they seek to bring about as one of the most fruitful preventives of war, and which it will be one of the first duties of the League of Nations to promote."

Vague as is the language alike of the Treaty, the Covenant, and the Clemenceau letter, in the matter of time and detail, it is clear that at Paris the victors gave a solemn engagement, not alone to the Germans but to the world as well, that disarmament was to be a major objective of the League and that the disparity between their armed forces and those of the recent enemy was to be eliminated by reduction to the German level.

A decade and a half after these commitments were made, it remained still unmistakable that practically nothing had been done in the field of land armaments to fulfill the pledges of 1919, and also that the prospects of disarmament were less hopeful than at any moment since the completion of the labors of the Paris Conference. In fact, as the year 1933 saw upwards of $4,000,-000,000 expended for armaments, 1934 witnessed a further intensification of competition on the part of nations great and small, alike in Europe, Asia, and America. And the signal for this new race was given by the evident collapse of the Disarmament Conference, which had undertaken to put into effect the promises of Paris.[1]

When one undertakes to grasp the reasons for the total failure of all attempts to bring about reduction or even limitation of land armaments, it is necessary first of all to state the problem.[2] In giving their assurances

[1] Foreign Policy Association, "The World Disarmament Conference: First Stage," *Foreign Policy Reports*, Vol. VIII, No. 5, 1932; also "The World Disarmament Conference: Second Stage, May 17, 1932–January, 1933," Vol. VIII, No. 23, 1933.

[2] Foreign Policy Association, "Limitation of Land Armaments," *Information Service*, Vol. VI, No. 2, 1930; also "Limitation of Air Armaments," Vol. VI, No. 17, 1930; Lefebure, V., *Scientific Disarmament*, 1931.

at Paris, the statesmen of the Allied and Associated Powers saw that problem in different lights. For Wilson, the assumption was that the League would presently constitute an effective guarantee for the security of all the member nations. For Clemenceau, the calculation was that the Treaty of Guarantee, bestowed upon France by Great Britain and the United States, would insure French security against later aggression. For Lloyd George, the goal was British return to the traditional policy of the balance of power.

When, however, the United States Senate repudiated the Treaty of Guarantee and refused to permit American membership in the League, the calculations of all three statesmen were brought to nothing. The nascent League was, as yet, patently incapable of guaranteeing the security of any member. The Anglo-Saxon guarantee of the security of France was destroyed. The policy of the balance of power had become inapplicable because France demanded assurances of her own security in advance of permitting the recovery of Germany to the point where the Reich could serve Great Britain as a counterweight to France.

The withdrawal of the United States had thus, on the one hand, destroyed French calculations for security and, on the other, left France, by reason of her military strength, supreme upon the Continent. Henceforth, in the very nature of things, the French were certain to cling to their existing military supremacy until they were able to establish other guarantees of their safety, either through alliance with the Anglo-Saxon nations or through organization of the League into an international body clothed with the authority and provided with the force to restrain aggression. Thus under all circumstances the French consistently maintained the thesis that security came before disarmament.

The British and the Americans, by contrast, being secure themselves by reason of their navies, and therefore content with small land forces, steadily pressed the thesis that military armaments themselves were a cause of insecurity and that the way to peace was through the reduction of armies. Always, however, their attention was concentrated upon land armaments. For themselves both nations demanded a superiority in naval strength, in the regions vital to them, far in excess of the advantage possessed by France on land. Actually, they strove to bring about the reduction of the land armaments of the European Continent because they were fearful of becoming involved in another European struggle, as they had been in the World War, and calculated that a disarmed Continent could not fight.

Between the French and the Anglo-Saxon powers, the issue was clear. There was no question of possible conflict. The French were not fearful lest British or American fleets should be employed to attack them. The Anglo-Saxon peoples were equally undisturbed as to the possibility of direct aggression by the French army. But the French demanded Anglo-Saxon guarantees of French security in advance of reducing their military forces, while the British and the Americans sought to persuade the French to consent to reduction without guarantees.

On this point, however, the French were from first to last immovable, because for them there existed a danger absent in the case of both the British and the Americans. Four times within a century, Prussian or German armies had approached Paris and on three of these occasions had entered it victoriously. The second Treaty of Paris

had in 1815 deprived France of the Saar, and the Treaty
of Frankfort had cost her Alsace-Lorraine. In the phase
of the World War when the Central Powers were
confident of victory, the German press and public had
proposed new mutilations and demanded new cessions.

In the World War, France had escaped the partitions
of the Franco-Prussian conflict solely because she had
been supported first by the British and then by the
American armies and fleets. Alone, she would have been
overwhelmed in 1914; and in any future war, if she were
isolated, the superiority of German numbers and industrial organization would insure defeat. Thus the supreme objective of France in the World War had been
security, and the dominating purpose of Clemenceau at
the Paris Conference had been the same. No security
for France could, however, be absolute, could in fact
approximate the safety bestowed upon both Anglo-
Saxon powers by sea barriers, save that provided either
by military alliance or by collective insurance obtained
through an effective League.

The German thesis, in turn, differed both from the
British and from the French. The Treaty of Versailles
had reduced German military resources to the level of
those of Belgium and prohibited any future rearmament.
But in the Treaty there had been the clear declaration of
purpose on the part of the victors to make German disarmament the first step in a general process. That was
a contract, and the fulfillment of this contract the Germans demanded unconditionally.[1]

In addition, apart from all questions of treaty promises, it was in itself contrary alike to right and reason

[1] Rohde, Hans, *Franco-German Factors of Power*, 1932.; Schmidt, Richard, and
Grabowsky, Adolf, *The Problem of Disarmament*, 1933; same authors, *Disarmament and
Equal Rights*, 1934.

to attempt to keep a nation of sixty-odd millions of inhabitants effectively disarmed in a Europe where other Great Powers were armed, and where Germany was surrounded by a circle of a million French, Polish, and Czech bayonets to which she could oppose but the hundred thousand allowed her by the Treaty of Versailles. In addition, her frontiers were demilitarized and her ancient fortresses either lost or demolished by the terms of the same treaty.

Three years after Waterloo, the armies of occupation of the victors had left French soil and automatically France had recovered her freedom of action in the matter of armaments. Within an equal time after Sedan, evacuation on the same terms had taken place, and but a few years later the rapidity and extent of French rearmament had gravely alarmed German military leaders. But when in 1932 the League Disarmament Conference actually assembled, German helplessness had already endured for a dozen years after the Armistice.

France asked security, Great Britain and the United States urged military disarmament, but the Germans demanded parity with France either through the reduction of French forces to the German level or through the expansion of the German forces to the proportions of those of her neighbor beyond the Rhine. Unless, however, the British and Americans, either by direct contract or through the medium of the League, guaranteed France against any evil consequences from the recognition of the German right to parity, it lay within the power of France, by invoking the terms of the Treaty of Versailles, to prohibit German rearmament legally, as it also did to prevent it physically.

When Great Britain, the United States, and Japan at

Washington and at London agreed to adjust their naval forces in accordance with the ratio of 5–5–3, each had, in effect, surrendered the power to molest either of the other two states in their domestic waters. Parity between Great Britain and the United States thus automatically insured the security of both. Parity in military forces between Germany and France, by contrast, would fatally compromise French security, because it would bestow upon Germany the power, once equality was attained, to proceed with complete immunity from danger to organize its superior numbers and resources for a new war of aggression.

Possession of naval parity by the United States, while in theory permitting a similar performance, in practice had no such implications, because there was no clash of policy between Great Britain and the United States. Fleets, like armies, are instruments of policy, but as no conflict of policy between Great Britain and the United States existed, parity in instruments was without significance. By contrast, French and German policies were in shock because French purpose envisaged the preservation and German purpose the revision of the status quo of the Paris Settlement. While the ratio between French and German military power was 3–1 or 4–1, as the Treaty of Versailles permitted, the disparity in the instruments of policy between the two countries precluded any challenge of the status quo by the Germans. As that disparity was reduced, however, the chances of successful challenge mounted *pari passu*.

All the problem of disarmament in the postwar years centers in this question of policy. For France, German policy constituted a direct and deadly threat, but for the British and the Americans it had no menace. For Germany, French resolution to preserve the status quo was a barrier to future greatness, and French insistence upon military supremacy in Europe a direct threat to national safety. Alike to the British and to the Americans, however, an armed and quarrelling Continent seemed the promise of a new war and a fresh danger of involvement, and therefore reduction of French armaments to German levels appeared a program of peace.

In this situation, the Anglo-Saxon powers concentrated their efforts upon persuading the French to consent to reduce their military forces. They did not concomitantly endeavor to bring the Germans to renounce their policy of territorial revision, because that was out of the question. But since it was German policy which explained French insistence upon military superiority, neither the British nor the Americans, acting now together and now separately, were able to accomplish anything of importance. Inevitably a deadlock in the matter of policy insured a deadlock in the discussion of the instruments of policy.

By contrast, in the field of naval armaments, agreement in policy between the British, American, and Japanese governments, an agreement set forth in the Nine-Power Treaty and in the Anglo-American renunciation of the right to fortify various naval bases, had originally made possible an adjustment of naval forces. When, however, the Japanese by their Manchurian operation precipitated a clash of policies, then the prospects of agreement upon naval armaments in the conference of 1935 became slight. For, having at last openly adopted a policy which conflicted alike with British and with American interests, the Japanese naturally sought to acquire a larger measure of naval strength than that which they had accepted either at Washington or at London. But in the light of the newly revealed policy of Japan, the British and American governments disclosed a common resolution not to suffer disproportionate increase in the instruments by which Japan could pursue her policy.

Turning now to the details of the discussions of disarmament in the postwar period, these present three phases. From 1920, when the League was actually launched, until 1925, when the Pacts of Locarno were made and German entrance into the League assured, all discussion at Geneva was concentrated not upon disarmament but upon security. In that time there were formulated both the Cecil Agreement of Mutual Assistance and the far more important Protocol of Geneva. Both of these projects were directed at investing Geneva with the authority and means of preventing aggression and therefore of preserving peace by binding the member nations to use their collective forces, both military and naval, to protect a member nation wantonly assailed.

Both of these programs, although the former bore the name of a British representative at Geneva, were rejected by the British parliament because they committed Great Britain to specific duties on the call of Geneva. The same considerations which led the United States Senate to reject the League because of the implications of Articles X and XVI of the Covenant, inspired British action in respect of the later engagements. Only when a crisis arrived, and even then solely on the basis of their own material interests, were the British prepared to share in any collective system to maintain order and prevent war.

In this first phase, from 1920 to 1925, the discussions

at Geneva did not lead to any solution of the problem of security. Nevertheless, with the coming of the Germans to Geneva, further delay in facing the question of disarmament became impossible. The years from 1925 to 1932, therefore, constitute a second phase, during which in a Preparatory Commission, acting in the name of the League, the attempt was made to deal directly with the issue of armaments and to discover some way of combining the French insistence on security with the German demand for parity.

All the various attempts failed, however. While an elaborate Draft Convention was eventually framed, in it those columns which were designed to be filled with the figures of the military forces of future armies were left significantly blank. On minor points there was agreement but in every case where differences among the French, Germans, and British over basic issues had developed, no viable compromise had been possible. During six years these discussions dragged on interminably and fruitlessly while German impatience mounted steadily, until at last the dangerous expedient was employed of transferring the still unsettled problem from the Preparatory Commission to a full-fledged Disarmament Conference with all the League powers, and the United States as well, represented therein.

Even before this Conference assembled in February, 1932, events in Europe and in Asia had foredoomed it to failure. In Europe the Truce of Locarno had expired, and Stresemann's successors, impelled by the growing menace of National Socialism, had embarked upon two catastrophic ventures. Thus before the Reichstag election of September, 1930, one member of the Brüning Cabinet had publicly reopened the question of the Polish

Corridor, and after it, in March, 1931, another had renewed the dispute over the *Anschluss* by proposing the
Austro-German tariff union.

The result had been a new shock between French and
German policies, a fresh period of turmoil, and ultimately still another German defeat in the Austrian
affair produced by French financial coercion exerted
both in Vienna and Berlin. As a consequence of this
conflict, Franco-German relations had reverted to the
pre-Locarno condition, and alarm as to German purpose
was acute alike in Paris, in Warsaw, and in Prague.
Thus on the eve of the convening of the Disarmament
Conference the question of security had acquired new
importance in the eyes of France and of her allies. On
the other hand, defeat in the Austrian affair, the onset
of the Great Depression, and the ever-rising tide of Hitlerism supplied new force to the demand of the Brüning
Government for parity.

Even less propitious were Asiatic events, for the Disarmament Conference actually assembled to the overture
of Japanese artillery about Shanghai. And these Japanese guns, in fact, demolished the whole case which the
British and the Americans had brought to Geneva. Both
came to urge reduction of armaments and each was similarly prepared to plead with France and her allies to
meet German demands, although neither was ready to
meet the French demand for security. But now, day by
day, events in Asia, the military campaign which had
opened with the Japanese occupation of Manchuria in
defiance of the ultimatum of the Council of the League,
demonstrated with increasing clarity that there was no
power in Geneva to restrain a nation bent on aggression,
and no means to protect a state which was the innocent

victim of such assault. And that, after all, was the French case. That was what France had been saying through the mouths of Clemenceau, Poincaré, and Briand ever since the Armistice. That was what she now proceeded to say with fresh emphasis in the voice of Tardieu.

What Japan had done Germany obviously could do, once she had obtained military parity with France. That she was resolved to do it, the double offensive revealed by the speech of Treviranus about the Polish Corridor and by the agreement of Curtius about Austrian affairs, satisfied the French and their allies. Therefore even before the delegates met, Tardieu set forth in crystal-clear phrase the old familiar demand of France that security should precede disarmament and that the League must be furnished with a force, this time in the air, adequate to insure that no European state should presently be overtaken by the fate of China.

The Disarmament Conference which constituted the third phase of the discussions, therefore, inevitably ended like the second. Agreement, which could not be reached in the Preparatory Commission, was equally unattainable in a regular Conference. Although eventually the French under British and American pressure did accept in principle the right of Germany to parity, in practice they insisted upon such postponements in attainment as to make the concession appear derisory in German eyes.

Two American Presidents intervened sensationally but unsuccessfully. Mr. Hoover, lightly brushing aside the political issues, in the midsummer of 1932 called for a cut of one third alike in naval and military forces. But for once the British and French were able to agree and both with polite finality dismissed the Hoover project. A year later, Roosevelt, with greater appreciation of the realities, proffered his pledge that if substantial disarmament took place he would refrain from pressing American neutral rights against powers engaged in the coercion of a state which had resorted to violence and, in American judgment, was guilty of aggression. But while this proposal awakened apprehension in the United States, it found little favor in France. The French, seeing that the promise was personal and recalling the episode of the Treaty of Guarantee which Wilson had bestowed and the Senate repudiated, rejected the Roosevelt proffer as they had dismissed the Hoover proposal. If it was a matter of concern to the United States to procure the reduction of French military forces, then it was for the American government to pay the price, which was—and always had been—the guarantee of French security. That was the view of Paris.

Last of all, Ramsay MacDonald made an eleventh-hour effort to save the Conference. His program envisaged a standard army of 200,000 for each of the Great Powers, and for Poland as well, intricate regulations of so-called defensive and offensive armaments, and progressive approach to parity by Germany. But although the British proposal found favor in American eyes, it failed to satisfy a Germany now wholly in the hands of Hitler, and in October, 1933, the dictator impatiently swept his country out of Conference and League alike and proclaimed the purpose to rearm without regard for the restrictions of the Treaty of Versailles.

For the larger part of a year after the German withdrawal the Conference staggered toward inevitable collapse. Without Germany, further discussion had become futile and even foolish. But it was not until midsummer, 1934, that the British Government faced the fact squarely and in the House of Commons simultaneously proclaimed its conviction that the failure of the Disarmament Conference was definitive and that its purpose to expand its own armaments, particularly in the air, could no longer be postponed. Thus, like the Economic Conference of 1933, the Disarmament Conference, while technically surviving, practically came to an end. It could be reconvened, but to reassemble it had now become fruitless so long as the causes of its failure continued unmodified.

Like the Hague Conferences of 1899 and 1907, the Geneva Conference of 1932–1934 came to grief because nations whose policies were irreconcilable were unwilling to consent to any curtailment of the means by which they had to pursue these policies. And, like the earlier failures, the later collapse proved the preface to new competitions in armaments because it was followed by fresh collisions of policy.[1] Nor was there the smallest basis for hoping, after the failures of the three conferences of the past, that there could be success in any new international gathering save as such an assembly was preceded by a compromise in policy between the Great Powers at odds.

In reality, armaments are no more than the thermometer upon which are recorded the stages of fever of a sick world. But to restore the health of that world it is necessary to abolish the fever and not by the application of ice to the thermometer to reduce the reading on the glass. When Herbert Hoover and Ramsay Mac-

---

[1] Einzig, Paul, *The Economics of Rearmament*, 1934; Foreign Policy Association, "Impending Naval Rivalries," *Foreign Policy Reports*, Vol. X, No. 3, 1934.

Donald, sitting beside the waters of the Rapidan, had been able to come to agreement as to the details of Anglo-American naval parity, then the fact and the figures of that agreement insured the adjustment which was later achieved at the London Naval Conference. But the Agreement of the Rapidan was possible only because a century of peace between the two Anglo-Saxon countries had removed all thought of aggression from the minds of both. And it testified convincingly to the absence of any clash of national policies.

If and when France and Germany ever reach an agreement in the matter of policy, such as existed between the United States and Great Britain on the eve of the London Naval Conference in the autumn of 1929, then an adjustment of their armed forces will be simple. While the present clash of policies endures, however, it must be equally impossible to persuade the French to abandon the superiority which they possess and the Germans to accept the inferiority which is theirs. And if in the future either Great Britain or the United States shall desire to promote disarmament by means of German parity it must be prepared to pay for French reduction by underwriting French security.

Chapter XXIX

FIFTEEN YEARS

LOOKING back over the fifteen years which separate Wilson from Hitler and the Paris Peace Conference from the midsummer *Putsch* in Vienna, it is clear that the facts of 1934 bore little resemblance to the hopes of 1919. During this decade and a half, efforts without precedent have been made to establish world order by the substitution of a system of organized peace for the old chaos produced by the pursuit of individual and irreconcilable national policies by the several states.

To that end, the League of Nations was created in 1919, and besides the original Covenant there have since been made the Pact of Paris and many other agreements, all designed to bring about a condition of international order. For the same purposes, conferences have again and again been convened to reach international accord in respect of tariffs, currencies, and armaments. This fifteen-year period has thus seen a multiplication of the means for the prevention of war which has no parallel in history.

Thanks to such untiring industry, the world found

itself in 1931 far more richly endowed with resources to prevent war and to promote international co-operation than ever before. The League of Nations was organized, the World Court established, the habit and technique of international conference acquired. By that time, too, Germany had actually joined the League and, although the United States still remained outside, long steps had been taken toward effective co-operation between Washington and Geneva.

Nevertheless in 1931, and in the immediately succeeding years, a series of events came to shatter the illusion of international association which had been created between 1925 and 1930, that is, during the period of the Truce of Locarno. The Manchurian affair in 1931, the fiasco of the London Economic Conference in 1932, and the failure of the Geneva Disarmament Conference in 1933, together disclosed the fact that public opinion had not kept pace with the expansion of the machinery of peace, and that, as a consequence, peoples had remained nationalistic and their governments were therefore unable or unwilling to make use of the machinery now available.

All the various assumptions upon which the League of Nations had originally been founded started from the primary calculation that as a consequence of the lessons of the World War, if not by reason of the instinctive will for peace and order of majorities, peoples were at last prepared to seek and to accept international accommodation of national policies where these conflicted. The League had therefore been created to do two things: to prevent war growing out of an immediate conflict of interests of nations, and to remove those issues which were the historic causes of conflict.

Success or failure for the great experiment, however, always turned upon the willingness of the majorities in all countries, in moments of crisis, to agree to international determination of their disputes and, in times of calm, to consent to similar adjustment of issues which otherwise would one day precipitate crises. In a word, the fate of the League of Nations was at all times contingent upon the extent to which all peoples, but primarily those of the Great Powers, were prepared to subordinate their sovereignties and to engage their resources in collective action to organize and to maintain world peace.

It is perfectly clear that the sixty-odd nations of the globe could not at the same time retain for themselves every prerogative of sovereignty and also co-operate effectively in a League of Nations. They had either, in advance of all crises, to undertake to submit voluntarily to the decision reached by the League where their own interests were at stake, or else to invest this League with the power to impose its decisions by force when these were made. Both courses, however, involved a modification of sovereign rights, a delegation of power, a restriction of national policy.

In point of fact, however, no Great Power was prepared to sacrifice any portion of its sovereignty, and no great people was even aware of the impossibility of reconciling the mutually exclusive systems of the sovereign state and of the League of Nations. On the contrary, each people, satisfied that its own rights, policies, and possessions were established in justice and reason, conceived that in an international parliament its cause must prevail. And none accepted the idea of going to Geneva as having any implication of the sacrifice of national interest. To every people, on the contrary, the League seemed an instrument for establishing the inherent justice of its cause without recourse to arms.

The champions of Geneva believed that because the majorities in most of the nations of the world had accepted the League, they had also accepted that idea of it which had existed in the mind of its founder, Woodrow Wilson. And, in the same fashion, the advocates of the Fourteen Points had been satisfied that when these had been accepted by both the Allies and the Central Powers, the character of the Paris Settlement had been determined in advance. But in reality each nation had interpreted Wilson's proposals in terms of its own interests, and when later the terms of the Peace Treaties did violence to the interests of any nation, it saw therein a breach of the contract of the Armistice.

Woodrow Wilson was able to persuade the statesmen of other nations to accept his Fourteen Points and to adopt his League of Nations. But in each case acceptance blinded him to the fact that peoples without exception saw the League not as a means for co-ordinating national policies at the sacrifice of national interests but as an instrument to carry out those policies. Once the League was established, they looked to Geneva to provide the double blessing of peace and the protection and promotion of national interest.

The League was thus established upon a gigantic equivocation; but between 1920 and 1924 that equivocation was not disclosed, because all of the Great Powers ignored Geneva utterly and transacted their business elsewhere. Nor was it exposed between 1925 and 1930, because, although Germany, France, and Great Britain, operating under the terms of the Truce of Locarno, came to Geneva, they tacitly excluded from their discussions those vital and unsettled issues which, had they been raised, must have precipitated controversy and produced deadlock.

During the first ten years of its existence, therefore, the League was never called upon to deal with an immediate clash between Great Powers over a vital issue and thus to remove the continuing causes of conflict. It had viewed the Franco-German struggle over the Ruhr from the sidelines. It had refrained from any attempt to find solution for such problems as the Polish Corridor, the *Anschluss*, or the chaos in China.

In 1931, however, the League was suddenly called upon to act in a crisis precipitated by an undisguised act of violence by one Great Power against a weaker nation. In 1933, it was asked to provide an accommodation between the tariff and currency policies of nations. Between 1932 and 1934, it was required to bring about an adjustment among the armaments of states. And in each case it failed. The Japanese continued to impose their will in Manchuria. The Economic Conference in London collapsed in swift fiasco. The Disarmament Conference in Geneva suffered a lingering and tragic fate.

Common to all these episodes was an identical resolution of each Great Power to serve its own national interests without regard for international consequences. Japan was resolved to have Manchuria. The American administration was determined to proceed with its own program of domestic recovery. France insisted upon security without regard to the German demand for parity, and Germany upon parity without concern for the French claim to security. And in every instance, although the action of the government of one state was

fatal to the co-operation of the many, that government
was supported by its own citizens unquestioningly.

The League had no power of persuasion and no resource for coercion. Japan, the United States, France
would not yield to the will of the majority in the matter
of Manchuria, stabilization, or disarmament. Nor in
any case would the majority consent to provide the force
for achieving by authority what could not be attained
by consent. Patently the three questions were of varying
importance; practically, however, the same issue was
involved, that of internationalism versus nationalism.
And in every case it was nationalism which prevailed.

The fact that must be evident to all objective minds
is that in each of these three episodes both the theory
and the practice of the League of Nations were subjected
to tests which were at once fair and final. To prevent
aggression, promote economic co-operation, forestall a
race in armaments, these were tasks properly and inevitably set for any international institution. To have failed
in all three was to demonstrate one of two things, either
that the machinery of Geneva was inadequate, or that
the will of peoples to employ it was nonexistent.

But in every case the machinery functioned efficiently
up to the point where it became necessary for member
nations, on the one hand, to consent to sacrifice their
interests or, on the other, to permit the employment of
their forces. In the Manchurian affair, for example,
Japan had to give in or the other Great Powers had to
join in the application of force. But Japan would not
obey the law and the other nations would not enforce
it. What was then at fault was not the machinery of the
League but the assumption that peoples would subordinate national interests to international consideration.

The consequences of the failure of the League in Manchuria and in the London and Geneva Conferences were fully disclosed in the Austrian crisis of July, 1934. The murder of Dollfuss in Vienna produced a situation ominously reminiscent of that precipitated by the assassination of the Archduke in Serajevo just twenty years before. European peace was again in the balance. It was of the earlier situation, too, that Sir Edward Grey had written, after the war, that had the League machinery been available in 1914 he was satisfied that the catastrophe could have been averted.

But in 1934 the League did exist, its machinery was in order, everything was ready and waiting. Nevertheless, as Russia had mobilized in 1914 to protect Serbia, Italy mobilized two decades later to defend Austrian independence. It was not to Geneva but to London and Paris that Mussolini turned to seek and to obtain a mandate for his program of action. And in the presence of a force beyond German power to overcome, Hitler bowed to necessity and the "Nazi" campaign in Austria collapsed instantly and ingloriously.

In effect, moreover, the Austrian affair was quite as disastrous for the prestige of the League as the events in Manchuria. In the Manchurian case, the machinery of Geneva had been invoked unsuccessfully. In the Austrian affair, the futility of appeal to Geneva was assumed in advance and Europe reverted to the old familiar technique of mobilization and the Concert. To have waited for Geneva would have insured the success of the *Putsch*, and such delay could have added nothing to the resources of an Italian dictator who saw the security of his country at stake.

Unmistakably, therefore, that world which the

League of Nations was designed to serve does not yet exist. World public opinion whose instrument it was to become is as yet lacking. Those majorities within countries which were to drive their governments to enter and follow pathways of peace are still undiscoverable. On the contrary, the masses everywhere today support governments which build great navies, organize large armies, or construct huge air fleets. These masses are equally responsive to appeals based upon considerations of ethnic nationalism and those of economic nationalism. Wherever in any country the issue between nationalism and internationalism has been raised, it is the former which has prevailed.

The successive triumphs of Mussolini, Pilsudski, Hitler, and half a score of other dictators, each in his own country the incarnation of nationalistic faith, were in themselves clear evidence of the direction the minds of the masses were taking. Between dictatorship, whether Fascist or National Socialist, and Geneva there can be no basis of co-operation, because at bottom the League of Nations was designed to abolish precisely that spirit of which the dictator is invariably the symbol. In a world half democratic and half dictatorial, international co-operation is always out of the question.

In a word, the League of Nations was conceived as the lasting expression of the meaning of the World War. It was to be the instrument of a new world made wise by the mistakes of the old. It was to provide the machinery for creating collective order in the place of the anarchy of the individualism of the past. But like a sailing ship on the sea or a water-wheel mill beside a river, the League depended upon something outside itself for motive power. And that something was the effective will of the majorities within countries to seek international peace and order by the only means possible, namely the subordination of national policy to international adjustment.

If the majorities within states supported statesmen and policies which were nationalistic, then precisely as long as that situation endured, the League of Nations was bound to be like a ship in a calm or a mill in a drought. And when, after 1930, the majorities in all countries turned to nationalistic camps, the present plight of the League became inescapable. As early as 1920, Woodrow Wilson had described the presidential election of that year as a "solemn referendum." He had appealed to the American people over the heads of his opponents and on behalf of an international as contrasted with national conceptions. But he was beaten.

Elsewhere in the world similar struggles had the same ending. The Italian, British, Japanese, and German peoples each in turn followed the American example. The Manchurian episode was the epitome of the history of the pursuit of peace in the postwar years. What the Japanese wanted, they took. When the League protested, the Japanese turned a deaf ear to Geneva. When the League called upon the member nations to make good the principles of the Covenant and the Pact of Paris, by upholding the law which had been broken and by defending a victim of unprovoked aggression, these member nations put a blind eye to the telescope, and thus ignored the signals flying from the Quai Wilson.

But if one nation would not obey the law voluntarily and the others would not enforce it, a League without moral authority to persuade or physical resource to coerce had become at the best an ideal and at the worst an illusion. In sharp contrast to the failure of the League in Manchuria in 1931, however, was its success in the Saar in 1935. For the peace of Europe and for the prestige of Geneva as well, the plebiscite of January 13, 1935, which registered the will of the inhabitants of the Saar Region to return to Germany, was an equally significant gain. The dispatch of British and Italian troops to insure order during the election was, too, an example of international co-operation as rare as it was impressive.

Nevertheless, it is essential to note that both the election itself and the dispatch of international forces were predicated upon prior Franco-German accord. And it was the consent of both countries to the submission of the issue to an election supervised by the League and to abide by the results, which actually exorcised the perils inherent in the question.

If, by contrast, either France or Germany had adopted in the Saar the policy Japan followed in Manchuria, the machinery of Geneva would have been again ineffective. But France preferred peace with Germany to precarious possession of the Saar, and Germany was satisfied that— as the event proved—a fair election would insure her triumph.

In fact, then, the Saar Plebiscite constituted a fitting postlude to the first fifteen years of League history; for it demonstrated anew the basic truth that the creation of the League had constituted not a solution but a revision of the problem of peace. Thenceforth there existed a machine capable of producing peaceful adjustment of international disputes, but the problem of persuading peoples to employ that machine when their vital interests are in question still remained.

CONCLUSION

No student of contemporary history can fail to note the obvious parallel between the decade and a half following the Congress of Vienna and the fifteen years which came after the Conference of Paris. Politically, both were eras of reaction provoked by earlier convulsions: the first by the French Revolution, and the second by the Russian.

Between 1815 and 1830 what existed was clearly a truce of exhaustion. After a quarter of a century of almost continuous conflict, France was in no condition to challenge the territorial decisions of the two Treaties of Paris which had reduced her to the limits of 1789. By contrast, the later pause which lasted from the July Revolution to the Crimean War was, primarily, a peace of calculation. War was then no longer beyond the resources of France but it was unattractive to those who directed French policy.

Precisely in the same fashion, the years from 1920 to 1934 constituted another truce of exhaustion dictated by the conditions in which Germany found herself at the close of the World War. When, too, Adolf Hitler, like Louis Philippe, came to power as a result of a domestic upheaval, he found himself face to face with a political problem strangely reminiscent of 1830; for, as the possibility of recovering Belgium confronted the

Citizen King, so the Reichsfuehrer was faced by the chance to join his native Austria to the Reich.

In 1934 as in 1830, however, the pathway of ambition was blocked by the combined strength of the other Great Powers of Europe. As Great Britain, Russia, and Prussia had closed the pathway of France down the Scheldt to Antwerp, so France, Italy, and the Little Entente now barred the road of Germany southward along the Danube to Vienna. Like Louis Philippe, therefore, Adolf Hitler in his turn was forced, temporarily at least, to renounce a program of national expansion.

So far, then, the resemblances between the two postwar periods were at once striking and, for those who lived in the later time, not without a measure of reassurance, since, despite contemporary fears, the July Revolution had proved a preface not to a new convulsion but to two decades of further peace among the Great Powers. Nevertheless there was in 1934 one circumstance which was without parallel in 1830 and went far toward dissipating the optimism inspired by precedent. Whereas after 1830 the government and people of France had found peace, if not distinguished, at least tolerable and even profitable, neither the German dictator nor the German people could discover promise of a similar situation in 1934.

In 1830 the French Bourgeoisie had aided and abetted the July Revolution because they saw in the stupid and oppressive policies of the restored Bourbons the seeds of a new upheaval like that of the Great Revolution. To prevent such a catastrophe, they successfully intervened, so that Charles X made way for Louis Philippe. When that change had been accomplished, however, French Business and Finance were under no temptation to permit domestic upheaval to be followed by foreign war, because in that direction lay the danger of a new Napoleon. Peace was then their chief concern, and for two decades the French people found that peace tolerable because it was increasingly prosperous.

Much the same circumstances at first attended the Fascist upheaval in Italy in 1922. High Finance and Big Business in Italy saw in the continuing weakness of parliamentary democracy in the peninsula the growing menace of a Communist triumph. To protect property from the dangers this Red threat had for it, Italian Capitalism followed the example of the French Bourgeoisie and gave their decisive aid to a change in regime. Thus in Italy Mussolini served the purposes of Louis Philippe in France a century earlier.

Once Fascism had triumphed, however, Italian Capitalism could have no interest in seeing the program of foreign aggression, which Mussolini had preached, translated into fact. For when the new regime had consolidated its position, the Red Peril was definitely exorcised. Thereafter, no further danger of Communism in Italy could exist unless the strain and disillusionment of still another war should restore the conditions out of which the crisis of 1922 had emerged.

Mussolini, therefore, despite his warlike utterances, was as little able—and perhaps as little anxious—to undertake the seizure of Dalmatia as Louis Philippe had been ready for the annexation of Belgium. To gratify Italian pride without risking foreign war became the aim of policy, and as a consequence the Duce was as cautious in action as he was reckless in phrase. Like Louis Philippe, however, he was able in the opening years of his rule to provide Capitalism with profits and

Labor with employment, since these years were a time of relative prosperity and considerable recovery.

When in 1933 Hitler, in his turn, mounted to absolute control in the Reich, he was faced by an economic problem without parallel in the experience of Louis Philippe or Mussolini. To his rise to power the same forces had contributed as had supported the Citizen King and the Duce. Heavy Industry and High Finance in Germany had, in the domestic consequences of the Great Depression, seen a threatening prospect of disruptive upheaval. To arrest the visible growth of Communism, they had exploited Hitler and his National Socialist movement to overthrow the Republic.

The major purpose of Capitalism in Germany, as in Italy, however, had been, not to clear the way for foreign war, but to insure domestic order. Having put absolute power in the hands of their selected agent, those who had favored and financed Hitler would normally have viewed war in the same light as did those who had similarly supported Mussolini. For, in the existing circumstances of Germany, the odds against her victory were very great, while the domestic consequences of another military defeat would be disastrous. And since National Socialism had been far less successful than Fascism in crushing opposition on the home front, its hold upon power was correspondingly more precarious.

Unhappily for Hitler and for German Capitalism which had backed him, however, there was in Germany a problem of domestic prosperity that was lacking in the Fascist experience in Italy. At the moment the Reichsfuehrer's control became absolute, Germany was confronted by the devastating consequences of the economic nationalism of the rest of the world. Under the stress of the Great Depression all countries, large and small, had committed themselves to the passionate pursuit of autarky.

Since Germany was completely dependent upon the outside world for most of the essential raw materials of industry and could obtain these only as she could give her manufactures in exchange, her situation was bound to become increasingly desperate as the world refused her goods. Deprived of foreign raw materials, her factories would run down, her industry would halt, and as unemployment mounted, the Red menace was certain to revive. Raised to power under a pledge to abolish all danger of Communism, Hitler thus found himself faced by a situation in which the economic nationalism of other nations inevitably fostered Communism within the Reich.

It was, moreover, self-evident that whatever regime ruled in the Reich, whether imperial, republican, or dictatorial, it could not hope to survive permanently unless it was able to provide the working masses with food and employment, and the capitalistic classes with order and prosperity. It was inability to perform this primary function of government that had, in the end, sealed the fate of the Weimar Republic. As long as that regime had been able to provide domestic prosperity, it had also been able to repulse Communism and National Socialism.

On the prospectus of material well-being supplied by the Dawes Plan, Stresemann had been able to take his fellow-countrymen both to Locarno and to the League. Recovery at home had permitted him to pursue policies of peace abroad. It was only when, after the death of

Stresemann, Brüning was forced to multiply the taxes of the rich and to increase the privations of the poor in order to counteract the effects of the Great Depression, that Labor had turned to the example of Moscow, and Capital to that of Rome.

Thereupon Hitler had marched to power to the accompaniment of music which was martial, but the forces which were operating to insure his triumph were economic. To satisfy the needs of Capitalism which had supported him, he had now to provide Labor with employment, and thus with food; for masses long deprived of food and employment must in the end constitute the stuff of which revolutions are made, and while people can exist without glory, they will not long endure a shortage of bread.

In the same fashion, while Capital will instinctively reject the hazards of foreign war as long as it is assured of domestic order, it will accept the risks of such war if these constitute the sole alternative to revolution at home. And in 1934 a hundred voices charged publicly that German Heavy Industry and High Finance already accepted war as the only alternative to revolution otherwise inescapable by reason of the economic policies of other nations, and that as a consequence the peace which persisted was a peace of preparation.

What was true of the economic circumstances of Germany was becoming true also, if to a lesser degree, of those of Italy. Like Germany, Italy was dependent upon the outside world for most of the raw materials essential to its industry. To exchange for these, Italy possessed little but labor. When the world closed its doors to her laborers the consequences to the domestic economy of Italy were therefore disastrous. And upon the Fascist regime was placed the responsibility for domestic conditions which were beyond its power to remedy. Far away in Asia, too, Japan as early as 1931 had undertaken to solve the same problem by foreign aggression, deliberately exploiting national patriotism to provide the means of national existence.

Thus by the end of 1934 it was becoming clear that a new note had crept into international relations. Half a generation after the Armistice the old, familiar issues dividing peoples still seemed on the surface to retain their traditional vitality. Lost provinces, defenseless frontiers, suffering minorities, these continued to supply the material out of which nationalistic campaigns were manufactured. Even those peoples whose material circumstances were becoming intolerable still thought of their wrongs in terms of the old ideology. The Treaty of Versailles and not the tariffs of other nations seemed to the Germans the major cause of their contemporary sufferings. But what peoples perceived only dimly, dictators were already seeing plainly, namely that it was the economic and not the political status quo which had become intolerable. And the consequences of this economic status quo could not be abolished by any revision of the territorial decisions of the Paris Peace Conference.

Thus while it was possible after 1934, as after 1830, that the caution of dictators, the concern of capitalists, the exhaustion of countries might in Europe postpone a conflict which in recent years had come to seem not only inevitable but also imminent, it was no longer possible to believe that enduring peace could be founded upon the existing circumstances. And that, after all, constituted the final lesson of the experience of the previous century. The system created by the Congress of Vienna had survived for four decades, but it had eventually gone down in ruin following a long series of wars, because it had totally disregarded that spirit of political nationalism which was born of the French Revolution.

In the end the subject and divided nationalities of the Continent had set liberty above peace, and, since national unity was to be had only by force, had unhesitatingly accepted the hazards and hardships of war. By the close of the World War, however, this principle of nationality was everywhere triumphant. All the peoples of the Old World had acquired liberty and, with only one important exception, substantial unity. At most what remained were boundary disputes. The right of every nationality to freedom had been established; only the details of adjustment of rival interests remained to be regulated.

But in the place of the old problem of political nationalism a new issue of economic nationalism was coming to the fore. The right of peoples to national unity had been recognized, but the ability of free and united peoples to exist decently and prosperously was not yet established. What the implications of this new issue were, the Great Depression plainly disclosed alike in Germany, in Italy, and in Japan. What the consequences of failure to solve the new problem peacefully would be, the example of Japan and the menace of Germany also clearly indicated.

In a word, it was becoming more and more unmistakable that the world's real problem at the time of the Paris Peace Conference had not been to make the world safe for Democracy but to make it tolerable for those democracies which already existed in 1914 or had emerged from the World War. And that problem had been primarily economic and not political. If the French Revolution had aroused nationalities to consciousness of their political rights, the Industrial Revolution had just as clearly awakened nations to their economic necessities. And against inequalities in economic circumstances countries were as certain to react violently as they had been to resist political injustices. To expect the German, Italian, or Japanese people to accept as definitive the economic status quo of 1919 was therefore as absurd as to expect the Italians, Poles, or Balkan peoples to accept the political status quo of 1815 as final.

But for the peaceful solution of this new problem the machinery of the League and the provisions of the Pact of Paris were useless. Nor was public international law of any avail, for, like the municipal law, it constituted a guarantee of the rights of those possessors of property whose titles were clear. The Covenant of the League made it an aggression to undertake by violence to disturb the status quo; the Pact of Paris made such action a crime. But to enact a law against theft while permitting starvation to exist, could not prevent stealing but only populate prisons. And to abolish war without providing some other means of remedying economic circumstances which insure national misery for some peoples while bestowing national prosperity upon others, must prove equally futile.

It was on this rock of the status quo that the League of Nations ultimately came to grief. Had the League existed in 1777, it must have made American independence impossible, for the British could have invoked its Covenant to restrain the French intervention which alone made the victory of the colonists possible. Had it existed in 1859, it must have been a similar weapon of Austria, and equally fatal to Italian unification. For the Americans of the Revolution and the Italians of the Risorgimento, however, theirs was the battle of Liberty against Tyranny, of Justice against Oppression; and had the League intervened against them, for both it would have lost all moral value. But both in 1777 and in 1859 the League would have been compelled to intervene; for French and American policy in the earlier year, and Sardinian in the later, constituted a clear threat to peace and an employment of war as an instrument of national policy.

In 1919, in the immediate presence of the devastation of the World War, and also in the conviction that, with the liberation of subject peoples, the old causes of conflict had been abolished, it was possible to believe that the memories of the horrors of the past struggle would preclude their repetition in a new. A decade and a half later, however, it was evident that while all peoples had largely forgotten the agonies of the distant war, many were finding the conditions of present peace intolerable. And since war constituted the sole means of escape from these conditions, it was coming to appear, alike to the masses and to the classes in several states, a lesser evil.

* * * * * *

The student of international relations must, therefore, perceive that so far from solving the problem of peace the postwar world has, at most, only succeeded in stating it. To prevent war it is not enough to interpose legal or moral obstacles to war. That is like damming a river without providing an exit for the flood waters, thus merely causing extension of the area of inevitable inundation and destruction. Nor is it sufficient to prove war terrible thereby to prevent it. On the contrary it is also necessary to demonstrate that the existing peace is equitable and therefore tolerable.

Since, too, various nations find the existing peace inequitable and unendurable as a consequence of their own material circumstances and of the economic practices of more fortunate peoples, the world is faced with the problem, not of keeping the peace but of creating it.

Today, however, the doctrine of absolute sovereignty bars the way to the establishment of any system of international order, because it is the rights of nations, everywhere reckoned imprescriptible, which are responsible for the present condition of anarchy. The price of peace, therefore, is the readjustment of national rights to international necessities. The alternative is new wars for old; but such wars are not inevitable.

Only those wars are inevitable which result from the decisions of peoples that their present conditions are not to be endured and cannot be changed save by war. In the nineteenth century many peoples found their political circumstances intolerable because these constituted a denial of independence or unity. As a consequence, they took up arms and no effort to preserve peace was successful because none proposed any substitute for war as a means for ending what appeared injustice to those who were ready to fight rather than endure.

Today economic conditions have largely replaced political as causes for conflict. But this transformation has neither changed the nature of the problem nor modified the resolution of peoples. Thus the contemporary question is whether peaceful means can be found for removing economic inequalities which nations will not endure; for in the end, if these nations discover no alternative, they will resort to arms. If mankind actually believed that war is the greatest of human evils, there would be no problem of peace. But such has never been the case in the past and obviously is not in the present.

On the contrary, Italian Fascism, Japanese Imperialism, and German National Socialism, each in its turn, has put the world on notice that it has rejected all the postwar prescriptions of peace because these would guarantee the permanence of disparities in economic circumstances fatal to national well-being, and is now openly training its youth for battle.

In the face of this clear warning the more fortunate nations, Great Britain, France, and the United States, have not modified their economic practices but instead have multiplied their military and naval preparations. And in this respect the Soviet Union has significantly followed their example. Nor is it possible to discover any alternative to this course consonant with policies which these countries are pursuing.

In the first days of 1935 at least two great countries in Europe and many smaller nations as well were confronted by the fact that what they were witnessing within their frontiers was a race between recovery and revolution, for, under the stress of the Great Depression, the conditions of their national existence were becoming more and more onerous and the temper of their masses progressively more dangerous.

In the face of this patent danger, too, the statesmen of these countries were without adequate resources to resolve the crisis. The poverty of their countries in the essential raw materials and minerals of industry rendered them dependent upon foreign supplies to keep domestic industrial machinery in operation. But penury in the means of procuring the necessary foreign supplies paralyzed their efforts.

Having to choose between foreign war and domestic collapse to Communism, governments backed by Industry, Finance, and Business, would unquestionably invite the hazards of the former to escape the horrors of the latter. Thus the problem of peace for the future had patently become a question of reconciling the traditions of absolute sovereignty with the conditions of contemporary economic existence. On the one hand the peoples of the Great Powers which together possessed an approximate monopoly of the world's resources in the essentials of industry remained firm in their assertion of the right to the exclusive exploitation of these essentials. On the other hand, the less well-favored nations made parity in prosperity the price of peace.

To bridge the gap between these two seemingly irreconcilable conceptions is, therefore, the problem of the peacemakers of a new era in which economic self-sufficiency has replaced ethnic self-determination as the chief objective of the national policies of Great Powers.

Appendix A

THE COVENANT OF THE LEAGUE OF NATIONS [1]

The High Contracting Parties,

In order to promote international cooperation and to achieve international peace and security:

by the acceptance of obligations not to resort to war,

by the prescription of open, just and honourable relations between nations,

by the firm establishment of the understandings of international law as the actual rule of conduct among Governments, and

by the maintenance of justice and a scrupulous respect for all treaty obligations in the dealings of organised peoples with one another,

Agree to this Covenant of the League of Nations.

ARTICLE I

1. The original Members of the League of Nations shall be those of the Signatories which are named in the Annex to this Covenant and also such of those other States named in the Annex as shall accede without reservation to this Covenant. Such accession shall be effected by a Declaration deposited with the Secretariat within two months of the coming into force of the Covenant. Notice thereof shall be sent to all other Members of the League.

2. Any fully self-governing State, Dominion or Colony not named in the Annex may become a Member of the League if its admission

---

[1] The Covenant is given with annotations as found in *Ten Years of World Cooperation*. Amendments in force, as mentioned in footnotes, are included in the text in italics; other proposed amendments have been added in footnotes. The paragraphs are given as officially numbered by an Assembly resolution of September 21, 1926.

is agreed to by two-thirds of the Assembly, provided that it shall give effective guarantees of its sincere intention to observe its international obligations, and shall accept such regulations as may be prescribed by the League in regard to its military, naval and air forces and armaments.

3. Any Member of the League may, after two years' notice of its intention so to do, withdraw from the League, provided that all its international obligations and all its obligations under this Covenant shall have been fulfilled at the time of its withdrawal.

ARTICLE II

The action of the League under this Covenant shall be effected through the instrumentality of an Assembly and of a Council, with a permanent Secretariat.

ARTICLE III

1. The Assembly shall consist of Representatives of the Members of the League.

2. The Assembly shall meet at stated intervals and from time to time as occasion may require at the Seat of the League, or at such other place as may be decided upon.

3. The Assembly may deal at its meetings with any matter within the sphere of action of the League or affecting the peace of the world.

4. At meetings of the Assembly, each Member of the League shall have one vote, and may have not more than three Representatives.

ARTICLE IV

1. The Council shall consist of Representatives of the Principal Allied and Associated Powers,[1] together with Representatives of four[2] other Members of the League. These four[2] Members of the League shall be selected by the Assembly from time to time in its discretion. Until the appointment of the Representatives of the four Members of the League first selected by the Assembly, Representatives of Belgium, Brazil, Spain and Greece shall be Members of the Council.

[1] The Principal Allied and Associated Powers were the following: The United States of America, the British Empire, France, Italy, and Japan (see Preamble of the Treaty of Peace with Germany); but the United States did not accept membership.
[2] See following Paragraph 2 and note.

2. With the approval of the majority of the Assembly, the Council may name additional Members of the League, whose Representatives shall always be Members of the Council;[1] the Council with like approval may increase the number of Members of the League to be selected by the Assembly for representation on the Council.[2]

2 bis.[3] *The Assembly shall fix by a two-thirds majority the rules dealing with the election of the non-permanent Members of the Council, and particularly such regulations as relate to their term of office and the conditions of re-eligibility.*

3. The Council shall meet from time to time as occasion may require, and at least once a year, at the Seat of the League, or at such other place as may be decided upon.

4. The Council may deal at its meetings with any matter within the sphere of action of the League or affecting the peace of the world.

5. Any Member of the League not represented on the Council shall be invited to send a Representative to sit as a member at any meeting of the Council during the consideration of matters specially affecting the interests of that Member of the League.

6. At meetings of the Council, each Member of the League represented on the Council shall have one vote, and may have not more than one Representative.

ARTICLE V

1. Except where otherwise expressly provided in this Covenant or by the terms of the present Treaty, decisions at any meeting of the Assembly or of the Council shall require the agreement of all the Members of the League represented at the meeting.

2. All matters of procedure at meetings of the Assembly or of the Council, including the appointment of Committees to investigate particular matters, shall be regulated by the Assembly or by the Council and may be decided by a majority of the Members of the League represented at the meeting.

[1] In virtue of this paragraph of the Covenant, Germany was nominated as a permanent Member of the Council on September 8, 1926.

[2] The number of Members of the Council selected by the Assembly was increased to six instead of four by virtue of a resolution adopted at the third ordinary meeting of the Assembly on September 25, 1922; and it was further increased to nine by a resolution adopted by the Assembly on September 8, 1926.

[3] This amendment came into force on July 29, 1926, in accordance with Article XXVI of the Covenant.

3. The first meeting of the Assembly and the first meeting of the Council shall be summoned by the President of the United States of America.

ARTICLE VI

1. The permanent Secretariat shall be established at the Seat of the League. The Secretariat shall comprise a Secretary-General and such secretaries and staff as may be required.

2. The first Secretary-General shall be the person named in the Annex; thereafter the Secretary-General shall be appointed by the Council with the approval of the majority of the Assembly.

3. The secretaries and staff of the Secretariat shall be appointed by the Secretary-General with the approval of the Council.

4. The Secretary-General shall act in that capacity at all meetings of the Assembly and of the Council.

5.[1] *The expenses of the League shall be borne by the Members of the League in the proportion decided by the Assembly.*

ARTICLE VII

1. The Seat of the League is established at Geneva.

2. The Council may at any time decide that the Seat of the League shall be established elsewhere.

3. All positions under or in connection with the League, including the Secretariat, shall be open equally to men and women.

4. Representatives of the Members of the League and officials of the League when engaged on the business of the League shall enjoy diplomatic privileges and immunities.

5. The buildings and other property occupied by the League or its officials or by Representatives attending its meetings shall be inviolable.

ARTICLE VIII

1. The Members of the League recognise that the maintenance of peace requires the reduction of national armaments to the lowest point consistent with national safety and the enforcement by common action of international obligations.

2. The Council, taking account of the geographical situation and circumstances of each State, shall formulate plans for such reduction for the consideration and action of the several Governments.

[1] This paragraph came into force August 13, 1924, in accordance with Article XXVI.

3. Such plans shall be subject to reconsideration and revision at least every ten years.

4. After these plans shall have been adopted by the several Governments, the limits of armaments therein fixed shall not be exceeded without the concurrence of the Council.

5. The Members of the League agree that the manufacture by private enterprise of munitions and implements of war is open to grave objections. The Council shall advise how the evil effects attendant upon such manufacture can be prevented, due regard being had to the necessities of those Members of the League which are not able to manufacture the munitions and implements of war necessary for their safety.

6. The Members of the League undertake to interchange full and frank information as to the scale of their armaments, their military, naval and air programmes, and the condition of such of their industries as are adaptable to warlike purposes.

ARTICLE IX

A permanent Commission shall be constituted to advise the Council on the execution of the provisions of Articles I and VIII and on military, naval and air questions generally.

ARTICLE X

The Members of the League undertake to respect and preserve as against external aggression the territorial integrity and existing political independence of all Members of the League. In case of any such aggression or in case of any threat or danger of such aggression the Council shall advise upon the means by which this obligation shall be fulfilled.

ARTICLE XI

1. Any war or threat of war, whether immediately affecting any of the Members of the League or not, is hereby declared a matter of concern to the whole League, and the League shall take any action that may be deemed wise and effectual to safeguard the peace of nations. In case any such emergency should arise the Secretary-General shall on the request of any Member of the League forthwith summon a meeting of the Council.

2. It is also declared to be the friendly right of each Member of

the League to bring to the attention of the Assembly or of the Council any circumstance whatever affecting international relations which threatens to disturb international peace or the good understanding between nations upon which peace depends.

ARTICLE XII[1]

1. The Members of the League agree that if there should arise between them any dispute likely to lead to a rupture they will submit the matter either to arbitration *or judicial settlement* or to enquiry by the Council and they agree in no case to resort to war until three months after the award by the arbitrators *or the judicial decision* or the report by the Council.

2. In any case under this Article, the award of the arbitrators *or the judicial decision* shall be made within a reasonable time, and the report of the Council shall be made within six months after the submission of the dispute.

ARTICLE XIII[1]

1. The Members of the League agree that whenever any dispute shall arise between them which they recognise to be suitable for submission to arbitration *or judicial settlement*, and which cannot be satisfactorily settled by diplomacy, they will submit the whole subject-matter to arbitration *or judicial settlement*.

2. Disputes as to the interpretation of a treaty, as to any question of international law, as to the existence of any fact which, if established, would constitute a breach of any international obligation, or as to the extent and nature of the reparation to be made for any such breach, are declared to be among those which are generally suitable for submission to arbitration *or judicial settlement*.

3. *For the consideration of any such dispute, the court to which the case is referred shall be the Permanent Court of International Justice, established in accordance with Article XIV, or any tribunal agreed on by the parties to the dispute or stipulated in any convention existing between them.*

4. The Members of the League agree that they will carry out in full good faith any award *or decision* that may be rendered, and that

[1] The amendments printed in italics in Articles XII and XIII came into force on September 26, 1924, in accordance with Article XXVI of the Covenant.

they will not resort to war against a Member of the League which complies therewith. In the event of any failure to carry out such an award *or decision*, the Council shall propose what steps should be taken to give effect thereto.

ARTICLE XIV

The Council shall formulate and submit to the Members of the League for adoption plans for the establishment of a Permanent Court of International Justice. The Court shall be competent to hear and determine any dispute of an international character which the parties thereto submit to it. The Court may also give an advisory opinion upon any dispute or question referred to it by the Council or by the Assembly.

ARTICLE XV

1.[1] If there should arise between Members of the League any dispute likely to lead to a rupture, which is not submitted to arbitration *or judicial settlement* in accordance with Article XIII, the Members of the League agree that they will submit the matter to the Council. Any party to the dispute may effect such submission by giving notice of the existence of the dispute to the Secretary-General, who will make all necessary arrangements for a full investigation and consideration thereof.

2. For this purpose the parties to the dispute will communicate to the Secretary-General, as promptly as possible, statements of their case with all the relevant facts and papers, and the Council may forthwith direct the publication thereof.

3. The Council shall endeavour to effect a settlement of the dispute and, if such efforts are successful, a statement shall be made public giving such facts and explanations regarding the dispute and the terms of settlement thereof as the Council may deem appropriate.

4. If the dispute is not thus settled, the Council either unanimously or by a majority vote shall make and publish a report containing a statement of the facts of the dispute and the recommendations which are deemed just and proper in regard thereto.

5. Any Member of the League represented on the Council may

[1] The amendment to the first paragraph of this article came into force on September 26, 1924, in accordance with Article XXVI of the Covenant.

make public a statement of the facts of the dispute and of its conclusions regarding the same.

6. If a report by the Council is unanimously agreed to by the Members thereof other than the Representatives of one or more of the parties to the dispute, the Members of the League agree that they will not go to war with any party to the dispute which complies with the recommendations of the report.

7. If the Council fails to reach a report which is unanimously agreed to by the members thereof, other than the Representatives of one or more of the parties to the dispute, the Members of the League reserve to themselves the right to take such action as they shall consider necessary for the maintenance of right and justice.

8. If the dispute between the parties is claimed by one of them, and is found by the Council, to arise out of a matter which by international law is solely within the domestic jurisdiction of that party, the Council shall so report, and shall make no recommendation as to its settlement.

9. The Council may in any case under this Article refer the dispute to the Assembly. The dispute shall be so referred at the request of either party to the dispute provided that such request be made within fourteen days after the submission of the dispute to the Council.

10. In any case referred to the Assembly, all the provisions of this Article and of Article XII relating to the action and powers of the Council shall apply to the action and powers of the Assembly, provided that a report made by the Assembly, if concurred in by the Representatives of those Members of the League represented on the Council and of a majority of the other Members of the League, exclusive in each case of the Representatives of the parties to the dispute, shall have the same force as a report by the Council concurred in by all the members thereof other than the Representatives of one or more of the parties to the dispute.

Article XVI

1.[1] Should any Member of the League resort to war in disregard of its covenants under Articles XII, XIII or XV, it shall *ipso facto*

---

[1] The following proposal for the amendment of Paragraph 1 of Article XVI was awaiting ratification in 1935:

"Should any Member of the League resort to war in disregard of its covenants under Articles XII, XIII, or XV, it shall *ipso facto* be deemed to have committed an act of be deemed to have committed an act of war against all other Members of the League, which hereby undertake immediately to subject it to the severance of all trade or financial relations, the prohibition of all intercourse between their nationals and the nationals of the covenant-breaking State, and the prevention of all financial, commercial or personal intercourse between the nationals of the covenant-breaking State and the nationals of any other State, whether a Member of the League or not.

2. It shall be the duty of the Council in such case to recommend to the several Governments concerned what effective military, naval or air force the Members of the League shall severally contribute to the armed forces to be used to protect the covenants of the League.

3. The Members of the League agree, further, that they will mutually support one another in the financial and economic measures which are taken under this Article, in order to minimise the loss and inconvenience resulting from the above measures, and that they will mutually support one another in resisting any special measures aimed at one of their number by the covenant-breaking State, and that they will take the necessary steps to afford passage through their territory to the forces of any of the Members of the League which are cooperating to protect the covenants of the League.

war against all other Members of the League, which hereby undertake immediately to subject it to the severance of all trade or financial relations and to prohibit all intercourse at least between persons resident within their territories and persons resident within the territory of the covenant-breaking State and, if they deem it expedient, also between their nationals and the nationals of the covenant-breaking State, and to prevent all financial, commercial or personal intercourse at least between persons resident within the territory of that State and persons resident within the territory of any other State, whether a Member of the League or not, and, if they deem it expedient, also between the nationals of that State and the nationals of any other State whether a Member of the League or not.

"It is for the Council to give an opinion whether or not a breach of the Covenant has taken place. In deliberations on this question in the Council, the votes of Members of the League alleged to have resorted to war and of Members against whom such action was directed shall not be counted.

"The Council will notify to all Members of the League the date which it recommends for the application of the economic pressure under this Article.

"Nevertheless, the Council may, in the case of particular Members, postpone the coming into force of any of these measures for a specified period where it is satisfied that such a postponement will facilitate the attainment of the object of the measures referred to in the preceding paragraph, or that it is necessary in order to minimise the loss and inconvenience which will be caused to such Members."

4. Any Member of the League which has violated any covenant of the League may be declared to be no longer a Member of the League by a vote of the Council concurred in by the Representatives of all the other Members of the League represented thereon.

ARTICLE XVII

1. In the event of a dispute between a Member of the League and a State which is not a Member of the League, or between States not Members of the League, the State or States not Members of the League shall be invited to accept the obligations of membership in the League for the purposes of such dispute, upon such conditions as the Council may deem just. If such invitation is accepted, the provisions of Articles XII to XVI inclusive shall be applied with such modifications as may be deemed necessary by the Council.

2. Upon such invitation being given the Council shall immediately institute an enquiry into the circumstances of the dispute and recommend such action as may seem best and most effectual in the circumstances.

3. If a State so invited shall refuse to accept the obligations of membership in the League for the purposes of such dispute, and shall resort to war against a Member of the League, the provisions of Article XVI shall be applicable as against the State taking such action.

4. If both parties to the dispute when so invited refuse to accept the obligations of membership in the League for the purposes of such dispute, the Council may take such measures and make such recommendations as will prevent hostilities and will result in the settlement of the dispute.

ARTICLE XVIII

Every treaty or international engagement entered into hereafter by any Member of the League shall be forthwith registered with the Secretariat and shall as soon as possible be published by it. No such treaty or international engagement shall be binding until so registered.

ARTICLE XIX

The Assembly may from time to time advise the reconsideration by Members of the League of treaties which have become inapplicable, and the consideration of international conditions whose continuance might endanger the peace of the world.

Article XX

1. The Members of the League severally agree that this Covenant is accepted as abrogating all obligations or understandings *inter se* which are inconsistent with the terms thereof, and solemnly undertake that they will not hereafter enter into any engagements inconsistent with the terms thereof.

2. In case any Member of the League shall, before becoming a Member of the League, have undertaken any obligation inconsistent with the terms of this Covenant, it shall be the duty of such Member to take immediate steps to procure its release from such obligations.

Article XXI

Nothing in this Covenant shall be deemed to affect the validity of international engagements, such as treaties of arbitration or regional understandings like the Monroe doctrine, for securing the maintenance of peace.

Article XXII

1. To those colonies and territories which as a consequence of the late war have ceased to be under the sovereignty of the States which formerly governed them and which are inhabited by peoples not yet able to stand by themselves under the strenuous conditions of the modern world, there should be applied the principle that the well-being and development of such peoples form a sacred trust of civilization and that securities for the performance of this trust should be embodied in this Covenant.

2. The best method of giving practical effect to this principle is that the tutelage of such peoples should be entrusted to advanced nations who, by reason of their resources, their experience or their geographical position, can best undertake this responsibility, and who are willing to accept it, and that this tutelage should be exercised by them as Mandatories on behalf of the League.

3. The character of the mandate must differ according to the stage of the development of the people, the geographical situation of the territory, its economic conditions and other similar circumstances.

4. Certain communities formerly belonging to the Turkish Empire have reached a stage of development where their existence as independent nations can be provisionally recognised subject to the

rendering of administrative advice and assistance by a Mandatory until such time as they are able to stand alone. The wishes of these communities must be a principal consideration in the selection of the Mandatory.

5. Other peoples, especially those of Central Africa, are at such a stage that the Mandatory must be responsible for the administration of the territory under conditions which will guarantee freedom of conscience and religion, subject only to the maintenance of public order and morals, the prohibition of abuses such as the slave trade, the arms traffic and the liquor traffic, and the prevention of the establishment of fortifications or military and naval bases and of military training of the natives for other than police purposes and the defence of territory, and will also secure equal opportunities for the trade and commerce of other Members of the League.

6. There are territories, such as Southwest Africa and certain of the South Pacific islands, which, owing to the sparseness of their population, or their small size, or their remoteness from the centres of civilisation, or their geographical contiguity to the territory of the Mandatory, and other circumstances, can be best administered under the laws of the Mandatory as integral portions of its territory, subject to the safeguards above mentioned in the interests of the indigenous population.

7. In every case of mandate, the Mandatory shall render to the Council an annual report in reference to the territory committed to its charge.

8. The degree of authority, control or administration to be exercised by the Mandatory shall, if not previously agreed upon by the Members of the League, be explicitly defined in each case by the Council.

9. A permanent Commission shall be constituted to receive and examine the annual reports of the Mandatories, and to advise the Council on all matters relating to the observance of the mandates.

Article XXIII

Subject to and in accordance with the provisions of international conventions existing or hereafter to be agreed upon, the Members of the League:

(a) will endeavour to secure and maintain fair and humane conditions of labor for men, women, and children, both in their own countries and in all countries to which their commercial and industrial relations extend, and for that purpose will establish and maintain the necessary international organisations;

(b) undertake to secure just treatment of the native inhabitants of territories under their control;

(c) will entrust the League with the general supervision over the execution of agreements with regard to the traffic in women and children and the traffic in opium and other dangerous drugs;

(d) will entrust the League with the general supervision of the trade in arms and ammunition with the countries in which the control of this traffic is necessary in the common interest;

(e) will make provision to secure and maintain freedom of communications and of transit and equitable treatment for the commerce of all Members of the League. In this connection, the special necessities of the regions devastated during the war of 1914–1918 shall be borne in mind;

(f) will endeavour to take steps in matters of international concern for the prevention and control of disease.

Article XXIV

1. There shall be placed under the direction of the League all international bureaux already established by general treaties if the parties to such treaties consent. All such international bureaux and all commissions for the regulation of matters of international interest hereafter constituted shall be placed under the direction of the League.

2. In all matters of international interest which are regulated by general conventions but which are not placed under the control of international bureaux or commissions, the Secretariat of the League shall, subject to the consent of the Council and if desired by the parties, collect and distribute all relevant information and shall render any other assistance which may be necessary or desirable.

3. The Council may include as part of the expenses of the Secretariat the expenses of any bureau or commission which is placed under the direction of the League.

Article XXV

The Members of the League agree to encourage and promote the establishment and cooperation of duly authorised voluntary national Red Cross organisations having as purposes the improvement of health, the prevention of disease and the mitigation of suffering throughout the world.

Article XXVI[1]

1. Amendments to this Covenant will take effect when ratified by the Members of the League whose Representatives compose the Council and by a majority of the Members of the League whose Representatives compose the Assembly.

2. No such amendment shall bind any Member of the League which signifies its dissent therefrom, but in that case it shall cease to be a Member of the League.

ANNEX

1. ORIGINAL MEMBERS OF THE LEAGUE OF NATIONS
[names omitted]

11. FIRST SECRETARY-GENERAL OF THE LEAGUE OF NATIONS

The Honorable Sir James Eric Drummond, K.C.M.G., C.B.

[1] The following amendment has been offered to replace Article XXVI, and was awaiting ratification in 1935:

"Amendments to the present Covenant the text of which shall have been voted by the Assembly on a three-fourths majority, in which there shall be included the votes of all the Members of the Council represented at the meeting, will take effect when ratified by the Members of the League whose Representatives composed the Council when the vote was taken and by the majority of those whose Representatives form the Assembly.

"If the required number of ratifications shall not have been obtained within twenty-two months after the vote of the Assembly, the proposed amendment shall remain without effect.

"The Secretary-General shall inform the Members of the taking effect of an amendment.

"Any Member of the League which has not at that time ratified the amendment is free to notify the Secretary-General within a year of its refusal to accept it, but in that case it shall cease to be a Member of the League."

Appendix B

WILSON'S FOURTEEN POINTS, ETC.

1. The Fourteen Points, Part of President Wilson's Address to Congress on January 8, 1918

I. Open covenants of peace, openly arrived at, after which there shall be no private international understandings of any kind, but diplomacy shall proceed always frankly and in the public view.

II. Absolute freedom of navigation upon the seas, outside territorial waters, alike in peace and in war, except as the seas may be closed in whole or in part by international action for the enforcement of international covenants.

III. The removal, so far as possible, of all economic barriers and the establishment of an equality of trade conditions among all the nations consenting to the peace and associating themselves for its maintenance.

IV. Adequate guarantees given and taken that national armaments will be reduced to the lowest point consistent with domestic safety.

V. A free, open-minded and absolutely impartial adjustment of all colonial claims, based upon a strict observance of the principle that in determining all such questions of sovereignty the interests of the populations concerned must have equal weight with the equitable claims of the Government whose title is to be determined.

VI. The evacuation of all Russian territory and such a settlement of all questions affecting Russia as will secure the best and freest coöperation of the other nations of the world in obtaining for her an unhampered and unembarrassed opportunity for the independent determination of her own political development and national policy and assure her of a sincere welcome into the society of free nations under institutions of her own choosing; and, more than a welcome, assistance also of every kind that she may need and may herself desire. The treatment accorded Russia by her sister nations will be the acid test of their good will, of their comprehension of her needs as distinguished from their own interests, and of their intelligent and unselfish sympathy.

VII. Belgium, the whole world will agree, must be evacuated and restored, without any attempt to limit the sovereignty which she enjoys in common with all other free nations. No other single act will serve as this will serve to restore confidence among the nations in the laws which they have themselves set and determined for the government of their relations with one another. Without this healing act the whole structure and validity of international law is forever impaired.

VIII. All French territory should be freed and the invaded portions restored, and the wrong done to France by Prussia in 1871 in the matter of Alsace-Lorraine, which has unsettled the peace of the world for nearly fifty years, should be righted, in order that peace may once more be made secure in the interest of all.

IX. A readjustment of the frontiers of Italy should be effected along clearly recognizable lines of nationality.

X. The peoples of Austria-Hungary, whose place among the nations we wish to see safeguarded and assured, should be accorded the freest opportunity of autonomous development.

XI. Rumania, Serbia, and Montenegro should be evacuated; occupied territories restored; Serbia accorded free and secure access to the sea; and the relations of the several Balkan states to one another determined by friendly counsel along historically established lines of allegiance and nationality; and international guarantees of the political and economic independence and territorial integrity of the several Balkan states should be entered into.

XII. The Turkish portions of the present Ottoman Empire should be assured a secure sovereignty, but the other nationalities which are now under Turkish rule should be assured an undoubted security of life and an absolutely unmolested opportunity of autonomous development, and the Dardanelles should be permanently opened as a free passage to the ships and commerce of all nations under international guarantees.

XIII. An independent Polish state should be erected which should include the territories inhabited by indisputably Polish populations, which should be assured a free and secure access to the sea, and whose political and economic independence and territorial integrity should be guaranteed by international covenant.

XIV. A general association of nations must be formed under specific covenants for the purpose of affording mutual guarantees of political independence and territorial integrity to great and small states alike.

2. Part of President Wilson's Address at Mount Vernon, July 4, 1918

There can be but one issue. The settlement must be final. There can be no compromise. No halfway decision would be tolerable. No halfway decision is conceivable. These are the ends for which the associated peoples of the world are fighting and which must be conceded them before there can be peace:

I. The destruction of every arbitrary power anywhere that can separately, secretly, and of its single choice disturb the peace of the world; or, if it cannot be presently destroyed, at the least its reduction to virtual impotence.

II. The settlement of every question, whether of territory, of sovereignty, of economic arrangement, or of political relationship, upon the basis of the free acceptance of that settlement by the people immediately concerned, and not upon the basis of the material interest or advantage of any other nation or people which may desire a different settlement for the sake of its own exterior influence or mastery.

III. The consent of all nations to be governed in their conduct toward each other by the same principles of honor and of respect for the common law of civilized society that govern the individual citizens of all modern States in their relations with one another; to the end that all promises and covenants may be sacredly observed, no private plots or conspiracies hatched, no selfish injuries wrought with impunity, and a mutual trust established upon the handsome foundation of a mutual respect for right.

IV. The establishment of an organization of peace which shall make it certain that the combined power of free nations will check every invasion of right and serve to make peace and justice the more secure by affording a definite tribunal of opinion to which all must submit and by which every international readjustment that cannot be amicably agreed upon by the peoples directly concerned shall be sanctioned.

These great objects can be put into a single sentence. What we seek is the reign of law, based upon the consent of the governed and sustained by the organized opinion of mankind.

Appendix C

THE LOCARNO PACT

Annex A: Treaty of Mutual Guarantee Between Germany, Belgium, France, Great Britain, and Italy

(*Translation*)

The President of the German Reich, His Majesty the King of the Belgians, the President of the French Republic, His Majesty the King of the United Kingdom of Great Britain and Ireland and of the British Dominions beyond the Seas, Emperor of India, and His Majesty the King of Italy;

Anxious to satisfy the desire for security and protection which animates the peoples upon whom fell the scourge of the war of 1914–18;

Taking note of the abrogation of the treaties for the neutralization of Belgium, and conscious of the necessity of ensuring peace in the area which has so frequently been the scene of European conflicts;

Animated also with the sincere desire of giving to all the signatory Powers concerned supplementary guarantees within the framework of the Covenant of the League of Nations and the treaties in force between them;

Have determined to conclude a treaty with these objects, and have appointed as their plenipotentiaries: [names omitted]

Who, having communicated their full powers, found in good and due form, have agreed as follows:—

Article 1. The high contracting parties collectively and severally guarantee, in the manner provided in the following articles, the maintenance of the territorial status quo resulting from the frontiers between Germany and Belgium and between Germany and

France and the inviolability of the said frontiers as fixed by or in pursuance of the Treaty of Peace signed at Versailles on the 28th June, 1919, and also the observance of the stipulations of articles 42 and 43 of the said treaty concerning the demilitarized zone.

Article 2. Germany and Belgium, and also Germany and France, mutually undertake that they will in no case attack or invade each other or resort to war against each other.

This stipulation shall not, however, apply in the case of—

1. The exercise of the right of legitimate defence, that is to say, resistance to a violation of the undertaking contained in the previous paragraph or to a flagrant breach of articles 42 or 43 of the said Treaty of Versailles, if such breach constitutes an unprovoked act of aggression and by reason of the assembly of armed forces in the demilitarized zone immediate action is necessary.

2. Action in pursuance of article 16 of the Covenant of the League of Nations.

3. Action as the result of a decision taken by the Assembly or by the Council of the League of Nations or in pursuance of article 15, paragraph 7, of the Covenant of the League of Nations, provided that in this last event the action is directed against a State which was the first to attack.

Article 3. In view of the undertakings entered into in article 2 of the present treaty, Germany and Belgium and Germany and France undertake to settle by peaceful means and in the manner laid down herein all questions of every kind which may arise between them and which it may not be possible to settle by the normal methods of diplomacy:

Any question with regard to which the parties are in conflict as to their respective rights shall be submitted to judicial decision, and the parties undertake to comply with such decision.

All other questions shall be submitted to a conciliation commission. If the proposals of this commission are not accepted by the two parties, the question shall be brought before the Council of the League of Nations, which will deal with it in accordance with article 15 of the Covenant of the League.

The detailed arrangements for effecting such peaceful settlement are the subject of special agreements signed this day.

Article 4. (1) If one of the high contracting parties alleges that a violation of article 2 of the present treaty or a breach of articles 42 or 43 of the Treaty of Versailles has been or is being committed, it shall bring the question at once before the Council of the League of Nations.

(2) As soon as the Council of the League of Nations is satisfied that such violation or breach has been committed, it will notify its finding without delay to the Powers signatory of the present treaty, who severally agree that in such case they will each of them come immediately to the assistance of the Power against whom the act complained of is directed.

(3) In case of a flagrant violation of article 2 of the present treaty or of a flagrant breach of articles 42 or 43 of the Treaty of Versailles by one of the high contracting parties, each of the other contracting parties hereby undertakes immediately to come to the help of the party against whom such a violation or breach has been directed as soon as the said Power has been able to satisfy itself that this violation constitutes an unprovoked act of aggression and that by reason either of the crossing of the frontier or of the outbreak of hostilities or of the assembly of armed forces in the demilitarized zone immediate action is necessary. Nevertheless, the Council of the League of Nations, which will be seized of the question in accordance with the first paragraph of this article, will issue its findings, and the high contracting parties undertake to act in accordance with the recommendations of the Council provided that they are concurred in by all the members other than the representatives of the parties which have engaged in hostilities.

Article 5. The provisions of article 3 of the present treaty are placed under the guarantee of the high contracting parties as provided by the following stipulations:—

If one of the Powers referred to in article 3 refuses to submit a dispute to peaceful settlement or to comply with an arbitral or judicial decision and commits a violation of article 2 of the present treaty or a breach of articles 42 or 43 of the Treaty of Versailles, the provisions of article 4 shall apply.

Where one of the Powers referred to in article 3, without committing a violation of article 2 of the present treaty or a breach of articles 42 or 43 of the Treaty of Versailles, refuses to submit a dispute to peaceful settlement or to comply with an arbitral or judicial decision, the other party shall bring the matter before the Council of the League of Nations, and the Council shall propose what steps shall be taken; the high contracting parties shall comply with these proposals.

Article 6. The provisions of the present treaty do not affect the rights and obligations of the high contracting parties under the Treaty of Versailles or under arrangements supplementary thereto including the agreements signed in London on the 30th August, 1924.

Article 7. The present treaty, which is designed to ensure the maintenance of peace, and is in conformity with the Covenant of the League of Nations, shall not be interpreted as restricting the duty of the League to take whatever action may be deemed wise and effectual to safeguard the peace of the world.

Article 8. The present treaty shall be registered at the League of Nations in accordance with the Covenant of the League. It shall remain in force until the Council, acting on a request of one or other of the high contracting parties notified to the other signatory Powers three months in advance, and voting at least by a two-thirds' majority, decides that the League of Nations ensures sufficient protection to the high contracting parties; the treaty shall cease to have effect on the expiration of a period of one year from such decision.

Article 9. The present treaty shall impose no obligation upon any of the British dominions, or upon India, unless the Government of such dominion, or of India, signifies its acceptance thereof.

Article 10. The present treaty shall be ratified and the ratifications shall be deposited at Geneva in the archives of the League of Nations as soon as possible.

It shall enter into force as soon as all the ratifications have been deposited and Germany has become a member of the League of Nations.

The present treaty, done in a single copy, will be deposited in the archives of the League of Nations, and the Secretary-General will be requested to transmit certified copies to each of the high contracting parties.

In faith whereof the above-mentioned plenipotentiaries have signed the present treaty.

Done at Locarno, the 16th October, 1925.

Appendix D

THE PACT OF PARIS

(Also called the Kellogg Pact or the Kellogg-Briand Pact)

The President of the German Reich, the President of the United States of America, His Majesty the King of the Belgians, the President of the French Republic, His Majesty the King of Great Britain, Ireland and the British Dominions beyond the Seas, Emperor of India, His Majesty the King of Italy, His Majesty the Emperor of Japan, the President of the Republic of Poland, the President of the Czechoslovak Republic;

Deeply sensible of their solemn duty to promote the welfare of mankind;

Persuaded that the time has come when a frank renunciation of war as an instrument of national policy should be made to the end that the peaceful and friendly relations now existing between their peoples may be perpetuated;

Convinced that all changes in their relations with one another should be sought only by pacific means and be the result of a peaceful and orderly process, and that any signatory Power which shall hereafter seek to promote its national interests by resort to war should be denied the benefits furnished by this Treaty;

Hopeful that, encouraged by their example, all the other nations of the world will join in this humane endeavor and by adhering to the present Treaty as soon as it comes into force bring their peoples within the scope of its beneficent provisions, thus uniting the civilized nations of the world in a common renunciation of war as an instrument of their national policy;

Have decided to conclude a Treaty . . .

ARTICLE I

The High Contracting Parties solemnly declare in the names of their respective peoples that they condemn recourse to war for the solution of international controversies, and renounce it as an instrument of national policy in their relations with one another.

ARTICLE II

The High Contracting Parties agree that the settlement or solution of all disputes or conflicts of whatever nature or of whatever origin they may be, which may arise among them, shall never be sought except by pacific means.

ARTICLE III

The present Treaty shall be ratified by the High Contracting Parties named in the Preamble in accordance with their respective constitutional requirements, and shall take effect as between them as soon as all their several instruments of ratification shall have been deposited at Washington.

This Treaty shall, when it has come into effect as prescribed in the preceding paragraph, remain open as long as may be necessary for adherence by all the other Powers of the world. Every instrument evidencing the adherence of a Power shall be deposited at Washington and the Treaty shall immediately upon such deposit become effective as between the Power thus adhering and the other Powers parties hereto.

It shall be the duty of the Government of the United States to furnish each Government named in the Preamble and every Government subsequently adhering to this Treaty with a certified copy of the Treaty and of every instrument of ratification or adherence. It shall also be the duty of the Government of the United States telegraphically to notify such Governments immediately upon the deposit with it of each instrument of ratification or adherence.

Appendix E

FINAL TEXT OF THE PROPOSED FOUR-POWER TREATY

Signed at Rome, July 15, 1933

Agreement of Understanding and Coöperation

PREAMBLE

The President of the German Reich, the President of the French Republic, His Majesty the King of Great Britain, Ireland, and the British Dominions beyond the Seas, Emperor of India, and His Majesty the King of Italy;

Conscious of the special responsibilities incumbent on them as possessing permanent representation on the Council of the League of Nations, where the League itself and its members are concerned, and of the responsibilities resulting from the common signature of the Locarno agreements;

Convinced that the state of disquiet which obtained throughout the world can only be dissipated by reinforcing their solidarity in such a way as to strengthen confidence in peace in Europe;

Faithful to the obligations which they have assumed in virtue of the Covenant of the League of Nations, the Locarno Treaties, and the Briand-Kellogg Pact, and taking into account the declaration of the renunciation of force, the principle of which was proclaimed in the declaration signed at Geneva on December 11, 1932, by their delegates at the Disarmament Conference and adopted on March 2, 1933, by the Political Commission of that Conference;

Anxious to give full effect to all the provisions of the Covenant of the League of Nations, while conforming to the methods and procedure laid down therein, from which they have no intention of departing;

Mindful of the rights of every State, which cannot be affected without the consent of the interested party;

Have resolved to conclude an agreement with these objects, and have appointed as their plenipotentiaries: [names omitted]

Who, having exchanged their full powers, found in good and due form, have agreed as follows:

ARTICLE 1

The High Contracting Parties will consult together as regards all questions which appertain to them. They undertake to make every effort to pursue, within the framework of the League of Nations, a policy of effective co-operation between all Powers with a view to the maintenance of peace.

ARTICLE 2

In respect of the Covenant of the League of Nations, and particularly Articles 10, 16, and 19, the High Contracting Parties decide to examine between themselves, and without prejudice to decisions which can only be taken by the regular organs of the League of Nations, all proposals relating to methods and procedure calculated to give due effect to these articles.

ARTICLE 3

The High Contracting Parties undertake to make every effort to insure the success of the Disarmament Conference and, should questions which particularly concern them remain in suspense on the conclusion of that Conference, they reserve the right to re-examine these questions between themselves under the present agreement with a view to insuring their solution through the appropriate channels.

ARTICLE 4

The High Contracting Parties affirm their desire to consult together as regards all economic questions which have a common interest for Europe, and particularly for its economic restoration, with a view to seeking a settlement within the framework of the League of Nations.

ARTICLE 5

The present agreement is concluded for a period of 10 years from the date of its entry into force.

If before the end of the eighth year none of the High Contracting Parties shall have notified to the others its intention to terminate the agreement, it shall be regarded as renewed and will remain in force indefinitely, each of the High Contracting Parties possessing in that event the right to terminate it by a declaration to that effect on giving two years' notice.

Article 6

The present agreement, drawn up in English, French, German, and Italian, of which the French text prevails in case of divergence, shall be ratified and the ratification shall be deposited at Rome as soon as possible. The Government of the Kingdom of Italy will deliver to each of the High Contracting Parties a certified copy of the *procès-verbaux* of deposit.

The present agreement will enter into force as soon as all the ratifications have been deposited.

It shall be registered at the League of Nations in conformity with the Covenant of the League.

Done at Rome, the _____ day of _____, 1933, in a single copy, which will remain deposited in the archives of the Government of the Kingdom of Italy; certified copies will be delivered to each of the High Contracting Parties. In faith whereof the above-mentioned plenipotentiaries have signed the present agreement.

Appendix F

GERMAN-POLISH DECLARATION
(Translation)

The Polish and German Governments consider that the time has come to begin a new era in the relations between Poland and Germany through a direct contact between the two countries. They have therefore agreed through the present declaration to establish the basis for the future development of these relations.

Both Governments start with the assumption that the maintenance and consolidation of permanent peace between their respective countries constitutes an essential condition to the general peace of Europe. They have, therefore, agreed to base their own relations upon the principles set forth in the Pact of Paris of August 27, 1928. Furthermore, in respect of the relations between Poland and Germany, they desire to clarify the application of these principles.

Accordingly both Governments assert that the peaceful development of their mutual relations will not impair any international obligations which they have hitherto undertaken in respect of other states prior to the making of this Declaration. And they further affirm that this Declaration does not repudiate these obligations but on the contrary leaves them undisturbed. Nor does this Declaration include within its purview such questions as are, by international law, recognized to be purely domestic issues of either state.

Both Governments announce their intention to communicate directly with each other in all questions which may arise pertaining to their mutual relations. Should disputes arise notwithstanding and should settlement not be attained by direct negotiations, then they agree, in such special instance, to seek solution through some other peaceful means and by common understanding so that the possibility of such settlement may not be disturbed. And, in case of necessity, they agree to employ those measures of procedure which have already been fixed by them, to arrive at future accord. And they further agree under no circumstances to use force to settle such disputes.

The guarantee of peace based upon these foregoing principles will facilitate the task of the two nations in finding solutions of the political, economic, and cultural problems, which must be discovered in settlements equally just and reasonable for the interests of both nations.

Both Governments are convinced that, in this fashion, the relations between their respective countries will develop fruitfully and will lead to the establishment of a good neighborly intercourse which will be a blessing not alone for their two nations but also for all Europe as well.

The present agreement shall be ratified and the documents of ratification shall be exchanged in Warsaw at the earliest possible date. It shall remain in force for a period of ten years, starting from the date of the notification of ratification. In case it is not denounced by one of the two contracting nations six months before the expiration of that period it shall remain in force thereafter. But it can then be denounced by either Government upon six months' notice.

Prepared in double original in Polish and in German.

Berlin, 26 January, 1934.

BIBLIOGRAPHY*

Academy of Political Science, *Proceedings*, New York, Columbia University:
  "Tariffs and Trade Barriers," Vol. XV, No. 3, 1933.
Adams, J. T., *The Epic of America*, Boston, Little, Brown, 1931.
Adriacus, *pseud.*, *From Trieste to Valona*, Rome, Alfieri and Lacroix, 1919.
American Academy of Political and Social Science, *The Annals*, Philadelphia:
  *"Raw Materials and Foodstuffs in the Commercial Policies of Nations," Vol. CXII, 1924.
  "American Policy in the Pacific," Vol. CLXVIII, 1933.
  "Prerequisites of Japanese Security" July, 1933.
*American Council, Institute of Pacific Relations, *Memoranda*, New York, fortnightly.
————, *Conflict in the Far East, 1931–1932*, New York, 1932.
————, *Behind the Far Eastern Conflict*, 1933.
American Foundation, *The World Court's Advisory Opinion on the Austro-German Customs Union Case*, New York, 1931.
American Journal of International Law, Washington, D.C.
Amery, Rt. Hon. L. S., *Empire and Prosperity*, London, Faber and Faber, 1931.
Ancel, Jacques, *Les Balkans Face à l'Italie*, Paris, Delagrave, 1928.
Andreades, A. M., *Philip Snowden*, London, King, 1930.
*Angell, J. W., *The Recovery of Germany*, New Haven, Yale University Press, 1932.
————, *Financial Foreign Policy of the United States*, New York, Council on Foreign Relations, 1933.
Angell, Sir Norman, *The Press and the Organization of Society*, London, Labor Publishing Company, 1922.
————, *The Unseen Assassins*, New York, Harper, 1932.
————, *The Great Illusion*, New York, Putnam, 1933.

*NOTE.—*Books, periodicals, and pamphlets which are recommended in the text for general reference are indicated by an asterisk.*

*Anonymous, *Der Kampf um die Deutsche Aussenpolitik*, Leipzig, Liszt, 1931.

Apponyi, Albert, Gróf, *et al.*, *Justice for Hungary*, London, Longmans, 1928.

Aranitović, Relja, *Les Ressources et l'Activité Économique de la Yougoslavie*, Paris, Bossuet, 1930.

Archimbaud, Léon, *La Conférence de Washington*, Paris, Payot, 1923.

Argus, *pseud.*, *The Economic Aspect of the Austro-German Customs Union*, Prague, Orbis, 1931.

Armstrong, H. F., *The New Balkans*, New York, Harper, 1926.
—————, *Hitler's Reich*, New York, Macmillan, 1933.
—————, *Europe Between Wars?*, New York, Macmillan, 1934.

Arnot, R. P., *Soviet Russia and Her Neighbors*, New York, Vanguard, 1927.

Atchley, W. W., *Finland*, London, Sidgwick and Jackson, 1931.

*Bain, H. F., *Ores and Industry in the Far East*, New York, Council on Foreign Relations, 1933, rev. ed.

Baker, C. W., *Government Control and Operation of Industry in Great Britain and the United States During the World War*, New York, Oxford University Press, 1921.

Baker, P. J. N., *The Geneva Protocol*, London, King, 1925.
—————, *Disarmament*, New York, Harcourt, 1926.
—————, *Disarmament and the Coolidge Conference*, London, Hogarth, 1927.
—————, *The Present Juridical Status of the British Dominions in International Law*, New York, London, Longmans, 1929.

*Baker, R. S., *Woodrow Wilson and the World Settlement, 1922*, New York, Doubleday, 1922, 3 vols.

Balla, V. de, *The New Balance of Power in Europe*, Baltimore, Johns Hopkins Press, 1932.

Ballard, G. A., *The Influence of the Sea on the Political History of Japan*, New York, Dutton, 1921.

Banse, Ewald, *Germany Prepares for War*, New York, Harcourt, 1934.

*Barnes, H. E., *World Politics in Modern Civilization*, New York, Knopf, 1930.

Barnes, Joseph, *ed.*, *Empire in the East*, New York, Doubleday, 1934.

Baruch, B. M., *The Making of the Reparation and Economic Sections of the Treaty*, New York, Harper, 1920.

Batsell, W. R., *Soviet Rule in Russia*, New York, Macmillan, 1929.

*Bau, M. J., *The Foreign Relations of China*, New York, Revell, 1922.
—————, *The Open Door Doctrine in Relation to China*, New York, Macmillan, 1923.

Beales, A. C. F., *The History of Peace*, New York, Dial Press, 1931.

*Bean, R. B., *The Races of Man: Differentiation and Dispersal of Man*, New York, The University Society, 1932.

Beard, C. A., *The Navy: Defense or Portent?*, New York, Harper, 1932.

————, and Beard, Mary, *The Rise of American Civilization*, New York, Macmillan, 1927, 2 vols.

————, and Radin, George, *The Balkan Pivot: Jugoslavia*, New York, Macmillan, 1929.

Beauchamp, Joan, *Agriculture in Soviet Russia*, London, Gollancz, 1931.

Beaverbrook, W. M. A., Baron, *My Case for Empire Free Trade*, London, Empire Crusade, 1930.

*Beer, G. L., *African Questions at the Paris Peace Conference*, New York, Macmillan, 1923.

Beer, Max, *The League on Trial*, Boston, Houghton Mifflin, 1933.

Bellquist, E. C., *Some Aspects of the Recent Foreign Policy of Sweden*, Berkeley, University of California Press, 1929.

Bemis, S. F., *ed.*, *The American Secretaries of State and their Diplomacy*, New York, Knopf, 1927–1929, 10 vols.

Benn, Sir E. J. P., *About Russia*, New York, Appleton, 1930.

Benoist, Charles, *La Question Méditerranéenne*, Paris, Attinger, 1928.

Bentwich, Norman de Mattos, *The Mandates System*, New York, Longmans, 1930.

*Bérard, Victor, *British Imperialism and Commercial Supremacy*, New York, Longmans, 1906.

Berdahl, C. A., *The Policy of the United States with Respect to the League of Nations*, Geneva, Kundig, 1932, (also New York, Oxford University Press, 1933).

Besiedovskiǐ, G. Z., *Revelations of a Soviet Diplomat*, London, Williams and Norgate, 1931.

Beveridge, Sir W. H., *British Food Control*, New Haven, Yale University Press, 1928.

————, *ed.*, *Tariffs: the Case Examined*, New York, Longmans, 1931.

Bihlmans, Alfred, *Latvia in the Making 1918–1928*, Riga, Riga Times, 1928.

Bitterman, M., *Austria and the Customs Union*, Prague, Orbis, 1931.

Blakeslee, G. H., *The Pacific Area*, Boston, World Peace Foundation, 1929.

Bland, J. O. P., *China: The Pity of It*, London, Heinemann, also New York, Doubleday), 1932.

*Bogardus, J. F., *Europe, A Geographical Survey*, New York, Harper, 1934.

Bogart, E. L., *Direct and Indirect Costs of the Great World War*, New York, Oxford University Press, 1920.

Boggs, T. H., *The International Trade Balance*, New York, Macmillan, 1923.

Bonnamour, George, *Le Rapprochement Franco-Allemand*, Paris, Delpeuch, 1927.

Booth, C. D., and Bridge, Isabelle, *Italy's Aegean Possessions*, London, Arrowsmith, 1928.

Borchard, E. M., *The Diplomatic Protection of Citizens Abroad*, New York, Banks Law Publishing Company, 1927.

Borovička, J., *Ten Years of Czechoslovak Politics*, Prague, Orbis, 1929.

Boucke, O. F., *Europe and the American Tariff*, New York, Crowell, 1933.

Bouy, Raymond, *Le Désarmement Naval*, Paris, Presses Universitaires, 1931.

*Bowman, Isaiah, *The New World*, Yonkers, World Book Company, 1928, 4th ed.

Boycott, A. G., *The Elements of Imperial Defence*, London, Gale, 1931.

Brady, R. A., *The Rationalization Movement in German Industry*, Berkeley, University of California Press, 1933.

Bratt, K. A., *That Next War?*, New York, Harcourt, 1931.

Brierly, James L., *The Law of Nations*, New York, Oxford University Press, 1928.

Brigham, A. P., *Geographic Influences in American History*, Boston, Ginn and Company, 1903.

*Brunhes, Jean, and Vallaux, Camille, *La Géographie de l'Histoire*, Paris, Colin, 1921.

Bryce, J., *The Holy Roman Empire*, New York, Macmillan, 1914.

Buday, László, *Dismembered Hungary*, London, Grant Richards, 1923.

Budish, J. M., and Shipman, S. S., *Soviet Foreign Trade: Menace or Promise*, New York, Liveright, 1931.

Buell, R. L., *The Washington Conference*, New York, Appleton, 1922.
————, *Europe, a History of Ten Years*, New York, Macmillan, 1928.
————, ed., *New Governments in Europe*, New York, Nelson, 1934.

Bülow, B., Fürst von, *Memoirs*, Boston, Little, Brown, 1931–32, 4 vols.

*Burns, C. D., *1918–1928; A Short History of the World*, New York, Harcourt, 1928.

Butler, Sir Geoffrey G., and Maccoby, Simon, *The Development of International Law*, New York, Longmans, 1928.

*Butler, N. M., *The Path to Peace*, New York, Scribner, 1930.

Bywater, H. C., *Sea-Power in the Pacific*, Boston, Houghton Mifflin, 1921.

——————, *Navies and Nations*, Boston, Houghton Mifflin, 1927.

Cabot, J. M., *The Racial Conflict in Transylvania*, Boston, Beacon Press, 1926.

Cambon, J. M., *The Diplomatist*, London, P. Allan, 1931.

Campbell, T. D., *Russia, Market or Menace?*, New York, London, Longmans, 1932.

*Carnegie Endowment for International Peace, Carnegie Series, *Economic and Social History of the World War*, New York.

*——————, *International Conciliation*, New York, monthly:
  "Final Protocol of the Locarno Conference 1925, and Treaties Between France and Belgium, and France and Czechoslovakia," No. 216, 1926.
  "The Sixth International Conference of American States," No. 241, 1928.
  "The Soviet Security System," No. 252, 1928.
  "The Final Settlement of the Reparations Problems Growing Out of the World War," No. 262, 1930.
  "The International Trade of Manchuria," No. 269, 1931.
  "The Co-operation of the United States with the League of Nations and with the International Labour Organization," No. 274, 1931.
  "What Follows the Pact of Paris," No. 276, 1932.
  "The Present Economic State of Germany," No. 279, 1932.
  "Disarmament," No. 285, 1932.
  "The U.S.S.R. and Disarmament," No. 292, 1933.
  "The Montevideo Conference, Antecedents and Accomplishments," No. 300, 1934.

*Carr-Saunders, A. M., *Population*, New York, Oxford University Press, 1925.

Carroll, E. M., *French Public Opinion and Foreign Affairs 1870–1914*, New York, Century, 1931.

*Carter, J. F., *Conquest: America's Painless Imperialism*, New York, Harcourt, 1928.

——————, *Man is War*, Indianapolis, Bobbs-Merrill, 1926.

Chamberlain, Sir Austen, *Peace in Our Time*, London, Allen, 1928.

Chamberlin, W. H., *Soviet Russia*, Boston, Little, Brown, 1931, rev. ed.

——————, *Russia's Iron Age*, Little, Brown, 1934.

——————, *The Soviet Planned Economic Order*, Boston, World Peace Foundation, 1931.

Chang, Chung Fu, *The Anglo-Japanese Alliance*, Baltimore, Johns Hopkins Press, 1931.

Charles-Roux, François, *Trois Ambassades Françaises à la Veille de la Guerre*, Paris, Plon, 1928.

Charques, R. D., *The Soviets and the Next War; the Present Case for Disarmament*, London, Secker, 1932.

Cheyney, A. S., *ed.*, *The International Labor Organization*, Philadelphia, American Academy of Political and Social Science, 1933.

Chidell, Fleetwood, *Australia—White or Yellow*, London, Heinemann, 1926.

Cippico, Antonio, Conte, *Italy, the Central Problem of the Mediterranean*, New Haven, Yale University Press, 1926.

Clapham, J. H., *An Economic History of Modern Britain*, Cambridge, Eng., University Press, and New York, Macmillan, 1931–32.

Clark, Evans, *ed.*, *Boycotts and Peace*, New York, Harper, 1932.

Clark, Grover, *Economic Rivalries in China*, New Haven, Yale University Press, 1932.

Clausewitz, Karl von, *On War*, New York, Dutton, 1914.

Codresco, Florin, *La Petite Entente*, Paris, Les Presses Modernes, 1930.

Cole, Captain D. H., *Imperial Military Geography*, London, Sifton, Praed, 1930, 6th ed.

—————, *Changing Conditions of Imperial Defence*, London, Sifton, Praed, 1930.

Cole, G. D. H., *British Trade and Industry*, London, Macmillan, 1932.

*—————, and Cole, Margaret, *The Intelligent Man's Review of Europe Today*, New York, Knopf, 1933.

Condliffe, J. B., *China Today: Economic*, Boston, World Peace Foundation, 1932.

Connoly, Violet, *Soviet Economic Policy in the East*, London, Oxford University Press, 1933.

*Conwell-Evans, T. P., *The League Council in Action*, New York, Oxford University Press, 1929.

Cook, Sir Edward, *The Press in War-Time*, London, Macmillan, 1920.

Coolidge, A. C., *Origins of the Triple Alliance*, New York, Scribner, 1926, 2d ed.

Cooper, C. S., *Latin America: Men and Markets*, Boston, Ginn, 1927.

Copeland, M. T., *International Raw Commodity Prices and the Devaluation of the Dollar*, Cambridge, Harvard University Press, 1934.

*Cornéjo, M. H., *The Balance of the Continents*, London, Oxford University Press, 1932.

Coste, Pierre, *La Lutte pour la Suprématie Financère*, Paris, Payot, 1932.

*Council on Foreign Relations, *Permanent Bases of Foreign Policy*, New York, Council on Foreign Relations, 1931.

*————, *Foreign Affairs*, New York, quarterly. (See entry *Foreign Affairs*.)

Cowan, A. R., *War in World History*, New York, Longmans, 1929.

Crane, J. O., *The Little Entente*, New York, Macmillan, 1931.

Cressey, G. B., *China's Geographic Foundations*, New York, McGraw-Hill, 1934.

Cresson, W. P., *The Holy Alliance; the European Background of the Monroe Doctrine*, New York, Oxford University Press, 1922.

————, *Diplomatic Portraits: Europe and the Monroe Doctrine One Hundred Years Ago*, Boston, Houghton Mifflin, 1923.

Croce, Benedetto, *A History of Italy, 1871–1915*, New York, Oxford University Press, 1929.

*Crocker, W. R., *The Japanese Population Problem, The Coming Crisis*, New York, Macmillan, 1931.

Crowther, Samuel, *America Self-Contained*, New York, Doubleday, 1933.

Culbertson, W. S., *International Economic Policies; a Survey of the Economics of Diplomacy*, New York, Appleton, 1925.

Cumming, Sir J. G., ed., *Political India, 1832–1932*, New York, Oxford University Press, 1932.

Cunningham, William, *The Rise and Decline of the Free Trade Movement*, Cambridge, Eng., University Press, 1912, (also New York, Putnam, 1907).

Current History, New York, New York Times Company, monthly.

Currey, M. I., *Italian Foreign Policy, 1918–1932*, London, Nicholson and Watson, 1932.

Custance, Sir R. N., *A Study of War*, Boston, Houghton Mifflin, 1925.

D'Abernon, E. V., Viscount, *The Diary of an Ambassador*, New York, Doubleday, 1929–31, 3 vols.

Davies, D. D., Baron, *The Problem of the Twentieth Century*, New York, Putnam, 1931.

Davis, S. C., *Reservoirs of Men*, Geneva, Librairie Kundig, 1934.

Davis, Col. W. J., *Japan: The Air Menace of the Pacific*, Boston, Christopher, 1928.

Dawson, W. H., *The Future of Empire; the World Price of Peace*, London, Williams and Norgate, 1930.

*————, *Germany Under the Peace Treaty*, London, Allen and Unwin, 1933.

Day, Clive, *A History of Commerce*, New York, Longmans, 1928.

Daye, Pierre, *L'Europe en Morceaux*, Paris, Plon, 1932.

*Delaisi, Francis, *Les Deux Europes; Europe Industrielle et Europe Agricole*, Paris, Payot, 1929.

Delbrück, Clemens von, *Die Wirtschaftliche Mobilmachung in Deutschland*, Munich, Verlag für Kulturpolitik, 1924.

Delle-Donne, O., *European Tariff Policies Since the World War*, New York, Adelphi, 1928.

Denikin, A. I., *The White Army*, London, Cape, 1930.

*Dennery, Étienne, *Asia's Teeming Millions*, London, Cape, 1931.

Dennett, Tyler, *Americans in Eastern Asia*, New York, Macmillan, 1922.

Dennis, A. L. P., *The Anglo-Japanese Alliance*, Berkeley, University of California Press, 1923.

——————, *The Foreign Policies of Soviet Russia*, New York, Dutton, 1924.

Derry, Kingston, *Outlines of English Economic History*, London, Bell, 1932.

Dewey, A. G., *The Dominions and Diplomacy*, New York, Longmans, 1929, 2 vols.

Dickinson, G. L., *The International Anarchy, 1904–1914*, New York, Century, 1926.

Diesel, Eugen, *Germany and the Germans*, New York, Macmillan, 1931.

*Dixon, Roland, *The Racial History of Man*, New York, Scribner, 1923.

Dobb, M. H., *Soviet Russia and the World*, London, Sidgwick and Jackson, 1932.

——————, and Stevens, H. C., *Russian Economic Development Since the Revolution*, New York, Dutton, 1928.

Dobbert, Gerhard, *ed.*, *Red Economics*, Boston, Houghton Mifflin, 1932.

——————, *ed.*, *Soviet Economics; a Symposium*, London, John Lane, 1933.

Donham, W. B., *Business Adrift*, New York, McGraw-Hill, 1931.

Douglass, P. F., *The Economic Dilemma of Politics: A Study of the Consequences of the Strangulation of Germany*, New York, Europress, 1932.

*Dublin, L. I., *ed.*, *Population Problems*, Boston, Houghton Mifflin, 1926.

Duboscq, André, *La Pacifique et la Rencontre des Races*, Paris, Fayard, 1929.

Dulles, F. R., *America in the Pacific*, Boston, Houghton Mifflin, 1932.

Dumas, Samuel, and Vedel-Petersen, K. O., *Losses of Life Caused by War*, Oxford, Clarendon Press, 1933.

*Duncan, H. G., *Race and Population Problems*, New York, Longmans, 1929.

Duranty, Walter, *Duranty Reports Russia*, New York, Viking Press, 1934.

Durham, M. E., *Twenty Years of Balkan Tangle*, London, Allen and Unwin, (also New York, Putnam), 1920.

Dyboski, Roman, *Outlines of Polish History*, London, Allen and Unwin, (also New York, Oxford University Press), 1931, 2d ed.

*Earle, E. M., *Turkey, The Great Powers, and the Bagdad Railway; A Study in Imperialism*, New York, Macmillan, 1923.

*East, E. M., *Mankind at the Crossroads*, New York, Scribner, 1923.

Eckardt, Hans von, *Russia*, New York, Knopf, 1932.

Eckel, E. C., *Coal, Iron and War*, New York, Holt, 1930.

Eckhart, Ferenc, *A Short History of the Hungarian People*, London, Grant Richards, 1931.

Edwards, William, *British Foreign Policy from 1815 to 1933*, London, Methuen, 1934.

Einzig, Paul, *Behind the Scenes of International Finance*, New York, Macmillan, 1931.

————, *The Fight for Financial Supremacy*, New York, Macmillan, 1931.

————, *Finance and Politics*, London, Macmillan, 1932.

————, *The Economic Foundations of Fascism*, London, Macmillan, 1933.

————, *The Sterling-Dollar-Franc Tangle*, New York, Macmillan, 1933.

*————, *Germany's Default: The Economics of Hitlerism*, New York, Macmillan, 1934.

————, *The Economics of Rearmament*, London, Routledge, Kegan Paul, 1934.

Eldridge, F. R., *Dangerous Thoughts on the Orient*, New York, Appleton-Century, 1933.

Elliott, W. Y., *The New British Empire*, New York, McGraw-Hill, 1932.

Emeny, Brooks, *The Strategy of Raw Materials; A Study of America in Peace and War*, New York, Macmillan, 1934.

Engely, Giovanni, *The Politics of Naval Disarmament*, London, Williams and Norgate, 1932.

Etherton, P. T., and Tiltman, H. H., *Japan: Mistress of the Pacific?*, London, Jarrolds, 1933.

————, *Manchuria, The Cockpit of Asia*, New York, Stokes, 1932.

Fabre-Luce, Alfred, *La Crise des Alliances*, Paris, Grasset, 1922.

Fachiri, A. P., *The Permanent Court of International Justice*, New York, Oxford University Press, 1932, rev.

Fairburn, W. A., *The International Goal of Russian Communism*, New York, Nation Press Printing Company, 1931.

*Fairgrieve, James, *Geography and World Power*, London, University of London Press, 1924, (also New York, Dutton, 1921).

*Febvre, L. P. V., and Bataillon, Lionel, *A Geographical Introduction to History*, New York, Knopf, 1925.

Feinberg, Nathan, *La Question des Minorités à la Conférence de la Paix*, Paris, Rousseau, 1929.

*Feis, Herbert, *Europe the World's Banker; 1870–1914*, New Haven, Yale University Press, 1930.

Ferdinand-Lop, S., *Les Ressources du Domaine Colonial de la France*, Paris, Dunod, 1924.

Ferguson, W. S., *Greek Imperialism*, Boston, Houghton Mifflin, 1913.

*Field, F. V., *American Participation in the China Consortiums*, Chicago, University of Chicago Press, 1931.

*————, ed., *Economic Handbook of the Pacific Area*, New York, Doubleday, 1934.

*Finot, Jean, *Race Prejudice*, New York, Dutton, 1924.

Fischer, Louis, *The Soviets in World Affairs*, London, Jonathan Cape, (also New York, Robert Ballou), 1930, 2 vols.

————, *Machines and Men in Russia*, New York, Smith and Haas, 1932.

Fleming, D. F., *The United States and the League of Nations*, New York, Putnam, 1932.

Fletcher, J. G., *Two Frontiers*, New York, Coward-McCann, 1930.

Florinsky, M. T., *The End of the Russian Empire*, New Haven, Yale University Press, 1931.

————, *World Revolution and the U.S.S.R.*, New York, Macmillan, 1933.

Flournoy, F. R., *Parliament and War*, London, King, 1927.

Foerster, R. F., *The Italian Emigration of Our Times*, Cambridge, Harvard University Press, 1919.

Folks, Homer, *The Human Costs of the War*, New York, Harper, 1920.

Foreign Affairs, New York, Council on Foreign Relations, quarterly:
"The Permanent Bases of Japanese Foreign Policy" by Viscount Kikujiro Ishii, Vol. 11, No. 2, 1933.
"Germany and the Crisis in Disarmament" by Allen W. Dulles, Vol. 12, No. 2, 1934.
"The Foreign Policy of the Duce," by Dino Grandi, Vol. 12, No. 4, 1934.
"The Strategy of Another Russo-Japanese War" by T. J. Betts, Vol. 12, No. 4, 1934.

*Foreign Policy Association, *Foreign Policy Reports*, New York, fortnightly (Vols. VII to X); *Information Service*, New York, fortnightly (Vols. I to VI):

"Protection of Minorities in Europe," Vol II, No. 19, 1926.

"Italian Foreign and Colonial Policy," Vol. III, No. 1, 1927.

"Developments in Russia's Foreign Relations," Vol. III, No. 10, 1927.

"Pan-American Arbitration Treaty," Vol. V, No. 18, 1929.

"Unsettled Boundary Disputes in Latin America," Vol. V, No. 26, 1930.

"Limitation of Land Armaments," Vol. VI, No. 2, 1930.

"The London Naval Conference January 21–April 22, 1930," Vol. VI, No. 6, 1930.

"Limitation of Air Armaments," Vol. VI, No. 17, 1930.

"Recent Balkan Alignments," Vol. VII, No. 1, 1931.

"The Franco-Italian Naval Dispute," Vol. VII, No. 8, 1931.

"The Political Structure of the Soviet State," Vol. VIII, Nos. 1 and 2, 1932.

"The World Disarmament Conference: First Stage," Vol. VIII, No. 5, 1932.

"The Soviet Union and Japan in the Far East," Vol. VIII, No. 12, 1932.

"The Lausanne Reparation Settlement," Vol. VIII, No. 19, 1932.

"The World Disarmament Conference: Second Stage, May 17, 1932–January, 1933," Vol. VIII, No. 23, 1933.

"Hitler and the German Political Crisis," Vol. VIII, No. 26, 1933.

"Political Realignments in Europe," Vol. IX, No. 5, 1933.

"German-Polish Disputes: Danzig, the Polish Corridor and East Prussia," Vol. IX, No. 9, 1933.

"The Soviet Union as a European Power," Vol. IX, No. 11, 1933.

"The Disarmament Crisis," Vol. IX, No. 17, 1933.

"The Balkans in the World Crisis," Vol. IX, No. 20, 1933.

"The New Status in the Pacific," Vol. IX, No. 23, 1934.

"Impending Naval Rivalries," Vol. X, No. 3, 1934.

"The Dismemberment of China," Vol. X, No. 4, 1934.

"Seventh Pan-American Conference," Vol. X, No. 7, 1934.

"The International Labor Organization," Vol. X, No. 9, 1934.

"Two Years of the Manchoukuo Regime," Vol. X, No. 14, 1934.

"Economic Structure of the Third Reich," Vol. X, No. 15, 1934.

——————, certain other publications listed in the separate entry for *World Affairs Pamphlets* (*q.v.*)

Foreman, Clark, *The New Internationalism*, New York, Norton, 1934.

Fortescue, Sir John, *The Empire and the Army*, London, Cassell, 1932.

Frank, Tenney, *Roman Imperialism*, New York, Macmillan, 1914.

Friedman, E. M., *Russia in Transition*, New York, Viking Press, 1932.

*Friedman, Samuel, *Le Problème des Minorités Ethniques*, Paris, Librairie Générale de Droit et de Jurisprudence, 1927.

Fuller, Major-General J. F. C., *Imperial Defence, 1588–1914*, London, Sifton, Praed, 1926.

————, *War and Western Civilization, 1832–1932*, London, Duckworth, 1932.

————, *Empire Unity and Defence*, London, Arrowsmith, 1934.

*Furness, J. W., and Jones, L. M., *Mineral Raw Materials*, Trade Promotion Series No. 76, Bureau of Foreign and Domestic Commerce, Washington, Government Printing Office, 1929.

Garner, J. W., *Prize Law During the World War*, New York, Macmillan, 1927.

————, *International Law and the World War*, New York, Longmans, 1920.

*Garth, T. R., *Race Psychology*, New York, McGraw-Hill, 1930.

Geneva Research Center, *Geneva Special Studies*, Geneva, monthly:
"The Covenant and the Pact," Vol. I, No. 9, 1930.
"The United States and the League," Vols. II, III, and IV, January of years 1931–32–33.
"Sanctions and Security; An Analysis of the French and American Views," Vol. III, No. 2, 1932.
"The League and Manchuria," Vol. II, Nos. 10, 11, and 12, 1931, also Vol. III, No. 5.
"Problem of World Economic Conference," Vol. IV, No. 3, 1933.
"The League and Manchukuo," Vol. V, No. 3, 1934.
"Duties of Non-Recognition in Practice 1775–1934," Vol. V, No. 4, 1934.

Gerig, Benjamin, *The Open Door and the Mandates System*, London, Allen and Unwin, 1930.

*Gini, Corrado, *Report on Certain Aspects of the Raw Materials Problem*, League of Nations, 1922, (or *Report on the Problem of Raw Materials and Foodstuffs*, Boston, World Peace Foundation, 1922).

*————, and others, *Population*, Chicago, University of Chicago Press, 1930.

Glasgow, George, *From Dawes to Locarno, 1924–25*, London, Benn, 1925, (also New York, Harper, 1926).

*Goad, H. E., *The Making of the Corporate State*, London, Christophers, 1932.

Gobineau, J. A. de, *The Inequality of Human Races*, New York, Putnam, 1915.

Goebel, O. H., *Deutsche Rohstoffwirtschaft im Weltkrieg*, New Haven, Yale University Press, 1930.

Golovin, N. N., *The Problem of the Pacific in the Twentieth Century*, London, Gyldendal, (also New York, Scribner), 1922.

Gooch, G. P., *Nationalism*, New York, Harcourt, 1920.

——————, *History of Modern Europe, 1878–1919*, New York, Holt, 1923.

*——————, *Franco-German Relations, 1871–1914*, London, Longmans, 1923.

Goode, W. T., *Is Intervention in Russia a Myth?*, London, Williams and Norgate, 1931.

*Gowen, H. H., *Asia, A Short History from the Earliest Times to the Present Day*, Boston, Little, Brown, 1926.

Graham, M. W., *The League of Nations and the Recognition of States*, Berkeley, University of California Press, 1933.

Graham, Stephen, *The Dividing Line of Europe*, New York, Appleton, 1925.

Grant, Madison, *The Passing of the Great Race*, New York, Scribner, 1921.

Graves, W. S., *America's Siberian Adventure 1918–20*, New York, Peter Smith, 1931.

*Greaves, H. R. G., *The League Committees and World Order*, New York, Oxford University Press, 1931.

Gregory, J. W., *The Menace of Colour*, London, Seeley, (also Philadelphia, Lippincott), 1925.

*——————, *Race as a Political Factor*, London, Watts and Company, 1931.

Gregory, T. E. G., *The Gold Standard and Its Future*, New York, Dutton, 1932.

Grison, Philippe, *La Liberté des Mers et la Rivalité Anglo-Américaine de 1920 à 1930*, Paris, Bossuet, 1930.

Gubkin, I. M., *The Natural Wealth of the Soviet Union and Its Exploitation*, Moscow, Cooperative Publishing Society of Foreign Works in the U.S.S.R., 1932.

Guichard, Louis, *The Naval Blockade*, New York, Appleton, 1930.

Gurian, Waldemar, *Bolshevism: Theory and Practice*, London, (and New York), Sheed and Ward, 1932.

Guyot, Georges, *L'Italie devant le Problème Colonial*, Paris, Société d'Editions Géographiques, 1927.

*Haddon, A. C., *The Races of Man and Their Distribution*, New York, Macmillan, 1925.

Haig, R. M., *The Public Finances of Post-War France*, New York, Columbia University Press, 1929.

Hall, J. W., *The Revolt of Asia: The End of the White Man's World Dominance*, New York, Putnam, 1927.

Haller, Johannes, *France and Germany, the History of One Thousand Years*, London, Constable, 1932.

Hamel, J. A. van, *Danzig and the Polish Problem*, New York, Carnegie Endowment for International Peace, 1933.

Hankins, F. H., *The Racial Basis of Civilization; a Critique of the Nordic Doctrine*, New York, Knopf, 1931.

Hara, Katsuro, *Introduction to the History of Japan*, New York, Putnam, 1920.

Haring, C. H., *South America Looks at the United States*, New York, Macmillan, 1928.

Harper, S. N., *Civic Training in Soviet Russia*, Chicago, University of Chicago Press, 1929.

——————, *Making Bolsheviks*, Chicago, University of Chicago Press, 1931.

*Haskins, C. H., and Lord, R. H., *Some Problems of the Peace Conference*, Cambridge, Harvard University Press, 1920.

Hawtrey, R. G., *Economic Aspects of Sovereignty*, New York, Longmans, 1930.

*Hayes, C. J. H., *A Political and Social History of Modern Europe*, New York, Macmillan, 1924, 2 vols.

——————, *Essays on Nationalism*, New York, Macmillan, 1926.

——————, *France: A Nation of Patriots*, New York, Columbia University Press, 1930.

——————, *The Historical Evolution of Modern Nationalism*, New York, R. R. Smith, 1931.

Hazen, C. D., Thayer, W. R., and Lord, R. H., *Three Peace Congresses of the Nineteenth Century*, Cambridge, Harvard University Press, 1917.

Heiden, Konrad, *History of National Socialism*, London, Methuen, 1934.

Heinecke, Gunther-Erfrid, *No More Reparations*, New York, Europress, 1932.

*Hennig, Richard, *Geopolitik*, Leipzig, Teubner, 1931.

Hertz, F. O., *Race and Civilization*, New York, Macmillan, 1928.

Hervey, J. G., *The Legal Effects of Recognition in International Law*, Philadelphia, University of Pennsylvania Press, 1928.

Hill, Chesney, *Recent Policies of Non-Recognition*, Worcester, Carnegie Endowment for International Peace, 1933.

*Hill, N. L., *International Administration*, New York, McGraw-Hill, 1931.

Hindmarsh, A. E., *Force in Peace*, Cambridge, Harvard University Press, 1933.

Hirst, F. W., *From Adam Smith to Philip Snowden*, New York, Adelphi, 1925.

——————, *The Consequences of the War to Great Britain*, New Haven, Yale University Press, 1934.

Hitler, Adolf, *My Battle*, Boston, Houghton Mifflin, 1933.

Hodgson, J. G., *Economic Nationalism*, New York, H. W. Wilson, 1933.

*Hoetzsch, Otto, *Germany's Domestic and Foreign Policies*, New Haven, Yale University Press, 1929.

Holcombe, A. N., *The Chinese Revolution*, Cambridge, Harvard University Press, 1931.

Holland, Sir T. E., *European Concert in the Eastern Question*, New York, Oxford University Press, 1885.

Hoover, C. B., *The Economic Life of Soviet Russia*, New York, Macmillan, 1931.

——————, *Germany Enters the Third Reich*, New York, Macmillan, 1933.

*Hoskins, H. L., *European Imperialism in Africa*, New York, Holt, 1930.

*Howard-Ellis, Charles, *The Origin, Structure and Working of the League of Nations*, London, Allen and Unwin, (also Boston, Houghton Mifflin), 1928.

*Howland, C. P., *ed.*, *American Foreign Relations*, New Haven, Yale University Press, 1928–1931, 4 vols.

Hsü, L. S., *Sun Yat-Sen, His Political and Social Ideals*, Los Angeles, University of Southern California Press, 1933.

Huddleston, Sisley, *War Unless—*, London, Gollancz, 1933.

Hudson, M. O., *The World Court, 1921–34*, Boston, World Peace Foundation, 1934, rev. ed.

Hull, W. I., *The War Method and the Peace Method*, New York, Revell, 1929.

*Huntington, Ellsworth, *The Character of Races*, New York, Scribner, 1924.

——————, *The Pulse of Progress*, New York, Scribner, 1926.

Imperial Economic Conference, *Report of the Conference*, Ottawa, Acland, 1932.

Inman, S. G., *Problems in Pan Americanism*, New York, Doubleday, 1925.

*Institute of Pacific Relations, *Problems of the Pacific*, Chicago, University of Chicago Press, 1925-27-29-31-33.

International Conciliation, New York, Carnegie Endowment for International Peace, monthly.

International Institute of Intellectual Cooperation, *The State and Economic Life*, Paris, 1934.

*International Union for the Scientific Investigation of Population Problems, 2d Assembly, *Problems of Population*, London, Allen and Unwin, 1932.

Inter-Parliamentary Union, *What Would Be the Character of a New War?*, London, King, 1931.

*Jackson, Judith, and King-Hall, Stephen, *The League Year-Book*, New York, Macmillan, annual since 1932.

Jaffe, L. L., *Judicial Aspects of Foreign Relations, in Particular of the Recognition of Foreign Powers*, Cambridge, Harvard University Press, 1933.

Jaquin, Pierre, *La Question des Minorités entre l'Italie et la Yugoslavie*, Paris, Sirey, 1929.

Jászi, Oszkár, *The Dissolution of the Hapsburg Monarchy*, Chicago, University of Chicago, 1929.

Jessup, P. C., *The United States and the World Court*, Boston, World Peace Foundation, 1929.

Johnson, W. F., *America's Foreign Relations*, New York, Century, 1921, 2 vols.

Jones, C. F., *Commerce of South America*, Boston, Ginn, 1928.

*Jones, C. L., *Caribbean Backgrounds and Prospects*, New York, Appleton, 1931.

Jones, J. M., *Tariff Retaliation*, Philadelphia, University of Pennsylvania Press, 1934.

Jones, R. L., *History of the Foreign Policy of the United States*, New York, Putnam, 1933.

Josey, C. C., *Race and National Solidarity*, New York, Scribner, 1923.

*Junghann, Otto, *National Minorities in Europe*, New York, Covici Friede, 1932.

Kantorowicz, H. U., *The Spirit of British Policy and the Myth of the Encirclement of Germany*, New York, Oxford University Press, 1932.

Kawakami, K. K., *Japan's Pacific Policy*, New York, Dutton, 1922.
————, *Manchoukuo, Child of Conflict*, New York, Macmillan, 1933.

Keith, A. B., *The Sovereignty of the British Dominions*, New York, Macmillan, 1929.

—————, *Dominion Autonomy in Practice*, New York, Oxford University Press, 1929.

—————, *The Constitutional Law of the British Dominions*, New York, Macmillan, 1933.

Kelchner, W. H., *Latin American Relations with the League of Nations*, Boston, World Peace Foundation, 1930.

Kennedy, Capt. M. D., *Some Aspects of Japan and Her Defence Forces*, London, Kegan Paul, 1929.

Kenworthy, J. M., and Young, G., *Freedom of the Seas*, New York, Liveright, 1929.

Keynes, J. M., *The Economic Consequences of the Peace*, New York, Harcourt, 1920.

*King, Bolton, *Fascism in Italy*, London, Williams and Norgate, 1931.

King, Joseph, *The German Revolution; Its Meaning and Menace*, London, Williams and Norgate, 1933.

Kleinwächter, F. F. G., *Self-Determination for Austria*, London, Allen and Unwin, 1929.

Knickerbocker, H. R., *The Red Trade Menace; Progress of the Soviet Five-Year Plan*, New York, Dodd, 1931.

*Koch-Weser, E. F. L., *Germany in the Post-War World*, Philadelphia, Dorrance, 1930.

Kohn, Hans, *Nationalism and Imperialism in the Hither East*, New York, Harcourt, 1932.

—————, *Orient and Occident*, New York, John Day, 1934.

Korf, Baron S. A., *Russia's Foreign Relations During the Last Half Century*, New York, Macmillan, 1922.

Kosok, Paul, *Modern Germany. A Study of Conflicting Loyalties*, Chicago, University of Chicago Press, 1933.

Krishnaswami, A., *The New Indian Constitution*, London, Williams and Norgate, 1934.

*Kühlmann, Richard von, *Thoughts on Germany*, New York, Macmillan, 1932.

Ladas, S. P., *The International Protection of Industrial Property*, Cambridge, Harvard University Press, 1930.

—————, *The Exchange of Minorities: Bulgaria, Greece and Turkey*, New York, Macmillan, 1932.

Lambert, Charles, *La France et les Étrangers*, Paris, Delahaye, 1927.

Lanessan, J. L. de, *Histoire de l'Entente Cordiale Franco-Anglaise*, Paris, Alcan, 1916.

Langer, W. L., *European Alliances and Alignments, 1871–1890*, New York, Knopf, 1931.

*Langsam, W. C., *The World Since 1914*, New York, Macmillan, 1933.

*Laski, H. J., *Studies in the Problem of Sovereignty*, New Haven, Yale University Press, 1917.

Lasswell, H. D., *Propaganda Technique in the World War*, New York, Knopf, 1927.

Latané, J. H., *The United States and Latin America*, New York, Doubleday, 1926.

————, *A History of American Foreign Policy*, New York, Doubleday, 1927.

Latourette, K. S., *The Development of Japan*, New York, Macmillan, 1926, 2d ed.

————, *The Chinese, Their History and Culture*, New York, Macmillan, 1934, 2 vols.

Lattimore, Owen, *Manchuria, Cradle of Conflict*, New York, Macmillan, 1932.

Lauterpacht, H., *The Function of Law in the International Community*, New York, Oxford University Press, 1933.

Lautman, Jules, *Les Aspects Nouveaux du Protectionnisme*, Rivière, Paris, 1933.

Lawton, Lancelot, *An Economic History of Soviet Russia*, London, Macmillan, 1932.

*League of Nations, *Annotated Bibliography on Disarmament and Military Questions*, Geneva, 1931.

*————, *Armaments Year Book*, Boston, World Peace Foundation annual.

*————, *Preparatory Commission for the Disarmament Conference*, 1925–1934.

————, *Report and Proceedings of the World Economic Conference*, 1927.

*————, *Ten Years of World Co-operation*, Boston, World Peace Foundation, 1930.

Lee, T. F., *Latin American Problems; Their Relation to Our Investors' Billions*, New York, Brewer, 1932.

Lefebure, V., *Scientific Disarmament*, New York, Macmillan, 1931.

*Leith, C. K., *World Minerals and World Politics*, New York, McGraw-Hill, 1931.

Lémonon, E., *L'Italie d'apres Guerre, 1914–1921*, Paris, Alcan, 1922.

*Lessing, O. E., *ed.*, *Minorities and Boundaries*, New York, Van Riemsdyck, 1931.

Lichtenberger, Henri, *Relations Between France and Germany*, Washington, Carnegie Endowment for International Peace, 1923.

Lindsey, Edward, *The International Court*, New York, Crowell, 1931.

*Lippincott, I., *Economic Resources and Industries of the World*, New York, Appleton, 1929.

*Lippmann, Walter, and Scroggs, W. O., *The United States in World Affairs*, New York, Harper, annual since 1931.

Litvinoff, Maksim, *The Soviet's Fight for Disarmament*, New York, International Publishers, 1932.

Liu Shih Shun, *Extraterritoriality, Its Rise and Its Decline*, New York, Columbia University Press, 1925.

Lloyd George, David, *The Truth About Reparations and War Debts*, New York, Doubleday, 1932.

Lockey, J. B., *Pan-Americanism; Its Beginnings*, New York, Macmillan, 1920.

Lockhart, J. G., *The Peace Makers, 1814–1815*, London, Duckworth, 1932.

Lorwin, L. L., *Labor and Internationalism*, Washington, Brookings Institution, 1929.

Lowell, A. L., *Public Opinion in War and Peace*, Boston, Harvard University Press, 1923.

Luboff, Edouard, *Soviet Dumping*, London, Anglo-Russian Press, 1931.

*Luehr, Elmer, *The New German Republic*, New York, Minton, Balch, 1929.

Lyautey, Pierre, *L'Organisation de l'Empire Colonial Français*, Paris, Editions de France, 1931.

Maanen-Helmer, Elizabeth van, *The Mandates System in Relation to Africa and the Pacific Islands*, London, King, 1929.

*Macartney, C. A., *National States and National Minorities*, New York, Oxford University Press, 1934.

*McClure, Wallace, *World Prosperity as Sought Through the Economic Work of the League of Nations*, New York, Macmillan, 1933.

McCrea, R. C., et al., *International Competition in the Trade of Argentina*, Worcester, Carnegie Endowment for International Peace, 1931.

McCurdy, C. A., *Empire Free Trade*, London, Hutchinson, 1930.

MacDonald, J. N., *A Political Escapade*, London, Murray, 1921.

McFadyean, Sir Andrew, *Reparation Reviewed*, London, Benn, 1930.

McGuire, C. E., *Italy's International Economic Position*, New York, Macmillan, 1926.

Machray, Robert, *The Little Entente*, New York, R. R. Smith, 1930.

——————, *Poland, 1914-1931*, London, Allen and Unwin, (also New York, Dutton), 1932.

McIver, D. T., *Debased Currency and the London Monetary Conference*, Chicago, The Homewood Press, 1933.

*MacIver, R. M., *The Modern State*, New York, Oxford University Press, 1926.

*Mackinder, H. J., *Democratic Ideals and Reality*, New York, Holt, 1919.

MacNair, H. F., *China in Revolution*, Chicago, University of Chicago Press, 1931.

Madariaga, Salvador de, *Disarmament*, New York, Coward-McCann, 1929.

——————, *Englishmen, Frenchmen, Spaniards*, New York, Oxford University Press, 1931, rev. ed.

——————, *I Americans*, New York, Oxford University Press, 1931.

Maddox, W. P., *Foreign Relations in British Labour Politics*, Cambridge, Harvard University Press, 1934.

Maestracci, Noël, *L'Empire Colonial Français Contemporain*, Paris, C. Lavauzelle, 1931.

Malin, J. C., *The United States After the World War*, Boston, Ginn, 1930.

Malynski, Emmanuel, *Problèmes de l'Est et la Petite Entente*, Paris, Cervantes, 1931.

Manchuria Year Book, East-Asiatic Economic Investigation Bureau, (London, Stechert), annual since 1930.

Mangin, Gen. J. E., *Comment Finit La Guerre*, Paris, Plon, 1920.

Margalith, A. M., *The International Mandates*, Baltimore, Johns Hopkins Press, 1930.

Marriott, Sir John Arthur R., *The Makers of Modern Italy*, New York, Oxford University Press, 1931.

Martel, René, *The Eastern Frontiers of Germany*, London, Williams and Norgate, 1930.

Martin, P. A., *Latin America and the War*, Baltimore, Johns Hopkins Press, 1925.

Mathews, J. M., *American Foreign Relations*, New York, Century, 1928.

*Mattern, Johannes, *Concepts of State Sovereignty and International Law*, Baltimore, Johns Hopkins Press, 1928.

——————, *The Employment of the Plebiscite in the Determination of Sovereignty*, Baltimore, Johns Hopkins Press, 1920.

Maurice, Sir Frederick, *Governments and War*, London, Heinemann, 1926.

Maurois, André, *Lyautey*, New York, Appleton, 1931.

*Mavor, James, *An Economic History of Russia*, New York, Dutton, 1925, 2 vols.

Meuvret, J., *Histoire des Pays Baltiques*, Paris, Colin, 1934.

Michels, R. K., *Cartels, Combines and Trusts in Post-War Germany*, New York, Columbia University Press, 1928.

Michon, Georges, *The Franco-Russian Alliance, 1891–1917*, London, Allen and Unwin, 1929.

Migot, Robert, and Gusthal, Comte, *La Guerre Est Là*, Paris, Soubiron, 1932.

Milenkovitch, V. M., *Le Probléme de la Sécurité Européenne d'après les Accords de Locarno*, Paris, Pedone, 1928.

Miller, D. H., *The Geneva Protocol*, New York, Macmillan, 1925.

*————, *The Peace Pact of Paris*, New York, Putnam, 1928.

————, *The Drafting of the Covenant*, New York, Putnam, 1928.

Miller, H. A., *Races, Nations and Classes*, Philadelphia, Lippincott, 1924.

Miller, H. G., *The Isthmian Highway; A Review of the Problems of the Caribbean*, New York, Macmillan, 1929.

*Miller, M. S., *The Economic Development of Russia, 1905–1914*, London, King, 1926.

Miller, W., *The Ottoman Empire and Its Successors, 1801–1927*, Cambridge, Eng., University Press, 1927.

Mitrany, David, *The Problem of International Sanctions*, New York, Oxford University Press, 1925.

Moncado, H. C., *America, the Philippines and the Orient*, New York, Revell, 1932.

Moon, P. T., *Imperialism and World Politics*, New York, Macmillan, 1926.

Moore, Frederick, *America's Naval Challenge*, New York, Macmillan, 1929.

Moore, J. B., *International Law and Some Current Illusions*, New York, Macmillan, 1924.

————, *A Digest of International Law*, Washington, Government Printing Office, 1906.

Moore, W. G., *France and Germany; A Study of National Character and Opinion*, London, S.C.M., 1932.

Morley, Felix, *The Society of Nations*, Washington, Brookings Institution, 1932.

Morrison-Bell, Sir Clive, *Tariff Walls; a European Crusade*, London, J. Murray, 1930.

*Morse, H. B., and Macnair, H. F., *Far Eastern International Relations*, Boston, Houghton Mifflin, 1931.

*Motherwell, Hiram, *The Imperial Dollar*, New York, Brentano, 1929.

*Moulton, H. G., and Ko, Junichi, *Japan; An Economic and Financial Appraisal*, Washington, Brookings Institution, 1931.

Moulton, H. G., and Pasvolsky, L., *War Debts and World Prosperity*, Washington, Brookings Institution, 1932.

Mousset, Albert, *L'Albanie devant l'Europe*, Paris, Delagrave, 1930.

*Mowat, R. B., *The European States System; A Study of International Relations*, London, Oxford University Press, 1929, enl.

————, *The Concert of Europe*, New York, Macmillan, 1931.

*————, *European Diplomacy, 1815–1914*, New York, Longmans, 1922.

*Mower, E. C., *International Government*, Boston, Heath, 1931.

*Muir, Ramsay, *Political Consequences of the Great War*, London, Butterworth, 1930.

————, *A Short History of the British Commonwealth*, Yonkers, World Book Co., 1922–23, 2 vols.

Munro, D. G., *The United States and the Caribbean Area*, Boston, World Peace Foundation, 1934.

*Munro, I. S., *Through Fascism to World Power; a History of the Revolution in Italy*, London, Maclehose, 1933.

Muntz, E. E., *Race Contact*, New York, Century, 1927.

Murdoch, James, *A History of Japan*, London, Kegan Paul, (also New York, Greenberg), 1926.

*Muret, Maurice, *The Twilight of the White Races*, New York, Scribner, 1926.

*Myers, D. P., *World Disarmament*, Boston, World Peace Foundation, 1932.

*————, *Handbook of the League of Nations Since 1920*, Boston, World Peace Foundation, 1930.

*————, *Origin and Conclusion of the Paris Pact*, Boston, World Peace Foundation, 1929.

Nathan, Manfred, *Empire Government*, Cambridge, Harvard University Press, 1929.

National Bureau of Economic Research, *Recent Economic Changes in the United States*, New York, McGraw-Hill, 1929, 2 vols.

National Industrial Conference Board, *Rationalization of German Industry*, New York, National Industrial Conference Board, 1931.

————, *Trends in the Foreign Trade of the United States*, New York, National Industrial Conference Board, 1930.

*Nearing, Scott, and Freeman, Joseph, *Dollar Diplomacy*, New York, Huebsch, 1925.

Newbigin, M. I., *The Mediterranean Lands*, New York, Knopf, 1924.

Nickerson, Hoffman, *Can We Limit War?*, New York, Stokes, 1934.

*Nicolson, H. G., *Peacemaking 1919*, London, Constable, (also Boston, Houghton Mifflin), 1933.

Normano, J. F., *The Struggle for South America*, Boston, Houghton Mifflin, 1931.

Offutt, Milton, *The Protection of Citizens Abroad by the Armed Forces of the United States*, Baltimore, Johns Hopkins Press, 1928.

Ogburn, W. F., and Jaffé, William, *The Economic Development of Post-War France*, New York, Columbia University Press, 1929.

*Ogg, F. A., *European Governments and Politics*, New York, Macmillan, 1934, rev. ed.

Olden, Rudolf, *Stresemann*, New York, Dutton, 1930.

*Orchard, J. E., *Japan's Economic Position*, New York, McGraw-Hill, 1930.

*Owen, D. E., *Imperialism and Nationalism in the Far East*, New York, Holt, 1929.

Pacific Affairs, edited by Owen Lattimore, Honolulu, quarterly.

Papanastassiou, A. P., *Vers l'Union Balkanique*, Paris, Dotation Carnegie, 1934.

*Pares, Sir Bernard, *History of Russia*, New York, Knopf, 1930.

Pargiter, R. B., and Eady, H. G., *The Army and Sea Power*, London, Benn, 1927.

Patterson, E. M., *The World's Economic Dilemma*, New York, McGraw-Hill, 1930.

————, *America: World Leader or World Led?*, New York, Century, 1932.

*Peffer, N., *The White Man's Dilemma*, New York, Day, 1927.

————, *China, the Collapse of a Civilization*, New York, Day, 1930.

*Penrose, E. F., *Food Supply and Raw Materials in Japan*, Chicago, University of Chicago Press, 1930.

Percy, Lord Eustace, *Maritime Trade in War*, New Haven, Yale University Press, 1930.

Perquel, Jules, *Les Vicissitudes des Placements Français à l'Étranger*, Paris, Éditions du Capital, 1929.

Pezet, Ernest, and Simondet, H., *La Yougoslavie en Peril?*, Paris, Bloud et Gay, 1933.

Phelps, Phelps, *Our Defenses Within and Without*, New York, Powers, 1932.

*Phillimore, Sir W. G. F., *Three Centuries of Peace Treaties*, London, 1919.

*Pitigliani, Fausto, *The Italian Corporative State*, London, King, 1933.

*Pitt-Rivers, G. H. L. F., *ed.*, *Problems of Population*, London, Allen and Unwin, 1932.

————, *The Clash of Culture and the Contact of Races*, London, Routledge, 1927.

Pollard, R. T., *China's Foreign Relations, 1917–1931*, New York, Macmillan, 1933.

Popovici, Andrei, *The Political Status of Bessarabia*, Washington, Ransdell, 1931.

Porritt, Arthur, *ed.*, *The Causes of War*, New York, Macmillan, 1932.

Pribram, A. F., *England and the International Policy of the European Great Powers, 1871–1914*, New York, Oxford University Press, 1931.

Radin, Paul, *The Racial Myth*, New York, McGraw-Hill, 1934.

Ramsay, Alexander, *The Economics of Safeguarding*, London, Benn, 1930.

Rawles, W. P., *The Nationality of Commercial Control of World Minerals*, New York, American Institute of Mining and Metallurgical Engineers, 1933.

Ray, Parimal, *India's Foreign Trade Since 1870*, London, Routledge, 1934.

Reale, Egidio, *La Politique Fasciste et la Société des Nations*, Paris, Pedone, 1932.

*Recouly, Raymond, *De Bismarck à Poincaré*, Paris, Éditions de France, 1932.

Redlich, M. D. de, *International Law as a Substitute for Diplomacy*, Washington, Independent Publishing Company, 1929.

Reinsch, P. S., *Secret Diplomacy*, New York, Harcourt, 1922.

Reiss, R. A., *The Comitadji Question in Southern Serbia*, London, Hazell, 1924.

Remer, C. F., *Foreign Investments in China*, New York, Macmillan, 1933.

————, and Palmer, W. B., *A Study of Chinese Boycotts with Special Reference to Their Economic Effectiveness*, Baltimore, Johns Hopkins Press, 1933.

*Remington, W. E., *World States of the Machine Age*, Columbus, Ga., Gilbert Printing Company, 1932.

Reut-Nicolussi, E., *Tyrol Under the Axe of Italian Fascism*, London, Allen and Unwin, 1930.

*Reuter, E. B., *Race Mixture*, London, McGraw-Hill, 1931.

Richmond, Admiral Sir H. W., *Economy and Naval Security*, London, Benn, 1931.

————, *Imperial Defence and Capture at Sea in War*, London, Hutchinson, 1932.

Rippy, J. F., *Latin America in World Politics*, New York, Crofts, 1931, rev. ed.

*Roberts, S. H., *Population Problems of the Pacific*, London, Routledge, 1927.

——————, *History of French Colonial Policy, 1870–1925*, London, King, 1929, 2 vols.

Robertson, W. S., *History of the Latin-American Nations*, New York, Appleton, 1932, rev. ed.

*Robinson, G. T., *Rural Russia Under the Old Régime*, New York, Longmans, 1932.

Rodick, B. C., *The Doctrine of Necessity in International Law*, New York, Columbia University Press, 1928.

Rogers, J. H., *America Weighs Her Gold*, New Haven, Yale University Press, 1931.

Rohde, Hans, *Franco-German Factors of Power*, Berlin, Berliner Börsen Zeitung, 1932.

*——————, *Der Kampf um Asien*, Stuttgart, Deutsche Verlagsanstalt, 1924–1926, 2 vols.

Roorbach, G. B., *Problems in Foreign Trade*, New York, McGraw-Hill, 1933.

Roosevelt, Nicholas, *The Restless Pacific*, New York, Scribner, 1928.

Rosenberg, Arthur, *A History of Bolshevism*, New York, Oxford University Press, 1934.

*——————, *The Birth of the German Republic*, New York, Oxford University Press, 1931.

Ross, E. A., *The Russian Soviet Republic, 1918–1922*, New York, Century, 1923.

Rouček, J. S., *The Working of the Minorities System under the League of Nations*, Prague, Orbis, (also Hackettstown, N. J., the author), 1929.

——————, *Contemporary Roumania and Her Problems*, Stanford, Stanford University Press, 1932.

Rouma, Georges, *Les Ressources Économiques de l'Amérique Latine*, Brussels, Renaissance du Livre, 1923.

Rowland, S. W., *Depreciation Reconsidered*, London, Gee and Company, Ltd., 1933.

Rutherford, V. H., *War or Peace? England and America*, London, Williams and Norgate, 1930.

Rutter, Owen, *The New Baltic States and Their Future*, Boston, Houghton Mifflin, 1926.

Salter, Sir Arthur, *Allied Shipping Control: An Experiment in International Administration*, New York, Oxford University Press, 1921.

——————, *Recovery, The Second Effort*, New York, Century, 1932.

*Salvemini, Gaetano, *The Fascist Dictatorship in Italy*, New York, Holt, 1927.
————, *Mussolini Diplomate*, Paris, Grasset, 1932.
Sansom, G. B., *Japan, A Short Cultural History*, New York, Century, 1931.
Sargent, Arthur, *Seaways of Empire, Notes on Geography of Transport*, London, A. and C. Black, (also New York, Macmillan), 1930.
Satow, Sir Ernest M., *A Guide to Diplomatic Practise*, London, Longmans, 1932, 2 vols., 3d ed. rev.
*————, *International Congresses*, London, H. M. Stationery Office, 1920.
Schacht, Hjalmar, *The End of Reparations*, New York, Ballou, 1931.
Scheffer, Paul, *Seven Years in Soviet Russia*, New York, Macmillan, 1932.
Schevill, Ferdinand, and Gewehr, W. M., *The History of the Balkan Peninsula*, New York, Harcourt, 1933, rev.
Schiff, Victor, *The Germans at Versailles*, London, Williams and Norgate, 1930.
*Schmidt, C. T., *German Business Cycles*, New York, National Bureau of Economic Research, 1934.
Schmidt, Richard, and Grabowsky, Adolf, *Disarmament and Equal Rights*, Berlin, Heymanns, 1934.
————, *The Problem of Disarmament*, Berlin, Heymanns, 1933.
Schmitt, B. E., *England and Germany*, Princeton, Princeton University Press, 1918.
*Schneider, H. W., *Making the Fascist State*, New York, Oxford University Press, 1928.
*Schneider, H. W., and Clough, S. B., *Making Fascists*, Chicago, University of Chicago Press, 1929.
Schoonmaker, E. D., *Our Genial Enemy France*, New York, Long and Smith, 1932.
*Schuman, F. L., *War and Diplomacy in the French Republic*, New York, McGraw-Hill, 1931.
*Scott, J. B., ed., *Preliminary History of the Armistice*, New York, Oxford University Press, 1924.
————, *The International Conferences of American States, 1889–1928*, New York, Oxford University Press, 1931.
Sears, L. M., *A History of American Foreign Relations*, New York, Crowell, 1927.
Semple, E. C., *The Geography of the Mediterranean Region*, New York, Holt, 1931.
————, *American History and Its Geographic Conditions*, Boston, Houghton Mifflin, 1933.

Seton-Watson, R. W., *Treaty Revision and the Hungarian Frontiers*, London, Eyre and Spottiswoode, 1934.

Seymour, Charles, *American Diplomacy During the World War*, Baltimore, Johns Hopkins Press, 1934.

Shiel, M. P., *The Yellow Peril*, London, Gollancz, 1929.

*Shotwell, J. T., *War as an Instrument of National Policy and Its Renunciation in the Pact of Paris*, New York, Harcourt, 1929.

Shuster, G. N., *The Germans; an Inquiry and an Estimate*, New York, Dial Press, 1932.

Sieburg, Friedrick, *Who Are These French?*, New York, Macmillan, 1932.

Siegfried, André, *France: A Study in Nationality*, New Haven, Yale University Press, 1930.

Silvio, Trentin, *Le Fascisme à Genève*, Paris, Riviere, 1932.

Simonds, F. H., *Can America Stay at Home?*, New York, Harper, 1932.

——————, *Can Europe Keep the Peace?*, New York, Harper, 1934, rev. ed.

——————, *America Faces the Next War*, New York, Harper, 1933.

——————, *How Europe Made Peace Without America*, New York, Doubleday, 1927.

——————, *The A B C of War Debts*, New York, Harper, 1933.

Simpson, Kemper, *Introduction to World Economics*, New York, Harper, 1934.

Sipple, C. E., *British Foreign Policy Since the World War*, Iowa City, University of Iowa, 1932.

*Slosson, P. W., *Twentieth Century Europe*, Boston, Houghton Mifflin, 1927.

——————, *The Great Crusade and After, 1914–1928*, New York, Macmillan, 1930.

Smith, George O., *The Strategy of Minerals*, New York, Appleton, 1919.

Smogorzewski, Casimir, *Poland, Germany and the Corridor*, London, Williams and Norgate, 1930.

——————, *La Politique Polonaise de la France*, Paris, Gebethner and Wolff, 1926.

Sobolevitch, E., *Les États Baltes et la Russie Soviétique*, Paris, Presses Universitaires, 1930.

*Soltau, R. H., *French Parties and Politics, 1871–1930*, New York, Oxford University Press, 1930.

* ——————, *French Political Thought in the 19th Century*, New Haven, Yale University Press, 1931.

Sombart, Werner, *ed.*, *Volk und Raum*, Hamburg, Hanseatische Verlagsamstalt, 1928.

Somervell, D. C., *The British Empire*, London, Christophers, 1930.

South American Handbook, London, South American Publications, (also New York, Sanderson), annual since 1924.

Southard, F. A., Jr., *American Industry in Europe*, Boston, Houghton Mifflin, 1931.

Southworth, Constant, *The French·Colonial Adventure*, London, King, 1931.

*Spencer, H. R., *Government and Politics of Italy*, Yonkers, World Book Company, 1932.

*Spengler, Oswald, *The Decline of the West*, New York, Knopf, 1926–1928, 2 vols.

——————, *The Hour of Decision*, New York, Knopf, 1934.

Stamp, Sir J. C., *The Financial Aftermath of War*, New York, Scribner, 1932.

Stegemann, Hermann, *The Struggle for the Rhine*, New York, Knopf, 1927.

Stern, S., *Fourteen Years of European Investments, 1914-1928*, New York, Bankers Publishing Company, 1929.

Stewart, George, *The White Armies of Russia*, New York, Macmillan, 1933.

Stoddard, Lothrop, *Europe and Our Money*, New York, Macmillan, 1932.

——————, *The Rising Tide of Color*, New York, Scribner, 1920.

Stone, Julius, *International Guarantees of Minority Rights*, New York, Oxford University Press, 1932.

Stowe, Leland, *Nazi Means War*, New York, McGraw-Hill, 1934.

Stowell, E. C., *International Law; a Restatement of Principles in Conformity with Actual Practice*, New York, Holt, 1931.

——————, *Intervention in International Law*, Washington, Byrne, 1921.

Strupp, Karl, *La Situation Juridique des Macédoniens en Yougoslavie*, Paris, Presses Universitaires, 1930.

——————, *Intervention in Finanzfragen*, Leipzig, Noske, 1928.

Stuart, G. H., *French Foreign Policy from Fashoda to Serajevo, 1898–1914*, New York, Century, 1921.

Sturzo, Luigi, *The International Community and the Right of War*, New York, Long & Smith, 1930.

Surface, F. M., *The Grain Trade during the World War*, New York, Macmillan, 1928.

Takekoshi, Yosaburo, *The Economic Aspects of the History of the Civilization of Japan*, New York, Macmillan, 1930, 3 vols.

T'Ang Leang Li, *The Inner History of the Chinese Revolution*, New York, Dutton, 1930.

Tardieu, André, *France and America*, Boston, Houghton Mifflin, 1927.

Taussig, E. W., and White, H. D., *Some Aspects of the Tariff Question; An Examination of the Development of American Industries Under Protection*, Cambridge, Harvard University Press, 1931, 3d enl. ed.

——————, *The Tariff History of the United States*, New York, Putnam, 1931, 8th ed.

*Taylor, T. G., *Environment and Race*, New York, Oxford University Press, 1927.

*Temperley, H. W., ed., *A History of the Peace Conference of Paris*, London, Frowde and Hodder, (also New York, Oxford University Press), 1920–1924, 6 vols.

*Thomas, Franklin, *The Environmental Basis of Society*, New York, Century, 1925.

Thompson, E. J., and Garratt, G. T., *Rise and Fulfilment of British Rule in India*, London, Macmillan, 1934.

Thompson, H. C., *The Case for China*, New York, Scribner, 1933.

*Thompson, W. S., *Danger Spots in World Population*, New York, Knopf, 1929.

Thomson, Valentine, *Briand, Man of Peace*, New York, Covici Friede, 1930.

*Tilley, Arthur, *Modern France*, Cambridge, Eng., University Press, 1923.

Timoshenko, V. P., *Agricultural Russia and the Wheat Problem*, Stanford, Stanford University Press, 1932.

Tittoni, T., *Italy's Foreign and Colonial Policy*, London, Smith, Elder, 1914.

Toynbee, A. J., *The World after the Peace Conference*, London, Oxford University Press, 1925.

*——————, *Survey of International Affairs*, annual, Royal Institute of International Affairs, New York, London, Oxford University Press.

——————, *The Conduct of British Empire Foreign Relations Since the Peace Settlement*, London, Oxford University Press, 1928.

——————, ed., *British Commonwealth Relations*, New York, Oxford University Press, 1934.

*Trampler, Kurt, *Die Krise des Nationalstaates*, Munich, Knorr, 1932.

*Treat, P. J., *The Far East*, New York, Harper, 1928.

Trotsky, Leon, (or Trotskiĭ, Lev), *L'Internationale Communiste après Lénine*, Paris, Rieder, 1930.

——————, *The Real Situation in Russia*, New York, Harcourt, 1928.

——————, *The History of the Russian Revolution*, New York, Simon and Schuster, 1932–1933, 3 vols.

Tryon, F. G., and Eckel, E. C., *eds.*, *Mineral Economics*, New York, McGraw-Hill, 1932.

Tryon, G. C., *A Short History of Imperial Preference*, London, P. Allan, 1931.

Tuohy, F., *Occupied, 1918–1930*, London, Thornton, Butterworth, 1931.

Turner, C. C., *Britain's Air Peril*, London, Pitman, 1933.

Turner, F. J., *The Frontier in American History*, New York, Holt, 1921.

United States, *Limitation of Naval Armaments*, Records of the Conference at Geneva, June 20 to August 4, 1927, Washington, Government Printing Office, 1928.

Urrutia, F. J., *Le Continent Américain et le Droit International*, Paris, Rousseau, 1928.

Utley, Freda, *Lancashire and the Far East*, London, Allen and Unwin, 1931.

*Uyeda, Teijiro, *The Future of Japanese Population*, New York, Institute of Pacific Relations, 1933.

Vallentin, Antonina, *Stresemann*, New York, Long & Smith, 1931.

*Vernadsky, A. G., *A History of Russia*, New Haven, Yale University Press, 1929.

*Viallate, Achille, *Economic Imperialism and International Relations during the Past Fifty Years*, New York, Macmillan, 1923.

Viereck, G. S., *Spreading the Germs of Hate*, New York, Liveright, 1930.

Villari, Luigi, *The Expansion of Italy*, London, Faber, 1930.

——————, *The Awakening of Italy*, London, Methuen, 1924.

*Vinacke, H. M., *A History of the Far East in Modern Times*, New York, Crofts, 1928.

——————, *Problems of Industrial Development in China*, Princeton, Princeton University Press, 1926.

Viner, Jacob, *Dumping: a Problem in International Trade*, Chicago, University of Chicago Press, 1923.

Vrieslander, Wismann, *Lloyd-George*, Munich, Wieland-Verlag, 1923.

Wallace, B. B., and Edminster, L. R., *International Control of Raw Materials*, Washington, Brookings Institution, 1930.

*Walp, P. K., *Constitutional Development of the League of Nations*, Lexington, University of Kentucky, 1931.

Wambaugh, Sarah, *Plebiscites Since the World War*, Washington, Carnegie Endowment, 1933.

Ward, Sir A. W., and Gooch, G. P., *eds.*, *The Cambridge History of British Foreign Policy, 1783–1919*, Cambridge, Eng., University Press, (also New York, Macmillan), 1922.

Weale, Putnam, *pseud.*, *An Indiscreet Chronicle from the Pacific*, New York, Dodd, Mead, 1922.

Webster, C. K., *The Foreign Policy of Castlereach 1812–1815*, London, G. Bell and Sons, Ltd., 1931.

Wedel, O. H., *Austro-German Diplomatic Relations, 1908–1914*, Stanford, Stanford University Press, 1932.

*Wehberg, Hans, *The Outlawry of War*, Washington, Carnegie Endowment, 1931.

Wheare, K. C., *The Statute of Westminster*, New York, Oxford University Press, 1933.

Wheeler-Bennett, J. W., *The Wreck of Reparations*, New York, Morrow, 1933.

*————, *Information on the Renunciation of War, 1927–1928*, London, Allen and Unwin, 1928.

*————, *ed.*, *Documents on International Affairs*, annual since 1930, Royal Institute of International Affairs, New York, London, Oxford University Press.

————, *Disarmament and Security Since Locarno, 1925–1931*, New York, Macmillan, 1932.

Wheeler-Bennett, J. W., and Longemann, F. E., *Information on the Problem of Security, 1917–1926*, London, Allen and Unwin, 1927.

*Whitbeck, R. H., and Thomas, O. J., *The Geographic Factor, Its Role in Life and Civilization*, New York, Century, 1932.

White, H. D., *The French International Accounts, 1880–1913*, Cambridge, Harvard University Press, 1933.

Whitton, J. B., *Isolation: An Obsolete Principle of the Monroe Doctrine*, New York, Carnegie Endowment, 1933.

Whyte, Sir A. F., *China and the Foreign Powers*, New York, Oxford University Press, 1928, rev.

Whyte, A. J. B., *The Political Life and Letters of Cavour, 1848–1861*, New York, Oxford University Press, 1930.

Wild, P. S., *Sanctions and Treaty Enforcement*, Cambridge, Harvard University Press, 1934.

Willert, Sir Arthur, *Aspects of British Foreign Policy*, New Haven, Yale University Press, 1928.

Williams, B. H., *Economic Foreign Policy of United States*, New York, McGraw-Hill, 1929.

————, *The United States and Disarmament*, New York, McGraw-Hill, 1931.

Williams, E. T., *A Short History of China*, New York, Harper, 1928.

Williams, H. G., *Through Tariffs to Prosperity*, London, P. Allan, 1931, 2d ed.

Williams, Sir J. F., *International Change and International Peace*, New York, Oxford University Press, 1932.

───────, *Some Aspects of the Covenant of the League of Nations*, New York, Oxford University Press, 1934.

Williams, Roth, *The League, the Protocol and the Empire*, London, Allen and Unwin, 1925.

Williamson, J. A., *A Short History of British Expansion*, London, Macmillan, 1922.

Willoughby, W. W., *China at the Conference*, Baltimore, Johns Hopkins Press, 1922.

*Winkler, Max, *Investments of United States Capital in Latin America*. Boston, World Peace Foundation, 1929.

───────, *Foreign Bonds, an Autopsy*, Philadelphia, Roland Swain. 1933.

Wittmann, Ernö, *Past and Future of the Right of National Self-Determination*, Amsterdam, Van Holkema, 1920.

Wood, Ge-Zay, *China, the United States and the Anglo-Japanese Alliance*, New York, Revell, 1921.

Wood, J. B., *Incredible Siberia*, New York, Dial Press, 1928.

Woodhouse, E. J., and Woodhouse, C. G., *Italy and the Jugoslavs*. Boston, Badger, 1920.

Woog, Claude, *La Politique d'Émigration de l'Italie*, Paris, Presses Universitaires, 1931.

Woolf, L. S., *After the Deluge*, New York, Harcourt, 1931.

*───────, *Imperialism and Civilization*, New York, Harcourt, 1928.

World Affairs Pamphlets, published jointly by the Foreign Policy Association, New York, and World Peace Foundation, Boston:
"The Spirit of Modern France" by Helen Hill, No. 5, 1934.
"Soviet Russia, 1917–1933" by V. M. Dean, No. 2, 1934.
"America Must Choose," by H. A. Wallace, No. 3, 1934.
"Conflicts of Policy in the Far East" by G. H. Blakeslee, No. 6, 1934.

*World Peace Foundation, Boston:
Blakeslee, G. H., *The Pacific Area*, 1929.
Chamberlin, W. H., *The Soviet Planned Economic Order*, 1931.
Condliffe, J. B., *China Today: Economic*, 1932.
Hudson, M. O., *The World Court, 1921–34*, 1934, rev. ed.
Jessup, P. C., *The United States and the World Court*, 1929.
Kelchner, W. H., *Latin American Relations with the League of Nations*, 1930.

(Continued on next page)

*World Peace Foundation, Boston (continued):

  Myers, D. P., *Handbook of the League of Nations Since 1920*, 1930.
  ————, *Origin and Conclusion of the Paris Pact*, 1929.
  ————, *World Disarmament*, 1932.
  Winkler, Max, *Investments of U. S. Capital in Latin America*, 1929.
*————, *The International Labour Organization*, 1931.
*————, *Ten Years of International Jurisdiction*, 1932.
*————, *Publications*, Vols. I–XII, 1917–1930:
  "Protocol of Arbitration, Security and Disarmament," Vol. VII, No. 7, 1924.
  ————, *World Affairs Pamphlets*, see separate entry above.
  ————, For other publications, see entries for League of Nations.

Worsfold, W. B., *France in Tunis and Algeria*, London, New York, Brentano, 1930.

*Wrench, G. T., *The Causes of War and Peace*, London, Heinemann, 1926.

Wright, P. G., *The American Tariff and Oriental Trade*, Chicago, University of Chicago Press, 1931.

Wright, Quincy, *Mandates Under the League of Nations*, Chicago, University of Chicago Press, 1930.
  ————, ed., *Public Opinion and World Politics*, Chicago, University of Chicago Press, 1933.

Wright, R. F., *Medieval Internationalism, the Contribution of the Medieval Church to International Law and Peace*, London, Williams and Norgate, 1930.

*Young, C. W., *Japan's Special Position in Manchuria*, Baltimore, Johns Hopkins Press, 1931.
  ————, *The International Relations of Manchuria*, Chicago, University of Chicago Press, 1929.

Young, George, *Diplomacy Old and New*, New York, Harcourt, 1921.

Younghusband, Sir F. E., *Dawn in India*, New York, Stokes, 1931.

*Zimmermann, E. W., *World Resources and Industries*, New York, Harper, 1933.

Zimmern, L. A., *Must the League Fail?*, London, Hopkinson, 1932.

Zurcher, A. J., *The Experiment with Democracy in Central Europe*, New York, Oxford University Press, 1933.

INDEX